Blue Rhythm Fantasy

MUSIC IN AMERICAN LIFE

A list of books in the series appears at the end of this book.

Blue Rhythm Fantasy

Big Band Jazz Arranging in the Swing Era

JOHN WRIGGLE

UNIVERSITY OF
ILLINOIS PRESS
Urbana, Chicago,
and Springfield

Supported by the AMS 75 PAYS Endowment of the American Musicological Society, funded in part by the National Endowment for the Humanities and the Andrew W. Mellon Foundation.

1 2 3 4 5 C P 5 4 3 2 1
♾ This book is printed on acid-free paper.

Library of Congress Cataloging-in-Publication Data
Names: Wriggle, John.
Title: Blue rhythm fantasy: big band jazz arranging in the swing era / John Wriggle.
Description: Urbana : University of Illinois Press, 2016. | Series: Music in American life | Includes bibliographical references and index.
Identifiers: LCCN 2016000553 (print) | LCCN 2016002206 (ebook) | ISBN 9780252040405 (cloth : alk. paper) | ISBN 9780252082269 (pbk : alk. paper) | ISBN 9780252098826 (ebook)
Subjects: LCSH: Big band music—History and criticism. | Jazz—1931–1940—History and criticism. | Jazz—1941–1950—History and criticism. | Arrangement (Music)—History—20th century.
Classification: LCC ML3518 .W75 2016 (print) | LCC ML3518 (ebook) | DDC 784.4/8165137—dc23
LC record available at http://lccn.loc.gov/2016000553

Contents

Blue Rhythm Fantasy

Introduction

> Musical arrangers ply their trade behind the scenes, out of the spotlight's glare and away from the sound of applause. Though they make indispensable contributions to theater, radio, film, television, and recordings, most labor in obscurity, their faces unrecognizable and names unknown. Viewed more as industrious artisans than creative artists, arrangers have received far less attention and acclaim than their colleagues who compose, play, and sing for a living.
>
> Parting the curtain of anonymity that has kept these musicians hidden from view reveals the central position that they have occupied on the main stage of American cultural life.[1]
>
> —Mark Tucker, "In Search of Will Vodery"

Appreciations of music arrangers and their work are not unusual in chronicles of American popular music. After acknowledging the more celebrated contributions of composers and performers, observation that much of the music audiences actually hear has been "arranged" by a third party generally doesn't stir much controversy. Yet detailed or probing historical studies of the discipline remain surprisingly rare. As Mark Tucker suggests, this dearth may be due to the frequent exclusion of music arranging from consideration as creative art—a designation often reserved for "original" composition or "inspired" performance—or the difficulties inherent in documenting the legacy of figures typically removed from the public spotlight. There also may be a perception of technical arranging topics as too esoteric for general audiences; even among scholars, Tucker suggests that "no consensus has developed around aesthetic criteria and technical features that distinguish an arranger's art."[2] Given these potential obstacles, arrangers have maintained a hazy presence in historical narratives.

Music arranging generally comprises the process of adapting a composition to fit a specific performance format or ensemble, like voice and piano, marching band, four-part vocal choir, or symphony orchestra.[3] Orchestration—assigning the roles of individual performers within the ensemble—is usually incorporated into the arranger's job, though large-scale commercial operations like radio networks, film studios, or publishing companies may employ a "production-line" process that divides the tasks of arranging and orchestration between specialists.[4] In popular music, arrangers often manipulate the original source music to fit into a recognized idiom, genre, or style. During the Swing Era of the 1930s and '40s, these manipulations could be as potentially broad as the incorporation of "swing" jazz rhythm, or as narrow as emulating the style of the John Kirby sextet—one of many popular ensembles of the period to feature a specific set of arranging techniques.[5] In particular, the jazz dance orchestra—or "big band"—format proved an attractive universal framework for popular music, as the versatility of these large ensembles also allowed for a variety of stylized interpretations. Swing Era music arrangers enjoyed something of a golden age in terms of artistic stature and public awareness, although that recognition has also complicated their critical reception and historical portrayal.[6]

What did these "indispensable" musicians set out to accomplish when they put pencil to paper? Even among histories that celebrate the importance of arrangers in building the reputations of Swing Era stars, few have explored the practical or artistic imperatives behind an arrangement's construction, let alone pointed to specific examples. On the other hand, technical "how-to" textbooks designed for aspiring composers and arrangers rarely offer a cultural context for the music, often ignoring the reasons that a given arrangement may have been created in the first place. This present study is not intended as a comprehensive history of Swing Era jazz or a reference manual on period arranging technique (although it admittedly hopes to engage with both of those fields). Instead, it aims to explore some of the motivations and ideologies behind the different arranging strategies that defined Swing Era music and to consider the broader legacy of arrangers in American culture. An arranger's personal biography and artistic style can offer crucial insights about a musical work's social power and purpose that have often been missing from jazz and popular music narratives.

Cultural studies of the Swing Era have celebrated the artistic and economic importance of New York City.[7] It was this entertainment center where established traditions of Broadway stage scoring and a commercial dance band market intersected with recent developments in jazz and a recovery of the music publishing and recording business following the initial calamity of the Great Depression. Arrangers held an integral role within each of these fields, and the emergent popularity of the big band format intensified demand for their skills. By 1935, high-profile big band leaders like Benny Goodman might commission or purchase hundreds of arrangements by many different writers within a single year.[8] This material was often provided by band member side-musicians who doubled in the task of arranging, or—as frequently found in the top echelons of the industry—independent freelance arrangers dedicated to the discipline.

As with most freelance occupations, professional Swing Era arrangers participated in a range of income-generating activities in order to survive. Fortunately, an arranger's services were required at some step—or many steps—in just about every entertainment medium of the period, whether studio orchestras, nightclub floor shows, radio broadcasts, song publications, theatrical productions, or films. Assignments might not only call for scoring band orchestrations, but also creating piano leadsheets, setting lyrics, collaborating with stage choreographers, transcribing (notating by ear) other arrangers' work off recordings, editing older orchestrations to fit new combinations of players (most successful big bands grew in size throughout the Swing Era), or serving as a "copyist" (notating individual musicians' parts from an arranged score).[9]

But while the accepted career description of *arranger* has always been diplomatically broad, attempts to combine that title with *composer*, *swing*, or *jazz* quickly run up against decades of politicized debate. Although this study considers creative applications of musical form and orchestration, it is not invested in establishing hierarchies between arrangement and composition, or between arrangers and "composer-arrangers" (or the more nebulous tag "re-composer").[10] Even Duke Ellington, whose career marketing explicitly celebrated his stature as a composer, rarely cited any conceptual or practical differentiation between composition and arrangement as applied to big band scoring. Musicians who arranged music composed by others will be considered alongside those who orchestrated their own original compositions, as both partake in the art of arrangement.

Questions of *swing* and *jazz* arise not only as a consideration of period styles, but also because most criticism and historical studies on Swing Era music have been written from a jazz-centric perspective. The Swing Era is often recalled as the period when black jazz found its largest—and whitest—popular audience; responses to this phenomenon have ranged widely, due in large part to the racism and segregation that dominated the era's entertainment industry. As discussed later, the controversial relationship between swing—often defined as mainstream white commercial entertainment—and jazz—often differentiated as African American vernacular art—fostered music criticism that worked to distance favored jazz personalities or musical works from contextual "entertainment" concerns like variety stage programming, social dancing, or even singing. Critical responses have also included efforts to separate the jazz of the Swing Era from both earlier and later jazz styles, especially post–World War II bebop or "modern jazz." As David Ake explains, "Ever since the rise of bebop, a cadre of musicians, aficionados, and critics has worked to paint jazz as a serious art from . . . guided in large measure by the desire to counteract racist notions that reduced creative African American musicians to charismatic but unthinking entertainers in the service of a predominantly white clientele."[11] Alex Stewart notes a resulting tendency to view the big band era as "a decade of excess sandwiched between two periods of 'authentic' jazz."[12] Examples might include the legacies of arrangers Tadd Dameron, Gil Evans, or Dizzy Gillespie: musicians whose work in the modern jazz idiom is broadly embraced by jazz fans, but whose earlier Swing Era arranging contributions tend to be overlooked.

This present study—provided, perhaps problematically, by yet another jazz-focused scholar—approaches jazz as less of a fixed repertoire or cadre of musicians (although there are times when that definition can be useful) than a broad tradition of African American musical expression that has been applied to multiple styles, genres, or client demands.[13] Efforts to identify exactly which of these expressions—improvisation, rhythm, timbre, performer ethnicity, gender, or venue—are most important in determining an artifact's "jazziness" will always remain somewhat, if not entirely, subjective. As Scott DeVeaux points out, "Even when a swing band was led by an acknowledged jazz virtuoso, improvisation was only one part of a carefully balanced packaged of entertainment."[14] More to the point—during the Swing Era, it appears that the term *jazz* represented whatever attributes the client holding the checkbook wanted it to. Whether this makes big band swing any different from earlier or later jazz idioms is a larger debate beyond the scope of this study, but discourses surrounding jazz versus popular music's role in commerce and cultural identity will resurface throughout the following chapters.

For musicians working in the competitive field of arranging, the almighty client checkbook provided for, among other provisions, the physical space to write scores and dry the ink on manuscript orchestra parts. While necessarily considering the work of multiple arrangers, much of this study focuses on the activities in suite 203 at 156 West Forty-Fourth Street, just east of Broadway in Manhattan. From 1936 until 1950, this address was home to the Broadway Music Clinic, where African American arranger Francis "Chappie" Willet (1907–76) shared office space with musicians including Porter Grainger, Donald Heywood, and Russell Wooding—all seminal, if now obscure, figures on the black Broadway entertainment scene. This focus serves multiple purposes: to narrow the scope of an otherwise overwhelming topic; to shine a small spotlight on the contributions of these forgotten musicians; and to provide a case study of the different professional networks and cultural currents that Swing Era arrangers negotiated in building their careers. The story of the Broadway Music Clinic reminds us that although big band jazz was a major concern of the era—and indispensable as a means of income and visibility—that idiom did not develop in artistic isolation.

Chappie Willet's career in particular offers a poignant model for examining some of the controversies surrounding the arranging discipline. Willet was an ambitious entrepreneur—he established a music school, recording studio, talent agency, and publishing venture—and a celebrated "race man" in the black press, enjoying an unusually well-documented career that reflected many social concerns of the period. Like most of his peers, Willet largely avoided limiting himself to the title of "jazz arranger": his customized manuscript paper displayed the more inclusive moniker "arranger of music."[15] Yet, as a black musician working in a segregated entertainment industry where conceptions of musical identity were often informed by racial essentialisms (typically framed by conceptions of black-hot-jazz-improvised-authentic versus white-sweet-legit-composed-commercial), the jazz label may have been inevitable. Popular music is, above all, a cultural product; all the activities in Willet's offices were influenced by trends in contemporary politics, business marketing, variety stage-entertainment practices, media technology, and ideologies of urban modernism. Willet was keenly aware of the economic and political ramifications of taking on white clients as well as black; the ethnic identification of individual arrangers is acknowledged throughout this study in recognition of period power structures that starkly defined the living and working spaces of American musicians and their audiences.[16]

To consider the work of a freelance arranger—as opposed to better-known bandleader-arranger icons like Duke Ellington or Fletcher Henderson (whose legacies also reflect decades of additional jazz history baggage and criticism)—requires a reframing of previous interpolations of biography and historical repertoire. Willet's projection of his own individual style into arrangements created for a variety of clients known for *their* own individual styles challenges the performer-centered focus of most jazz and popular music narratives. Another feature that makes Willet an attractive study is that his music—though vaguely lauded as "advanced for the period"—was not necessarily *innovative* as compared to the rhythmic or textural developments usually credited to canonical jazz arrangers like Don Redman or Billy Strayhorn.[17] Perhaps more comparable to the legacy of freelancers like Andy Gibson (a black arranger who wrote for Charlie Barnet, Count Basie, and Cab Calloway) or Skip Martin (a white arranger who wrote for Barnet, Basie, and Benny Goodman), Willet's music generally met contemporary expectations of genre and style and demonstrates the cultural powers of arranging *within* the Swing Era big band idiom. This book considers music arranging as a legitimate, creative art form and celebrates Swing Era arrangers' central role in a fascinating—and still reverberating—period of American popular music.

* * *

Although many sources have been drawn upon, my intended focus is on testimony from arrangers active during the Swing Era and surviving manuscript music held in archival collections. Nine chapters are divided into three general sections: chapters 1, 2, and 3 overview the economic, political, and professional landscape of Swing Era arrangers, gradually narrowing to focus on the careers of Chappie Willet and his colleagues; chapters 4, 5, and 6 consider prevalent big band arranging techniques and stylistic concerns, including examples from Willet's arrangements; and chapters 7, 8, and 9 offer more detailed case studies that consider Willet's negotiation of genre, performer identity, and personal arranging style.

Early twentieth-century arrangers present a challenge for researchers. Arranging-related oral histories, for example, seem to suffer less from matters of technical esotericism than the fact that the importance of the job was so obvious to the primary participants as to simply preclude discussion. A three-reel Smithsonian Jazz Oral History Project (JOHP) interview of black arranger Tom Whaley, despite being conducted by the accomplished musician Milt Hinton, is frustratingly typical in its glib accounting of the arranger's technical education, applied craft, or artistic motivations.[18] Nevertheless, the JOHP transcriptions represent a valuable resource, including extensive interviews with black arranger Horace Henderson and white arranger Eddie Sauter; interviews with black Swing Era performers Harry "Sweets" Edison, David "Panama" Francis, and Russell Procope also consider issues related to arranging. Stanley Dance's *World of...* series of oral histories offers valuable documentation of jazz arrangers, if often paraphrased and limited in discussions of technique. Dance's interviews and biographies focus on black musicians, including Eddie Barefield, Benny Carter, Eddie Durham, Andy Gibson, Budd Johnson, Sammy Lowe, Jimmy Mundy, Fred Norman, Sy Oliver, Billy Strayhorn, Tom Whaley, and Ed Wilcox.[19] Interviews compiled by Gene Lees in *Arranging the Score*, also frequently paraphrased and avoiding technical topics, focus on white arrangers, including Les Brown, Bill Challis, Johnny Mandel, Billy May, and Mel Powell.[20]

Additional sources include testimonials scattered throughout jazz and popular music literature: the published memoirs of black trombonist-vocalist Clyde Bernhardt and white arranger Van Alexander, for example, provide critical eyewitness accounts of nightclub, theater, and ballroom venues in Swing Era New York.[21] Weekly black newspapers, including the *Baltimore Afro-American*, *Chicago Defender*, *New York Amsterdam News*, *Philadelphia Tribune*, and *Pittsburgh Courier*, offer vital data, especially in their coverage of black performers, venues featuring black entertainment, and entertainment industry news both black and white. These publications' celebration of racial pride through professional accomplishment also provides an informative alternative to mainstream (white) news sources like the *New York Times*, *Billboard*, or *Variety*, which have a tendency to emphasize reportage of commerce over culture (for example, citing a venue's box-office income without identifying who the featured entertainers were).

Gunther Schuller's monumental critique *The Swing Era* (1989) stands as one of the first works to shed light on a number of Swing Era arrangers.[22] However, many twentieth-century jazz commentaries tend to overlook (if not explicitly dismiss) the Swing Era's popular ballad and novelty-song genres—and their performers—in favor of instrumental arrangements featuring solo improvisation. As Elijah Wald points out, "When we seek to understand jazz—or . . . any other style—while dismissing massively influential [popular] figures as irrelevant mediocrities, . . . we're not dealing with the reality of what the players at that time were doing, of the societies they were working in, or of how their music evolved."[23] Among other efforts to address this issue, it will be conceded that the present study's focus on freelance arrangers tends to ignore "head arrangements": unwritten or collectively improvised routines created by the performers, often cited as a prized component of the jazz tradition—indeed, for some purists, one of the few redeeming aspects of the big band legacy—but which are not representative of most Swing Era popular music.

As Jeffrey Magee notes in his 2005 study of Fletcher Henderson, "Only recently have scholars begun to mine written music as a viable and revealing source for jazz research."[24] Many significant sources of notated music, including the vast archives of Swing Era performers Louis Armstrong, Duke Ellington, Benny Goodman, and Artie Shaw, were only made available to scholars beginning in the late 1980s and '90s. When these archival sources were finally introduced, they were met with the academic phenomenon of the "new musicology" (ca. 1985–2005), which shifted music histories toward more interdisciplinary, extramusical topics. Although resulting studies of the Swing Era provided valuable groundwork for more broadly inclusive efforts, one initial symptom of musicology's corresponding "new jazz studies" movement was to place the study of notated music texts on the back burner.[25]

Nevertheless, the late date of this effort does allow one advantage: more sound recordings from the Swing Era are currently available than ever before. In addition to the continued unearthing of previously unissued studio recordings (also made more readily available in digital format), the release of radio transcription recordings (studio recordings originally designated for radio play only) and live radio airchecks (recordings of broadcast radio transmissions) reveal performances and arrangements potentially heard by more contemporary listeners than some of those represented on commercial disc releases. This development radically expands the breadth of material available for study, and may even provide a more accurate representation of period repertoire—a "popular" alternative to the studio-recorded "jazz canon" selections repeatedly reissued in historical anthologies.[26] Chappie Willet is a terrific case in point: the number of Willet's verifiable arrangements issued on record has roughly doubled since the arranger's death in 1976, including a number of aircheck recordings only made available during the past decade.[27]

Another of the present study's admitted prejudices lies in the presumption that swing big band audiences are as conscious of the ensemble orchestra unit as any other component of a performance, including featured vocalists or instrumental soloists. Climbing a bit further out on this limb, some of the following music examples reference archival scores or orchestra parts for arrangements that are not documented in period sound recordings. In selectively emphasizing the work of arrangers (versus that of the performers), this written evidence is afforded as much documentary weight as that of recorded works. Granted that these instances do presume of the reader some technical knowledge or notation-reading skills, the majority of the notated examples are documented in period recordings, and listening to the cited audio sources (reference timings are provided in parentheses) will significantly enhance the discussion at hand, regardless of score-reading ability.

A preference for excerpted score reductions in notated examples follows a precedent set by Schuller and extended in subsequent musicological studies. Surviving manuscript notation has been referenced where possible, though in some cases scores have been transcribed off of audio recordings. In a few instances, manuscript sources are referenced in combination with transcribed scores (to fill in missing manuscript parts, or when there are scores or orchestra parts relating to the same piece and written by the same arranger, but commissioned by a different bandleader). Staves labeled *rhythm* represent the combined scoring of piano, guitar, and bass; for purposes of reduction, bass parts are notated at sounding pitch unless stated otherwise. Rhythm section chord symbols reflect manuscript guitar part notation; in the absence of archival guitar parts—or in the case of transcribed scores—chord symbols reflect the full ensemble voicing.[28] Manuscript and archive sources are indicated in all examples and figures; complete citations are provided in the list of abbreviations. All measure number indications run consecutively (repeated measures are included in the count); in the case of transcribed scores, the audio source is cited in accompanying notes. A listing of Chappie Willet's publications, manuscripts, and related audio sources is provided in the appendix.

The Arranger in Jazz History

A 1937 *Amsterdam News* article proclaimed: "As the arranger for Louis Armstrong's band and all the music heard on the recent Fleischmann's program on NBC, Chappie [Willet] is literally the unseen power behind the throne, considering that Louis is the king. However, he is perfectly satisfied, for the moment at least, to take the proverbial back seat, for arrangers, like Rome, just aren't made overnight."[29] Given his position in the "back seat," it may be expected that Chappie Willet's name doesn't appear very often in jazz and popular music histories. Neither do his Swing Era peers Edgar Battle, Margie Gibson, Buster Harding, Elton Hill, Dean Kincaide, Billy Moore Jr., or Lou Singer. Even those arrangers whose careers were documented in oral history efforts remain unknown to many fans of Swing Era music; to date, no comprehensive analytical studies of freelance arrangers' work has been widely published, if undertaken. Billy Strayhorn—who enjoyed a lengthy association with Duke Ellington and penned a number of hit compositions—arguably broke through the wall of public awareness, if mostly after his death. Arrangers Benny Carter, Sy Oliver, and Mary Lou Williams may be exceptional in their relative historical visibility, due in part to their reputations as performers, and for arranging "hot" big band jazz and its descendant genres—a decidedly selective portrayal by jazz critics and historians. But even these arrangers fall under the shadows of their clients; it is stars like Louis Armstrong, Count Basie, Tommy Dorsey, or Benny Goodman who capture the headlines of jazz histories. Indeed, why shouldn't they—isn't jazz a performer's art? Enter the world of jazz historiography.

Despite the relegation of arrangers to the backseat of music histories, one might be surprised to discover just how revered, reviled, and politicized the discipline has been in writings on jazz. Arrangements themselves have inspired a wide array of suppositions regarding cultural identity and artistic authenticity. Does an arrangement represent the stain of commercial formula upon the freedom of jazz improvisation, or did arranging play a central role in creating jazz as we know it?[30] Do arrangements represent the antithesis of jazz's vital spontaneity, or does arranging itself comprise an act of artistic invention—even improvisation?[31] The Casa Loma Orchestra's Swing Era recordings of pieces titled "White Jazz" and "Black Jazz"—written by white arranger Gene Gifford and performed by a white band—referenced widespread perceptions of arrangements as embodying essentialized racial attributes; at the same time, arrangers were among the first musicians to cross color lines in America's segregated entertainment industry. Freelance arrangers in particular have posed a dilemma in discourses of art versus commerce—not solely committed to any single performer's individual style, they nonetheless played a crucial role in defining that style.

The Swing Era is typically recalled as the period when jazz had its greatest impact on popular music, including arranging. But arrangers were involved in instrumental and vocal jazz since its inception, including the earliest New Orleans ragtime bands. Lawrence Gushee's study of the 1914–18 Creole Band considers the arranging capabilities of that group and arrangements they performed in World War I–era stage productions in New York.[32] Early New Orleans jazz appears to have evolved in part from printed arrangements of ragtime marching band music—like the publications distributed by midwestern publisher John Stark—and a tradition of dance band performance requiring "note-reading ability in order to be able to play the latest hits from the New York publishers."[33] Techniques of jazz performance gradually made inroads into a preexisting, orchestral-based entertainment industry, represented by successful dance bandleaders and arrangers like James Reese Europe and, by the 1920s, Paul Whiteman.[34]

During the Swing Era, commentaries on American jazz by European critics Stanley Nelson (*All about Jazz*, 1934) and Hugues Panassié (*Hot Jazz*, translated to English in 1936) featured discussions of the dance band arranging field, including freelance arrangers.[35] Nelson essentially equated jazz with the dance band format and focused primarily on white musicians like Paul Whiteman—a bandleader whose "symphonic"-style orchestra held broad appeal in mainstream music markets—to suggest "it is the arrangement which characterizes many of our best bands, as well as the stars who play with them."[36] Panassié celebrated the "hot" dance band arranging styles of Benny Carter, Gene Gifford, Don Redman, and Luis Russell to argue that an arranger "takes the tune as a starting point and makes it undergo transformations quite as profound as hot soloists. In other words, the arranger, too, is a creator."[37] Panassié was also quick to establish that he will not "study those persons who make arrangements

Arranger-bandleader Benny Carter, ca. October 1946. Carter arranged music for Cab Calloway, Benny Goodman, and Chick Webb. Photo by William P. Gottlieb. Music Division, Library of Congress.

of a commercial sort," although he made allowances for the published dance band arrangements of Archie Bleyer and Jimmy Dale to display "considerable inventiveness."[38] A number of later historians similarly allowed for an arranger's creativity to potentially match that of composers or improvising performers.[39]

Parallel to ideologies of jazz performance, some arrangers' "genius" has been critically celebrated, and others have been dismissed as forgettable "craftsmen." Judgments like these frequently belie subjective tastes in repertoire and variable conceptions of instrumental jazz as a marker of artistic value. Swing Era critic George Simon seized upon arranger Eddie Sauter's claim that "writing commercially is not an art," and divided jazz big band repertoire into categories of "stupid pop" tunes eliciting "mere craftsmanship" versus "wonderfully fresh-sounding originals" revealing "artistic creativity"—more often than not taking the form of "inspiring instrumentals."[40] Similar rhetoric surrounding the jazz-arranging crimes of "chronic overwriting"—a charge leveled at the same Eddie Sauter—or veering "dangerously close to novelty" abound in swing big band criticism.[41] Professional requirements that may have prompted an arrangement's creation are rarely considered in these quests for purity and originality, especially in the arena of Tin Pan Alley repertoire; indeed, many jazz discographies and historical reissues identify arrangers only for instrumental performances, offering no attributions for vocal material.

At the height of the Swing Era in the early 1940s, a growing acknowledgment of African American contributions to jazz and widespread economic inequities prompted critics and historians to take more radical positions. As Peter Townsend describes, "An ethic of [jazz] authenticity was beginning to be manifested in writings in the music press, . . . a process of sifting out the 'real' jazz" that was dependent upon a "separation of jazz from its performance contexts."[42] This ideological scramble to differentiate performers from their repertoire or presentation format required a recasting of the role of dance band arrangers. Contrary to Nelson and Panassié, arrangements could be pegged as a necessary-evil component of the music business—a symptom of commercial conformity and a dilution of performer-centered jazz ideals like solo improvisation.[43] By the end of the 1940s, the entire discipline of arranging was open to attack in discourses on jazz authenticity and the corollary threat of cultural appropriation. The industry saturation and economic viability of swing drew attacks from dogmatic traditionalists like Rudi Blesh, whose *Shining Trumpets* (1946) relegated "the arranged playing of instrumental sections" as heard in the black dance bands of Fletcher Henderson, Duke Ellington, Count Basie, or Jimmie Lunceford to the "outmost fringes" of jazz.[44] Blesh argued that "deceptive elements" of this music (presumably including his identification of African-identified jazz techniques like "call-and-response" or "dirty tone") made "present-day commercial swing falsely seem another form of that [jazz] music"—an ideal represented in its purest form by virtuosic New Orleans soloists like Louis Armstrong, whose extensive legacy of arranged ensemble performance Blesh ignores.[45] Music notation itself, with its socioeconomic implications of education and literacy, offered a target for jazz "primitivists" like clarinetist Mezz Mezzrow, whose 1946 autobiography charged that "written music is like handcuffs" for "pure-and-simple jazzmen" like himself; Mezzrow not only compared symphony orchestra performances to "a goose-stepping army . . . one-hundred-men-with-a-fuehrer," but also questioned jazz trumpeter Bix Beiderbecke's interest in music composition.[46]

Other commentators cast post–Swing Era musicians who performed outside of the big band format as demonstrating a reaction against artistic constraints endemic to the popular music industry. Under this theme, 1940s bebop stylists Dizzy Gillespie and Charlie Parker are often cited as figures antithetical to swing big band music. Ross Russell—writing in 1959—interpreted Gillespie's and Parker's music as embodying a "revolt against big bands, arrangers . . . [and] against commercialized music in general."[47] By the 1990s, the *Grove Dictionary of Jazz* entry for "arrangement" claimed: "It is unthinkable that great improvisers and virtuoso players such as Charlie Parker and Dizzy Gillespie should need an arranger or should need to write out an arrangement of one of their pieces. At most they might write out the theme statement."[48] This growing emphasis on the differences between bebop and swing ignored both Parker's and Gillespie's repeated return to heavily arranged formats—including big bands, string orchestras, and vocal choirs—throughout their careers, and even the prevalence of obviously arranged introduction, interlude, and coda passages found in (especially Gillespie's) bebop music for smaller combos.[49]

The discussion of Swing Era dance band arrangers in Amiri Baraka's *Blues People* (1963) takes a similarly anti-orchestral turn even as it emphasizes stratifications of social and economic class. Baraka argues that black big bands "were largely middle-class Negro enterprises," and that the arranger's role as "one of the most important men in big-band jazz [was] demonstrating how far jazz had gotten from earlier Afro-American musical tradition."[50] Casting the entire discipline of swing dance band arranging to reflect a dilution of rural black folk values by white middle-class ideals, he concludes that "swing music, which was the result of arranged big-band jazz . . . had very little to do with black America."[51] Yet Baraka also allows for the celebration of Duke Ellington's work during this period, suggesting that this bandleader, composer, and arranger—generally portrayed by historians as a representative of the black middle class—was able to "integrate so perfectly the older blues traditions with the 'whiter' styles of big-band music."[52]

Baraka is careful to delineate between black "big-band jazz" and white "swing"; in writings by other commentators, similarly nuanced use of these terms (as well as the differentially diagnosed entities "swing big band," "dance band," "stage band," or "jazz orchestra")—often paralleled by oppositions of "artist" instrumental improvisers against "novelty" vocalists or "hack" arrangers—has never resulted in a consistent taxonomy.[53] Even when focusing on freelance arrangers (as opposed to bandleader-arrangers like Ellington, Fletcher Henderson, or Stan Kenton), some commentators have followed Panassié in attempting to separate "jazz" practitioners (a status frequently assigned to Benny Carter and Gil Evans, for example) from "commercial" laborers.[54] The latter ilk are often left unnamed, though perhaps this epithet might be applied to jingle writer Leon Carr or—Panassié notwithstanding—stock arranger Jimmy Dale. (Or perhaps Chappie Willet—readers are encouraged to consider their own standards of jazz authenticity regarding the study that follows.)

As record reissues and historical anthologies built up a selective jazz "canon" repertoire through the late twentieth century, another emergent theme was the establishment of aesthetic ideals that legitimize favored arrangers—or even individual arrangements—as having transcended the artistic impositions of a capitalist-driven music industry that forced mediocrity upon the masses. In the *Oxford Companion to Jazz* (2000), Max Harrison isolates "distinguished instances of the craft" that "addressed the more awakened minds among listeners, whereas arrangers' energy was devoted mainly to current popular songs ranging in quality from excellent to—more often—abysmal."[55] In *The Swing Era* (1989), Gunther Schuller judges the success of arrangers based on degrees of artistic authenticity, arguing that "an arrangement is by definition a reworking of some other creator's original material, and only in rare instances . . . can it achieve the authenticity of full creation."[56] This case-by-case gatekeeper mandate accompanies a critique of black bandleader Jimmie Lunceford, whose college training, "retinue of arrangers," and "exacting musicianship" is compared to that of the financially successful white bandleader Paul Whiteman, a long-established foil to "authentic" big band jazz (forgetting Stanley Nelson for the moment).[57] Schuller's framework nevertheless allows for exceptions—briefly opening the gate—including his suggestion that the departure of arranger Sy Oliver from the Lunceford orchestra resulted in nothing less than that ensemble's loss of "creative force and imagination."[58]

Perhaps the potential for contradiction in writings by Blesh, Baraka, Schuller, and others simply highlights the breadth of influence and variety of musical product that music arrangers are responsible for. But there have been tangible repercussions from these efforts to legitimize jazz as an autonomous art form, including jazz's perceived antagonism toward the stage entertainment medium. Stanley Dance's *World of Count Basie* (1980), for example, cited the practice of Swing Era dance bands "playing from theater stages and accompanying increasingly ostentatious floorshows" to decry a "tendency in [Swing Era] jazz toward elaboration and decoration . . . fat, in the form of commercial concessions or exotic coloring."[59] Attempts to isolate Broadway or vaudeville-inspired revue and stage show performance as artistically incongruous with jazz ignore the deep musical ties between these mediums and their shared role in defining American popular entertainment.[60]

It has been some twenty years since Scott DeVeaux warned against "the assumption that the progress of jazz as art necessitates increased distance from the popular."[61] Regardless of jazz's argued presence or purity in arranging, this study considers stage entertainment as an integral component of Swing Era popular music, whether white swing or black jazz (if such a division is possible). This consideration offers ample opportunity and motivation for revisiting previously historicized—and ostracized—music, especially vocal genres. Recent studies of Swing Era arranging by scholars including Andrew Berish, John Howland, Jeffrey Magee, Catherine Tackley, and Walter van de Leur have begun to offer analyses of big band jazz in social context.[62] Cultural studies by Kenneth Bindas, Patrick Burke, Todd Decker, Joel Dinerstein, Lewis Erenberg, David Stowe, Peter Townsend, Sherrie Tucker, and Christopher Wilkinson have similarly initiated a more comprehensive look at this vast body of music.[63] For scholars of jazz and American popular culture, the complexity of artistic, racial, gender, economic, and political forces at work during the Swing Era continues to provide a rich and rewarding field of investigation.

1

Business and Politics

The Landscape

> It kind of was a weird existence. . . . You didn't have time. Either you couldn't get a job at all, or you were smothered in work. . . . In other words, they don't want to hear anything about you until you're well-known—I don't want to say famous—they don't want to know anything about you until there's a demand for you, then they all want to know all about you. . . . It's rags to riches, you know. And then back down again if you're not careful.[1]
>
> —Arranger Spud Murphy

The first three chapters consider the economic, political, and professional landscape of popular-music arrangers working during the Swing Era. Arrangers are often portrayed to represent the business side of music—the individuals responsible for making a piece of music marketable toward a target audience. Music arranging was a steadily growing field in America during the 1930s and '40s, when the job was integral to many areas of the entertainment industry. New York in particular supported a large and lucrative nightclub and theater scene, where institutions such as the Shuberts' Winter Garden Theatre on Broadway had established themselves in the early decades of the twentieth century. These venues presented stage revue programs comprising dancers, singers, comedians, acrobats, and chorus lines with arranged musical accompaniment, a "variety" medium that remains associated with Broadway to this day. Indeed, the name *Broadway* grew to represent the geographic and cultural axis of American popular entertainment.

The Times Square district, located on and around Broadway in midtown Manhattan, encompassed music-publishing companies, booking agencies, radio and recording studios, and performance venues stretching from the prestigious Pennsylvania Hotel on Thirty-Third Street to the seedy bars of Fifty-Second "Swing Street." By the mid-1930s, nightclub operators who had been trying to lure wealthy white patrons uptown to see black vaudeville performers and jazz bands at Harlem stage revue venues like the Cotton Club, Connie's Inn, and

Ubangi Club also began a strategic move into the midtown district. Here they could cater to a larger mainstream market, described by Lewis Erenberg as "a mass audience of moderate spenders, businessmen and their wives, and out-of-town visitors."[2] Performers representing Harlem remained a premier attraction throughout the period, as Broadway packaged swing jazz music for popular audiences through the dramatic medium of the stage "production number." Incorporation of black performers into midtown's white entertainment structure was celebrated in production titles like *Harlem on Broadway*—a 1941 nightclub revue written by black Broadway veterans Andy Razaf and Eubie Blake and presented at the new Ubangi Club on Broadway at Fifty-Second Street.[3]

The music format most commonly associated with the Swing Era is the jazz dance big band: typically a group of ten or more musicians, comprising one or more vocalists, a woodwind—or "reed"—section (three or more saxophones, usually doubling clarinet), brass section (a combination of three or more trumpets and trombones, possibly subdivided into individual sections in the case of larger ensembles), and rhythm section (piano, guitar, bass, and drums). David Stowe goes as far as to suggest that the sectional orchestration strategies of the big bands may have reflected the "larger, more bureaucratic, and more rationalized characteristics" of New Deal America during the Great Depression.[4] But regardless of metaphoric potential, these large musical organizations required the services of someone to do the musical rationalizing. Although a number of bandleaders were notably capable arrangers themselves (including Count Basie, Glenn Miller, and Artie Shaw), most Swing Era stars lacked either the time or inclination to write large numbers of works for their own bands. As some production- and recording-date deadlines may have been physically impossible for a single arranger to meet, even prolific bandleader-arrangers (like Benny Carter, Duke Ellington, and Fletcher Henderson) turned to others for material. For dance bands, this crucial commodity might be found in the form of a commercial "stock" arrangement printed and sold by the song's publisher, an individualized "special" arrangement designed for a specific client or occasion (sometimes including original compositions), or an aural transcription based on another band's recorded performance.

Music arrangers found a central role within the business apparatus that supported the rise of big bands during the mid-1930s—an entertainment industry expansion enabled in part by a consolidation of radio, recording, and management enterprises during the Depression. The management agencies that dominated the new Swing Era corporate landscape included Music Corporation of America (MCA), the William Morris Agency, and Rockwell-O'Keefe (later General Artists' Corporation, or GAC).[5] Arranger Fred Norman recalled being offered a job at Rockwell-O'Keefe, whose New York office "was supplying [their dance bands] with arrangements written by specially hired arrangers.

They needed someone to sit in the office and grind out the scores."[6] New York also served as the headquarters for national radio networks and their client advertising firms. The popular success of swing big bands bolstered demand for new arrangements to be broadcast over the radio on commercially sponsored "sustaining" programs; the mediums of radio and live performance were merged in "remote" on-site programming from dance venues like the Roseland Ballroom or Pennsylvania Hotel.[7]

Bandleaders trying to meet ten or more side-musician salaries generally took as much work as possible, and rigorous performance and broadcast schedules necessitated a daunting number of arrangements. For example, the Benny Goodman orchestra's weekly appearances on the NBC radio program *Let's Dance* prompted a supporting budget to commission eight new arrangements per week for thirteen weeks, followed by four per week for a second thirteen weeks.[8] Swing Era performers were also approached by "song pluggers" representing Tin Pan Alley publishers, who offered bands new arrangements in order to stay up to date with the latest hits—hopefully to be included in the bands' broadcast programming. Lewis Erenberg suggests that this relationship was not entirely equal; it was "expensive for publishers to hire special arrangers, but sheet music firms needed the bands to play their work and had to give them wider creative latitude."[9]

Music industry trade publications highlighted the central role arrangers played in the process of creating and marketing new songs. *Metronome* magazine, for example, covered behind-the-scenes topics like publication bootlegging ("$2,000,000 Theft of Orchestrations") and the "Evolution of Song Plugging."[10] In "Seeing a Song through the Mill," arranger Harold Rubenstein described the extensive infrastructure and personnel required by the publishing industry of the period, as well as the frantic work pace associated with production-line industry:

> From [the melody and harmony] lead sheet the piano part is made . . . the guitar symbols are added and the lyric is checked for the correct division of words into syllables and punctuation. The piano part is then rushed over to the engravers to be engraved . . . on a metal plate. This is a very slow process as the notes, stems and accidentals are all separate dies and have to be hammered into the plate by hand. When the plates have been completed they strike off green proofs that are sent back to the publisher to be proof read. . . .
>
> The vocal orchestration is scored [by an arranger], extracted and autographed [by a copyist]; a process of writing on yellow waxed paper with a brown or black acid resisting ink. . . . The autographed sheets are placed on a wet zinc plate and put under a great pressure which forces the ink notes and staff to leave the paper for the plate. . . . The plate is immersed in an acid bath which eats away the surface of the plate leaving the notes raised. The plate is now ready for the press from which printed orchestrations grow. . . . Parts have to be proof read. . . .

> When the dance arranger has completed his score, it is extracted [into orchestra parts by the copyist] and the parts are taken . . . to a band for tryout. . . . The dance arrangement then goes through the same steps as the vocal arrangement.[11]

In this labor-intensive environment, the services of competent arrangers—whether employed by publishers, radio networks, management agencies, or bandleaders—were at a premium. Professional arranging and copying work (differentiated tasks, but often done by a single laborer) were technical skills that commanded respectable wages, an especially attractive incentive for musicians struggling through the Depression economy. A fee schedule for copyists contracted by publisher Chappell and Company for work on the Shuberts' 1935 Broadway stage production *At Home Abroad* specified time wages of two dollars per hour (approximately thirty-four dollars in 2015 currency), or work by the page ranging from twenty-five to fifty cents per page, depending on instrument and transposition; the schedule includes a stipulation for ten cents extra per page for "all night work," as well as coverage of additional expenses for travel from outside New York City.[12] In March 1936, arrangers and copyists represented by New York's American Federation of Musicians (AFM) Local 802 organized a strike over wage rates and work hours for full-time employees of forty-four music publishers.[13] Eight hundred union-represented network radio musicians had recently negotiated for weekly wages including $100 for arrangers (approximately $1,700 in 2015 currency) and $50 for copyists, with a thirty-five-hour workweek.[14] The publishing-house employees—estimated to comprise about 150 workers—eventually settled for weekly wages of seventy-five dollars for arrangers and thirty-five dollars for copyists, with a thirty-seven-hour workweek.[15] Included in the agreement was a stipulation for the continued "use of Local 802's identifying stamp on all music manuscripts."[16]

As the demand and reward for arrangers grew, advertisements in music trade magazines *Billboard*, *Down Beat*, and *Metronome* offered opportunities to "increase your income by studying arranging" and "learn right at home to compose and arrange music" ("in ½ the usual time"), and enrollment in correspondence courses offering instruction in "modern arranging and orchestration."[17] Hungry freelance arrangers advertised "orchestral arranging of any kind: hot—sweet—concert."[18] The 1938 AFM Local 802 directory listed 235 union arrangers and copyists (the category is combined, and does not include arrangers and copyists listed elsewhere in the directory as performing musicians); by 1941, the ranks had grown to 349; by 1947, the number was 632.[19]

Dance band arrangers could command wages competitive with their publishing house and radio-studio counterparts. In 1943, for example, Billy Strayhorn received a weekly salary of $100 working for Duke Ellington.[20] One of the most frequently cited—though perhaps least typical—arranging contracts was negotiated in 1939, when Tommy Dorsey offered to pay arranger Sy Oliver the equivalent of his former salary with Jimmie Lunceford, plus a yearly salary raise of $5,000.[21] But often the repertoire was commissioned only as needed. Freelance arrangers typically earned their income through the sale of individual arrangements, prices for which varied depending on demand and reputation. Benny Goodman's 1935 *Let's Dance* arrangers, including Fletcher Henderson, were reportedly paid $37.50 per arrangement (approximately $630 in 2015 currency).[22] By the height of the Swing Era, top-tier arrangers like Benny Carter might charge bandleaders like Cab Calloway as much as $100 per arrangement.[23] In March 1945, Artie Shaw paid George Siravo $235 for two arrangements ("I Could Write a Book" and "Thrill of a Lifetime")—not including a $28 fee paid to a Los Angeles contractor for part copying.[24]

For freelancers who charged by the score (as opposed to the hourly or weekly wages earned by their contract counterparts), speed was a critical factor. Mary Lou Williams claimed to have been writing "for some half-dozen bands each week . . . one week I was called upon for twelve arrangements."[25] Arranger Lyle "Spud" Murphy recalled turning out one arrangement daily, Monday through

Arranger Mary Lou Williams, ca. 1946. Williams arranged music for Duke Ellington, Benny Goodman, and Andy Kirk. Photo by William P. Gottlieb. Music Division, Library of Congress.

Thursday, for Benny Goodman's orchestra—writing the score in the morning and having the individual orchestra parts "extracted" in the afternoon—and two arrangements on Friday for the Joe Haymes and Casa Loma orchestras.[26] Murphy's four-per-week deal with Benny Goodman even entailed temporarily moving to Chicago during 1935 and 1936, where the band held residency at the Congress Hotel.

Murphy's extended relationship with Goodman highlights an important, if somewhat murky, practice in the dance band business. Some bandleaders offered freelance arrangers a type of semi-salaried position loosely referred to as a "staff arranger," whereby the client could obtain arrangements at low cost (often below union wage rates) in exchange for the financial security of regular commissions. In 1936, for example, Chick Webb hired Van Alexander to provide three arrangements per week for a total of seventy-five dollars—a fee that included part copying.[27] Arranger Les Brown recalled his 1938 agreement with bandleader Rube Newman to provide four arrangements per week for seventy-five dollars; that same year, Billy May received seventy dollars weekly in a four-arrangements-per-week deal with bandleader Charlie Barnet.[28] Regarding the title of "staff arranger," Spud Murphy explained:

> The way it usually worked out was you would do arrangements—two or three for somebody. And if they liked them, they tried to give you as many as they could. It *kind* of became a staff arranger, but nobody looked at it that way. In other words, I was Goodman's "staff arranger," but I was also Casa Loma's "staff arranger," you know? I was also arranger for Joe Haymes. It didn't make any difference, you took whatever jobs there were. Unless somebody wanted to sign you to a contract. And nobody did, 'cause they could get you any time they wanted anyway.[29]

Freelance music arranging offered an opportunity for ambitious musicians to play the market in one of Depression-era America's relatively thriving industries. The job offered many of the same freedoms that had drawn performers into professional dance music: as Scott DeVeaux describes, swing band entertainment represented "a wide-open field"—one that may have been especially attractive to African Americans seeking a route to respectable economic or social advancement—and could reward those who made it to the top levels of the business with sizable incomes.[30] But arrangers were also subject to many of the same social and economic struggles faced by musicians who performed under the spotlight. Indeed, the relatively low public profile of arranging may have generated as much controversy as it avoided.

In 1941, the *New York Times* ran a story on white radio arranger Paul Baron, who complained that "'the conductor and the vocalist stand up for the cheers—whether radio, vaudeville, the theatre—and the arranger slinks off to do another exacting job so that someone else can earn more cheers.'"[31] But despite Baron's perception of the "general public's lack of knowledge of the art of orchestration and arrangement," Swing Era press coverage championing their work is not rare.[32] *Metronome* presented brief biographical sketches of arrangers, accompanied by photos and sample arrangements ("Your Arranger This Month"); by the late 1930s, black musicians like Fred Norman were featured alongside white arrangers like Joe Lipman.[33] In 1941, Don Redman was the subject of a special tribute, highlighting the arranger's contributions as a "style-setter and a pacemaker" during the preceding twenty years.[34] *Down Beat* magazine's "Men behind the Bands" column followed suit in the early 1940s, presenting biographical spotlights on black arrangers (like Billy Moore Jr.) as well as white (like Jiggs Noble).[35] In the black press, the *New York Amsterdam News* embraced successful "race" arrangers like Jimmy Mundy and Chappie Willet as "the unseen power behind the throne" and "unsung heroes of swing."[36]

The descriptors *unseen* and *unsung* indicated not only perceptions of music arranging in general, but also the position of black arrangers in a white-controlled music industry. Arranging work—especially in New York—represented a significant locus of cross-racial interaction in the largely segregated Swing Era popular music market (Benny Goodman's integrated band providing the most celebrated exception). Efforts by white bandleaders to include black performers might preclude touring the South, or even involve instances of black musicians "passing" for white; in any case, most of these associations were short-lived.[37] Off the performance bandstand, the "behind-the-scenes" nature of arranging allowed for white bandleaders to hire black arrangers (such as Gene Krupa hiring Jimmy Mundy, Charlie Barnet hiring Andy Gibson, or Tommy Dorsey hiring Sy Oliver), and for black bandleaders to hire white arrangers (such as Chick Webb hiring George Bassman, Cab Calloway hiring Will Hudson, or Jimmie Lunceford hiring Roger Segure).

The integration efforts of black bandleaders, however, never garnered as much attention in mainstream media, where efforts to fight social injustice were usually framed as the province of white power brokers like producer, critic, and NAACP board member John Hammond.[38] Indeed, as integration remained mediated by white institutions, efforts to promote swing dance bands as representations of American democracy at work may have proved more apt than proponents of the metaphor intended.[39] Black arranger Phil Moore provided his own observations of industry practice in the September 1946 issue of *Negro Digest*: "There are two musicians unions in practically every principal city in the country, except New York. . . . [Jurisdiction] zones are set up more or less by the white locals. . . . Whenever a [black] man wants to get a job that pays decent money he has to be okayed by the white local."[40]

Some historians have cited instances of bandleaders crossing color lines in their hiring of arrangers to suggest that commercial competition fostered the breakdown of racial barriers in the arranging business.[41] Hidden from public view, arranging jobs in corporate booking or publishing offices—like that offered to Fred Norman by Rockwell-O'Keefe—could present opportunities for black musicians to cross lines of racial segregation in the entertainment industry, albeit working under white management. But these backroom relationships could also be interpreted as merely another form of exploitation. A 1941 *Chicago Defender* article by Major Robinson—"Harlem's Music Arrangers Make Broadway's Tops [*sic*] Leaders"—highlighted the dependence of "Broadway" (i.e., mainstream white entertainment) on the unheralded contributions of black arrangers and songwriters, including Fletcher Henderson, Edgar Battle, and Andy Razaf. Robinson cited the results of radio disc jockey Martin Block's nationwide orchestra popularity contest to claim that "of the majority of topflight white bands that copped choice spots, more than seventy-five percent of their arranged scores are turned out by colored arrangers."[42] The details of Robinson's statistics were not provided, but others shared his perception.[43] A 1939 *Baltimore Afro-American* column by Lillian Johnson similarly raised the issue of black arrangers writing anonymously for white bands:

> I certainly disapprove of the lily white bands that use the arrangements of the colored musicians, without giving them the chance to play. By that, I mean that if a man is a good musician and a good arranger, I feel that it is unfair to himself and to his people to go over to a white band where he will be used solely in the back room of the band, and often at a salary that is much less than that paid any other person connected with the outfit. If he is a professional arranger and has an office for that service alone, such as Chappie Willet has, then that is a horse of another color. . . . The white boys may not have the native ability, but they have plenty of ambition and perseverance, and that's a combination that's hard to beat.[44]

The exception for Chappie Willet was likely in deference to the arranger's well-publicized work for white bandleader Gene Krupa. A 1938 *Pittsburgh Courier* article announcing Krupa's invitation for Willet to join his "staff of arrangers" revealed the potential reservations behind such a relationship:

> Should Willet accept the spot which is vacant for him, this will mark the first time in his career that he has done such for an ofay [white] leader. In the past he has devoted his talent to the colored field exclusively, not because of any difference of feeling said he, but just because the colored boys seemingly needed someone to devote their time to them and them alone, as everybody was doing such work for white bands.[45]

Johnson's comment regarding "native ability" referenced long-held presumptions of blacks as possessing innate musical talent, especially for jazz. David

Stowe cites instances of Swing Era performers drawing distinctions between black orchestras, perceived as "loose and swinging," and white orchestras, associated with "sophisticated arrangements and precise ensemble execution . . . sweet bands not generally respected by swing critics."[46] Likewise, the "sweet" bands were "not associated with 'race' outfits"—at least in the emerging imagination of jazz authenticity, which tended to prize up-tempo dance numbers, novel orchestration devices, or displays of solo improvisation.[47] As Andrew Berish notes, most views of sweet or hot repertoire during this period were "gross simplifications that could never encompass the fluid world of jazz-inflected dance band music."[48]

But the perceptions of difference ran deep. Black bandleader Lucky Millinder complained that "the colored arranger steals ideas from colored bands, ideas which are completely new, and sells them to the white orchestras as well as teaching them the 'feel' of the music."[49] Competitive associations between race and artistic authenticity were also reflected in period conceptions of "special" arrangements: unpublished orchestrations portrayed as focusing on the "hot"—often read "black"—jazz idiom, highlighting rhythmic syncopation and improvisation.[50] A 1944 *Billboard* magazine review offered similar opinions on the provenance of "special" arrangements via claims of an exception that purportedly proved the rule:

> Unlike most Negro bands around, [Claude] Hopkins's doesn't depend upon fancy and over-harmonized effects. Band, instead, dishes up very commercial type of dance music with little frill, fuss or trimming. . . . Tunes in the books are current pops for the most part, another deviation from most colored jump bands around. Latter usually have plenty of specialties in the books.[51]

Perhaps reflecting a corollary image of commercially published stock arrangements as the domain of white musicians, a 1941 *Billboard* bandleader poll listed black arrangers Fletcher Henderson and Sy Oliver in the top two "best special arranger" slots, whereas all seven arrangers listed in the "best stock arranger" category were white.[52] Of course, black "special" arranger Sy Oliver also scored stock arrangements (for publisher Embassy Music), as did Edgar Battle (Lewis Music and Exclusive Publications), Eddie Durham (Famous Music), Fred Norman (Broadcast Music and Paramount), Edgar Sampson (Southern Music), and Jimmy Mundy (Exclusive, Regent, Robbins, and Stasny). Nevertheless, the stock arrangers most heavily advertised in trade publications like *Metronome* were white (at a ratio of more than ten to one from 1936 to 1939).[53]

Chappie Willet's business model may be instructive. Although the arranger accepted stock arrangement assignments (see chapter 4)—fees for which were cited as comparable to top-tier "special" arrangement rates, perhaps between $75 and $125 per score—he primarily advertised himself as a creator of the more artistically prestigious special arrangements.[54] In fact, Willet's considerable efforts to market himself throughout the Swing Era reveal a side of the arranging business that performer-focused music histories have tended to obscure. For example, many arrangers' efforts included the entertainment-industry custom of publicity photo distribution: Willet sent Louis Armstrong photos of himself, including a personalized note—"working like this is really a pleasure when it's for King Louis, the greatest of the great"—clearly serving as a reminder of his availability for services.[55]

Bolder publicity efforts by arrangers might be seen as a delicate task because their backroom status suggests that they somehow publicize their contributions without stealing the spotlight from their clients. On the other hand, the 1936 opening of Willet's midtown Manhattan offices and talent school—later to include a recording studio and publishing venture (see chapter 2)—not only marked the arranger's establishment on the Times Square scene, but also initiated a period of media coverage in the black press that easily rivals that of any performer. In several instances, the publicity suggests a conscious campaign

Arranger Chappie Willet in his Broadway Music Clinic office, ca. December 1937. Willet arranged music for Louis Armstrong, Gene Krupa, and Jimmie Lunceford. Courtesy of the Louis Armstrong House Museum.

by Willet and his media champions to invent the role of celebrity arranger. The 1938 *Amsterdam News* feature "Unsung Heroes of Swing"—just one of the generous photo spreads to hype Willet's career during this period—positioned Willet first in a list of celebrated black arrangers that included Jimmy Mundy, Edgar Sampson, and Will Vodery, among others.[56] Even a series of newspaper advertisements for Harlem's Garden Barber Shop, which featured photos and endorsements from performer celebrities like Armstrong and Millinder, included an unlikely endorsement from Willet ("tools always SHARP; atmosphere never FLAT; courtesy ever NATURAL").[57]

Print media were not the only avenue for arrangers wishing to advance their careers. Dance band performers like saxophonist Jimmy Mundy, trumpeter Eddie Sauter, and pianist Mary Lou Williams built up their reputations as side-musician-arrangers prior to establishing themselves as dedicated freelancers.[58] Billy May claims to have performed on trumpet primarily to arrange, believing that "to be a successful arranger, you had to be a decent player first to get recognized. . . . I played enough to be established, so I could write."[59] Like other aspiring arrangers looking for greater access to clients, May's career aspirations entailed moving to New York, where he was able to join the Charlie Barnet orchestra (and later Glenn Miller and Ozzie Nelson) as a side-musician.[60] In 1937, Count Basie's manager Willard Alexander offered arranger, trombonist, and guitarist Eddie Durham "seventy-five dollars a week to play with Basie, and another seventy-five to write for the band, so it was a hundred-and-fifty a week."[61] In 1939, erstwhile bandleader Fletcher Henderson attempted to reinvigorate his career by taking a side-musician role that highlighted his continued arranging work for Benny Goodman.[62]

Whether freelance "staff" or full-time side-musician, an arranger's long-term relationship with a bandleader might be viewed as a sort of creative partnership, shaping a band's signature sound and style. In 1938, a two-part article published in *Billboard* offered two professionals' thoughts on "What the Band Leader Means to the Arranger" and "What the Arranger Means to the Orchestra Leader."[63] Aside from predictably congenial accolade swapping, white arranger George Duning and bandleader Kay Kyser offered some carefully delimited definitions of the arranger's role in the dance band business. Duning discussed the issue of public recognition and the establishment of a band's musical style:

> After all, what possible good can it do the arranger to get his name into print so that the public knows he arranges for a certain band? Of course, it is important that other people in the profession know what you are doing and with whom you are identified. The word gets around. . . . No arranger goes to a leader and dictates style or policy. . . . Arrangements, like clothing, can go "out of fashion." Today we might be using an arrangement "lick" that is well liked. Tomorrow that same "lick" will go out of style. But how will the arranger know when it does?

> Simple enough—the band leader tells him, for his (the bandsman's) is the finger on the public pulse. . . . The intelligent leader will listen to his arranger. He will argue with him—providing there is a point in contention—but both leader and arranger are concerned with musical values, so inevitably the right side wins. . . . Except for a few bands with recognizable styles, the public doesn't know why it likes one band better than the other. More often than not it is the leader, thru sheer personality and showmanship.[64]

Kyser responded:

> The arranger, musically speaking, is the most important member of the band. . . . From the creative viewpoint, he is the leader's "other brain." . . . The arranger must be able to tell in a minute when a tune is good for a band and when it isn't. . . . I also believe that an arranger should never listen to other bands on the air or elsewhere. The temptation to copy a phrase or lick is often too great a temptation to resist. . . . The arranger is at a loss to decide upon coming trends in music. The band leader can't be—if he wants to stay up there.[65]

Duning's concern about dictating style might well apply to a bandleader like Benny Goodman, who seems to have resented the stylistic impositions of some of his staff arrangers. In an interview with Richard Sudhalter, Goodman recalled: "I never liked that [1941] band as well as some others. To me it was—it was a rather affected kind of band. Good musicians—but with all respect to [arranger] Eddie Sauter, he wasn't really a jazz man. Too involved, too fussy: you had to watch your P's and Q's so goddamn much you could never play."[66] Trumpeter Jimmy Maxwell recalled how Benny Goodman "used to edit [Sauter's] arrangements brutally . . . he would take whole chunks out of them, leaving an open space for rhythm here, taking out a measure there, trying to make them swing."[67] Pianist and arranger Mel Powell also complained of Goodman's musical conservatism, lamenting how Goodman would cut down Sauter's music and "sometimes get the credit for it being a hit, getting it past the a&r men." Contrary to the submissive arranging ideals espoused by Duning, Powell argued: "Eddie, and I to a lesser degree, were exploring harmonic worlds that ought to have been encouraged, rather than set aside."[68]

It is worth noting that artistic tensions like these tended to air well after the Swing Era had ended; as with any freelance work, arrangers who were vocally at odds with their clients risked immediate unemployment. Perhaps not quite the "brain-sharing" partnership advertised by Kyser, this power dynamic may have been another attraction of the casual "staff arranger" system—arrangers could be easily replaced on a moment's notice, leaving the client bandleader or musical director with substantial artistic as well as financial control. Bandleader Artie Shaw seems to have reveled in the freedom to indulge his changing tastes, boasting that he "must have gone through three dozen arrangers" during the

Left to right: Bandleader Benny Goodman, pianist Teddy Wilson, and arranger Eddie Sauter, ca. 1948. Sauter arranged music for Goodman, Red Norvo, and Artie Shaw. Courtesy of the Frank Driggs Collection at Jazz at Lincoln Center.

Swing Era.[69] Nevertheless, highly valued arrangers did hold some clout at the negotiating table; in discussing his own experiences working for Goodman, Jimmy Mundy revealed, "Benny and I didn't get along too well . . . I was always quitting, but then he would sweeten the pot."[70]

With the exception of original compositions or arrangements of public-domain material, U.S. law provides no copyright protection for an arranger's creation. Arrangers created and sold a "for-hire" product for which they were paid a onetime fee; what happened to that product after this transaction was at the discretion of the owner. For many ensembles, it was standard practice to make alterations wherever and whenever they felt it was necessary; for bandleaders like Glenn Miller and Artie Shaw—who were also experienced arrangers—the temptation to make adjustments may have been irresistible. According to Billy May, Miller liberally revised his arrangers' work: "He messed with everybody's charts . . . merciless. The intro would be *beautiful*. 'Take that out.'"[71] Arranger Bill Finegan dubbed Miller an arrangement "meat-grinder."[72] Artie Shaw compared his own relationship with arrangers to "the role of an editor. If the same arrangement was handed to Dorsey, Goodman, Miller and me, it would have ended up four different arrangements."[73]

Jeffrey Magee, in his study of Fletcher Henderson, suggests that Goodman's frequent alterations to his arrangers' submissions reflected motivations ranging from "practical"—as often the case with Henderson—to "aesthetic"—as perhaps in the case with Sauter.[74] Ample evidence of the thinning and cutting of arrangements is preserved in archival manuscript collections. For example, Goodman orchestra parts for Sauter's 1940 "Superman" indicate cuts to the introduction for practical requirements of disc recording, but also additional edits for subsequent live performances.[75] Other alterations may have reflected performance issues or edits made in rehearsal. For example, Walter van de Leur identifies some of Billy Strayhorn's music that may have "landed on the cutting room floor" due to the technical limitations of Duke Ellington's vocal performers.[76]

More subtle changes can be found as well. While Swing Era performance practice typically allowed for dance band wind players to hold notes for durations shorter than notated, recordings of arrangements like Jerry Gray's 1937 "It's a Long Way to Tipperary" for Artie Shaw reflect explicit changes to phrasing and note duration—including the omission of held whole notes—which are not indicated in the manuscript score or orchestra parts.[77] Such alterations might reflect more gradual performance adaptations in response to breathing or phrasing preferences; section lead players might also take significant liberties in the interpretation of phrasing and rhythmic value. One of Red Norvo's trumpet players expressed annoyance at their leader's (or perhaps arranger's) directives, scribbling on their part "phrasing, value, blend, and, and, and. . . ."[78] Of course, changes in personnel—like adding a new soloist or removing a snarky side-musician—might also induce adaptations to an arrangement.

Even after practical performance edits were made, arrangements remained a flexible commodity. Time schedules and publishing interests of radio broadcast programs placed constraints on the arrangements that bands presented over the air. Billy May recalled the adaptations that Glenn Miller had to make for his band's fifteen-minute radio programs: "The [song] pluggers were busy in those days. . . . [Miller would] get all the plugs in he could for the [publishing] guys. . . . He was a demon at cutting here, and putting a bell note there, and then maybe he'd write a little thing for the saxes—dictate it to them—and it would be ready. He really knew how to run a rehearsal."[79] The limited durations of commercial recording formats—approximately three minutes for a ten-inch disc, or four-and-a-half minutes for a twelve-inch disc—also impacted arrangements; archival scores and orchestra parts often reveal arrangements longer than the performances issued on record. For example, manuscript parts for Chappie Willet's 1938 arrangement of "Jump Jump's Here" for Red Norvo includes solo passages for sax and xylophone that are cut or shortened in the performance recorded for commercial ten-inch disc.[80] Later Norvo performances of the same piece—as documented on a "transcription" recording designated for radio play—nevertheless reflect the full arrangement, suggesting that the omissions were temporary. It is unlikely that an outside arranger would be consulted in this perpetual editing process, a fairly accepted practice in popular music performance.

* * *

In a note left on a score delivered to Harry James, arranger Jimmy Mundy threatened: "Unless I receive the [$]600.00 that you owe within the next 24 hours, I shall instruct the county sheriff to proceed with legal judgment against you for same."[81] Mundy's memorandum reminds us that working in a freelance profession presumes a mastery of commerce and a willful participation in the negotiation of supply and demand. Any number of marketplace factors could influence employers' relationships with their employees; for their part, arrangers were expected to provide a functional product while catering to—or even creating—a client's personal style, taking a central role in determining a band's commercial success. At the same time, these "collaborators" may have had little say in the final execution or content of their arrangements, and could be as easily disposed of as any side-performer. On top of this, black arrangers (and bandleaders) had to negotiate what Duke Ellington biographer Harvey Cohen describes as "the range of talents attributed to African Americans": expectations of style and commercial format linked with racial stereotypes.[82] But this balancing act of musical invention and commercial patronage represented only part of an arranger's toils. The following chapters consider a range of experiences, activities, and relationships that might comprise an arranger's working world.

2

Ace Race Arranger

The Broadway Music Clinic

So last week one day I dropped in on Chappie Willet, the young arranger-partner of Russell Wooding, at their offices on West 44th Street just off Broadway. In shirt sleeves, open collar and with ink-stained fingers I found this youngest of Broadway arrangers seated behind a huge desk littered with score sheets. He was feverishly working on an arrangement of "I Hope Gabriel Likes My Music" which is to be used by Louis Armstrong.[1]

—Allan McMillan, *Chicago Defender*, 1936

Allan McMillan's February 1936 *Chicago Defender* feature may be the earliest media documentation of Chappie Willet's midtown Manhattan office space, known as the Broadway Music Clinic. The offices were located in the Mayfair Theatre Building at 156 West Forty-Fourth Street (still standing as of this writing), just east of Broadway in the Times Square district.[2] Designed by Apollo Theater architect George Keister in 1925 and built the following year, the Mayfair took the name of its 300-seat ground-floor theater; nine upper levels catered to the Broadway entertainment industry, housing at various times the offices of music publisher Harry Bloom, the American Federation of Actors, the Theater and Amusement Employees Union, the Theatrical Wardrobe Attendants Union, *New Theatre Magazine*, and multiple theatrical producers.[3] After the Mayfair Theatre folded in 1928, the building's owners split the high-ceilinged hall into three levels. The new street-level space initially housed a Chinese restaurant, then a barbershop speakeasy; in 1937, Jimmie Dwyer's Sawdust Trail—a bar and performance venue providing "continuous entertainment . . . 23 seconds from B[road]way"—took up residency, where it continued operation into the 1950s.[4] Willet occupied the new space directly overhead, in suite 203, for the duration of the Swing Era.

Born on September 6, 1907, Francis Robert Willet was raised by "musical parents"—Chester Willet and Elizabeth Hill—in the immigrant row-house neighborhood of South Philadelphia.[5] He attended the city's prestigious Central High School and enjoyed a successful athletic career that continued at West Virginia State College (formerly the West Virginia Colored Institute), where he enrolled in piano and composition studies in 1929.[6] Following graduation in 1933, Willet was recruited to serve as musical director of Edwards' Collegians, a local territory band. The group was renamed "Chappie Willet's Greystone Ballroom Orchestra" (referencing a high-profile Cincinnati residency previously held by the Collegians) and relocated to Willet's home base of Philadelphia, but disbanded by the fall of 1934.[7] At the end of that year, Willet obtained his first arranging work in New York City, scoring for stage shows at Harlem's Apollo Theater featuring Luis Russell's orchestra.[8] He appears to have joined the AFM Local 802 around 1937.[9] In the 1940s, Willet settled with his wife—stage performer Olena Hunter (1913–89)—at 147th Street and Broadway in Harlem, a straight shot from his Music Clinic office via the Interborough Rapid Transit (IRT) subway line.[10]

Aside from a roster of arranging clients that included bandleaders Willie Bryant, Jimmie Lunceford, and Lucky Millinder, Willet was engaged in a "staff" agreement with both Louis Armstrong and Gene Krupa.[11] The Armstrong relationship was probably mediated through Luis Russell, who served as the trumpeter's musical director from late 1935 until 1940 (although the Armstrong Museum holds Willet arrangements dated as late as 1944). Work with Krupa appears to extend from April 1938—the band's debut—until about 1940 as well, though it is possible that most of Willet's arrangements recorded by Krupa during 1939 and 1940 had been supplied in 1938. Other swing bandleaders who recorded Willet's arrangements during this period include Cab Calloway, Teddy Hill, and Red Norvo; additional clients reportedly included Bob Crosby, Glen Gray, and Chick Webb.[12]

Willet's arranging work and related Music Clinic activities were celebrated in the black press with remarkable regularity, especially at the height of the Swing Era during the late 1930s and early '40s. Just how much of this publicity was legitimate reportage of a meteoric career or the result of personal connections Willet had cultivated with entertainment columnists and news editors is open to speculation. In keeping with the editorial tone of the 1930s black press (and continuing a trend established during his earlier career as bandleader), much of Willet's media publicity framed his education and business success as a "race" achievement—a view that appears to have been embraced by the arranger himself. Frequently adopting the rhetoric of a press-release statement, some reports included a supporting theme of Willet having "long been fired by a desire to do something really helpful for young Negroes" and voicing concerns for "the future of Negro talent."[13] The following quote, first printed in a September 1940

New York Amsterdam News article, exemplifies the tenor of many Willet media statements:

> "I have a great many white students," explained Mr. Willet, "but I am here primarily to aid undiscovered talent in my own race, many of whom aren't aware of the fact that I am a Negro. It is time that we did something for our talent, instead of sitting idly by while countless white firms reap a fortune yearly from selfish exploitation of Negro entertainers. There is a great deal of new talent but white studios are not willing to train talented colored stars of tomorrow. If my efforts can do some little something to correct this present condition, I shall feel completely justified in my many sacrifices to build this organization."[14]

The same article, titled "Chappie Willet's Shoulders Broad Enough to Carry Load of Negro's in Showlife," summed up Willet's operations to date, including a wealth of names (and a permissible degree of publicity hype):

> Mr. Willet has wisely surrounded himself with the best possible staff to handle efficiently the various departments of his studio. Miss Derniece Harris, prominent pianist and vocal coach, is in complete charge of the music school which includes a hundred vocal and piano students. Russell Carrington assists Mr. Willet in the booking agency which has provided work for over fifty acts in the past three months. Many of these include not only some of our best talent, such as the Miller Brothers and Lois, Pete Nugent, Pearl Harrison, Myra Johnson, the Three Dukes, Norton and Norton, but many of the students trained in the music school.
>
> James Edwards, who handles amateurs, has formed a "Tomorrow's Headliners Club," which offers them a free audition and an opportunity to study at a cheaper, non-professional price. A new innovation of the Chappie Willet Studios is the "Song-Writers Club," organized by Charity Bailey, who is herself an authority on theory. It affords embryonic tunesmiths an opportunity to study the technicalities of writing songs as well as a chance to have their efforts played by topnotch bands. And efficiently checking on a smooth office routine is Connie Scott, Mr. Willet's private secretary.[15]

The Music Clinic staff reflected a range of entertainment careers and ambitions. Derniece Harris (1906–96) had studied music at Howard and Columbia Universities and performed in theater productions organized by Willet; she later toured with the USO during World War II, and went on to enjoy a successful performance career in Seattle under the name "Melody" Jones.[16] Russell Carrington was a former stage performer (he had shared a bill with the Miller Brothers dance act), and later worked as a coproducer of stage shows at Murrain's nightclub.[17] Pianist and singer Charity Bailey (1904–78) had studied at the Dalcroze and Juilliard conservatories, and went on to a distinguished career in music education, recording folk songs and hosting pioneering children's programming on public television in the 1950s.[18] James Edwards managed weekly amateur talent shows sponsored by Willet in Brooklyn, and—during World War II—at the Harlem Defense Recreation Center.[19] The later activities of pianist Connie Scott, herself the winner of an amateur competition at the Apollo, remain more elusive.[20]

Subsequent Music Clinic staff included publicist and *Amsterdam News* columnist Bill Chase and Harvard-educated pianist and arranger Gerald Cook (1921–2006), who studied with modernist composers Nadia Boulanger and Roger Sessions.[21] The histories of additional colleagues Susie Washington (pianist, lyricist, and arranger), Eulie (or perhaps Ulie) Saunders, and Thelma Keith (vocalist) are more difficult to trace.[22] Presumably, some (or all) of the music instructors and publicists worked on a freelance basis, or at least in shifts; a 1941 advertisement listed Willet's studio hours as 10:00 a.m. to 10:00 p.m.[23] Some of the song copyrights registered by Willet throughout the 1940s appear to include collaborations with songwriting students or other aspiring talents. Willet's reputation as a mentor for amateur musicians was celebrated in media coverage like "Powder Room Hit," a July 1946 *Ebony* magazine feature on songwriter Lucille Boone, who wrote the lyrics for "Put Your Brakes On, Papa" while working as a powder-room attendant at a Broadway nightclub.[24] Accompanying photos portrayed Boone and Willet working with a singer in the Music Clinic office.

Colleagues and Ventures

In addition to his affiliated instructors and assistants, Willet shared his Music Clinic headquarters with three veterans of New York's black Broadway scene. Arranger and bandleader Russell Wooding, composer and pianist Porter Grainger, and composer and producer Donald Heywood had all established their reputations in the 1920s. While they remained active through the Swing Era, their public profiles were arguably in decline at the time of their Music Clinic residencies; association with Willet's rising star may have been seen as beneficial to all parties.

In particular, the career of theater and studio arranger Alfred Russell Wooding (1891–1959) appears to have provided inspiration for Willet.[25] Wooding was formerly a messenger for the State Department and a National Guard band director during World War I; at the time of his Music Clinic affiliation, he served as bandmaster of Harlem's 369th New York National Guard Regiment (the outfit James Reese Europe had famously led in France), a post that led to his own well-publicized service in the Pacific during World War II.[26] The senior arranger's stage work with Ethel Waters—including Irving Berlin's *As Thousands Cheer* (1933) and the Shuberts' *At Home Abroad* (1935)—was repeatedly highlighted in publicity for Willet's offices.[27] Wooding was also credited in Swing Era productions at the Harlem Ubangi Club and Broadway Connie's Inn (see chapter 3); he also reportedly provided music for the CBS radio network.[28]

Porter Grainger (1891–ca. 1955) joined the Music Clinic in June 1937.[29] Perhaps best remembered today as a piano accompanist for blues singer Bessie Smith, Grainger also worked as composer on a number of celebrated stage projects, including *Get Set* (1923), *Hot Rhythm* (1930), and Zora Neale Hurston's folk project *The Great Day* (1932).[30] Grainger's Swing Era activities included writing revues for the Apollo, Small's Paradise, Ubangi Club, Club Mimo, Murrain's Cabaret, and Café Zanzibar (see chapter 3). In 1939, Grainger produced his own *Panorama of Negro Folklore* revue at the Alhambra Ballroom.[31] He also provided lyrics for at least two Willet compositions—"Nothin' to Do but Love" (1938) and "I Ain't Gettin' Nowhere Fast" (1939)—as well as Russell Wooding's "369th March" (1937).[32]

Despite reports that both Wooding's and Grainger's clinic quarters were bought out to make space for Willet's recording studio in 1939, Donald Gerard Heywood (1897–1967) moved into the suite in 1942.[33] Heywood's name is most frequently connected to the Jazz Age standard "I'm Coming, Virginia"—cocomposed with bandleader-violinist Will Marion Cook—but he also composed, arranged, conducted, or scripted numerous black Broadway productions, including the Ethel Waters feature *Africana* (1927; revival 1934), and worked alongside Grainger on *Get Set* and *Hot Rhythm*.[34] Heywood wrote and produced Swing Era stage shows for the Apollo, Plantation, and Ubangi Clubs, including further collaborations with Grainger (see chapter 3). He also composed for the film *Moon Over Harlem* (1939), the Sky Club floor show *The Mikado Jumps* (1939), the touring production *Tan-Americana* (1941), and the Carnegie Hall presentation *The Chocolate Soldier* (1942).[35] Many of Heywood's own production attempts, however—including *Caribbean Cruise* (1939, 1940), arranged by Willet and Lorenzo Cauldwell—appear to have folded soon after, if not prior to, opening.[36]

Archival manuscripts reveal an additional figure related to Willet's clique: arranger and conductor Thomas Le Roy Whaley (1892–1986).[37] Whaley is most often remembered for his later work with Duke Ellington (and then usually in the role of copyist), but during the Swing Era he was also in demand as an arranger, including work at the Apollo, Connie's Inn, Hurricane, Small's Paradise, and Café Zanzibar (see chapter 3). The Smithsonian Tom Whaley Collection (much of which is filed among the Smithsonian Duke Ellington Collection) includes music relating to all four Music Clinic residents. Representative artifacts include an undated leadsheet composition by Donald Heywood—"I'm Always on the Verge"—with instructions for Whaley to add "4 bar 2nd ending, 8 hot of chorus," and the message "Tom, please make these arrangements right away.

Dough on the line Friday. If you need me call." Corresponding orchestra parts in Whaley's hand include the requested additions.[38]

As explored later, Willet and his Broadway Music Clinic colleagues enjoyed an extensive reach in the nightclub and theater world of Swing Era New York. The Forty-Fourth Street offices also served as a base for additional business projects and political interests; efforts in the latter category included the hosting of community-activist meetings, though media documentation of these events is much scarcer than that relating to the entertainment field.[39] Following is a brief account of Willet's expansion into the fields of studio recording, talent management, and music publishing.

CHAPPIE WILLET RECORDING STUDIOS

In November 1938, Bill Chase's *Amsterdam News* column reported: "Chappie Willet, the arranger, is taking over the entire offices he formerly shared with Russell Wooding and Porter Grainger for one huge recording studio and music clinic."[40] A feature article printed the following July—"Ace Arranger Turns to Recording Field"—unveiled the resulting Music Clinic makeover. The new accommodations may not have been exactly "huge": Chase explained that Willet's "attractively appointed studios . . . are as completely equipped with [the] latest recording devices as those of the larger commercial companies, but naturally on a smaller scale."[41] An accompanying photo spread (which was indeed large) included shots of Willet and his recording gear outside a sound booth, singer "Sister" Rosetta Tharpe behind a microphone, and Willet's "capable secretary-accompanist, Miss Scott" at an upright piano. Willet announced that his new mobile recording gear could be used for everything from "recording the songs of famous Broadway stars in rehearsal to visiting private parties and banquets where guests delight in having recordings of their voices made." In Willet's words (as reported by Chase):

> "There are many recording studios such as mine along Broadway," the youthful arranger confessed, "but their interest in Negroes is usually a monetary one, giving little or no care to the results. That is the main reason for establishing my studio—so that I can be sure that each record made here has had my individual attention to the point where I am convinced that the performer has been given the best possible results."[42]

Chase also informed readers that the arranger-engineer could "record programs off the air" and that "many prominent personalities have commissioned him to make a disc of their participation in recent broadcasts." Some Chappie Willet Recording Studio discs survive in collections and archives, including artifacts connected to Louis Armstrong, Roy Eldridge, and Mary Lou Williams.[43] Clearly hoping to maximize potential clientele, Chase's article included more overt advertisements for the "House of Willet, dedicated to such people as you and me":

> "I wanted, too, to have a place where the amateur would feel at home as a professional. And it is surprising the number of every-day people who come in for recordings of their voices which they mail to the folks back home."
>
> More than anything else, Mr. Willet's studio is an experimental laboratory, where amateurs lose all fear of being self-conscious or of making mistakes. . . . It's a favorite spot of the "Cotton Club gang," where they come between shows to make records "for the fun of it," or listen to special numbers being recorded off the radio during the broadcasts of Cab Calloway's orchestra. This is of immense value to the average musician who uses this means of checking on mistakes, arrangements, etc.[44]

Social parties and jam sessions hosted at the Music Clinic studios (see chapter 3) offered opportunities for Willet to advertise his professional associations as well as flatter his clients. The *Amsterdam News*, for example, reported Willet entertaining European jazz composer-journalists Leonard Feather and Adrian

Arranger Chappie Willet (*center*) with recording gear at the Harlem Defense Recreation Center, ca. March 1942. Photograph by Austin Hansen, used by permission of Joyce Hansen and the Schomberg Center for Research in Black Culture.

de Haas, and—conveniently enough—*Amsterdam News* columnists Dan Burley and Bill Chase.[45] In September 1940, the *Pittsburgh Courier* printed a photo captioned "Handy Gives Congratulations"—composer and publisher W. C. Handy is shown shaking hands with Willet under a sign reading "Chappie Willet Recording Studios."[46] A similar photo in the *Amsterdam News* depicts Handy and Willet examining a phonograph disc Willet "has just made of the voice of the 'daddy of the blues' [Handy]."[47] Wartime publicity connected with the Harlem Defense Recreation Center—"Wax Letters Latest Fad for Soldiers"—provided another occasion for Willet to pose with his portable recording gear, as soldiers recorded spoken messages to send home to their families.[48]

CHAPPIE WILLET ARTISTS' ENTERPRISES

In February 1942, the *Chicago Defender* trumpeted the advantages of Donald Heywood having "recently aligned himself" with Willet:

> The Heywood-Willet tie-up, observers point out, should benefit promising sepia talent no end and should prove to be that springboard to success, which has long been lacking for our future stars. Heywood's fame as a producer and showman has placed him high in the opinion of Broadway bookers and producers, who are always on the lookout for new material and who will give young entertainers that "break" on his sayso alone, having known him as a shrewd picker of tomorrow's stars. Under Willet's handling the popular Bye Sisters were launched on their professional singing career and in two years have hit the top ranks of modern swi[n]gsters.[49]

As suggested by the descriptor "handling," the sister act cited represented not only the efforts of the Music Clinic talent school, but also Willet's booking and management agency, Chappie Willet Artists' Enterprises (later billed as Chappie Willet Enterprizes).[50] Similar to other Willet-managed "swingsters" like singer (Carrie) Belle Powell, who eventually performed with the Willie Bryant and Claude Hopkins orchestras and had an ensemble role in the Broadway musical *Swingin' the Dream* (1939), the Bye Sisters appear to have enjoyed some success—including a tour with Lionel Hampton in 1942—but never hit the truly big time.[51] Prior to the Heywood-Willet announcement, the Bye Sisters had appeared in Heywood's spring 1941 *Tropicana* revue at the Apollo and were featured in Willet's own *Rockin' in Rhythm* production staged at the Indigo Room in New Rochelle.[52]

The Indigo Room opened during the holiday season of 1941–42, supported by a flurry of publicity hyping an all–Artists' Enterprises talent lineup. Located outside New York City in suburban Westchester County (north of the East Bronx), Willet's "sin-den"—as designated by columnist Alvin Moses—was housed in the local Chauffeur and Domestic Workers' Club, at 4 Valley Place off Fifth

Avenue.[53] Print publicity claimed an opening attendance of over 500 members at the 250-capacity clubhouse.[54] The *Amsterdam News* provided Willet's explanation of the project: "'I've long been in search of a spot where I could break in young talent,' he stated, 'and now I feel that I have just the right spot. Unless we give embryo stars their chance they will never develop into stars of tomorrow. I intend to produce the entire revue using new material that has seldom been seen in nite clubs or theatres.'"[55]

It is not clear whether the suburban venue was intended as a permanent establishment or merely a temporary setup; nighttime blackout policies during the early months of America's involvement in World War II may have also influenced planning efforts. In any case, media coverage of Willet's production did not extend past a few weeks, and the Workers' Club itself was not listed in directories after 1942. A *Chicago Defender* advertisement plugging the Artists' Enterprises and the Indigo Room ("home of continuous fun") listed the Bye Sisters, Tick & Tock, the Reeves Sisters, Alicia & Arnesto, Derniece Harris, and blues singer Inez Washington as resident acts.[56] Additional Indigo Room publicity cited performers Jack Meredith, Short & Shorty, Sandra & Lakeeta, and Lou [*sic*] & Bebe; the latter duo consisted of Helen Watkins and Llewellyn (or "Lew") "200 Pounds of Joy" Crawford.[57] Crawford was already an established comedian, emcee, and floor-show dance director, including work on the 1935 *Ubangi Club Revue* and Ralph Cooper's film *The Duke Is Tops* (Million Dollar, 1938).[58] During the mid-1940s, Crawford was affiliated with the Harlem talent agency Suntan Studios, located at 217 West 125th Street, a sort of uptown parallel to Willet's midtown operation that advertised songwriters Andy Razaf and Porter Grainger among its residents.[59]

Few of the Indigo Room acts are traceable after World War II. Inez Washington is presumably the performer by that name who recorded for the obscure Cincinnati label around 1946, but does not appear to have been connected to Willet at that time.[60] Billie Hayes, another blues singer affiliated with Willet during World War II (although not connected to the Indigo Room productions), may be the only Artists' Enterprises talent documented on commercial disc.[61] In 1943, Hayes's recordings of "I Can't Get Enough," "Man Shortage Blues," "Blackout Blues," and "You Ain't Had No Blues" were released on Joe Davis's Beacon label; it has been suggested that the uncredited piano accompanist was Porter Grainger.[62] Willet leadsheet arrangements for at least three additional songs also designate use by Hayes.[63]

Disc releases may not be the best measure of the Artists' Enterprises activities, however, as the more prominent names on Willet's roster tended to be dancers. As cited earlier, these included the tap acts of Pete Nugent (1909–73) and the Miller Brothers & Lois (Bright Miller); both were featured in high-profile touring revues, backed by star bandleaders like Count Basie and Cab Calloway.[64] In any case, it is not clear how exclusive or extensive Willet's association with the different acts on his booking roster was. For example, the "adagio"—or more generally termed "ballroom"—dancer Harold Norton performed with various partners in addition to the Norton & Norton (husband and wife) combination cited in Willet's publicity.[65] And Willet's arranging work for headliner acts like the Nicholas Brothers, Peters Sisters, and the Three Chocolateers does not appear to have included a booking or management relationship.

Publicity for Willet's booking agency crested again during 1946 and 1947, including press plugs for vocalists Mae Iris Davis (a former USO performer), Kathie McAdams, and Jimmie Anderson—none of whom appear to have achieved significant long-term success.[66] Willet's office continued advertising through May 1947, a few months after All-American Newsreel reportedly distributed a film short that included a segment featuring the Music Clinic.[67] A *Pittsburgh Courier* description of this film describes Willet maintaining an office staff of six, including music teachers and publicity agents.[68] Also in spring 1947, All-American Pictures produced *Hi-De-Ho*, a film musical revue featuring Cab Calloway's orchestra, the Miller Brothers & Lois, and the Peters Sisters. Buster Harding is the only arranger listed in the film's credits, but the talent lineup, floor-show repertoire (which included Willet's own publication "A Rainy Sunday"), and relationship with All-American hints at Willet's hand somewhere in the production.

DUO MUSIC AND TEXT MUSIC PUBLISHING

Another facet of the Music Clinic emerged with the inauguration of two publishing companies, Duo Music and Text Music. In July 1944, the *Chicago Defender* announced Willet's Duo Music venture in "Willett [*sic*] Heads Music Firm"; the arranger was later quoted to declare that "of 1500 music publishers, only 15 are Negro-owned and most of these inactive."[69] Duo Music's initial concerns included two vocal ballads relating to bandleader Lucky Millinder. "Darlin'," by Millinder and Frances Kraft Reckling, had been previously published by Douglas Publishing in 1943 (with Reckling listed as sole composer); the new version registered by Duo Music reflected revisions to the melody and lyrics as heard on Millinder's May 1944 Decca recording with vocalist Judy Carol.[70] "A Rainy Sunday" is credited to Millinder, Art Franklin, and "Blackie" Warren.[71] The latter name—described in one notice as "Dr. Blackie Warren (of Chicago)"—is not documented elsewhere, and seems likely to be a pseudonym for Chappie Willet; a *New York Age* plug for the song included a photo of Willet with the Peters Sisters captioned "Songwriter congratulates Peters Sisters for harmonizing his tune."[72]

"A Rainy Sunday" was debuted by the Peters Sisters with Cab Calloway's orchestra at the Café Zanzibar in September 1944.[73] Publicity for the song peaked that fall, with the *Amsterdam News* claiming "U.S. Orders 250,000 Records of 'A Rainy Sunday' for Overseas"; a radio broadcast featuring the sisters reportedly announced plans to record a disc for free military distribution, indicating "a new spirit of inter-racial cooperation." The un-bylined report further offered that "if the present popularity of this latest Duo Music presentation continues, only the current paper shortage will prevent it from reaching the million mark in sheet music alone."[74] Even if such a recording was planned, no evidence of its production or distribution has been discovered, and it is doubtful that Willet's sheet-music sales (or those of any small publisher) were in danger of reaching the million mark. "Rainy Sunday" may not have been recorded to disc until 1946, when Apollo Records waxed a performance by Luis Russell's orchestra featuring vocalist Lee Richardson.[75] The Peters Sisters eventually performed the number onscreen with Calloway's orchestra in the 1947 film *Hi-De-Ho*.[76]

Text Music represented what appears to have been a onetime collaboration on the occasion of Adam Clayton Powell Jr.'s first congressional campaign. In October 1944, the *Chicago Defender* announced: "Langston Hughes, world famous poet, and Chappie Willet, noted song writer and arranger, have collaborated in writing a rousing, militant new song."[77] Their resulting publication, "'Let My People Go'—Now!," was arranged as a spiritual for four-part vocal choir with piano accompaniment, and included the following dedication:

> With thanks to ADAM CLAYTON POWELL, Jr. whose phrase "LET MY PEOPLE GO—NOW" inspired the writing of this song with the hope that it may help make this a free world for all mankind regardless of race, creed, or color.—The Publisher.[78]

The address provided for the Text Music Publishing Company is that of the Broadway Music Clinic. Hughes and Willet's racial uplift/protest song consists of a four-bar piano introduction, an eight-bar ensemble chorus, and four sixteen-bar verses decrying "Jim Crow" and "Uncle Tom" to be "spoken or sung" over ensemble vocal humming.[79] These lyrics are augmented by an additional type-written page providing three "extra verses for Adam Clayton Powell, Jr.," extolling the subject's political virtues.[80] Celebrated by the *Baltimore Afro-American* as a "stirring song that rings out with a message," the piece was performed by vocalist Elwood Smith and pianist-arranger Mary Lou Williams on the latter's *Piano Workshop* WNEW radio program during the summer of 1945; the *Chicago Defender* also anticipated the possibility of Lucky Millinder's orchestra performing the piece.[81]

For reasons unknown, Willet's interest in music publishing appears to have been relatively fleeting. Following a January 1945 copyright deposit for a batch of Caribbean-themed songs composed by veteran stage performer Tosh Hammed, Willet does not appear to have registered any more material under Duo or Text Music—although he did continue to register additional copyrights under his

The Peters Sisters (*left to right:* Mattie Jane, Virginia, and Anna Louise), ca. 1939. The Peters Sisters were featured at the Apollo Theater, Cotton Club, and Café Zanzibar. Courtesy of the Louis Armstrong House Museum.

own name. One such item was filed in October 1944: "Japan: An American Battle Song" credited words and music to Willet and black Broadway composer Andy Razaf. This patriotic war song was scored in two-beat marching meter with a sixteen-bar verse, a thirty-two-bar chorus, and a sixteen-bar refrain asking citizens to "buy, buy bonds" (with additional calls to "exterminate Japan").[82] "Japan" is almost certainly connected to the committee of "outstanding colored personalities in the musical and theatrical world" assembled in fall 1944 to promote war bonds. Advertised members included Harlem composers Razaf, Willet, Langston Hughes, Duke Ellington, W. C. Handy, J. C. Johnson, Luckeyeth Roberts, James P. Johnson, and J. Rosamond Johnson.[83]

* * *

In 1937, reporter Bill Chase's *Amsterdam News* profile on Chappie Willet declared:

> [Willet's] only formula for success is hard work—but definitely. An indefatigable person, he often puts in eighteen hours a day, sometimes going entirely without sleep if he has a "rush" job to do. He fully realizes the music business is a "tricky"

> affair, and the public may soon tire of "swing" or any other fad in music. So, it's his business to "keep in the know" as to what the public wants, prepare it, and serve it while it's hot—and he does.[84]

As promised, Willet continued to adapt to changing tastes in popular music throughout his career. In late 1945 he collaborated with songwriters Claude Demetrius and Rudolph Toombs—two rising stars in the emerging "rhythm and blues" field—to compose the song "Cherry Tree," and "jump blues" vocalist Eddie "Cleanhead" Vinson cited Willet among his orchestra's arrangers.[85] Overall, Willet's broad embrace of the entertainment industry appears to have been fairly successful; in addition to his arranging work, the Broadway Music Clinic school, recording studio, and talent agency remained active through the late 1940s. Perhaps the less persistent efforts of Willet's publishing venture reflected its relatively late entry in the Swing Era—which, by 1944, was arguably already in decline. Nevertheless, an elaborate stage entertainment network in Harlem and Times Square extended the Music Clinic's run for a few more years. Willet's stage music career provides a necessary background for exploring orchestration and arranging techniques that contributed to the Swing Era big band sound.

3

Harlem on Broadway

Nightclub and Theater Revues

During the war former $25-a-week men making $80 came to know and like us. Old-timers who never thought they could afford a club had to do something with money that formerly bought cars, refrigerators, and washing machines, so they gave a night to us and continued to do so.[1]

—Carl Erbe, Café Zanzibar, 1945

For an ambitious music arranger in Swing Era New York, work at prominent floor-show venues like the Café Zanzibar could offer not only professional prestige, but also substantial cash income. While exact statistics from tax-troubled establishments like the Cotton Club are predictably difficult to obtain (and entertainment reportage details may be skewed in any case), popular nightclubs like the New York branch of Billy Rose's Casa Mañana franchise cited gross incomes of $35,000 to $40,000 per week in 1938 (approximately $595,000 to $680,000 in 2015 currency).[2] Despite some ups and downs, nightclub business generally remained strong through World War II; in 1945, the Café Zanzibar cited patronage of 1,500 customers on weekdays and 2,300 on Saturdays—house band musician Clyde Bernhardt claimed "the place was sold out every night"—with a yearly gross of $2 million (approximately $26 million in 2015 currency).[3] At least some of this bounty was passed on to the clubs' entertainers: arranger Tom Whaley cited an early 1940s income of $400 (about $5,500 in 2015 currency) for a week's work scoring a Times Square nightclub revue.[4] By comparison, union-represented chorus dancers might earn fifty to sixty dollars per week.[5]

Louis Armstrong, writing to Don Redman during a residency at the Café Zanzibar, aired both frustration and gratefulness for his steady nightclub work: "I feel fine as ever. . . . Just the damn hours at the Club—are so long. . . . But one just has to get used to it—doesn't one? . . . They've added four more weeks on to these other six we had here. . . . Nice huh?"[6] Most large floor-show venues presented at least three shows nightly, with bands providing additional dinner or dance music between programs. But despite the extended hours, theater and nightclub residencies allowed performers a break from even more demanding road-trip touring schedules. Weeklong—or even season-long—nightclub engagements represented prized respites from life on the bus.

Duke Ellington's orchestra could earn a fairly modest $3,200 during a week's residency at the Hurricane Club in the fall of 1943; the club's total receipts earlier that year (as reported to Ellington) averaged around $18,000 per week.[7] While a top dance orchestra could bring in receipts as large as $1,500 for a well-attended "one-nighter" performance on tour, New York nightclub residencies at venues like the Cotton Club, Hurricane, and Café Zanzibar offered the added bonus of regular radio broadcasts, which helped build long-term publicity for the bands.[8] Theaters were another key source of income for many dance bands; venues like the Harlem Apollo or Broadway Strand presented as many as five or six revue programs a day. In 1935, a top swing act like Cab Calloway could earn as much as $10,000 for a weeklong theater engagement; a 1940 Paramount theater revue featuring Calloway's orchestra reportedly grossed a record-breaking $84,000 over two weeks.[9]

Swing Era nightclub and theater revues extended the vaudeville entertainment format of previous decades. Stage programs presenting multiple acts required an extensive support industry of musicians, composers, arrangers, scriptwriters, and choreographers. An act's accompanying music might be performed by a backing band touring with (and often headlining) the revue, or by local "house" bands attached to a specific venue. If the producers of a revue did not hire music arrangers, the individual acts hired one themselves. Dancer Al Williams of the "Four Step Brothers" offered one possible explanation: "Before the thirties, when we played colored theaters, the pit band could fake [improvise] the accents we needed . . . but the bands in white theaters didn't know how to do it. Eventually, we had to hire arrangers and hand out our own charts."[10] Margot Webb, one of Harold Norton's "adagio" dance partners, recalled their act paying fifty to seventy-five dollars for a stage show arrangement during the mid-1930s (approximately $850 to $1,275 in 2015 currency), noting that "a good arrangement had a potential performance life of two to three years."[11] Dance coaches or choreographers (*dance directors* in period lingo) represented another expenditure for stage acts; Webb cited choreographers charging as much as $250 per routine.[12] Typical of many specialty vaudeville acts, the Norton duo maintained a relatively focused working repertoire of three to five numbers.[13]

White Broadway arranger Robert Russell Bennett described the rigors of arranging music to dance choreography:

> Solo dancers and teams are the *bête noire* of the arranger. They seldom know what they want to dance to and, if they do, have no terms to communicate their wants to a musician. . . . Chorus dancing is staged by a director, who has names for all of the thousand and one tricky rhythms, steps, and formations he uses.

> Everything he creates should be echoed in the perfect orchestration, so, rather than spend months at a dancing school, this humble orchestrator takes down a sketch of every step, hop, twist, entrance, exit, stop, break, back-bend, split, nip-up or what-have-you—measure by measure.[14]

Bandleader Gene Krupa recalled Chappie Willet's contributions to stage show productions: "I'll never forget how much [Willet] did for bands that had to play shows; invariably vaudeville acts brought in music that was worse to listen to than to play, and it was murder to play from those sad, cut-up, marked-up, beat-up stocks. Chappie had the knack of being able to put down on paper what the performer wanted, and yet make it sound good."[15]

Cotton Club floor-show producer Leonard Reed (1907–2004) testified to the importance of pacing and variety in musical revue programming. An extended opening production number might begin with a chorus line of twelve to sixteen dancers, transition into a new tempo for a singing act, and then return to the original tempo; a solo tap or ballroom dance act might follow.[16] Following a large production number, a series of "middle number" specialty acts showcased vaudeville dancers, comedians, and singers in relatively brief routines. For additional variety, Reed's Cotton Club middle numbers included a troupe of "show girls" (as opposed to the chorus-line dancers, or "ponies"): "The show girls did no dancing. They walked and turned and spun—just picture: walk here and pose, and walk somewhere else."[17] The most spectacular of the middle numbers—typically dance acts like the Nicholas Brothers or the Three Chocolateers—would be placed in the penultimate program slot, building up applause for a return of the full ensemble in the finale production number (and preclude the discomfort of any early exits by audience members).[18]

Regardless of budget or venue size, many Swing Era floor-show programs appear to have reflected Reed's Cotton Club strategy—presenting an instrumental overture, an extended opening production number, a series of specialty vaudeville acts, and closing with another extended production number. A program for the Café Zanzibar's winter 1945–46 *Laugh-Lease Revue* indicates specialty acts—each of which usually performing two to three numbers—separated by larger production-style arrangements (featuring the Zanzibeaut dance chorus) positioned at the beginning, midpoint, and end of the program (see table 1).[19]

In a parallel with the Broadway stage musical format, floor-show revues might also utilize a dramatic script that served to tie together (if loosely) the variety acts into a single plot or theme. For example, an archival script titled "Halloween: A Musical Sketch by Donald Heywood" includes speaking parts for boys and girls carrying pumpkin lanterns, "an old witch stirring her boiling pot," and "Satan," whose entrance is accompanied by "frightening screams . . . lightning flashes and . . . wind machine."[20] Leadsheet music sketches for related dance numbers include "Halloween" and "Witch's Dance," both interpolating the classic "Mysterioso" theme associated with silent films; there is also an indication

Table 1. Café Zanzibar *Laugh-Lease Revue* program sequence (ca. December 1945).

Program Sequence	Act or Musical Number
1 (instrumental overture)	"Overture" (featuring the Cootie Williams orchestra)
2 (production number)	"Night Life" (featuring Ralph Brown and the Zanzibeauts)
3 (middle act)	Ella Fitzgerald (singer)
4 (middle act)	Howell & Bowser (comedians)
5 (production number)	"Dance Fantasy" (featuring Bert Howell and Ray Sneed Jr. with the Zanzibeauts)
6 (middle act)	Maurice Rocco (singer and pianist)
7 (middle act)	The Ink Spots (singers)
8 (production number--finale)	"House of Joy" (featuring the Cootie Williams orchestra and the entire company)

for some sort of "cat act."[21] Short dramatic sketches between musical numbers often incorporated the program's specialty performers, requiring a range of performance skills. As dancer Charles "Honi" Coles (1911–92) related to Mel Watkins, "You didn't just come into a show and do your dance routine. It was expected that you'd be in the comedy bits."[22]

Musicologist John Howland observes that interwar Broadway stage production number arrangements were "governed by a formal interest in building internal diversity through contrasting themes, textures, tempi, keys, and variations."[23] Some period film musicals offer documentation of stage revue production practices; Ralph Cooper's *The Duke Is Tops* (Million Dollar, 1938), for example, concludes with a stage show sequence explicitly aimed at re-creating the experience of visiting an exclusive New York nightclub, including performer names and song titles referencing contemporary Cotton Club programs.[24] The opening number of the film's climactic "Harmony Is Harlem" sequence features tap dancer Willie Covan, a veteran of black Broadway who had helped to popularize the "soft shoe" tap style.[25] Covan's orchestral accompaniment is scored in stop-time rhythm to frame his soft-shoe breaks, with multiple tempo and key changes providing dramatic tension and release (see table 2).[26] Harlem dance director Lew Crawford choreographed the accompanying ensemble dances.

Although relatively few scripts or scores from Swing Era floor shows survive, some artifacts connected with the career of arranger Tom Whaley provide a glimpse into the big band stage revue medium. One of New York's first-call stage show writers, Whaley boasted charging as much as $150—"a whole lot of money"—for a single arrangement.[27] A surviving Whaley production-number score labeled "Zanzibar Opening," for example, weaves together portions of "Daybreak Express," "Chattanooga Choo-Choo," "California, Here I Come," "Alabamy Bound," and "Take the 'A' Train" (see table 3).[28] This transportation-themed

Table 2. Formal structure of "Harmony Is Harlem" production number in *The Duke Is Tops*, possibly arr. by Phil Moore (1938). Transcription by the author.

Section	Bars	Performance	Tempo	Key
Intro	4	A cappella vocal ensemble	Slow	B major
Chorus	16 (8+8)			
Verse	16 (8+8)			
Chorus	8			
Interlude	8	Orchestra modulation, ensemble dancers enter	Up-tempo	D major
Chorus	32 (8+8+8+8)	Orchestra, ensemble dance		
Chorus	32 (8+8+8+8)	Orchestra, ensemble dance, instrumental solos		
Interlude	4	Orchestra modulation	Transition	
Chorus	32 (8+8+8+8)	Covan solo dance, rhythm section stop-time	Mid-tempo	B major
Chorus	32 (8+8+8+8)	Covan solo dance, orchestra stop-time		
Interlude	8	Orchestra modulation	Up-tempo	D major
Chorus	8	Covan solo dance, orchestra		

Table 3. Formal structure of "Zanzibar Opening" production number, arr. by Tom Whaley (ca. 1943–47). Manuscript score held in DEC.

Section	Bars	Theme	Key
Intro	16 (8+8)	"Daybreak Express"/"Chattanooga Choo-Choo"	C
Reh. A	32 (8+8+8+8)	"California, Here I Come"	
[Reh. B]	32 (8+8+8+8)	"Alabamy Bound"	A-flat
Reh. C	16 (8+8)	"California, Here I Come"	C
[Interlude]	16 (8+8)		E-flat
	12 (4+8)	"[Jumpin' at the?] Woodside" "4 bars piano, chos. 8 bars" (not notated)	
[Interlude]	8		A-flat
Reh. A [*sic*]	32 (8+8+8+8)	"Take the 'A' Train"	
	24 (8+8+8)	(Ensemble stop-time breaks)	
[Interlude]	8		C
	18	"Daybreak Express" ending, brass train-whistle effect	

medley includes three interludes, five modulations, and a chorus of stop-time breaks almost certainly designed to accompany a dance performance; a brief citation of Count Basie's "Jumpin' at the Woodside" may have been intended for comic effect.

Venues

Looking back on their Broadway heyday, *Variety* critics Abel Green and Joe Laurie Jr. claimed that "1936 and 1937 were such boom years for Harlem [*sic*—New York City] hotspots like the Cotton Club, the Kit Kat, the Harlem Uproar House, Ubangi, Small's Paradise, Plantation, Black Cat, Dicky [*sic*—Dickie] Wells and others, that there was a shortage of sepian [black] talent for the Negro theatres, which had to hire ofay [white] actors to round out their bills."[29] Even allowing for some entertainment-industry hyperbole, Chappie Willet's move to Times Square in the mid-1930s was well timed for entry into stage-arranging work. In addition to nightclubs featuring black entertainers, several large vaudeville theaters—including Loew's State, the Paramount, and the Strand—were a short walk from his Music Clinic offices. By 1941, pianist and *New York Age* columnist Herbie Nichols asserted that Willet "does most of his arranging for stage acts, practically dominating the field."[30] Despite the limited documentation (programs, payrolls, scripts, scores, etc.) of stage show productions from this period, intermittent media coverage traces some of the venues, revues, performers, choreographers, producers, and repertoire connected to Willet and his Music Clinic colleagues.

Few figures of the Swing Era roamed more widely than a freelance musician or a freelance arranger. While touring revues presented Willet's arrangements in venues across the country, his workspaces in New York City ranged from Broadway theaters to basement bars, from exclusive nightclubs to amateur talent shows. The following accounts are offered as a media snapshot of the arranger's working world—an extensive network of people and places that stretched from Harlem to Times Square. When available, performance fees and admission prices are cited to suggest the relative prestige of the different acts and venues. Some of the individuals identified are iconic figures in American entertainment; other Music Clinic associates may appear here in their only historical resurrection to date.

THE APOLLO THEATER

Willet claimed to have received his first New York break in late 1934, working with Luis Russell's orchestra at the 1,500-seat Apollo Theater, on West 125th Street off Eighth Avenue.[31] Russell's "Old Man River" orchestra played the Apollo's weeklong residencies twice that December, including a week with the Nicholas Brothers dance act.[32] Surviving financial records for the Apollo productions during 1934 and 1935 do not reflect direct payments to arrangers or conductors; perhaps they were paid out of the bandleaders' fees. Tom Whaley, who often worked at the Apollo circa 1935–41, reported that he received "a hundred dollars" for directing shows with Duke Ellington's band.[33] Weekly Apollo payments to featured orchestras ranged from $1,200 (paid to Luis Russell for the December 1934 show with the Nicholas Brothers) to $2,250 (paid to Lucky Millinder's orchestra the following month). A week's pay for headline acts like the Nicholas Brothers ranged from $525 (the December 1934 show) to $650 (November 1935). Other specialty acts, including Bessie Smith (February 1935), Harold Norton's dance duos (June 1935), the Three Dukes (February 1935), or Pete Nugent's Pete, Peaches, and Duke trio (February 1935) received between $125 and $350. Radio superstars like the Mills Brothers (April 1935) commanded as much as $3,000; unproven singles like Una Mae Carlisle (February 1935) or Belle Powell (debuting in December 1937) saw as little as $18 to $35.[34]

With a new revue program each week, arrangers like Willet or Whaley were on a tight schedule to tailor musical numbers to the needs of individual performers—which regularly included Willet-booked acts like the Three Dukes, Myra Johnson, the Miller Brothers & Lois, the Bye Sisters, or the Nortons.[35] As Harold Cromer of the comedy-dance act Stump & Stumpy declared of Willet, "He could write fast, I can tell you that!"[36] Cromer recalled witnessing Willet rehearse Lucky Millinder's orchestra in the Apollo basement, although it is not clear if Willet also conducted Apollo performances as Whaley had. A surviving Whaley orchestration labeled "Waters' Opening March 4 '38" coincides with an Ethel Waters performance at the Apollo backed by Eddie Mallory's orchestra; another Whaley score labeled "Ella Fitzgerald April 11 '41" corresponds to the Fitzgerald band's weeklong stand beginning on that date.[37] Other Apollo revue artifacts include Porter Grainger's script for a comedy stage routine titled "Miss High Brow and Mr. Tough"; Grainger's song "Harlem Has a Regiment for War" indicates use by Apollo favorites Ralph Cooper and comic-singer Dewey "Pigmeat" Markham.[38] Another Markham vehicle—Donald Heywood's "Pigmeat for President"—survives as a score comprising a ten-bar introduction, a two-bar repeating vamp, a series of odd-length vocal verse passages (twelve, eight, and eleven bars), a thirty-two-bar chorus, and a thirty-six-bar "vocal-dance" chorus.[39] Willet's arranging work was cited in publicity for Jimmie Lunceford's Apollo residency in January 1943 (Willet's arrangement of "East of the Sun"—with parts copied by Whaley—may date from this engagement) and Earl Hines's residency in September 1943.[40] Publicity for a June 1944 Millinder performance, promising a "stringless" thirty-piece orchestra and thirty-voice choir, touted arrangements by Willet and William Johnson.[41]

Another Apollo arranging task was to provide music for the chorus-line routines. Dance historians Marshall and Jean Stearns claimed that Sy Oliver's

"For Dancers Only" for Jimmie Lunceford (1937) was designed to accompany the Apollo dance chorus.[42] During the Swing Era, the "dance director" most often credited in Apollo productions was Leonard Harper (1899–1943), whose duties might have ranged from the grouping of stage-show scenes to the coaching of individual acts.[43] Clarence Robinson (1900–1979) occasionally served in the same capacity or as producer: organizing the roster of acts and perhaps assigning music-arranging duties.[44] Dancer Honi Coles, who went on to work as manager of the Apollo during the 1950s, praised Willet's stage work: "Finding an arranger who knew what we wanted was tough. . . . One of the best was Chappie Willett [*sic*]. We'd hum the crazy accents, along with the tune, and he put them in big-band arrangements."[45] Coles's dancing partner, Cholly Atkins, recalled their duo performing Willet's music on a theater tour with Count Basie in 1947: "A guy out of Philadelphia, Chappie Willet, arranged the music for our whole act. We had some real pretty melodic saxophone passages, and Basie's band just loved to get to a certain part. There would be no brass in there, nothing but rhythm and saxophones. And the cats would start singing."[46] The Apollo may have also been one of the last stage venues for Willet; Leonard Reed recalled Willet working with Apollo bandleader Reuben Phillips during the 1950s.[47] A 1958 production—from the period Reed is credited as producer at the Apollo—included Phillips's band, the Miller Brothers, and Stump & Stumpy.[48]

CONNIE'S INN

Russell Wooding arranged the *Hot Chocolates* floor shows at Connie's Inn—run by brothers Connie and George Immerman—during the spring and fall of 1935.[49] The spring production marked the reopening of the club after moving from Harlem (on Seventh Avenue off 131st Street, next to the Lafayette Theater) down to 200 West Forty-Eighth Street on Broadway (a site previously occupied by the Palais Royale).[50] Willet's work for Louis Armstrong began during the trumpeter's fall 1935 residency, where he was backed by Luis Russell's band; in addition to Willet's prior connection to Luis Russell, a recommendation or approval from Wooding at this time may have inspired the Broadway Music Clinic alliance. Armstrong recorded Willet's arrangement of "I've Got My Fingers Crossed" with Luis Russell's orchestra in November 1935; the *New York Amsterdam News* reported that Willet's compositions "Blue Rhythm Fantasy" and "Jungle Madness" were also included in broadcasts from Connie's during this period.[51] The Connie's residency culminated in the Luis Russell band becoming Armstrong's regular backing ensemble.

Connie's Inn was a "black-and-tan" venue—a term applied to establishments that allowed a degree of racial integration, but which usually implied the presentation of black entertainment to a white clientele. As Candice Love Jackson suggests, *tan* was also period slang for "whites who immersed themselves in black musical culture, pretending for a brief time that they belonged to the black community"; these venues could also maintain admission policies that "discouraged black patrons."[52] Prices at Connie's Inn were on the expensive side, though purchase of dinner was apparently not required (or perhaps depended on the patron); an advertisement for the Armstrong-Russell show, including "97 sepia stars," cited a cover charge of eighty-five cents, with a chicken dinner for $2.50 ($2.00 on weekends and holidays).[53] Like most midtown nightclubs during this period, the club presented three shows nightly. Leonard Harper staged many of the productions, which toured theaters in addition to (or, in some cases, aside from) the club venue; Willet may have "discovered" singer (Carrie) Belle Powell when she performed with the Three Melody Girls act in a 1937 touring production of *Connie's Hot Chocolates*.[54] The *Hot Chocolates* tours outlived the venue itself, which folded in the summer of 1936.[55]

THE COTTON CLUB

In September 1936, the Cotton Club moved from its Harlem location to midtown Broadway, at 200 West Forty-Eighth Street (previously the midtown location of Connie's Inn).[56] Managed by Herman Stark, the club continued to feature many

Arranger Chappie Willet and vocalist (Carrie) Belle Powell, ca. December 1937. Powell performed with the orchestras of Willie Bryant and Claude Hopkins. Courtesy of the Louis Armstrong House Museum.

of the same performers that had built the Harlem venue's reputation during the 1920s and early '30s, including Cab Calloway, Duke Ellington, Bill "Bojangles" Robinson, and Ethel Waters. Different "Cotton Club Parade" productions, featuring original music by Broadway composing teams like Bloom and Koehler or Fields and McHugh, were presented in the fall and spring, with an occasional third "summer" production staged in late spring.[57] Charlie Davis and Leonard Reed worked as producers for the club's programs during the late 1930s; Clarence Robinson often served as dance director.[58]

Willet cited the Cotton Club as a client by July 1937, although the arranger's exact position at the venue is unclear.[59] Leonard Reed recalled Willet working as the club's "house rehearsal pianist" from the period Reed first arrived (ca. 1937) until he left (ca. 1939), suggesting the arranger was a sort of fixture in the establishment.[60] Cab Calloway's trombonist Quentin Jackson also recalled Willet's work at the venue, praising him as an "extremely good arranger" who did "a lot of arranging for shows and for Cotton Club shows," including dance acts like the Cotton Club Boys.[61] Given the seasonal production schedule, however, it is not clear how regular Willet's employment was. Individual acts may have requested arrangers' services outside of the club rehearsals; for example, tap dancer Fayard Nicholas (1914–2006) worked with Willet privately to develop a routine for the Cotton Club. Their collaboration—possibly created at the Broadway Music Clinic—is related by Nicholas Brothers biographer Constance Valis Hill:

> Fayard danced the steps and hummed the accents as Willett [*sic*], on piano, improvised the melody. . . ."It was like we were in a rehearsal hall with mirrors and everything," Fayard recalls. "He wrote down everything I said and showed him—I even sang some of it to him—Da da, dat-da dee do dee daa, like that. That would be the introduction. No music." Unlike the thirty-two-bar musical structure the brothers most often used when working with big bands, Fayard's more openly structured solo "was more of a classical thing," he says, and it stretched past the eight-bar phrase. Instead of being episodic, with the B section following A, and so on, there was a more continuous weave of sound and movement. The resulting tapwork not only dovetailed with the melody but also included special accents that were reinforced by accompaniment. Fayard did not have a name for it, so he called it "Dance Specialty," and he performed it after his and Harold's "Specialty" act at the Cotton Club. Willett's [*sic*] formal, written arrangement of the music for big band enabled Fayard to perform the dance not only in the intimate setting of the Cotton Club but also on bigger stages and with other big-band orchestras.[62]

A program for the spring 1937 *Cotton Club Express* production (with Duke Ellington and Ethel Waters headlining) lists the Nicholas Brothers performing a number simply titled "Specialty," perhaps the routine cited by Fayard Nicholas.[63] Willet's relationship with the Cotton Club and its elite performers also provided a measure of professional prestige, as noted in an *Amsterdam News* plug for Willet's talent school titled "Plea for Training: Arranger Says Singers Need to Study":

> "Yes, sir, the plight of the amateur performer nowadays is very sad, and the future of Negro talent seems even less promising," declared Chappie Willet, ace Broadway arranger and talent discoverer. He made this declaration during the audition hours at the Cotton Club Wednesday, and aspirants were being turned down in droves either because they were just so-so or hadn't been properly rehearsed. . . ."The white performers realize the importance of the right training, but Negroes are still hoping for stardom, and at the same time are unwilling to prepare properly for it."[64]

In March 1938, *Billboard* magazine announced: "Chappie Willet, whose scorings have highlighted the leading colored combos, is handling the arrangement assignment for Duke Ellington at the Cotton Club."[65] Although Will Vodery was the only arranger credited in programs and other publicity for this production, Willet's union stamp is found on surviving manuscript music for one of the program numbers, "Swingtime in Honolulu."[66] Both Willet and Vodery were credited in a *Pittsburgh Courier* review of the club's fall 1938 production, featuring Cab Calloway, the Nicholas Brothers, the Dandridge Sisters, Rosetta Tharpe, and the Berry Brothers.[67] Cotton Club audiences also heard performances by various "house bands," including those led by Eddie Mallory, or Alberto Socarrás, whose Cuban dance band also appeared at the Harlem Uproar House and other venues.[68] Aircheck recordings of the Cotton Club's live radio broadcasts document Willet arrangements performed by Ellington ("Prelude in C-sharp Minor") and Louis Armstrong ("Struttin' with Some Barbecue").[69] Other Cotton Club acts reportedly connected to Willet included singers Avis Andrews (with the Cab Calloway orchestra) and June Richmond (with Andy Kirk).[70] The club closed in June 1940 amid investigations of tax fraud.[71] In addition to the loss of untaxed income, the demise of this prestigious venue may have been a factor in prompting Willet to devote more efforts toward publicizing his music school and booking agency during 1940 and 1941 or to undertake ventures like the Indigo Room production (chapter 2).[72]

THE ELKS' RENDEZVOUS CLUB

The Elks' Rendezvous Club, located at 464 Lenox Avenue off 133rd Street (south of the Elks' Henry Lincoln Johnson Lodge at 650 Lenox), opened in November 1937.[73] "America's Most Intimate Nite Club" presented floor shows staged by Leonard Harper and Lew Crawford, with the "Rendezvouettes" dance chorus and a number of Willet-roster acts including the Bye Sisters, Reeves Sisters, Tick & Tock, Inez Washington, and Zaro & Lakeeta (formerly Sandra & Lakeeta).[74] One of Porter Grainger's better-known compositions, "One Hour Mama," was recorded by Elks' Rendezvous performer Margaret Watkins; surviving manuscript music reflects the popular vaudeville device of an extended stop-time patter section between choruses.[75] Ralph Cooper (one of Crawford's associates from *The Duke Is Tops*) occasionally served as producer, and also appeared in the club's spring 1942 revue that included Sandra & Lakeeta and Myra Johnson (with the chorus "togged out in spiffy navy outfits").[76] The club operated until the mid-1950s.[77]

THE KIT KAT CLUB

Julie "Jules" Podell's Kit Kat Club, at 152 East Fifty-Sixth Street off Lexington Avenue, operated from 1935 until 1942.[78] Harold Cromer recalled George Immerman handling the Kit Kat talent booking; Chappie Willet's work at the venue was cited in March 1938.[79] Jazz critic and producer Hugues Panassié documented his viewing of the Jimmie Lunceford orchestra at the Kit Kat in November 1938, a possible source of his claim that Willet's "best arrangements have not been recorded."[80] Perhaps a step down from the Times Square venues, the club charged a $1.50 food and drink minimum at the time of Lunceford's residency.[81] After closing, the Kit Kat site was home to the Café Life, and then the Blue Angel.[82] Podell—a regular subject of law-enforcement investigations—also ran the Copacabana nightclub, originally located at 10 East Sixtieth Street.[83]

LOEW'S STATE THEATER

The 3,300-seat Loew's State Theater, at 1540 Broadway off Forty-Fifth Street, presented touring revues backed by bandleaders such as Lucky Millinder, Duke Ellington, and Louis Armstrong; admission for a 1937 show was fifty-five cents.[84] Willet's arrangement of "There's a Lull in My Life," cited in July 1937, could be the version Ella Fitzgerald performed with Chick Webb's orchestra during a Loew's State residency that August.[85] Cab Calloway's orchestra performed Willet arrangements at Loew's State in December 1938, including a feature for singer June Richmond titled "One Alone."[86] Willet client Myra Johnson, who had built her reputation singing with Fats Waller's band, made appearances at Loew's State throughout the late 1930s and early '40s.[87] In February 1944, the tap-dance trio the Three Hearts was featured in a vaudeville lineup accompanying the film *Swing Fever*; a subsequent *Billboard* review of the act noted "excellent jump music, arranged for them by Chappy [*sic*] Willet, Gotham Negro scorer. . . . Best effort was a rhythm tap done with chairs, which featured plenty of kicks and twists."[88]

CLUB MIMO

Bill "Bojangles" Robinson's Club Mimo, established in early 1938, was located at 2237 Seventh Avenue off 132nd Street.[89] Willet, Willie Bryant, and Clarence Robinson were among those listed in attendance at Robinson's sixty-first birthday party in 1939.[90] Porter Grainger provided music for Club Mimo revues in the spring and fall of 1941; the spring production, staged by Clarence Robinson and including Pete Nugent and Norton & Margot, made an additional run at the Apollo; the fall revue, *Rhythm Bound*, was produced by Charlie Davis.[91] A surviving Grainger script indicating use at Club Mimo—"Slaves de Orient"—offers a vehicle for growling brass and "oriental fanfare" music accompanying a troupe of "slave" women ("buds from Allah's garden . . . queens of innocence").[92]

MURRAIN'S CABARET

John Murrain's Cabaret—celebrated in Porter Grainger's song "When You're at Murrain's"—moved into the Club Mimo space around January 1942.[93] Publicity later that spring documented engagements for Willet-booked acts Tick & Tock and Sandra & Lakeeta (Sandra was apparently replaced by Zaro around this time).[94] Upon Leonard Harper's death, Lew Crawford took over the staging of a winter 1943 production that included Norton & Norton.[95] Pianist-composer Herbie Nichols recalled making Willet's acquaintance while Nichols was working at Murrain's with Walter Dennis's band during 1943 and 1944.[96] Danny "Prince of Joy" Henry, a former manager at the Elks' Rendezvous, produced the club's spring 1947 floor show, which continued to feature a number of specialty acts in addition to the "six lovely Murrainettes."[97] The club operated at the Seventh Avenue address through at least 1949, when a second location opened in the Bronx.[98]

THE PARAMOUNT THEATER

The 3,600-seat Paramount, at 1501 Broadway off Forty-Fourth Street, hosted residencies by big bands and touring revues, including a show with Red Norvo and Mildred Bailey in June 1938, and Gene Krupa in July 1939.[99] Cab Calloway's *Cotton Club Revue*, featuring Avis Andrews and the Three Chocolateers, appeared for two weeks during August–September 1940; the production included the debut of an original Willet-Chocolateers collaboration titled "The Hicky Ricky" (chapter 8).[100] The *Amsterdam News* noted Willet's office party for Erskine Hawkins's orchestra and the Ink Spots on the occasion of their Paramount stand in August 1941.[101]

THE PLANTATION CLUB

Joe Springer's Plantation Club opened in June 1936, occupying the Cotton Club's old location at 644 Lenox Avenue off 142nd Street.[102] When the Harlem Ubangi

Club closed in 1937, Grainger and Heywood's *Brevities in Bronze* show moved into the Plantation.[103] Heywood's song "(In My) Well of Loneliness"—a vehicle for Barrington Guy—was featured in the *Brevities in Bronze* production, and again in the 1939 Plantation revue *See Harlem First.*[104] Heywood was also credited on the 1938 revue *Swing-Copations.*[105] Teddy Blackman produced shows for the Plantation's "Tan Town Topics" productions, including the spring 1938 *Flirtation Fancies* revue featuring Pete Nugent.[106] Publicity citing Willet's arranging contributions appeared that same season; dance director Clarence Robinson worked at the club as well.[107] The Plantation closed in summer 1939, apparently relating to a liquor license revocation.[108]

SMALL'S PARADISE

Ed Small's Paradise, at 2294½ Seventh Avenue off 135th Street, was one of the few Harlem venues to enjoy success before, during, and after the Swing Era. Producer Al Richards and arranger Harry White worked with Porter Grainger on the club's fall 1936 and spring 1937 productions; Grainger composed and arranged (and may have written scripts for) revues including *Harlem Swing Hotel* (1936), *Paradise on the Nile* (1937), and *By the Spell of the Moon* (1943).[109] The Reeves Sisters performed in the spring 1942 *Chock Full of Rhythm* revue, staged by Leonard Harper and backed by Earl Bostic's band; Myra Johnson was also featured at the club.[110] Thelma Simmons served as producer for Grainger's fall 1943 show.[111] The ubiquitous Alberto Socarrás occasionally led the Small's house band as well.[112] Admission price in 1942 was $1.50.[113]

Both the Susie-Q (or Suzy-Q) and the Skronch (or Skrontch) dances were reported to have originated in Grainger's Paradise revues.[114] It is possible that Grainger's "Bowling Green Skronch" (from the 1937 revue *Paradise on the Nile*, but no doubt referencing Grainger's Kentucky roots) is related to Duke Ellington's 1938 "Skrontch" via the Broadway Music Clinic, when Willet worked on Ellington's Cotton Club show. As one report on Ellington's revue noted, "'The Skrontch' . . . it is said, was done a century ago in Kentucky."[115] Tom Whaley scores and leadsheets relating to another of Grainger's revues, labeled "Small's Paradise March 26 '44," include the titles "Daddy of Rhythm Opening," "Can't Wipe Us Out," "Congo Gal," "Mr. Tough," and a "Finale." Orchestra parts for a version of "Mr. Tough" include pasted-in excerpts from a stock arrangement of Noel Coward's "Zigeuner" waltz, and directions to continue into "St. Louis Blues."[116]

THE STRAND THEATER

Located at 1579 Broadway off Forty-Seventh Street, the 2,700-seat Strand Theater hosted revue tours backed by headliners like the Count Basie and Cab Calloway orchestras throughout the 1930s and '40s. Willet's office hosted a party for

Calloway's musicians during their July 1941 Strand residency, which also featured Avis Andrews.[117] In April 1947, another Calloway-backed revue—presenting five shows daily—included the Miller Brothers & Lois act.[118]

THE UBANGI CLUB

The first Ubangi Club opened in early 1934 at 2221 Seventh Avenue off 131st Street, in the space formerly occupied by the original Connie's Inn and the Immermans' short-lived Club Harlem.[119] Russell Wooding worked on the fall 1935 Ubangi production; before the venue closed in mid-1937, residencies were held by orchestra leaders Willie Bryant and Teddy Hill, backing floor shows with "a cast of 30" or "50 sepia stars."[120] Lew Crawford and Leonard Harper served as dance directors; at least one uptown *Ubangi Club Revue* was also presented at the Apollo.[121]

In 1941, Joe Springer opened a new Ubangi Club at 1678 Broadway off Fifty-Second Street (a site that later housed the jazz club Birdland). Donald Heywood wrote or produced stage shows for both Ubangi venues, including the uptown *Brevities in Bronze* (1937, a collaboration with Grainger), and midtown *Tan Manhattan* (1941, crediting orchestrations by Willet) and *Top Hats and Tom Toms* (1944).[122] Publicity for the establishment's 1941 opening gala presentation of *Tan Manhattan* offered dinner for a price of $1.25, with "never a cover charge" for floor shows in which "coffee colored belles" offered "lusty entertainment."[123] An undated postcard advertising the club's midtown location cited the same price for "the hottest colored show on Broadway," with photos of chorus dancers and dining-room seating under fake palm trees.[124]

Trombonist Clyde Bernhardt, who performed at the midtown Ubangi with Cecil Scott's orchestra from fall 1943 through spring 1944, provides a brief but invaluable description of the nightclub:

> Cecil had a six-month contract with the Ubangi but kept working there long after that. It was just a average looking club, some imitation pictures of Africa on the wall, but not a whole lot of them. The bandstand was suppose to be a old native hut or something. . . .
>
> They had a good floor show there, almost two hours long. Chappie Willet wrote the music and Donald Heywood produced. Alan Drew was master of ceremonies and male comedian. Used to have this big cigar stuffed in his mouth all the time—that was his trademark. His jokes was kind of smutty but he had the people laughing. [Jackie] Moms Mabley was the female comedian at the Ubangi. Mabel Lee, dancer Derby Wilson, and singer Myra Johnson was also on the bill. When Myra left, Margaret Watkins came in . . . could sure holler them blues.
>
> It was about January of 1944 that Joe Springer, the owner of the Ubangi, sent us down to the Center Street police station to get a cabaret card. There was a wartime rule in New York to make sure you didn't have no record of using dope

> and messing up. . . . After working the Ubangi for about five months, a rumor started going around that the club was cutting expenses. Something about a new war tax and they were going to drop a musician or two, maybe a couple chorus girls in order to break even. I thought they [were] doing terrific business but heard that's what they were going to do.[125]

New York Times publicity cited Charles Morrison as dance director for the *Top Hats and Tom Toms* production.[126] An April 1944 *Times* article, "Tax on Night Clubs Costs 5,000 Jobs of Entertainers," cited the Ubangi as one of many venues "contemplating abolishing entertainment on May 1"—the date that a new, nationwide amusement tax on patronage of nightclubs offering live entertainment would take effect.[127] While a number of clubs did continue their stage shows under the new tax (which was eventually lowered from 30 percent to 20 percent), the Ubangi appears to have ceased floor-show entertainment at that time.[128]

THE CAFÉ ZANZIBAR

After the Cotton Club, Joe Howard and Carl Erbe's Café Zanzibar may have been Willet's highest-profile nightclub venue. Opened in June 1943, the Zanzibar's first location was at 1634 Broadway and Fiftieth Street, above the Winter Garden Theatre (a space subsequently occupied by Ruby Foo's restaurant, and later host to an Applebee's franchise); in December 1944, the club moved across the street to the second floor of the Brill Building at 1619 Broadway and Forty-Ninth Street (a space previously occupied by Dave Wolper's Hurricane Club); in February 1947, the Zanzibar moved to a third, smaller venue, on Broadway "just above 47th Street" (previously occupied by the Ole South nightclub).[129] This last location presented a reduced floor show, as the "Zanzibeauts" chorus dancers took up residency at the Club 845 in the Bronx.[130] Despite claims of "never a cover charge," Zanzibar admission pricing varied; the Winter Garden location originally charged a $2.50 minimum, and the opening production at the Brill Building location charged $3.50, though frequent special promotions cited $2.00 (dinner included).[131]

Clyde Bernhardt described the contrast between the Zanzibar—where he performed in fall 1944 with the house band led by Claude Hopkins—and the seedier Ubangi: "The Zanzibar was very beautiful, and it had class. . . . There was a lot of mirrors in there, and all the reflections looked pretty. . . . Chappie Willet wrote the floor show as he did at the Ubangi. . . . White sports people, movie stars, politicians, and money big shots always came in there. But no Lindy Hopper dancers. It was strictly the fox-trot crowd."[132] Clarence Robinson and Jimmy Payne worked as dance directors on the different "Zanzibarabian Nights" productions.[133] Robinson, a native of Philadelphia, appears to have been a key associate of Willet throughout the Swing Era; Robinson's wife, Cotton Club and Zanzibar chorine Hyacinth Curtis, was even featured in Willet publicity photos.[134] Zanzibeaut chorus dancer Cleo Hayes fondly recalled working with Robinson, and remembered him working at the Zanzibar with Willet: "The last couple of days before the show would go in, [Willet] would come in and work with us and the band. . . . [Robinson] was the best, in every respect: he was easy to work with, you liked his work."[135] Hayes, who had also performed at the Cotton Club, described the Zanzibar epoch as the beginning of the end for Broadway nightclub floor shows: "By the time Zanzibar came along, they were beginning to use popular music. They were not having things [original compositions] that were written especially for the show. That was Cotton Club. . . . There was no repeat on that, black or white."[136] Some of the Zanzibar productions still featured original song material, created by composing teams like Benny Davis and Ted Murry.

Scattered archival music relating to the Zanzibar shows includes Porter Grainger's lyric sheet for a song titled "Zanzibar" (apparently not the Ellington composition of the same name) for "Clarence Robinson production Club Zanzibar"; a handwritten note on the document indicating "Miss Andrews" likely refers to Avis Andrews, who shared a bill at the Zanzibar with Ella Fitzgerald and Don Redman's orchestra in the summer and fall of 1943.[137] Grainger also wrote music for the following November 1943 production featuring Redman (alternating with Alberto Socarrás), Buck & Bubbles, Ella Fitzgerald, and boogie-woogie pianist Maurice Rocco.[138] A Tom Whaley big band score labeled "Opening Zanzibar Nov 24 '43" indicates stop-time breaks for a dance routine; a Redman-arranged score labeled "Zanzibar Finale"—including a note citing Grainger's "Mr. Tough" and an indication to continue into "Blue Skies"—may also stem from this production.[139]

A Willet arrangement of "Stardust" for Louis Armstrong's orchestra likely dates from the trumpeter's fall 1944 Zanzibar residency.[140] The Armstrong-headlined revue, which included Bill Robinson, the Nicholas Brothers, the Peters Sisters, Maurice Rocco, and the Delta Rhythm Boys vocal ensemble, made additional appearances at the Roxy Theater.[141] Willet's arranging contributions are cited in publicity for the Zanzibar's fall 1945 show, featuring Louis Jordan and Duke Ellington; partially surviving music includes Willet's arrangement of "Low Down Guy—High Class Girl."[142] The following December 1945–March 1946 *Laugh-Lease Revue* starring Cootie Williams and Ella Fitzgerald credited "special arrangements by Chappie Willet"; performers Ray Snead (the "sepia Ray Bolger") and Buddy Bowser also appear to have been affiliated with Willet's booking services.[143] A subsequent program featuring Bill Robinson and the Mills Brothers overlapped into the spring 1946 production; newly added talent included tap dancer Bunny Briggs, singer Marie Ellington, the Nat Cole trio, comedian Eddie "Rochester" Anderson, and the Teddy McRae orchestra, with

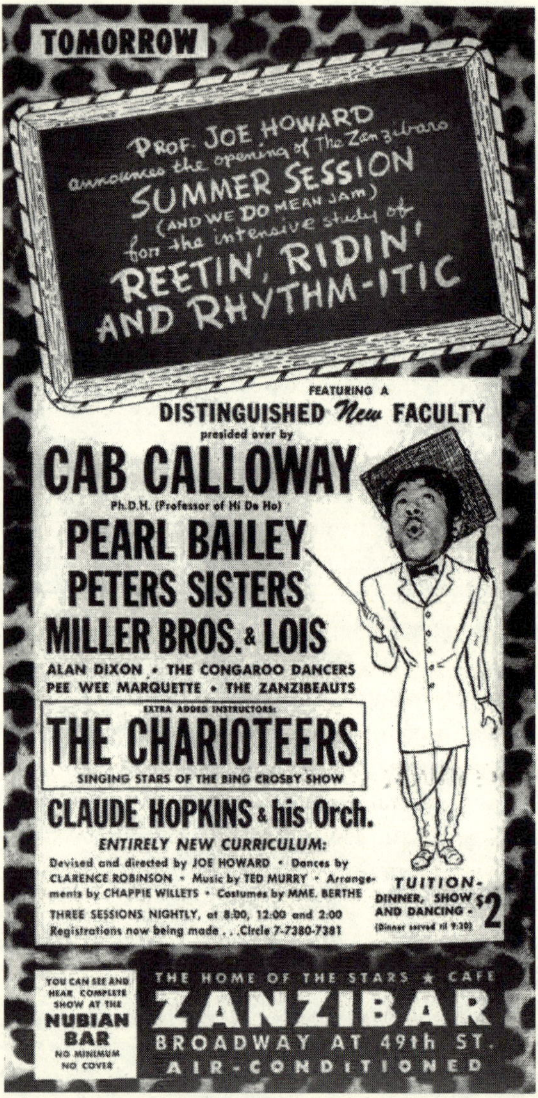

Café Zanzibar advertisement ("arrangements by Chappie Willets" [*sic*]), *New York Post*, June 25, 1946.

arrangements credited to Ted Murry and orchestrations to Willet.[144] Cab Calloway, the Peters Sisters, and the Miller Brothers & Lois headlined the summer 1946 lineup, again featuring Willet arrangements; the fall 1946 program, including the Ink Spots, Thelma Carpenter, Peg Leg Bates, and Eddie "Cleanhead" Vinson's orchestra, cited Murry arrangements and Willet orchestrations.[145]

After its final move in 1947, the Zanzibar reduced the size of its productions; Clarence Robinson conceded that "times are different now and we must cut down on overhead."[146] Willet reportedly obtained arranging work at Carl Erbe's new Vanity Fair nightclub, which opened in the Zanzibar's former Brill Building space.[147] When both the Vanity Fair and newly relocated Zanzibar opened that winter, the *Amsterdam News* noted that "an interesting commentary upon the difference between owners Joe Howard and Carl Erbe, . . . one [working] with colored entertainers and the other with white, is in the salary roll which will call for $8,000 a week at Zanzibar and $15,000 weekly at the Vanity Fair."[148] Even considering the reduced scale of the Zanzibar presentations, such extreme salary discrepancies reflected the brutal realities of the segregated entertainment industry. The fact that both clubs folded within a year was another indicator of the period, as even the lesser-paying jobs were becoming difficult to find.[149]

OTHER VENUES

Additional venues named in publicity relating to Willet, his talent roster, or the other Music Clinic residents include the Harlem Uproar House (operating January–November 1937, at 209 West Fifty-First Street off Broadway), Ben Marden's Riviera Club (operating ca. 1932–44 in Fort Lee, New Jersey, and another regular target of law-enforcement investigations), the Sky Club (operating ca. 1937–40, at 2195 Third Avenue off 120th Street), and Chu Jor's World Chinese Restaurant Cabaret (also referred to as "the World," operating ca. 1940–43, at 2387 Seventh Avenue off 139th Street).[150]

In January 1937, a *New York Times* review of the short-lived Harlem Uproar House described "a razzle-dazzle sort of place with an informal, hey-hey atmosphere and a thoroughly uninhibited show which boasts of several lively performers."[151] In addition to meeting the various legal and financial regulations intermittently enforced during the Swing Era (racketeering, taxes, etc.), New York nightclubs were occasionally pressured by authorities to clean up their presentations of "scantily-clad" chorus dancers.[152] A subsequent *Times* review that May reported that the Uproar House—"one of the hottest spots on Broadway"—fell under renewed pressure, and presented "what was solemnly called the 'funeral of the strip-tease' . . . and then discreetly passed out more wearing apparel to its comely dancing girls."[153] The following month, the *Times* reported the Cotton Club and Harlem Uproar House to be among the midtown nightclub venues cited by the New York City Police Department as presenting floor shows with "objectionable" content:

> Complaints had been lodged against the shows by plainclothes men who viewed the shows and reported them objectionable. [Police] Commissioner [John J.] Sullivan said:
>
> "Based on the contention and defense offered by the licensees they are given the benefit of the doubt with a warning that any repetition of the alleged occurrences would warrant drastic action being taken against them, with a view of revocation

> of licenses, and that in the future they may expect the same close supervision that they have been receiving in the past. . . ." [Harlem Uproar House manager] Mr. [Jay] Faggen . . . asserted that when his club opens in the Fall it will have a show that will be "99 per cent vaudeville."[154]

Faggen may have attempted to redeem the legal status of his establishment. A *Times* review in September described the Uproar House fall production to be a "somewhat warier and more chaste kermess than its predecessors," but also attempted to reassure readers that "still, the essential ingredients are there."[155] Perhaps audiences were more discerning, or the club's owners simply decided to cash out as their bookkeeping fell under closer scrutiny; the Uproar House filed for bankruptcy two months later.[156]

* * *

Chappie Willet's ability to work across a wide range of venues and clients was a critical factor to his success. His career in a white-dominated entertainment industry may have necessitated such movement, even as it also—in view of the demand for black talent—may have rewarded it. Between Harlem and Times Square, the music of a freelance arranger like Willet might be performed by more musicians and heard by more varied audiences than that of many figures who found their success limited to more specific markets. As explored in the following chapters, even Willet's music arrangements might be heard to reflect these crossings between different social strata and cultural backgrounds.

4

Theory and Practice

The Fundamentals

> As with most subjects, arranging can be divided into theory and practice. The first consists of fundamentals from study and books. . . . But knowledge of these subjects will not make an arranger, particularly one of modern music. Experience and practical application of original ideas are important, probably more so than fundamental knowledge.[1]
>
> —Arranger Jimmy Dale, *Metronome*, 1933

The next three chapters explore some of the musical techniques and tools favored by Swing Era big band arrangers. Jimmy Dale's discussion of "theory and practice" is a theme repeated in many accounts of the arranging discipline. Bandleader Kay Kyser claimed that arranging required "study and technical knowledge far beyond that of the average—or even the above-average—musician."[2] Musicologist Scott DeVeaux suggests that "specialized terminology of European music theory" may have been limited to those Swing Era musicians who "harbored the ambition to become composers or arrangers."[3] Access to professional experience, education, or training is a central concern in examining Depression-era America; parallels between education and career success were especially pertinent for black musicians subjugated to the doctrine of "separate but equal." Yet despite its recognized importance, the question of specific technical or theoretical musical knowledge—what did arrangers know and when did they know it—can be difficult to pin down.

Swing Era arrangers have been remarkably spare in revealing the details of their own education or techniques in published histories, and it seems that biographers or interviewers have rarely pressed them on the issue. As a result, explanations like that of Bill Challis or Jimmy Mundy—"I just picked it up"—may have added to the discipline's reputation as an enigmatic practice.[4] While many arrangers received training in music performance, their turn to arranging seems to reflect personal predilection more than any systematic tutoring.

In any case, more informative arrangers do not appear to have embraced any single school, teacher, or pedagogical resource more than any other, although a couple of potential exceptions may be offered.

Some arrangers reinforced Jimmy Dale's emphasis on "hands-on" education, claiming to have essentially learned the craft on their own. Most formal music training prior to World War II focused on the European classical tradition, so that musicians interested in popular idioms like dance band music had no structured pedagogy. Ed Wilcox, who trained in music at Fisk University and was a founding member of Jimmie Lunceford's orchestra, noted that "little of [the orchestration, harmony, and counterpoint courses at Fisk] meant anything where dance bands were concerned," and described his arranging education as "a matter of trial and error."[5] Sammy Lowe, who worked with the Erskine Hawkins orchestra, also cited "trial, hit and error" as his method of learning: "I took orchestrations and spread 'em out on the bed to see what each instrument was doing. . . . I thought I'd get some formal training at Tennessee State, but I soon found out that I knew more about writing arrangements than the instructors."[6] Benny Carter described a similar strategy: "Take each part from an orchestration, put them on the floor, and study them, part by part. . . . It was many years before I learned to make a score."[7] Fred Norman, who studied music at Howard University, explained that he "never had any training in arranging, and there weren't many books available then, so I used to go to the Library of Congress and sit and study the books on music they had there."[8]

Unavailability of academic instruction or avoidance of "how-to" publications could also be embraced as a source of pride, allowing arrangers to celebrate the development of their own artistic instincts and "original ideas." Indeed, the growing competition of the period may have rewarded reputations for innate talent or clandestine methodology. Spud Murphy's 1937 *Swing Arranging Method* publication touted its author as "devoid of a thorough academic knowledge; . . . he 'feels' his scores, rather than methodically plans them on score paper."[9] In a similar vein, Mary Lou Williams humbly boasted that her employer Andy Kirk "liked my ideas, though I could not set them down on paper. . . . I hadn't studied theory, but asked Kirk about chords and voicing and register. In about 15 minutes I had memorized what I wanted . . . the boys gave me a chance and each time I did better."[10] Concerns of developing and maintaining a uniquely individual style may in part explain why arrangers have identified relatively generic sources of technical information—like Cecil Forsythe's *Orchestration*, a text cited by arrangers Bill Challis, Glenn Miller, and Nelson Riddle—more readily than publications specifically devoted to dance band arranging technique.[11] Knowledge of orchestration was necessary for any arranger; as Williams rued, "my first attempt, 'Messa Stomp,' was beyond the range of half the instruments."[12] Bassist George Duvivier, who arranged for Lucky Millinder and Jimmie Lunceford, explained that he was familiar with harmonic theory, but "wrote one early arrangement in which there was something completely out of range of the poor trombone player. I didn't know what the problems were, so I got a book about all the instruments, what they could do and what they couldn't."[13]

Despite the reliance on self-education and the prizing of individual style, traditional school-music programs still represented an attractive avenue. Gerald Wilson, a trumpeter-arranger for Jimmie Lunceford, described his own pedigree in a prestigious high school program:

> I never actually used anything [arranging books or magazines]. . . . I had studied harmony at Cass Tech in Detroit—studied writing with some private teachers in Detroit, Michigan, where I attended school for about five years, at Cass Tech there. It was a very . . . recognized department. So I had studied harmony. . . . You had to [already have] a major instrument that you could play [before entering Cass]. So it was quite an experience.[14]

Big band pioneer Don Redman followed his musical training at Storer College with "advanced studies" at the Boston Conservatory of Music.[15] Trumpeter Dick Vance, who played and wrote for Fletcher Henderson's orchestra, went on to study composition at Juilliard.[16] Another eager student was Eddie Sauter. Prior to study with modernist concert music composer Stefan Wolpe in the 1940s, Sauter had taken composition lessons from instructors affiliated with the Chicago Music College (Louis Gruenberg), Columbia University Teacher's College (Howard Murphy), and Juilliard (Bernard Wagner).[17]

Other aspiring arrangers picked up knowledge informally from their peers working in the field. Tom Whaley, who was active prior to the arrival of the Swing Era, claimed that he had no formal training in arranging, and initially "made so many mistakes, leaving off sharps and flats. . . . I got [arranging fundamentals] from listening to [arrangers] Don Redman [and] Joe Jordan. . . . Joe Steele, who was at the New England Conservatory nine years, used to tell me a whole lot of things."[18] As a student in Pittsburgh, Billy Strayhorn listened to disc recordings by Ellington and Goodman, and discussed technical music issues with local guitarist-arranger Bill Esch.[19] Jimmy Mundy worked with arranger Cecil Irwin to create material for stage acts at Chicago's Grand Terrace nightclub: "Cecil was a great talent, a great writer. They'd call in Andy Razaf and Paul Denniker to do the composing and lyrics, and Leonard Harper was the choreographer. It was good experience, because we'd have to catch dance steps in the chorus routines, first this step, then that step."[20] Melba Liston, trombonist-arranger for Gerald Wilson and Count Basie, recalled picking up arranging skills in the mentorship role of copyist for Wilson's orchestra.[21] Horace Henderson, younger brother of bandleader Fletcher Henderson, enjoyed a privileged position in receiving his informal training:

> There weren't too many books out. . . . My greatest experience came from being in New York, seeing these giants of jazz execute it, and being able to ask them questions and them givin' me the correct answer. . . . We used to go up and have jam sessions at [Fletcher's apartment]. . . . I used to borrow the stock [arrangements] . . . [such as those by] the great Archie Bleyer. . . . Then when we finished that [performance], we would stop . . . and discuss what had transpired during that session . . . man, that was a lesson.[22]

Formal private lessons from established professionals were another source of education. Saxophonist Hart Leavitt took arranging lessons from clarinetist Clarence Hutchenrider, who let his student observe rehearsals of the Casa Loma Orchestra; Leavitt later took private lessons from Fletcher Henderson while freelancing in New York around 1934.[23] Henry Mancini recounted how theater conductor Max Adkins gave him "the parts of a stock arrangement . . . and had me reconstruct the full score from them. . . . I came to see what was

Arranger-bandleader Horace Henderson, ca. 1940. Henderson arranged music for Charlie Barnet, Benny Goodman, and Fletcher Henderson. Courtesy of the Frank Driggs Collection at Jazz at Lincoln Center.

important and what was expendable."[24] Chick Webb's side-musician-arranger Edgar Sampson reportedly took lessons from classical arranger John Sacco during the late 1930s, even after Sampson had established his own freelance career.[25] Jimmy Mundy, reputed as "a well-schooled musician with a solid background in the classics," likewise cited mid-career studies under classical concert and film composer Ernst Toch in California.[26] Van Alexander enrolled in more classically focused extension-course studies at Columbia—an experience shared by arranger Salvatore "Tutti" Camarata—and then took a year of lessons from composer and *Metronome* magazine columnist Otto Cesana, whose advertised students included Matty Matlock, Alvino Rey, and Buddy Weed.[27] Alexander himself later provided lessons to arranger Johnny Mandel, showing his pupil his own scores and the resulting recorded performances.[28]

Beginning in the mid-1930s, a number of New York arrangers—including Bill Challis, Franklyn Marks, Glenn Miller, Mel Powell, and Frank Skinner—followed George Gershwin in studying the numerically based composition system of music theorist Joseph Schillinger.[29] Instruction was available through Schillinger's private studio or in courses offered at Columbia and New York Universities.[30] As Horace Henderson recalled, "They had different systems in New York . . . it got to be a fad around there with the guys . . . [arranger] Dick Vance . . . the Schillinger system, you know. [Saxophonist-arranger] Eddie Barefield. . . . They all went to school and studied this system so I got in on this."[31] Although Glenn Miller's hit "Moonlight Serenade" was celebrated as the fruit of Schillinger studies—arranger Bill Finegan complained how Miller "always kept touting the Schillinger method"—the true extent of the instructor's wider influence on big band arranging remains speculative.[32] As reflected in published textbooks, Schillinger focused more on generating melody, harmony, and counterpoint material than on approaches to formal routine or orchestration specific to dance bands.[33] After World War II, jazz or "commercial" music-education programs at Schillinger House (later Berklee College of Music) and North Texas State College (later University of North Texas) finally offered formal training in scoring for the dance band or jazz orchestra format.[34]

Education programs of the 1920s and 1930s, however, were much more likely to provide a European classical curriculum. Chappie Willet advertised his training at West Virginia State College (WVSC) as a matter of pride; the affiliation provided him a link to violinist and composer Clarence Cameron White, a well-connected figure in the African American community who taught at WVSC from 1924 to 1930.[35] Publicity for recital performances by Willet's piano and composition instructors cite established classical repertoire including Bach's Toccata and Fugue in D minor, Beethoven's Piano Sonata No. 23, op. 57 ("Appasionata"), Schumann's Romanze No. 2 (op. 28), Chopin's Prelude No. 22 (op. 28), Schubert-Liszt's "Hark, Hark, the Lark," and Wagner-Liszt's "Tannhauser March," as well as "Juba (Dance)" (1913) by African American composer R. Nathaniel Dett.[36] A recital concert featuring the school's composition students included Willet's own "Binnorie," a fairy tale–inspired title that suggests a work out of the nineteenth-century European Romantic tradition.[37] For his solo piano graduation recital, Willet performed Christian Sinding's 1896 "Marche Grotesque" (op. 32, no. 1) and excerpts from Alexandre Tansman's more recent *Sonatine Transatlantique* (1930).[38]

However, like other arrangers of his generation, Willet went outside the classroom to explore the world of popular music and dance band arranging. By early 1932 he was leading his own local dance orchestra. Willet's Campus Revelers comprised twelve members, including a vocalist, and featured arrangements written by Willet and fellow WVSC student Richard Poore.[39] After graduation, Willet continued to develop his big band arranging skills "on the job" as musical director for a touring dance band prior to his entry into the New York scene.

Basic Arranging Techniques

In the absence of more extensive explanations from arrangers themselves, recorded performances and surviving manuscript music offer documentation of period arranging strategies. Despite the staggering quantity of music published during this period—the Swing Era has been described as the music industry's answer to American mass production—contemporary print sources outlining arranging technique are relatively few, and appear to have been almost exclusively the domain of white male authors.[40] Nevertheless, these publications intended as prescriptive texts offer some pertinent descriptions of universal practices. The remainder of this chapter references both print and manuscript sources to outline some of the most common techniques familiar to arrangers of the 1930s and early '40s. Subsequent chapters trace the application of these techniques to specific arranging assignments and individual styles, demonstrating the powers of an arranger working in the big band swing idiom.

White studio conductor and arranger Arthur Lange's pre–Swing Era text *Arranging for the Modern Dance Orchestra* (1926; reprinted 1927) appears to have had a significant influence on subsequent publications that emerged throughout the following decade.[41] Lange outlined the different dance orchestra sections, instrument ranges, and potential formal routines (an arrangement's sequence of verses, choruses, interludes, etc.); notated examples demonstrated various harmonic voicing techniques, textural scoring effects, and excerpts of his own scores. The basic design and content of Lange's book was reiterated in subsequent Swing Era publications, including Paul Weirick's *Dance Arranging: A Guide to Scoring Music for the American Dance Orchestra* (1934), Frank Skinner's *New Method for Orchestra Scoring* (1935), and Claude Lapham's *Scoring for the*

Modern Dance Band (1937).[42] Norman Ellis's *Instrumentation and Arranging for the Radio and Dance Orchestra* (1936) addressed a broader range of commercial formats, and Glenn Miller's *Method for Orchestral Arranging* (1943) focused more narrowly on the Miller band's individual style and instrumentation, but these works also reflected Lange's essential design.[43]

Skinner's *New Method* is an admirably practical and informative resource. In addition to covering the basic techniques found in competing publications (and often in a more succinct and better-organized presentation), Skinner includes discussions of voicing for "seventh chords with added sixths" (similar to dominant-thirteenth chords, which are also identified), scoring for string sections, analyses of sample score excerpts, and even techniques for part copying. Publisher Robbins Music followed up this mid-priced ($2.00) paperback edition with Skinner's *Simplified Method for Modern Arranging* ($1.50).[44] Other Swing Era publications included shorter, magazine-format texts like Spud Murphy's *Swing Arranging Method* (1937), or Van Alexander's relatively late entry *First Arrangement* (1947); additional publications are cited in contemporary trade magazines.[45] Trade publications themselves featured articles and reader-response columns dedicated to topics of arranging technique, including those written by arrangers Archie Bleyer, Jimmy Dale, and Otto Cesana for *Metronome*, and Will Hudson for *Down Beat*. Although these "how-to" books and articles range widely in terms of practical use or reliability, they do reinforce some prevalent techniques found in many period arrangements, whether "specials" or published "stocks." In acknowledgment of Lange's precedent, the following topics are organized by orchestral section.

SCORING FOR RHYTHM SECTION

In a 1933 *Metronome* article, "It Must Have That Swing: Cardinal Points in Arranging," arranger Eddie MacDonald outlined what he observed to be common attributes of contemporary dance band arrangements. In addition to his identification of "novel effects" and considerations of "orchestral weight" and "tone color," MacDonald discussed approaches to rhythm section scoring:

> The essential features of a danceable arrangement must be a smooth and unbroken rhythm, a prominent melodic line and the total absence of any extraneous musical material. The arranger must keep in mind at all times that the basic fox-trot rhythm is the familiar and much maligned "oom-pah." . . . There have been evolved many interesting patterns on this elementary rhythm, such as the press roll rhythm and the ride rhythm.[46]

In notated examples, MacDonald outlined the rhythm section "press roll" and "ride" patterns (see example 4.1), scoring techniques established during the 1920s that would nonetheless dominate American popular dance music through

Example 4.1. Rhythm section scoring patterns, after Eddie MacDonald's August 1933 *Metronome* examples I–II.

the Swing Era.[47] MacDonald defended the prevalence of these patterns, warning that the arranger should "forestall [the] tendency of the rhythm section to wander off by making his [written] parts as musically interesting as possible, within the bounds of sound rhythm."[48]

The "press roll" pattern is associated with a piano and bass two-beat or cut-time (2/2) rhythm (the fox-trot "oom-pah" per MacDonald); the "ride" pattern is typically associated with four-beat (4/4) rhythm.[49] Lange had declared two-beat fox-trot rhythm "the outstanding representative of American Dance Music"; the fox-trot's popularity appears to have resulted in the nearly universal application of the cut-time signature in dance band scores through the 1940s (including MacDonald's examples), regardless of the exact metric patterns invoked.[50] Howard Spring argues that the four-beat pattern, initially associated with slower-tempo dance music, became more prevalent with the rising popularity of the Lindy Hop and related swing dances requiring "four movements for each measure of accompanying music."[51] A 1937 Will Hudson column in *Down Beat* noted that "sophisticated" Swing Era arrangements might alternate between passages of cut-time and four-beat rhythm.[52]

Swing Era manuscript scores generally reflect the directives cited by MacDonald, requiring fairly intricate notation in rhythm section orchestration. Piano and bass parts are typically written out in full staff-line notation (as reflected in example 4.1); two-stave, chordal piano parts reflected especially painstaking labors in handwritten music copying. For piano rhythm parts, Hudson recommended an octave-and-a-half range for right-hand chords extending "from the

A on the staff [down] to E-flat below [the staff]," a strategy that appears to have been widely adhered to.[53] The piano left-hand part typically doubles the bass part in unisons or octaves, though special passages (usually interludes or breaks) might reinforce brass or woodwind scoring. Recordings reveal that while some rhythm section players did occasionally add their own variations to a written part (bass players in particular), many performers simply executed the arrangers' original scoring as notated. As Horace Henderson observed (perhaps with some understatement), "it takes time to write the notes": a shorthand notation system using chord symbol nomenclature and slashes for repeated chords or figures "was helpful to the arranger as far as the time element was concerned."[54] Nevertheless, staff-line notation remained the standard practice for piano and bass parts into the 1940s.[55]

Banjo parts of the 1920s and early '30s often included a combination of pitch notation, chord symbols, and slash notation (see example 4.1). Although the guitar had always been an option for dance band rhythm sections, developments in recording technology and the rising popularity of four-beat rhythm resulted in a widespread preference for the "smoother-sounding" guitar during the early 1930s.[56] This favoring of guitar was accompanied and reinforced by a comparable shift in bass players' embrace of the string bass over brass tuba, likewise contributing to a smoother rhythm section attack. Stock arrangement publications rarely differentiated bass parts as "brass" or "string," but did begin to favor guitar over banjo around 1933. Arrangers appear to have incorporated shorthand slash notation and chord symbols for guitar earlier than for bass or piano; slash notation for guitar parts had all but supplanted staff-line pitch notation by the end of the 1930s (though less often in the narrowing number of banjo parts).[57]

The different components of the American dance band drum kit—including the hi-hat cymbal and bass drum foot pedal—were not standardized until the close of the 1920s, and continued to develop through the Swing Era.[58] Techniques for notating drum parts could range widely in special arrangements; stock arrangements or instructional publications like *Gene Krupa Drum Method* (1938) tended to provide notation similar to that demonstrated by MacDonald.[59] The bottom space of the drum staff indicates the bass drum rhythm (usually reinforcing the bass part); the upper figure represents a snare drum or cymbal rhythm (the latter differentiated by *x* noteheads).[60] Drummers generally enjoyed a degree of latitude in the interpretation of their parts, and were often directed to "fake" or "ad lib" (improvise) depending on style and capability; Miller recommended that the drummer "should be allowed to improvise except where the arranger desires special effects."[61] In addition to outlining the standard fox-trot rhythm, Lange, Skinner, and Lapham also provided samples of rhythm section notation for Latin dance rumba or tango arrangements.[62]

SCORING FOR BRASS AND WOODWINDS

Lange addressed arranging techniques for a ten-piece dance band, comprising a four-piece rhythm section (piano, banjo, bass, and drums) and two wind sections: a three-piece saxophone or "reed" section (saxophones doubling clarinet) and a three-piece brass section (two trumpets and one trombone). His techniques for scoring these trio wind sections, based largely on triad or dominant-seventh chord voicings (for example, the pitches B—D—F for a G dominant-seventh chord), offer a fair summation of 1920s dance band arranging conventions. As bandleader Andy Kirk recalled, "Back in the 1920s . . . everything was based on triads and dominant chords. Then some bands, McKinney's Cotton Pickers among them, added a sixth [scale degree to the voicing]. . . . To get a full sound, they added a fourth sax, not doubling, but filling out the chord. I remember clearly that, when I first heard this change, it actually bothered my ear a little."[63] Kirk's observation highlights the increase in standard dance band ensemble size during the late 1920s and early '30s—perhaps encouraged by Don Redman's addition of a fourth sax to McKinney's orchestra (ca. 1928)—which allowed for an expansion of harmonic definition in passages voiced for section or ensemble. This new capability, in addition to the development of a more relaxed rhythm section attack (aided by the preference for string bass and guitar) and an emphasis on "antiphonal" texture (division of the brass and reed sections), has been heard to mark the arrival of the Swing Era big band idiom.[64]

On the topic of four-part harmony, Benny Carter—who also worked with McKinney's orchestra—cited the influence of Archie Bleyer's stock arrangements published during the early 1930s: "I think Archie was the first one who made a four-part harmony common [in big band arranging] by use of the sixth in the major chord, and of course in the minor chord as well."[65] Although Carter did not identify a specific example, this device does appear in Bleyer's popular 1931 stock arrangement "Business in F," where brass and/or saxes add the sixth scale degree to the rhythm section's major triads (for example, D added to the F triad pitches F—A—C).[66] Bleyer later outlined his procedure for adding a fourth harmony part in his January 1933 *Metronome* column.[67] Reed player Russell Procope credited Carter himself with popularizing "four-part harmony in 1929, 1930, which was, you know, just about unheard of. It just came into style . . . a complete turnaround because before that they were just playing triads mostly."[68] Regardless of its origins, this development was accompanied by a noticeable shift in big band arranging strategies, as the harmonic depth available in a four-piece section apparently offered enough sonic variety to encourage section-based antiphony or soli scoring *across* successive repetitions of chorus form (the term *chorus* indicating each complete song form refrain).[69] Contrary to the concern for textural variety *between*—or even within—common thirty-two-bar or twelve-bar chorus forms during the 1920s (hear the Fletcher

Henderson orchestra's 1924 "Copenhagen" or 1927 "Variety Stomp"), the acceptance of textural consistency across choruses is arguably another key tenet of the emerging Swing Era sound (hear the McKinney orchestra's 1928 "Cherry" or Carter's 1933 "Symphony in Riffs").

Redman, Bleyer, and Carter's strategy for scoring four-part harmony might appear obvious in hindsight; by the 1930s, sixth-chords were already fairly common in popular song leadsheet publications.[70] Yet their approach also signaled a broader interest in the exploration of upper chord "extensions" (chord tones beyond the seventh scale degree) in jazz harmony. It's worth noting that the progressive expansion of chord tones reflected in period arranging texts—from the sixth and ninth chords outlined by Lange, to the eleventh chords discussed by Weirick, to the thirteenth chords identified by Skinner—merely codified harmonic voicing strategies already in use for some time.[71] But by 1937, Will Hudson's tutorials advised "the use of the sixth whenever possible when writing ensemble passages."[72] In particular, the addition of the ninth scale degree to a dominant-seventh chord (for example, adding the pitch A to the G dominant–seventh chord tones B—D—F) emerged as a defining sound of the swing big band idiom.[73]

With larger ensembles and the allure of four-part harmony, Swing Era arrangers expanded Lange's trio voicing concepts into a five-voice ensemble (the term *voice* referring to an instrumental harmony part), typically built around a brass section of three trumpets and two trombones.[74] In the standard five-voice scoring technique, the three trumpets and first trombone are scored in four-part harmony (each instrument playing a different chord tone); the remaining (second) trombone commonly "doubles" (duplicates the pitch of) the lead trumpet in a lower register, or simply plays the root note of the chord.[75] The lowest four parts of this brass voicing are often doubled in unison or octave by the reed section (usually comprised of three alto saxes and one tenor, or two altos and two tenors).[76] This doubling strategy was popular in stock arrangements designed to maximize the harmonic capabilities of smaller ensembles, but the five-voice brass texture also served as the starting point for many "special" dance band arrangements through the 1930s.[77] For example, Benny Carter's manuscript score for "Swingin' the Blues" (ca. 1936) demonstrates some of the shorthand notation techniques that could be employed in creating this simple but dependable ensemble texture. After scoring three trumpets and two trombones in five-voice, four-part harmony, Carter directed the copyist to create saxophone section parts doubling the brass voicing, with the second tenor sax reinforcing the lead trumpet voice in octaves (see table 4).

Chappie Willet's arrangement of "A-Tisket, A-Tasket" offers another example of a five-voice brass ensemble with the lower four voices doubled by saxes (example 4.2). This technique—frequently found in scoring for ensemble melody passages—is referred to as "close" ensemble voicing: the scoring of instruments

Table 4. Indications for ensemble voicing doublings in manuscript score for "Swingin' the Blues," arr. by Benny Carter (ca. 1936). Manuscript score held in BCC.

Instrument	Copying Directions
Alto sax 1	[copy] 2nd trumpet
Alto sax 2	[copy] 3rd trumpet
Tenor sax 1	[copy] 1st trombone
Tenor sax 2	[copy] 1st trumpet [octave lower]

with minimal intervallic range between voices. Note also the addition of the sixth or ninth degrees in the wind section voicings (D for the F triad, G for the B-flat triad, and D for the C dominant–seventh chord), despite the triad or dominant-seventh chords assigned to the rhythm section parts.[78]

The scoring of larger intervals between voices—referred to as "open" voicing—was often reserved for rhythmic accent or punctuation effects.[79] These "percussive" or "fill-in" response figures typically reinforced antiphonal texture—a brass section figure responding to a passage scored for reeds, or vice versa.[80] Skinner also demonstrated a common technique for five-voice scoring where the second voice of a close-position voicing is uniformly dropped an octave, referred to in post–Swing Era texts as a "semi-open" or "drop-two" voicing.[81] The latter technique was popular in scoring for sax sections that included a baritone sax; the strategy may have even evolved out of the practice of alto saxophonists doubling on baritone (both instruments read in the same transposing key, but the baritone sounds an octave lower). For example, Skip Martin's arrangement of "Caprice XXIV Paganini" for Benny Goodman (example 4.3) uses "drop-two" open sax section voicings—with the "dropped" note assigned to a baritone

Example 4.2. Score reduction of five-voice ensemble scoring in "A-Tisket, A-Tasket" mm. 5–8 (0:05), arr. by Chappie Willet for Red Norvo (1938). Manuscript orchestra parts held in RNP.

Example 4.3. Score reduction of sax and brass open voicings in "Caprice XXIV Paganini" mm. 93–96 (1:59), arr. by Skip Martin for Benny Goodman (1941). Manuscript score held in BGP.

sax—as well as open brass voicings reflecting the drop-two technique (m. 93), lead doublings (also m. 93), and even five-part harmony (m. 95).

It might be noted that these basic five-voice scoring techniques could also be among the first elements of standard practice to be altered or expanded upon by an arranger. Indeed, that was the attraction of using such familiar voicings in the first place—to provide an effective and efficient contrast against other techniques. Jerry Gray's arrangement of "It's a Long Way to Tipperary" for Artie Shaw presents a brass soli passage where the initial close-position scoring unexpectedly expands to "open" voicings via contrary motion between the (ascending) trumpet and (descending) trombone sections (example 4.4)—a variation just noticeable enough to catch the ear.

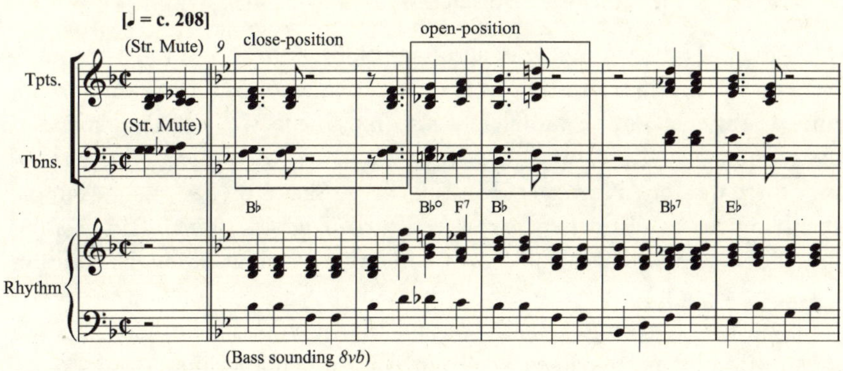

Example 4.4. Score reduction of mixed voicing passage in "It's a Long Way to Tipperary" mm. 9–13 (0:09), arr. by Jerry Gray for Artie Shaw (1937). Manuscript score held in ASC.

Spud Murphy's *Method* provided notated examples of brass-versus-reed call-and-response textures that dominated the Swing Era—a strategy traditionally attributed to Fletcher Henderson's orchestra.[82] Murphy even differentiated between two approaches to writing these "hot licks": the "Henderson style," marked by "accented notes falling on the off-beat most of the time" with brass rhythmic punctuations responding to reed melody figures (comprising two-bar phrases presumably similar to those heard in the head-chorus riff of Henderson's "Wrappin' It Up"); and the "Casa Loma style," marked by short reed figures "repeatedly" answering the brass section in rapid succession (comprising one-bar phrases similar to those heard in the out-chorus of Gene Gifford's "Casa Loma Stomp"), also including an antiphonal "fill-in" phrase ending.[83] Murphy's "fill-in" concept is explained in his discussion of background riffs: "When there is a hot trumpet solo, you will generally find it to be backed up by the Reed section, playing usually a simple swing phrase, which may vary in each bar or be repeated three times during the first six bars. The seventh and eighth bars always being different to 'send' the soloist, when the eight bar phrase repeats."[84]

By the early 1940s, Glenn Miller and Tommy Dorsey's larger brass sections of four trumpets and four trombones signaled another expansion of personnel in many dance bands. Combinations of up to five reeds and seven or eight brass encouraged scoring for six-part or seven-part harmony, or four-part harmony doubled in octaves between the trumpet and trombone sections. Trombonist and arranger Eddie Durham recalled responding to this gradual expansion in his first arranging assignments for Jimmie Lunceford back in the mid-1930s:

> They'd had only three trumpets, two trombones, and four saxes before . . . few of the bands had more instruments than that. I wrote a few things for them . . . stepping it up to five saxes. . . . Now [including Durham] we could have six brass too. . . . Where they had arrangements already set up, I wrote a part for myself, sometimes in the bass and sometimes above [the other trombones] . . . but it was hard to set some of their earlier arrangements in six-part harmony.[85]

Many archival scores reflect later additions of fifth saxophone, third or fourth trombone, or fourth trumpet parts to older arrangements; as Durham warned, some passages had to be completely rescored to effectively fit the expanded instrumentation. The more successful a band was, the more of this type of work there was for an arranger. Scores for Artie Shaw's orchestra, for example (including Gray's "Tipperary"), reveal recurring efforts to maintain existing repertoire for growing ensemble sizes, sometimes even including the addition of a string section.[86]

Despite the expanding size of dance bands, however, Swing Era approaches to brass-reed antiphony remained largely unchanged. While techniques for scoring different combinations of brass and reeds—"cross-section" scoring—remained a common topic in trade publications, the practice receded in prominence for much of the period. Stock arrangements often assigned players optional phrases to "cover" potential missing parts in other sections (e.g., a tenor sax filling out a trombone section voicing), but only as a means of necessary substitution.[87] In cases where arrangers worked outside these basic parameters—Duke Ellington and Billy Strayhorn offer well-documented examples—the exceptions may have proved the rule.[88]

In the assignment of "ad lib" brass or reed solos, the use of chord symbols and slash notation emerged more gradually than for rhythm section parts, depending on the arranger or publisher. Some Swing Era arrangements also provided melody or chord-tone outlines as references for the improvising performer, but there was no dominant standard practice. For example, Edgar Battle's 1936 stock arrangement of Chappie Willet's "Blue Rhythm Fantasy" provided soloists with both chord symbols and a notated melody line.[89]

SCORING FOR STRING SECTION

String instruments had been a central component of pre–Swing Era dance bands; scored as a section, they also played an important role in the "symphonic jazz" orchestrations performed by ensembles like Paul Whiteman's orchestra. By the mid-1930s, however, string sections had largely become the province of "sweet" dance bandleaders like Freddy Martin or studio arrangers like Andre Kostelanetz and Bill Challis. Stock arrangements also continued to include string parts, where violins were typically scored as optional doubles of ensemble lead or sax section parts. String sections briefly returned to broader popular favor in the early 1940s, inspired in part by Artie Shaw's successful recording of Alberto Dominguez's "Frenesi." Bandleaders including Harry James (as heard in Jack Matthias's arrangement of "Trumpet Blues"), Tommy Dorsey (as heard in Sy Oliver's arrangement of "Opus One"), Earl Hines, and Gene Krupa added string sections as well. Swing big band string sections typically comprised two to six violins (with the violins covering two, three, or four individual parts, which might be doubled), one or two violas, and one cello. Skinner's *New Method* included recommended string section "ratios"—the ideal number of violins, violas, and cellos to be used in different ensemble combinations. Based on surviving scores, band photos, and trade publication writings, a combination of three violin desks, one viola, and one cello appears to have been particularly popular.[90]

Swing Era string section scoring tends to follow one of three strategies: providing soft, sustained background harmonies for vocalists or other section soli scoring; providing a melodic counter-melody (usually scored in unison) to a vocal or instrumental solo passage; or providing an explicit textural and stylistic foil to more familiar dance band textures of syncopated brass and reeds. The latter strategy is often reinforced with non-swing, "legit" rhythmic phrasing, and even the omission of rhythm section accompaniment.[91] William Grant Still's arrangement of "Frenesi" for Shaw featured the first and third strategies: strings provide sustained harmonic backgrounds for the initial clarinet solo melody (0:06); a later interlude (0:54) sets the strings in "legit" counterpoint scoring without full rhythm section support, providing a stark juxtaposition to the brassy, syncopated eighth-note swing passage that immediately follows.[92] String interludes in Margie Gibson's "Deuces Wild" for Shaw follow a similar formula (example 4.5); Gibson's textural contrasts are reinforced by a directive for the drummer to "swing hard" upon the rhythm section's reentry with the brass (m. 85).[93]

An example of the counter-melody strategy is found in Chappie Willet's stock arrangement of "You Can Count on Me."[94] In addition to providing typical stock orchestration violin doublings of the sax section or lead parts, a sax soli passage over muted brass backgrounds is complemented by an upper-register unison violin counter-melody (example 4.6).[95]

Arranger Margie Gibson and bandleader Harry James, ca. 1941. Gibson arranged music for James, Benny Goodman, and Artie Shaw. Courtesy of the Frank Driggs Collection at Jazz at Lincoln Center.

Example 4.5. Score reduction of string section interlude passage in “Deuces Wild” (a.k.a. “Music and Rhythm”) mm. 77–86 (1:35), arr. by Margie Gibson for Artie Shaw (1942). Manuscript score held in ASC.

Example 4.6. Score reduction of string counter-melody passage in “You Can Count on Me” mm. 41–44, arr. by Chappie Willet for Exclusive Publications (1939).

SCORING FOR VOCALS

Relatively little instruction for vocal scoring is provided in Swing Era arranging texts. Weirick advocated options of doubling the vocal melody with unison violins, creating a unison string or woodwind obbligato counter-melody, or scoring sustained sax section backgrounds incorporating flute or clarinet.[96] Ellis also approved of the clarinet obbligato, but recommended "leaving out the melody in the orchestra as this has a tendency to conflict with the vocalist. . . . The vocalist must always be at liberty to interpret a number without the interference of any instrument . . . a harmony background with imitation and quasi-contrapuntal figurations is best."[97] In this regard, Willet's scoring for special vocal arrangements was relatively adventurous; background sax section figures like those in "I Ain't Gettin' Nowhere Fast" (for Cab Calloway) or "A-Tisket, A-Tasket" (for Red Norvo and Mildred Bailey) not only outline and anticipate the vocal melody, but also introduce additional rhythmic syncopation and harmonic variation (example 4.7). This strategy provides a swinging buoyancy to the passage, although—as Ellis warned—the constant ensemble motion underneath the vocal might risk distraction.

ROUTINES

Lange outlined a number of recommended "routines" for organizing the formal structure of dance band arrangements. Most dance arrangements were designed around repetitions of "chorus" form, where a single chorus represents one cycle through the song refrain (usually a thirty-two-bar sequence of four eight-bar phrases, or a twelve-bar "blues" form). The basic routine suggested by Lange comprised an introduction, two choruses of varied ensemble texture (including

Example 4.7. Score reduction of vocal chorus backgrounds in "A-Tisket, A-Tasket" mm. 52–55 (1:08), arr. by Chappie Willet for Red Norvo (1938). Manuscript orchestra parts held in RNP.

a vocal chorus, contrasting verse passage, or "patter" section, if applicable), an instrumental "arranger's chorus" (or comparable interlude, or "development," passage), a final ensemble chorus, and a coda ending.[98] Little variation from this strategy is offered in later publications of the 1930s.[99]

For introduction passages, Lange specified the importance of establishing "the sense of the rhythm that is required throughout the entire arrangement."[100] Weirick not only offered similar options of solo or ensemble scoring, but also included a description of "vamp" style introductions with a repeated phrase "containing some form of trick rhythm" (presumably an ear-catching syncopation or ensemble break figure); Ellis likewise endorsed the "tricky rhythm" strategy.[101] However, the recommended duration of an introduction varied among writers: Lapham suggested that introductions "should, as a rule, be only four measures"; Lange suggested that "if length is required . . . they may be long."[102]

After presenting the song's melody and lyrics in the first one or two choruses—scored in unison, duo, or the trio voicings cited earlier (counter-melodies are also discussed)—Lange recommends the insertion of an "arranger's chorus," where the arranger may "let his imagination take vent."[103] A significant emphasis on the arranger's chorus—also referred to as a "special chorus"—is maintained throughout the Swing Era; Lapham concurred that "this is the most special chorus of all, and displays the ingenuity of the arranger."[104] Writing in 1938, *Metronome* columnist Otto Cesana suggested different formal routines depending on the arrangement's status as a "special" or "stock," but preserved the arranger's chorus even in routines that might comprise only three choruses or less.[105]

Lange followed up the arranger's chorus (or a comparable interlude passage) with the final chorus, also referred to in later texts as a "swing" or "shout" chorus. According to Lange, the final chorus is to be "scored in ensemble form. . . . A rhythmic impression . . . can be done by employing occasional breaks or cymbal crashes."[106] Ellis reinforced the climactic nature of the shout chorus, warning that "it is not wise to have the Saxophones play soli [in a final chorus] as this has the tendency to cause a noticeable drop in the arrangement."[107] Cesana specified that "it is customary to modulate to the highest possible key and to arrange at least half of the [final] chorus in four part harmony in swing style."[108] Another important concept was stipulated by Cesana: a modulation leading into the final chorus "is best if it is in parallel harmony."[109] Cesana consistently advocated the parallel voicing of "triads, 7th, 9th, 11th, 13th, or augmented 15th chords, as well as . . . any other harmonic combination," recalling Lange's recommended chromatic modulations scored in "consecutive" parallel voicings.[110] Lapham observed that "modulations are one of the most important features of modern dance-band arranging"; Murphy directed that any modulation "should be very spectacular."[111]

On the subject of endings, Lange suggested that "the finish of an arrangement becomes more interesting" with the addition of a coda passage.[112] Ellis specified that "a number may end double *piano* [very quiet] or double *forte* [very loud]," depending on "the mood and style of the arrangement," and that the ending "may consist of four to eight bars."[113] He also warned that "all the good work previously done in the arrangement may be wasted by a slip-shod ending," though curiously little direction for the scoring of endings is provided by any of the writers cited.[114]

Stock Arrangements

Print stock arrangements played an integral role in many Swing Era dance bands. Although these publications are somewhat notorious for their varying degrees of artistry and quality, many period stock arrangements were in fact very well crafted and produced. The emergence of dance band stock arrangements in American popular music can been traced to the late nineteenth-century marching band tradition, as publishers sought to expand their market by providing arrangements that could be performed by ensembles of differing sizes and instrumentation.[115] Swing Era stock arrangements typically include parts for up to five brass, four saxes, and a four-piece rhythm section; by the early 1940s, parts for up to six brass and five saxes were not uncommon.[116] Presumably intended as publicity for more lucrative disc or piano-vocal sheet-music sales, stock arrangements comprising individual orchestra parts (an expanded violin or piano part usually served as a conductor's score) cost as little as seventy-five cents during the late 1930s.[117] Compared to the $100 or more that top freelance arrangers might charge for a special arrangement, the attraction of stock publications for bands in lower-income brackets is clear. *Down Beat* magazine offered regular "orchestration reviews" outlining the formal routines and performance styles ("blues," "hot," "Dixieland," etc.) of recent stock publications; as columnist Tom Herrick reported (or advertised) regarding the popularity of these arrangements, "The small time bandleader can now play big time stuff—and he loves it."[118]

Swing Era stock arrangements might be divided into three general categories: (1) arrangements commissioned by a song's publisher, with no specific relation to a previously existing arrangement or recorded performance; (2) arrangements reflecting a well-known orchestra's "special" arrangement, but scored by one of the publisher's "in-house" arrangers (often in the form of a loose transcription derived from a commercial recording); and (3) arrangements explicitly referencing an orchestra's "special" arrangement, perhaps even scored by the arrangement's original creator, and citing a specific recorded performance (including disc-release details advertised on the publication itself). The latter category not only carried clear advantages in advertising (which might also incorporate such blunt tactics as including photos of scantily clad female models), but can also provide a valuable record of historical performance practices—especially if scored by the original arranger.[119] But all stocks are informative in documenting common arranging techniques, as well as representing a vast portion of the music that was actually performed and heard in venues across the country.

Chappie Willet scored at least three stock arrangements that do not appear to have been documented in any recordings: "I'm Tellin' You in Front" (1937), coarranged with cocomposer Russell Wooding for Handy Brothers Music; "You Can Count on Me" (1939) for Exclusive Publications (a subsidiary of publisher Irving Mills); and "Push Out" (1939), again for Handy Brothers.[120] With the exception of Willet's consistent omission of the verse, all of these publications parallel the suggested formal routine for commercial arrangements outlined by Lange and reiterated in later Swing Era textbooks: an introduction, vocal "brace chorus," modulating transition, instrumental "special" (or "arranger's") chorus, and a final shout or "swing" chorus.[121] The "brace chorus" technique was a relic of earlier dance band publishing practices, but remained a preferred method for scoring stocks: sectional scoring for two adjacent choruses, usually with one orchestra section (brass or reeds) doubling the melody, and the other providing a counter-melody or fill-in phrases. These choruses (denoted in orchestra parts by two staves joined by a bracket, or "brace") could be selectively omitted or combined, depending on performance forces and durational requirements. Doubling of the vocal melody by the orchestra also allowed the option of an instrumental interpretation. For example, Tom Whaley created a set of orchestra parts for "Push Out" built from Willet's stock arrangement brace chorus; Whaley retained the eight-bar introduction as published, then created a thirty-two-bar AABA-form chorus that recombined the bridge (B section) of Willet's first brace chorus with the A sections of Willet's second brace chorus.[122] Norman Ellis's *Instrumentation and Arranging* provided suggestions for making alterations specifically to brace choruses, where an additional modulation could be inserted depending on what key the vocalist would be performing the piece in.[123]

The second category of stocks includes Les Brown's arrangement of "Jump Jump's Here" for Robbins Music. Elements of Willet's special arrangement as recorded by cocomposers Red Norvo and Mildred Bailey (example 4.8) are reflected in the clarinet-lead passage at the end of Brown's opening instrumental chorus (example 4.9).[124] But Brown's scoring also reflects variations typical of stock publications, including cross-section doublings and a replacement of

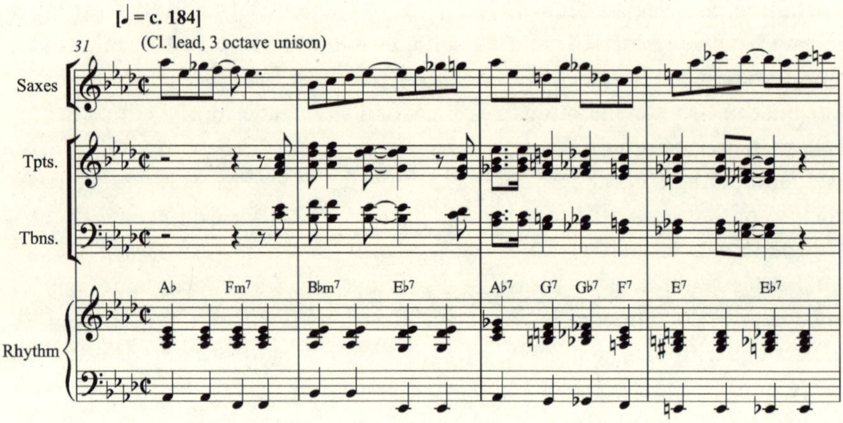

Example 4.8. Score reduction of clarinet-lead passage in "Jump Jump's Here" mm. 31–34 (0:36), arr. by Chappie Willet for Red Norvo (1938). Manuscript orchestra parts held in RNP.

Example 4.9. Score reduction of clarinet-lead passage in "Jump Jump's Here" (stock arrangement) mm. 31–34, arr. by Les Brown for Robbins Music (1938).

Willet's chromatic harmony substitutions with a chord progression lying closer to the tonic key (mm. 33–34).[125]

Robbins Music's publications of Willet arrangements "Prelude in C-sharp Minor" and "Grandfather's Clock" fall into the third category of "as recorded" stocks. However, both of these stocks are somewhat unusual within the Swing Era publishing world; scoring is credited to Spud Murphy "based on Chappie Willet's arr." The special citation of Willet may have reflected his "exclusive contract" with Robbins Music announced in April 1938.[126] Such secondary attributions are rare in stock publications, and many stocks—especially if scored by in-house orchestrators—did not bother to cite the original arranger in any form. Indeed, Murphy's scoring matches the corresponding special arrangements Willet provided to Duke Ellington and Gene Krupa quite closely, although some interlude material is truncated and the endings vary. While "Prelude" was only available as a radio transcription recording (as performed by Charlie Barnet), the "Grandfather's Clock" publication advertised Krupa's corresponding Brunswick disc release.[127]

Both Ellis and Weirick outlined strategies for the creation of commercial stock arrangements, and also discussed approaches to altering published stocks, referred to in jazz lingo as *doctoring*.[128] Alterations to stocks were also addressed in *Metronome* magazine: Archie Bleyer was somewhat dismissive of the practice, offering that "although it's a good idea to re-score a stock arrangement . . . I should think you would find it worthwhile to write specials."[129] As Jeffrey Magee explains in his examination of Don Redman's work, the degree of "doctoring" undertaken by an arranger can vary greatly, arguably even resulting in a completely new arrangement.[130] Swing Era examples of "doctored" stocks include Teddy Hill's 1937 recording of Larry Clinton's radio theme song "A Study in Brown," derived from Clinton's stock arrangement for Lincoln Music but employing variations in formal routine (e.g., adding a trombone solo chorus and eliminating some ensemble passages).[131]

Left to right: Studio bandleader Mack Shopnick, unknown, arranger Bob Haggart (at the bass), and drummer Morey Feld, ca. March 1947. Haggart arranged music for studio ensembles and the Bob Crosby orchestra. Photo by William P. Gottlieb. Music Division, Library of Congress.

Table 5. Roy Eldridge modifications to formal structure of "Muskat [*sic*] Ramble," arr. by Bob Haggart for Bob Crosby (1936) and published by Melrose Music [stock arrangement] (1936).

Crosby Routine (1936)	Melrose Stock Routine	Eldridge Routine (1939)
		Adds trumpet solo intro (8 bars)
Ensemble theme (16 bars)	[per Crosby]	[per Melrose]
Ensemble stop-time (16 bars)	[per Crosby]	[per Melrose]
Ensemble stop-time, tenor sax solo (16 bars)	[per Crosby]	[per Melrose]
Ensemble stop-time, trumpet solo (16 bars)	[per Crosby]	Trumpet solo, no stop-time
Ensemble stop-time, clarinet solo (16 bars)	*Omitted*	[omitted per Melrose]
Ensemble, trombone breaks (16 bars)	[per Crosby]	Alto sax solo, no breaks
	Adds ensemble passage (16 bars; Reh. F)	[per Melrose]
Ensemble shout chorus (16 bars)	[per Crosby]	[per Melrose]
Ensemble shout cont'd., trombone break, tag (10 bars)	[per Crosby]	[per Melrose]
		Adds ensemble tag (1 bar)

Another example of a lightly "doctored" stock is trumpeter Roy Eldridge's 1939 recording of the New Orleans–Dixieland standard "Muskrat [or 'Muscat'] Ramble." This performance reflects Bob Haggart's arrangement for the Bob Crosby orchestra as marketed in a 1936 Melrose Music publication (the stock routine varies a bit from the Crosby recording; see table 5).[132] Eldridge's alterations to the stock are simple enough to suggest that they may have been made during his studio recording session; the band adds an introduction and tag ending to the existing arrangement, and replaces one ensemble chorus with an improvised alto sax solo. Although the piece may have been part of Eldridge's regular book, it seems just as likely that the bandleader purchased this relatively simple seventy-five-cent stock arrangement as a sort of record-date insurance in the event that more ambitious numbers could not be completed within the allotted studio time. In any case, the stock publication proves functional, adaptable, and stylistically articulate.

* * *

Some Swing Era arranging texts augmented their discussions of orchestration technique and harmonic theory with hard-nosed business advice like that from Norman Ellis: "The arranger should never display anxiety or nervousness when the band starts to play their arrangement, and above all, should never ask the musicians for their opinion of the arrangement as this will indicate a lack of confidence on his part."[133] But these authors primarily advocated a universal musical framework upon which arrangers could create—as suggested in the introduction to Eddie MacDonald's article—"arrangements that are different and yet not too different."[134] A revealing descriptor of popular music ideals, this concept is critical in examining the legacy of freelance arrangers working in a variety of professional contexts. If the "theory" behind Swing Era arranging necessarily solicits generalizations due to the vast body of work created, the "practice" of Swing Era arrangers is represented by a wealth of historical documentation that has only begun to be examined. Big band arrangers developed a musical language that could be learned, shared, and adapted; as explored in the following chapters, musicians fluent in that language enjoyed the power to communicate much more than just a melody.

5

Episode and Interlude

Broadway Modernism

Theatre orchestration was undoubtedly the main source of ideas for dance orchestras, at first in its effect on the printed arrangements from which all dance bands played and, later, as the bands elaborated on these printed arrangements, in its more imaginative combinations. Dance orchestration has long since taken its place as the most imaginative and productive of all arranging.[1]

—Arranger Robert Russell Bennett, ca. 1939

Although he may be biased in favor of his field, Broadway theater arranger Robert Russell Bennett highlights the influence of theatrical orchestration on other areas of American popular music, especially Swing Era dance bands. Some musicians even considered work in orchestral theater music to represent a vocational class above that of touring dance bands or nightclub ensembles, a view suggesting that dance orchestras (or their arrangers) may have turned to theater-related musical forms as an exercise in upward mobility.[2] The reputation that Bennett and other Broadway arrangers enjoyed (or at least aspired to) as "composers of long classical training"—versus merely arrangers or orchestrators—may have also reinforced notions of the theater world as approaching the rarefied plane of "legitimate" music.[3]

There were also more tangible connections. One of the most lucrative employment opportunities for Swing Era arrangers arose when big bands were hired to work in Broadway-styled nightclub or theater revues—engagements also integral to the performers' professional status. In this setting, an ensemble might be required to temporarily shed their own stylistic identity in order to perform music designed to accompany the various stage acts comprising the program. As bandleader Andy Kirk noted, "Playing the Apollo was different from playing a dance hall, because in a dance hall the dancers had to dance to your music. At the Apollo, with a star like Bojangles [Bill Robinson], we had to play music for *him* to dance to. . . . We always had regard for the artist, whatever he was doing, and our music was background. We wanted to play it right—the way he wanted it."[4] But even with sympathetic musicians like Kirk, a touring revue or season-long nightclub production might cycle through a number of different backing bands or featured acts during its run. As Sammy Lowe of the Erskine Hawkins orchestra recalled, "You really had to be on the ball to play shows in theaters . . . what with all the new acts coming in and everything. The bands used to pride themselves on who could play the show the best . . . we would always have a soft-shoe number ready, just in case the chorus girls needed it."[5] New York stage producers turned to freelance arrangers like Will Vodery, Tom Whaley, or Chappie Willet to provide a stylistic continuity that could help unify their continually evolving program lineups.

Not surprisingly, some dance bandleaders sought out arrangers based on reputations established in the theater. Just as Willet's scores for vaudeville acts impressed client Gene Krupa, stage show music created by Whaley and Billy Strayhorn contributed to their obtaining regular work from Duke Ellington.[6] Nevertheless, the musical bonds between big bands and stage performance suffered jazz criticism that imagined *opposition* to dramatic idioms (and the entertainment industry in general) as an indicator of artistic value. Ellington, who had established his New York career working with nightclub floor shows, was a favorite target; *Metronome* critic (and Ellington biographer) Barry Ulanov condemned elements of musical variety in one of the maestro's Carnegie Hall concerts as reflecting a "glorified stage show."[7]

In tracing the development of urban entertainment combining music and theater, musicologist John Howland reclaims the term *glorified* as an aesthetic goal (not a pejorative adjective) in popular music arranging of the 1920s and '30s.[8] Stage revues comprising song, dance, and comedy acts out of the vaudeville tradition often invoked contrast and variety through programmatic representations of high and low culture. Arranged musical accompaniment reinforced this imagery through contrasting variations in melodic content, harmonic texture, tempo, key, and meter, techniques that were also well suited to the creation of extended production sequences that required controlled pacing or "spectacular" climaxes supporting dance choreography (chapter 3).[9]

As Howland observes, composers and arrangers working in New York during this period developed and shared a stage production–inspired musical language embraced by "dance bands, big band jazz, and the orchestral idioms of Hollywood and Broadway musicals, interwar radio, and the deluxe movie palace prologues of the day."[10] These arrangements often promoted "black folk music idioms"—like the blues—alongside "Euro-American classical form and style"—like symphonic concert music—by employing characteristic forms and orchestration effects.[11] Music arrangements described as "classical" or "symphonic" were typically marked by an avoidance of familiar Tin Pan Alley song forms, instead favoring "multithematic formal structures, and . . . 'sophisticated' introductions, interludes, and codas."[12] A commonly cited precedent for these concert-style arrangements is George Gershwin's "symphonic jazz" composition *Rhapsody in Blue*, debuted by Paul Whiteman's dance band in 1924. *Rhapsody*'s multithemed, "episodic" formal design was both celebrated and ridiculed as an attempt to inject European concert music devices into the realm of American popular music.[13]

Episodic form and symphonic-styled orchestrations were embraced by Swing Era dance bands as they performed material created for stage and film productions, and as arrangers searched for ways to expand their own musical vocabulary toward the establishment of a marketable style. Within this broad strategy, however, different approaches were explored; incorporation of devices like episodic form could range from subtle to obvious. For example, Jeffrey Magee describes how Fletcher Henderson's influential arrangements for Benny Goodman typically begin with "a swung version of [the song's] melody close to its original, published form," followed by a chorus "featuring improvising soloists accompanied by ensemble riffs and one more [chorus] featuring a written variation on the tune, a swing-era survival of what Arthur Lange had called the 'arranger's chorus.'"[14] Despite this formulaic approach to routine, Henderson's efforts still display a "flexible manipulation of highly commercialized idiomatic features."[15]

One illustration is Henderson's arrangement of "When Buddha Smiles" (recorded by Benny Goodman in 1935), where brief four-bar interlude and modulation passages (0:45; 2:14) between choruses are subtly melded into the formal structure by truncating the standard thirty-two-bar song form's last eight-bar phrase to only six bars (table 6; see reh. A and C). Recalling similar

Table 6. Formal structure of "When Buddha Smiles," arr. by Fletcher Henderson for Benny Goodman (1935). Manuscript score held in HFHC.

Section	Bars	Scoring	Key
Intro	4	Ensemble	G-flat
Chorus 1 (reh. A)	30 (8+8+8+6)	Ensemble theme; saxes versus brass	
Interlude	4	Sax soli	
Chorus 2 (reh. B)	32 (8+8+8+8)	Clarinet solo (originally trumpet solo)	
Chorus 3 (reh. C)	30 (8+8+8+6)	Sax solo and sax soli	
Interlude	4	Ensemble, modulation	
Chorus 4 (reh. D)	32 (8+8+8+8)	Ensemble shout chorus, clarinet solo	D major
Tag	1	Ensemble ending	

modulation techniques outlined by Arthur Lange, Henderson's transitional episodes feel more like an extension of the expected thirty-two-bar structure, providing a relatively smooth and unobtrusive adaptation to the familiar song form.[16]

Other arrangers might make more obvious efforts to manipulate popular forms. Historian Andrew Berish analyzes Eddie Durham's 1935 arrangement of "Avalon" for Jimmie Lunceford as "striking . . . in part, because of its adventurous digression from the conventional Tin Pan Alley [thirty-two-bar] form."[17] Musicologist Walter van de Leur critiques relatively conservative approaches to formal design—where "introductions, codas, modulations, and transitory sections . . . were typically short and of scant musical significance"—to differentiate the style of Billy Strayhorn, whose arrangements of "pop tunes" like "Flamingo" (recorded by Ellington in 1940) are marked by "carefully worked out introductions, transitions, and codas, which he uses as structuring elements to secure the internal logic of an orchestration."[18] Association of episodic form with classical concert music was explicit for arranger Bill Challis, who described

Arranger-bandleader Eddie Durham, ca. 1940. Durham arranged music for Count Basie, the International Sweethearts of Rhythm, Jimmie Lunceford, and Glenn Miller. Courtesy of the Frank Driggs Collection at Jazz at Lincoln Center.

his own strategy—"in those days we did an awful lot with interludes, modulations"—as being inspired by trumpeter Bix Beiderbecke's taste for composers Claude Debussy, Igor Stravinsky, Frederick Delius, Edward MacDowell, and Eastwood Lane.[19] Challis arrangements like "Blue Room" (recorded by the Dorsey Brothers orchestra in 1934) include modulations or interludes between every thirty-two-bar chorus, in addition to an introduction, verse, and coda.

Chappie Willet's work similarly emphasized episodic adaptations to repeated-chorus routines; some of his original compositions diverge significantly from standard popular song designs. Pieces like "Blue Rhythm Fantasy," "Jungle Madness," and "Prelude to a Stomp" (see table 7) employ a form built on two distinct choruses or themes: scoring for the first theme is essentially ensemble-based, while a second theme—built on a different chord progression and set in a different key—serves as a framework for improvised solos.[20] This strategy recalls a 1920s dance band vogue for contrasting, double-themed forms, as heard in Don Redman arrangements like "The Gouge of Armour Avenue" (recorded by Fletcher Henderson in 1924) and "The Stampede" (1926), or Duke Ellington's "East St. Louis Toodle-Oo" (1926).[21] Willet's emphasis on sixteen-bar structures—likewise reminiscent of strain forms favored during the 1920s—provides further contrast to the thirty-two-bar forms (usually comprising

Table 7. Formal structure of "Prelude to a Stomp," arr. by Chappie Willet for the Mills Blue Rhythm Band (1937). Transcription by the author.

Section/Theme	Bars	Scoring	Key
Theme 1	16 (8+8)	Ensemble theme	C major
Bridge	16 (8+8)	Sax solo	
Theme 1 (first variation)	16 (8+8)	Ensemble theme	
Bridge	16 (8+8)	Sax soli	
Theme 1 (second variation)	16 (8+8)	Ensemble theme	
Interlude	6	Ensemble, modulation	
Theme 2	8	Sax solo	D-flat major
	8	Sax solo, trombone riff	
Theme 2	8	Sax solo, trombone and sax riff	
	8	Sax solo, trombone, sax, and trumpet riff	
Theme 2	8	Sax solo, trombone, sax, and trumpet riff	
	8	Sax solo, ensemble riff, modulation	
Theme 1 (third variation)	16 (8+8)	Ensemble theme	C major

eight-bar phrases patterned AABA or ABAC) that dominated Swing Era popular music.

But even when working with more typical Tin Pan Alley song forms, Willet joined his peers in adding introductions, interludes, modulations, and codas to "glorify" his arrangements. Recalling Spud Murphy's directive that transitional modulation passages should be "spectacular," Willet's episodic insertions are often exploited as opportunities to inject rhythmic or harmonic surprise. One common strategy—and another association with classical concert music—was the application of chromatic harmony referencing the whole-tone scale.

Modernism, Chromaticism, and the Whole-Tone Scale

Musicologists have been fascinated by the cultural implications of tonal chromaticism in early twentieth-century American music. Carol Oja identifies chromaticism as an important technique of modernist composers "struggling to maintain an edge of cultivation and currency" in New York City during the 1920s, when the device was frequently invoked in "juxtaposing an experimental voice . . . with a traditional one."[22] These modernist contrasts often paired European concert music ideologies with African American jazz—as Oja argues, "crossing racial barriers in an era of segregation and blurring distinctions between art and entertainment."[23] Black composer William Grant Still's 1926 concert work *Levee Land*, for example, is described as "encircling popular African American gestures with chromaticism."[24] Samuel Floyd Jr. hears similar cultural juxtapositions of African American melody and European-derived "harmonic complexity" in R. Nathaniel Dett's 1921 "Chariot Jubilee," where "contrasts of lyricism and drama" suggest a "grand work of Call-Response."[25] John Howland identifies a comparable strategy in the legacies of pre–Swing Era black Harlem composers and arrangers like Will Marion Cook, Will Vodery, W. C. Handy, James Reese Europe, and Ford Dabney, musicians who—whether by artistic choice or commercial necessity—situated their careers and musical styles between or across the high and low idioms, and established a "middlebrow" aesthetic that employed dramatic stage-arranging techniques.[26] These musical works often juxtaposed stylized musical representations of a "high" European concert art (typically represented by symphonic orchestration textures like strings or flute, rubato tempo, or tonal chromaticism) and a "low" popular music (represented by syncopated jazz, ragtime marching band music, show tunes, folk songs, or African American blues and spirituals).[27]

By the 1930s and the arrival of the Swing Era, many "middlebrow" strategies were firmly established, even parodied. Composers and arrangers regularly combined concert music devices of episodic form or chromatic harmony with "jazzy" popular music techniques like blue notes, lip slurs, or growls.[28] One relevant example of this modernist approach comes from the other side of the Atlantic: Alexandre Tansman's 1930 *Sonatine Transatlantique*—the solo piano piece that Chappie Willet performed at his 1933 WVSC recital. In the foreword to the score, Tansman described the work to "record 'the reaction' of a European musician to contact with overseas dance rhythms," referencing a visit to the United States in the 1920s.[29] Movements titled "Fox-Trot" and "Charleston" bookend "Spiritual and Blues," where tonal chromaticism is woven into textures associated with the title. Notable instances include a chromatic sequence of parallel descending blue note phrases outlining a rhythmic formula identified with ragtime: a syncopated pattern (eighth-notes grouped 3+3+2) often referred to as "secondary rag" (example 5.1).[30] A student reviewer of Willet's recital performance rode the modernist-hybrid theme: "'Spiritual and Blues,' by Tansman . . . proved to be Mr. Willett's [*sic*] most impressive rendition for the evening. The blending of the Negroic notes into classic brilliance portrayed Mr. Willett's [*sic*] individual technique very beautifully."[31]

Bringing the concert music trope full circle, Oja suggests that modernist concert music allusions to chromatic scoring techniques (as heard in transitional passages of Gershwin's 1928 *Concerto in F*, for example) may have been intended as a programmatic representation of musical theater and popular music styles.[32] But whether the influence was concert to popular or vice versa, the attraction of bands, arrangers, and (apparently) audiences to the modernist—or even "futuristic"—Broadway "show band" sound was widespread.[33] This model was further popularized in early Hollywood film musicals produced during America's transition into the Swing Era; lavish productions like Eddie Cantor's *Whoopee!* (United Artists, 1930) and *Palmy Days* (United Artists, 1931) featured musical scores with episodic form and sudden chromatic transitions that supported expansive stage choreography directed by Busby Berkeley.[34]

An especially prominent chromatic device in popular music arrangements of the 1920s and '30s is the alteration of dominant-seventh chords through a lowered (flatted) or raised (augmented) fifth scale degree, employed as harmonic reference to a whole-tone scale (example 5.2). Among other attractions,

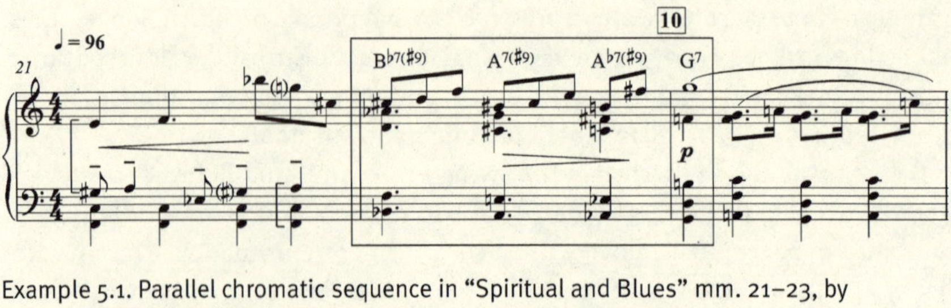

Example 5.1. Parallel chromatic sequence in "Spiritual and Blues" mm. 21–23, by Alexandre Tansman (1930). Chord symbols provided by the author.

Example 5.2. Common chord alterations referencing a whole-tone scale. The "+" symbol denotes an augmented fifth or other whole-tone-scale-derived chord tone.

the whole-tone scales' avoidance of a clear tonal center provides an immediately recognizable foil to more familiar scales (Western diatonic) associated with popular music. Jazz historians and critics have regularly cited use of the whole-tone scale by late Romantic-era European concert music composers like Claude Debussy in attempts to identify connections (or divisions) between jazz and classical music.[35] Scott DeVeaux traces the lineage of the "indisputably 'modern'" whole-tone effect from Debussy and Ravel to Horace Henderson's 1933 arrangement of Coleman Hawkins's composition "Queer Notions."[36] Ken Rattenbury posits that Duke Ellington's "use of bitonal clashes and whole-tone flurries" in "Ko-Ko" (1940) evokes Debussy.[37] Lawrence Kart suggests that such techniques of "conscious modernity" in big band jazz were intended as "exotic exceptions to a norm that is, in effect, being reinforced."[38] Indeed, a number of 1930s dance band radio theme arrangements, including "Chant of the Weed" (Don Redman's orchestra), "Jazznocracy" (Jimmie Lunceford), "Uptown Rhapsody" (Teddy Hill), "Blue Rhythm Fantasy" (Willie Bryant), and "Apurksody" (Gene Krupa)—the last three arranged by Chappie Willet—employ a sequence of altered-fifth dominant chords at some point (if not extensively), presumably intended as an aural attention-grabber.[39]

Musical efforts aimed at (or heard as) invoking discourse with European concert music have also been criticized as banal cliché or inauthentic pretense. Composer Will Marion Cook, writing to James P. Johnson in 1936, lamented that "Debussy seems to have set the whole world mad on [the] whole tone scale and every composer tries to be more modern, more dissonant than his predecessor."[40] In 1938, music critic Sayre Hillerson panned the Gene Krupa orchestra's "screeching and ponderous chords and screwy runs, with loving and frequent use of the whole-tone scale"; Edgar Jackson of *Gramophone* similarly criticized Krupa's whole-tone-infused radio theme "Apurksody" as "too symphonically clever."[41] Gunther Schuller asserts that "nothing dates more quickly than whole-tone writing," and lightly mocks Don Redman's 1931 "Chant of the Weed"—an arrangement featuring whole-tone scale melodies over altered-fifth chords in parallel half-step motion—as self-consciously "meant to be 'daring' and 'sophisticated,' representing the latest state of the jazz-tune art."[42] Intriguingly, Schuller goes on to laud Horace Henderson's arrangement of "Queer Notions"—a composition built on the same "harmonic modernity" of the whole-tone scale—as "one of the most advanced jazz instrumentals of the entire swing era," earning his highest accolade: "authentic jazz."[43]

Whether sophisticated, cliché, or simultaneously both, the whole-tone trope remained solidly entrenched in American dance band arranging throughout the Swing Era. Dance band arrangers' exploitation of introductions, codas, or interlude passages to inject chromaticism between choruses built on diatonic harmony extended the developments of New York stage and studio arrangers like Will Vodery, or ragtime-novelty composers like Zez Confrey.[44] Arthur Lange's 1926 *Arranging for the Modern Dance Orchestra* provided examples of harmonic voicings for dominant-seventh chords, dominant-ninth chords, and dominant-seventh chords with altered fifths, including voicings with the flatted-fifth degree voiced in the bass (example 5.3).[45] Lange specifically praised the "psychological effect" of scoring augmented-fifth chords in parallel chromatic motion for modulation passages.[46]

A climactic interlude passage of Will Hudson's "Jazznocracy," recorded by Jimmie Lunceford for Victor in 1934 (1:42), exemplifies the strategy outlined by Lange, as choruses built on diatonic harmony are separated by a sequence of whole-tone-flavored altered-fifth chords in parallel half-step motion.[47] Lunceford and Ray Bishop's 1934 "Stratosphere" likewise features an interlude passage comprising altered-fifth dominant voicings in parallel motion (see example 5.4), followed by unpredictable rhythm breaks and scoring for timpani drums that offers further programmatic associations with modernist concert music.[48] In this instance, the flatted-fifth dominant-chord voicings include the ninth

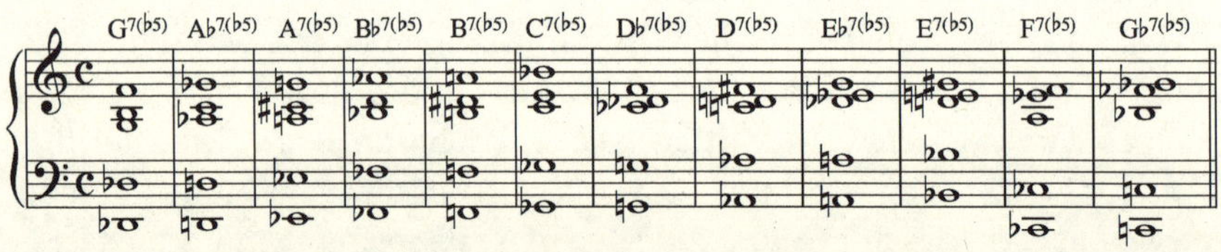

Example 5.3. Parallel chromatic sequences of dominant-seventh chords with "lowered fifth" in the bass, after Arthur Lange, ch. 2, ex. 7.

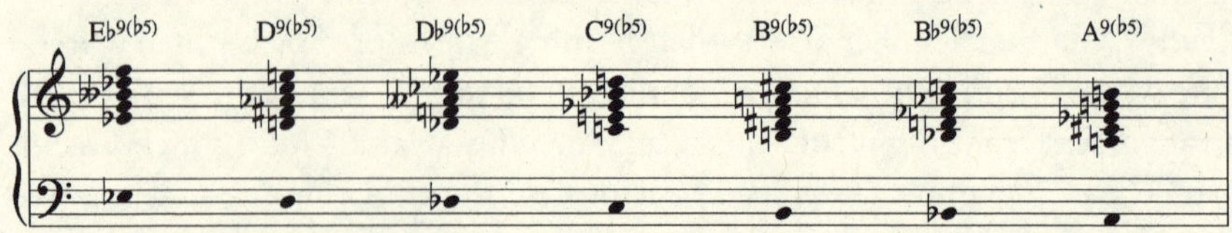

Example 5.4. Parallel whole-tone voicing sequence after "Stratosphere" (1:13) by Ray Bishop and Jimmie Lunceford (1934).

scale degree, a common Swing Era harmonic extension that also reinforces the whole-tone quality of the voicings.[49]

Chappie Willet's work for Louis Armstrong during 1936 to 1940 includes similarly episodic chromatic passages, as heard in aircheck recordings of "Rhythm Jam" (0:42) and "I Know That You Know" (2:18), or Decca studio recordings of "I've Got My Fingers Crossed" (2:24), "Struttin' with Some Barbecue" (1:35), and "You've Got Me Voodoo'd" (1:46). Similar to Lunceford's "Stratosphere," Willet's approach to whole-tone harmony frequently takes the form of augmented or flatted-fifth dominant voicings in sequences of parallel half-step motion—often with the flatted-fifth degree scored in the bass, recalling Lange's example.[50] The sequence of dominant-seventh chord voicings with raised and lowered fifths in an interlude passage of "After You've Gone" for Armstrong (example 5.5) is typical: Willet's temporary disruption of the rhythm section's swing (quarter-note) dance beat with a half-note stop-time pattern further emphasizes this modulation from the key of C major to E-flat.[51]

Passages reinforcing harmonic surprise with a dramatic interruption of the established dance groove abound in Swing Era big band music. The work of arranger Sy Oliver, for example, is described by Schuller to reveal a "love for transitions, breaks, and modulations without benefit of rhythm section, usually in highly chromatic passages"—strategies introduced to achieve "orchestral surprise."[52] Willet's work offers an individual refinement on this strategy, as his rhythmic-unison transitions for the full ensemble—usually reinforced by rhythm section stop-time scoring—often suggest the effect of an engine changing gears as the clutch releases the drive mechanism before building to a new rate of intensity.[53] Armstrong's Decca recording of "Wolverine Blues," for example, offers both descending (0:30) and ascending (2:56) half-note stop-time transitions that—along with a variety of breaks and interludes—suggest a readjustment of ensemble energy between choruses of smooth-running swing. Historian Joel Dinerstein cites examples of American streamline train imagery

Example 5.5. Score reduction of parallel whole-tone voicing interlude in "After You've Gone" mm. 129–33 (1:56), arr. by Chappie Willet for Louis Armstrong (1937). Transcription by the author.

Arranger-bandleader Sy Oliver, ca. September 1946. Oliver arranged music for Tommy Dorsey and Jimmie Lunceford. Photo by William P. Gottlieb. Music Division, Library of Congress.

to suggest that the Swing Era big bands reflected the "gear-and-piston efficiency" of industrialization, a mechanical metaphor that might well apply to Willet's technique.[54]

A more intensive application of chromaticism is found in Willet's "Opening" (example 5.6), a stage production fanfare written for Jimmie Lunceford's orchestra in 1938 or 1939 (perhaps for the Kit Kat Club or Apollo Theater).[55] "Opening's" rapid sequence of whole-tone chords in parallel half-step motion is disrupted by a climactic tempo change and modal sequence (mm. 23–24) before descending from another whole-tone chord (m. 25) to the long-awaited diatonic resolution. In this more uniformly chromatic context, Willet's significant delay in establishing a tonal center perhaps suggests parallels with the harmonic explorations of the European classical "fantasy" genre.

Other approaches combined whole-tone and half-step chromaticism, setting melodic themes derived from a whole-tone scale over sustained background harmonies featuring half-step voice-leading. The bridge to Krupa and Willet's "Apurksody" presents a whole-tone scale melody (played by saxes) over sustained backgrounds built on altered chords (played by brass); the use of dominant-ninth voicings provides additional half-step voice-leading opportunities (example 5.7).[56]

Example 5.6. Piano/conductor part for chromatic ensemble scoring in "Opening" mm. 13–26, arr. by Chappie Willet for Jimmie Lunceford (1938 or 1939). Manuscript orchestra part held in FDCJLO. Chord symbols provided by the author.

Example 5.7. Score reduction of chromatic voicings in "Apurksody" mm. 19–26 (0:44), arr. by Chappie Willet for Gene Krupa (1938). Transcription by the author.

Another tactic was to hold or repeat a single whole-tone chord voicing over a static pedal bass. In Willet's arrangement of "After You've Gone," the Armstrong orchestra crescendos on a held augmented dominant-ninth chord, building dramatic tension before launching into instrumental solo choruses (example 5.8). Willet also employed this device in a series of arrangements of European classical repertoire (chapter 7).

Modulations and interludes were not the only passages available for the application of chromatic effects, nor was the whole-tone scale the only tool available. Willet sometimes employed ascending or descending chromatic half-step motion to create harmonic substitutions for a song's original chord progression. In particular, brief passages of chromatic harmony substitution are found in arrangements written for Red Norvo during 1938, including "Jump Jump's Here" (example 4.8), and as heard in radio transcription recordings of "A-Tisket, A-Tasket" (0:21), "Blue Skies" (2:57), and "I'd Climb the Highest Mountain" (2:45). Perhaps the Norvo ensemble's reputation for "subtle" and "sophisticated" swing—a style established in part by Norvo's trumpeter-arranger Eddie Sauter—prompted Willet's turn to this device as a mark of urbane sophistication that would complement the bandleader's commercial identity.[57] Here, too, Willet takes care to score the rhythm section to reinforce the harmonic effect. In "Persian Rug"—another 1938 arrangement for Norvo—Willet first establishes the original (diatonic) chord sequence over swing rhythm (example 5.9), then scores a substitute chromatic progression in syncopated ensemble rhythmic unison for the climactic out-chorus (example 5.10).[58]

Willet's "Persian Rug" score also applies descending half-step motion in a unison sax figure that accompanies the solo trumpet melody (example 5.11). In this case, the rhythm section maintains the original diatonic harmony while the sax figure invokes half-step voice-leading to provide chromatic variation.

Another chromatic device is the brief insertion of a chord lying a half-step outside the local key area, typically scored in parallel voicings. This "side-slip"

Example 5.8. Score reduction of whole-tone voicing over pedal bass in "After You've Gone" mm. 44–49 (0:41), arr. by Chappie Willet for Louis Armstrong (1937). Transcription by the author.

Example 5.9. Score reduction of diatonic harmony scoring in "Persian Rug" mm. 109–11 (1:38), arr. by Chappie Willet for Red Norvo (1938). Manuscript orchestra parts held in RNP. Chord symbols provided by the author.

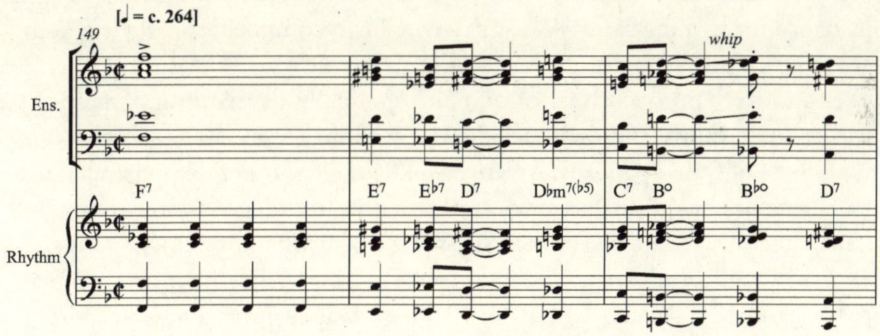

Example 5.10. Score reduction of chromatic harmony substitution in "Persian Rug" mm. 149–51 (2:14), arr. by Chappie Willet for Red Norvo (1938). Manuscript orchestra parts held in RNP. Chord symbols provided by the author.

Example 5.11. Score reduction of chromatic unison sax figure in "Persian Rug" mm. 21–28 (0:18), arr. by Chappie Willet for Red Norvo (1938). Manuscript orchestra parts held in RNP.

technique could add interest to a passage of otherwise static harmony, or perhaps even inject a touch of musical modernism. During the Swing Era, side-slips are especially prominent in the bridge of thirty-two-bar AABA chorus forms; one example is Edgar Sampson's "Stompin' at the Savoy" (recorded by Chick Webb for Vocalion in 1934), where half-step harmonic motion (0:22) is added to a

Example 5.12. Score reduction of harmonic side-step figure in the bridge of "Rhythm Jam" mm. 21–24 (0:21), arr. by Chappie Willet for Lucky Millinder with Mills Blue Rhythm Band (1937). Transcription by the author.

common "circle of fifths" harmonic progression that would otherwise sustain one chord for two measures. Willet's AABA-form composition "Rhythm Jam" uses a similar side-slip device in its bridge (example 5.12).[59]

Yet another approach was to set a chromatically descending bass line or counter-melody against a diatonic ii7—V7—I chord progression (another common "circle of fifths" pattern). Arrangers like Frank Skinner demonstrated use of a chromatic bass line that employs the flatted-fifth degree of the dominant chord, a technique referred to in post–Swing Era terminology as a *tri-tone substitution.*[60] For example, the chord sequence closing Willet's 1939 arrangement of "I Ain't Gettin' Nowhere Fast" for Cab Calloway features a bass line—reinforced by unison baritone sax and trombone—descending by half-step from C to B-natural (the flat-fifth of an F dominant–seventh chord) to B-flat (example 5.13, m. 166), then again from F to E-natural (the flat-fifth of a B-flat dominant–seventh chord) to E-flat (m. 167).[61] The chromatic half-step motion of the bass voice introduces a poignant dissonance (including a tri-tone interval against the lead trumpet voice), even as the accompanying diatonic chord progression reinforces its impending resolution.[62]

* * *

Example 5.13. Score reduction of chromatic bass line passage in "I Ain't Gettin' Nowhere Fast" mm. 165–68 (2:41), arr. by Chappie Willet for Cab Calloway (1939). Transcription by the author.

Jazz performers—and dance band arrangers like Don Redman and Arthur Lange—had embraced whole-tone and half-step chromatic devices since the emergence of jazz. These sounds may have been especially attractive to Swing Era big band arrangers because a period emphasis on textural consistency in orchestration (close-position voicings in diatonic four-part harmony, brass and sax antiphony, "smooth and unbroken rhythm") allowed these contrasting chromatic effects—often reserved for dramatic introduction, interlude, or modulation passages—to stand out even more. Arrangers like Chappie Willet and Sy Oliver regularly reinforced their injections of chromatic harmony and episodic form with surprise rhythm breaks or stop-time figures. Willet's predilection for writing heavily scored, densely packed arrangements also maximized opportunities to inject textural contrast and variety, a strategy that may have offered additional associations with "through-composed" concert music. But these glorified arranging techniques fulfilled only one side of the modernist equation; as examined in the following chapter, the use of contrasting and complementary popular music devices further demonstrates an arranger's negotiation of audience expectation and individual style.

6

Futuristic Ragtime

Style and Identity

Arrangements by [Jimmy] Mundy and Chappie Willet—he wrote for Chick [Webb], too—helped us achieve identity. People always said they could tell it was the Krupa band on the radio.[1]

—Bandleader Gene Krupa

Gene Krupa's statement raises an important issue: what exactly does it mean for an orchestra to "achieve identity," and how is it being measured? Although the development of a unique repertoire might appear to be an obvious strategy, few bands were willing to risk the abandonment of popular contemporary hits and familiar standards. And although arrangers like Jimmy Mundy and Chappie Willet might tailor their music to meet the needs of a specific client, arrangements could also be recycled or adapted. Indeed, similar versions of at least five of the Willet arrangements Krupa recorded from 1938 to 1940 had been previously performed by other bands, including Broadway standards ("I Know That You Know," previously performed by Louis Armstrong) and original compositions (like "Blue Rhythm Fantasy," performed by at least four other New York–based orchestras).[2] Soon after Krupa debuted Mundy's "Bolero at the Savoy," the same piece was recorded by Count Basie's orchestra; Basie also featured Mundy's "Fiesta in Blue," originally created for Benny Goodman's orchestra.

The repertoire shared among Swing Era bands highlights the complexities behind the establishment of a performer's individual sound and style, especially for those that relied on freelance arrangers who may have been trying to "achieve identity" on their own. For example, versions of Willet's original "Rhythm Jam" for Armstrong, Lucky Millinder with Mills Blue Rhythm Band, and Krupa are nearly identical in their ensemble scoring and solo assignments; one of the few variations in routine (the introduction to the Krupa version) was reportedly made by the performers themselves.[3] Of course, orchestras that featured an individual or select group of solo performers—like pianist Earl Hines with his own band, or trumpeter Cootie Williams with Benny Goodman—could certainly claim to retain a recognizable sonic identity independent of various arrangers' contributions (though some of these identifications may have been more limited to connoisseur listeners than is commonly acknowledged).[4] Even as trombonist Dicky Wells (side-musician with Fletcher Henderson, Teddy Hill, and Count Basie) claimed that audiences "in those days really were more arrangement conscious and less concerned with vocalists," vocalist-bandleaders like Louis Armstrong or Rudy Vallee undoubtedly enjoyed a significant advantage in the establishment of audience recognition, regardless of the arrangement.[5]

Bandleader-arranger Artie Shaw felt that "you face a problem that is more philosophical than musical in achieving a style, a recognizable sound. When you reach a point where you're so clear about what you want . . . your working materials have to give."[6] As discussed earlier (chapter 1), arrangers may not have had much say as to how their work would be interpreted by a performing ensemble; compared to side-musician arrangers, freelancers probably had even less input. While some critics attempted to celebrate a favored musician as a band's governing "chief arranger"—suggesting a conscious stylistic hierarchy within a band's repertoire—there is scant evidence of arrangers communicating with each other about their work for shared clients.[7] An orchestra's stylistic identity could also evolve over time, reflecting the changing tastes of the bandleader or their arrangers, or broader trends in music marketing.

Models of orchestra identity are further complicated by bandleaders like Benny Carter, Fletcher Henderson, or Don Redman, who all became successful freelance arrangers after honing personal styles leading their own distinctive bands. In the case of Henderson, arrangements designed for his own orchestra were later featured by Benny Goodman ("King Porter Stomp" is a well-documented example).[8] On the other hand, freelance arrangers like Van Alexander, Eddie Durham, Will Hudson, and Jimmy Mundy became bandleaders after establishing their reputations writing for other orchestras. More challenges to identity arose when the popularity of specific arrangements fostered the practice of transcribing (notating by ear) scores from recorded performances; arranger Henry Mancini referred to these jobs as "record takeoffs."[9] Clyde Bernhardt recalled the 1930s repertoire of Harlem bandleader Vernon Andrade:

> Andrade had a copy of all Jimmie Lunceford's top numbers. . . . Horace [Henderson] also brought over all the arrangements he made for his brother, Fletcher. We regularly played "Rug Cutter's Swing," "White Heat," and "For Dancers Only." If Andrade liked a hot record hit of some band, he got Joe Thomas or someone to take it off in the same key and make the exact arrangement.[10]

Sometimes arrangers borrowed ideas from other arrangers' routines, riffs, or orchestrations for their own creations. For example, the out-chorus riff in

Count Basie's 1939 recording of "Oh, Lady Be Good" is heard in Billy May's 1940 arrangement of "Leapin' at the Lincoln" for Charlie Barnet—the main theme of which served as the basis for Andy Gibson's 1941 "Special Delivery" for Cab Calloway. Arrangers even copied themselves; Gibson recycled the entire out-chorus of his 1945 "St. Louis Blues" arrangement for Calloway—an arrangement that also included Count Basie's "One O'clock Jump" riff—in his 1949 "D' Natural Blues" for Lucky Millinder. Mary Lou Williams's original score of "Riffs" for Benny Goodman (ca. 1937) closely mirrors her arrangement of "Dunkin' a Doughnut" as recorded by Andy Kirk (1938).[11] Jimmy Mundy's 1949 "Rank Frank" for Harry James is a virtual compendium of Mundy's—and other arrangers'—previous work for Basie.[12] Motivation for originality might not always outweigh considerations such as public recognition, studio recording deadlines, or the promotion of royalty-generating original compositions.

Yet despite what may appear in hindsight to be inconsistent or contradictory decisions regarding artistic originality and commercial competition—perhaps exemplified by Krupa's claim to "achieve identity" by playing arrangements designed for other bands—a bandleader at some point needed to choose which arrangers and which pieces to invest in, based on some concept of functionality and style. Hart Leavitt, saxophonist and arranger for the Yale Collegians dance band during the early 1930s, criticized his own inability to successfully "project a really good style": "Big bands, they were famous because of their arrangers. . . . Each arranger, they had a particular style. . . . Sometimes the arrangers would play in the band, but he had a particular *style*. If the guy running the band liked [that style], then he'd buy the arrangements. . . . It was very competitive."[13] Glenn Miller, writing for his own band, was able to boast a stylistic identity based on specific orchestration techniques: "Judging by our fan mail, we have a style too . . . you may have noticed the way, in our five-man sax section, the clarinet plays the lead along with one of the tenors [in octaves], while the others supply the rest of the four-part harmony."[14] Other ensembles have been identified to embrace a sort of orchestration "style guide" or rhythmic concept that might override the efforts of various freelance arrangers (or even the bands' improvising soloists); examples include Hal Kemp's "staccato brass" style (developed by arranger John Scott Trotter), Jimmie Lunceford's "behind-the-beat" style (attributed to Sy Oliver), or Jan Savitt's "shuffle" rhythm (developed by Jack Watson).[15]

Orchestration and performance technique were not the only factors in play. For Krupa, commissions from black arrangers like Mundy and Willet (and later Elton Hill and Fred Norman) and performance of repertoire associated with black orchestras (like the Mills Blue Rhythm Band) may have offered a competitive identity. Krupa's outspoken admiration of innovative black jazz performers (especially drummers Baby Dodds and Zutty Singleton), celebrated tenure in Benny Goodman's racially integrated quartet, and public statements against segregation have been interpreted as not only an indicator of personal integrity, but also of musical authenticity.[16] Krupa also differentiated himself from his white dance band peers: "My first major success in New York had *everything* to do with the Chicago drum style. Unlike the New Yorkers, we Chicagoans were raw, more primitive, on the black side."[17] One of Krupa's popular hits was Earl Bostic and Redd Evans's 1941 novelty song "Let Me Off Uptown," arranged by Elton Hill. Andrew Berish discusses the interracial dialogue in both the content and delivery of "Uptown," which featured black trumpeter Roy Eldridge conversing with white singer Anita O'Day in jive lingo "celebrating black culture through a musical journey to Harlem."[18] Some parallels to Krupa's strategy can be found in the career of Charlie Barnet, whose commercial identity was in part built around a repertoire associated with Duke Ellington and often scored by Barnet's black staff arranger Andy Gibson.[19] While these celebrations of black artistry represented important steps in the dismantling of segregation, the hiring of black talent by Barnet and Krupa—as well as Goodman and Shaw—added a marketable image of jazz authenticity to other advantages they enjoyed in the segregated Swing Era market.

Of course, the big band orchestrations created by Krupa's arrangers—including white side-musicians like George Siravo—also offer an audible musical identity. The remainder of this chapter explores some of the specific musical

Left to right: Manager Bill Harty, arranger Jimmy Mundy, Brunswick recording supervisor Mortimer Palitz, arranger Chappie Willet, and bandleader Gene Krupa, ca. April 1938. Mundy arranged music for Count Basie, Benny Goodman, and Earl Hines. Courtesy of the Frank Driggs Collection at Jazz at Lincoln Center.

gestures and devices that Chappie Willet drew upon in the construction of his own competitive, identifiable style. Following this preparatory review, we examine some instances where these different tools were effectively applied. Willet's strategy is especially pertinent to the consideration of freelancers' varied work for multiple clients, as arrangers negotiated conceptions of performer identity alongside their own artistic voice.

The Arranging Idiolect of Chappie Willet

As early as 1936, Allan McMillan of the *Chicago Defender* claimed that "there is something about the arrangement[s] of Chappie Willet which causes them to stand out."[20] Yet even after acknowledging the variable degree of innovation that might be desired in a given arranging assignment, it is notable that the orchestration techniques of Chappie Willet—and many of his freelance peers—tend to be fairly conservative, generally sticking to the basic scoring strategies of fox-trot rhythm, four-part harmony, and antiphonal brass/reed textures (see chapter 4). Granting a number of exceptions, Willet overwhelmingly relies on uniform close-position voicings doubled or split between brass and reed sections, creating relatively generic-sounding big band textures.[21] Within such a framework, how might a listener claim to hear an arranger's contributions to "stand out"?

In popular music studies, the term *idiolect* refers to the classification of musical traits associated with an individual musician or performing ensemble.[22] Similar to a singer or instrumentalist whose identity is immediately recognizable by their fans, arrangers can be identified through a personal idiolect embedded in their work—habitual gestures or favored techniques that recur in multiple arrangements, across a range of genres, or for different clients. For example, Walter van de Leur cites particular approaches to rhythmic ostinato scoring and unifying conceptions of form to argue that arranger Billy Strayhorn "combined a wide array of individual musical techniques—musical fingerprints—that in most cases leave little doubt as to the author of a given piece."[23] Examined broadly, these scoring strategies might be found in the work of any number of Swing Era big band arrangers; in their specific assignment or combination, however, these same devices have the potential to identify a creative voice.

As suggested in the preceding chapter, many Swing Era arrangers embraced a general strategy of episodic form and chromatic harmony that conjured associations with European classical and/or modernist concert music. But Willet's reinforcement of these devices with ensemble stop-time rhythm, combination of whole-tone scales with half-step chromaticism, and sudden juxtaposition of concert music tropes against familiar popular music signifiers (ragtime, blues, etc.) establishes a more individual style. An examination of Willet's favored orchestration techniques associated with these popular idioms—many of them otherwise generic to the language of big band arranging—helps to further define his arranging idiolect.

Willet's arrangements often feature representations of early twentieth-century ragtime marching band music. One such device is a brass band "bass run" or "tailgate" figure, typically scored for the trombones, low saxes, or rhythm section.[24] This musical trope includes a descending phrase familiar as the introductory trombone break in Duke Ellington's 1930 "Rockin' in Rhythm."[25] The "Rockin' in Rhythm" figure is pervasive in Willet arrangements from 1935 to 1940; examples include "Apurksody" (1:22), "I Ain't Gettin' Nowhere Fast" (0:16), "Push Out," "Washington and Lee Swing" (example 6.1), and "Wolverine Blues" (2:48).[26] Indeed, what sounds like Willet's self-conscious acknowledgment of the figure's prominence in his work is documented in a 1937 Louis Armstrong aircheck recording of "Them There Eyes," where the phrase is scored multiple times in an interlude passage (0:46), then humorously repeated in variation as a background riff.

Another ragtime device is a trombone section glissando or portamento—sliding from one pitch to another—heard in Willet arrangements for Armstrong like "Alexander's Ragtime Band" (0:03) and "Jubilee" (example 6.2).[27] In the case of "Jubilee," introductory drum rolls and sliding trombones provide

Example 6.1. Score reduction of ensemble break passage in "Washington and Lee Swing" mm. 36–39 (0:30), arr. by Chappie Willet for Louis Armstrong (1937). Transcription by the author.

Example 6.2. Score reduction of trombone portamento figures in "Jubilee" mm. 105–8 (1:59), arr. by Chappie Willet for Louis Armstrong (1938). Transcription by the author.

programmatic "parade" effects similar to those outlined by Matty Matlock and Bob Haggart—side-musician-arrangers for the Bob Crosby orchestra—in their "Dixieland Arranging" column in *Metronome*: "The trombone or trombones play . . . now and then a little glissando in the upper register of his horn to fill in a spot where the melody rests."[28] With the Swing Era expansion of the dance band trombone section to three players, the portamento would increasingly be employed in the shout-chorus of instrumental dance scores, as popularized in Bill Finegan's 1939 "Little Brown Jug" for Glenn Miller (2:28), Lionel Hampton's 1942 "Flying Home" (2:04), and Sy Oliver's 1943 "Opus One" for Tommy Dorsey (1:44).

Willet invoked another ragtime signifier through a syncopated "walking" bass line scored for brass or low saxes.[29] The out-chorus for "Prelude to a Stomp" presents the trombones in a unison bass line scored polyphonically—ragtime or New Orleans "Dixieland" style—against a trumpet theme and saxophone counter-melody (example 6.3).[30] Matlock and Haggart cited a similar device in their "Dixieland" column, explaining that "the trombones play a kind of a bass part with some notes anticipated"; in conformity with Willet's technique in "Prelude to a Stomp," they also advised to "not syncopate the bass part even though the trombones do."[31] Willet boldly extends this bass-line concept in "Alexander's Ragtime Band" for Armstrong (1:49) and "Swingtime in Honolulu" for Ellington (example 6.4), where a syncopated walking bass part is expanded into chord voicings for section or ensemble.[32] Matlock-Haggart and Spud Murphy highlighted additional ragtime or "Dixieland" techniques in swing dance band scoring; a Dixieland "trio" effect featuring clarinet, trumpet, and tenor sax (less often trombone, oddly enough) was popular, though Willet appears to have largely avoided it.[33]

Example 6.3. Score reduction of unison trombone bass line in "Prelude to a Stomp" mm. 137–40 (2:48), arr. by Chappie Willet for Mills Blue Rhythm Band (1937). Transcription by the author.

Example 6.4. Score reduction of harmonized trombone bass line in "Swingtime in Honolulu" mm. 111–18 (2:26), arr. by Chappie Willet for Duke Ellington (1938). Transcription by the author, referencing partial manuscript orchestra parts held in DEC.

Sometimes Willet scored phrases implying triple-meter against duple-meter by employing a ragtime metric displacement pattern (usually repeated groupings of three eighth-notes) referred to as "secondary rag."[34] The technique was also prevalent in stride piano music, where it might be reinforced by a "change-step" pattern in the left-hand bass part.[35] In the shout-chorus to his arrangement of "Persian Rug," Willet compressed the original melody into a shorter syncopated phrase that suggests an alternate triple-meter rhythm against the established four-beat swing, supported by the scoring of a "change-step" pattern bass line (example 6.5).[36]

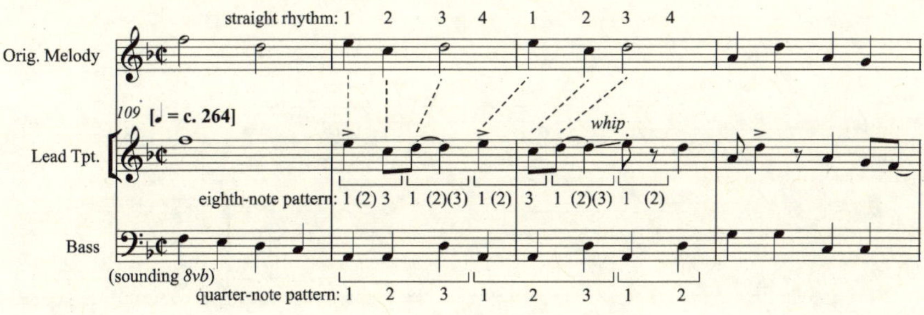

Example 6.5. Comparison of original melody and secondary rag passage in "Persian Rug" mm. 109–12 (1:38), arr. by Chappie Willet for Red Norvo (1938). Manuscript orchestra parts held in RNP.

Willet also favored a sax section trill (a rapid alternation between two pitches), perhaps mimicking the sound of a marching band piccolo or other high woodwind scoring. This device was invoked either in reinforcement of other marching band effects—as in "Struttin' with Some Barbecue" (2:15) and "Jubilee" (1:46)—or simply as a climactic rhythmic embellishment—as in "Memories of You" for Armstrong (2:18), "Rhythm Jam" (Millinder with Mills, 1:54), or "I Know That You Know" (example 6.6).[37] Sammy Lowe's arrangements for Erskine Hawkins also frequently use this device, from his 1939 "Hot Platter" (0:45) to his 1945 "Holiday for Swing" (1:18).

Additional popular music gestures that Willet juxtaposed against harmonic chromaticism or other concert music signifiers include more generic Swing Era orchestration techniques; repeated-note sax section figures, use of hat mutes (or "derbies"), and Duke Ellington–style growling brass were ubiquitous big band effects.[38] But again, Willet and other arrangers refined some of these techniques into personalized orchestration formulas that regularly recur in their work, establishing a recognizable idiolect. Some of Willet's preferred techniques include the fourth-beat hold, the stop-time vamp, the ensemble lip slur, the percussive "whip" (and its sibling, the "rip"), the piano chime effect, the *pomposo* triplet, the two-beat unison trombone bass line, and "tricky" ensemble scoring.

Willet frequently orchestrated an accented ensemble attack on the fourth beat of a measure, extending the note or chord across the following downbeat and reinforcing the effect with similar scoring for the rhythm section. Don Redman's 1931 "Chant of the Weed" provides an early Swing Era precedent (example 6.7).[39] Duke Ellington embraced this device for Cotton Club floor-show material, including his 1937 "Harmony in Harlem" (0:58) and 1938 "Skrontch" (0:04)—the latter song with lyrics directing dancers to "skrontch on the fourth beat" (followed by a sequence of parallel chord voicings in chromatic half-step

Example 6.6. Score reduction of sax trill figures in "I Know That You Know" mm. 151–54 (2:29), arr. by Chappie Willet for Louis Armstrong (1937). Transcription by the author.

Example 6.7. Score reduction of fourth-beat hold figure in "Chant of the Weed" mm. 65–68 (1:41), arr. by Don Redman (1931). Transcription by the author.

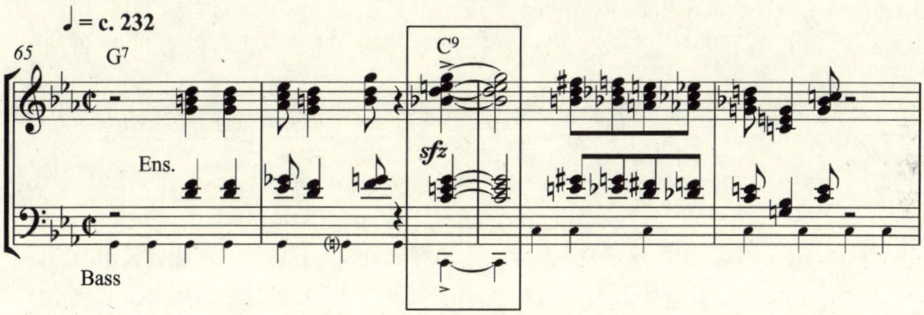

Example 6.8. Score reduction of fourth-beat hold figure in "Rhythm Jam" mm. 65–68 (1:06), arr. by Chappie Willet for Lucky Millinder with Mills Blue Rhythm Band (1937). Transcription by the author.

descent).[40] Other prominent examples of the fourth-beat hold include Sy Oliver's 1937 "For Dancers Only" for Jimmie Lunceford (0:09), Joe Garland's 1938 "In the Mood" for Edgar Hayes (0:24), or Avery Parrish's 1938 "Strictly Swing" for Erskine Hawkins (0:29). Willet tends to assign his fourth-beat holds to the middle of a two-bar or four-bar phrase, as in "Rhythm Jam" (example 6.8), "A-Tisket, A-Tasket" (0:38), "Prelude in C-sharp Minor" (Ellington, 2:06), or "Prelude to a Stomp" (Mills, 1:20).[41]

One of Willet's techniques for scoring the climactic ending of an arrangement was to employ a rhythm section "vamp" stop-time pattern, typically repeating accents on the second and fourth beats of a measure in support of a vocal or instrumental solo (or section soli), and often set in the tonality of the dominant (building tension prior to a final cadence on the tonic). The repeating vamp device has long been associated with vaudeville accompaniment or stage-production scoring, probably due to the need for cued repetitions of variable duration.[42] Brief stop-time vamps can be heard at the end of "Rhythm Jam" (2:34), "I Ain't Gettin' Nowhere Fast" (2:39), "I've Got My Fingers Crossed" (example 6.9), or "Alexander's Ragtime Band" (discussed later).[43]

Example 6.9. Score reduction of stop-time vamp in "I've Got My Fingers Crossed" mm. 107–12 (2:19), arr. by Chappie Willet for Louis Armstrong (1935). Transcription by the author.

For wind players, Willet often scores a "lip slur" effect associated with the blues tradition. In Willet's lip slur passages, the specified instruments execute a pitch bend down a half-step, then return to the original pitch.[44] This is indicated either by notating the half-step pitch change with slur line notation, or simply writing the words "lip slur"—examples include "A-Tisket, A-Tasket" (0:28, 1:53), "Grandfather's Clock" (example 6.10), "Rhythm Jam" (example 5.12), and "You've Got Me Voodoo'd" (1:07).[45] Willet usually assigns this device to accent the downbeat of a measure (often reinforced by a syncopated anticipation, as in example 6.10); Redman's "Chant of the Weed" again provides a precedent (example 6.11).

Another blues-inspired technique was the section or ensemble "whip," which requires the performer to either slur or glissando from one note up to a short accented note (the "rip" is a similar gesture, but presumably following a rest; see the following). Notated with a straight line connecting the relevant pitches or the written indication "whip," this effect could provide a surprise rhythmic accent in the midst of section or ensemble scoring; Redman's "Chant of the

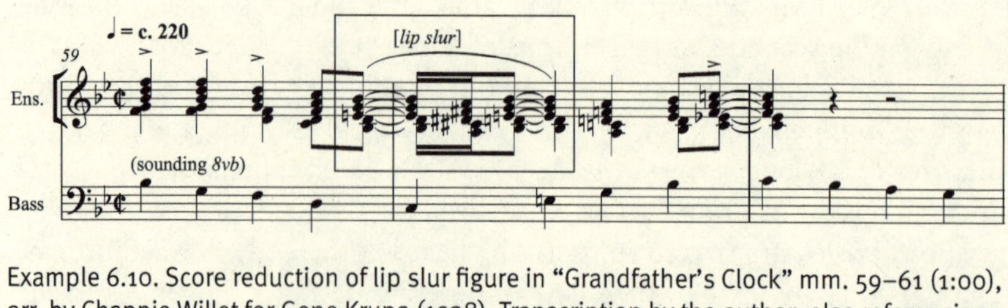

Example 6.10. Score reduction of lip slur figure in "Grandfather's Clock" mm. 59–61 (1:00), arr. by Chappie Willet for Gene Krupa (1938). Transcription by the author, also referencing stock arrangement scored by Spud Murphy for Robbins Music (1939).

Example 6.11. Score reduction of lip slur figure in "Chant of the Weed" mm. 102–5 (2:40), arr. by Don Redman (1931). Transcription by the author.

Weed" offers another big band precedent (see example 6.11, m. 102). The whip seems to have held particular currency with Willet around 1938, as reflected in work for Red Norvo such as "Blue Skies" (0:27) and "Persian Rug" (example 6.5, m. 111); additional examples include "Blue Rhythm Fantasy" (chapter 9) and "Prelude in C-sharp Minor" (example 6.12).[46] Willet does not appear to use this device more than once in a given passage.

Willet's ending for "Prelude in C-sharp Minor" (scored in C minor) also includes a percussive ensemble slur device—notated with wavy lines—highlighting an accented three-against-four rhythm (example 6.12, mm. 173–74). Willet provided similar notation in "Low Down Guy," where it is labeled in surviving parts as an "[air]plane effect"; the allusion to engine-revving or the Doppler effect can be heard in performances of "Rustle of Spring" (0:45) and "Grandfather's Clock" (2:28).[47]

Similar to the "whip" is the "rip"—a sudden slur or glissando ascent to a short accented note following a rest, or otherwise detached from the preceding note.[48] In arrangements like "Apurksody" (0:10) and "Blue Skies" (example 6.13), Willet used the "rip" device in the midst of a hat-muted brass passage, with the

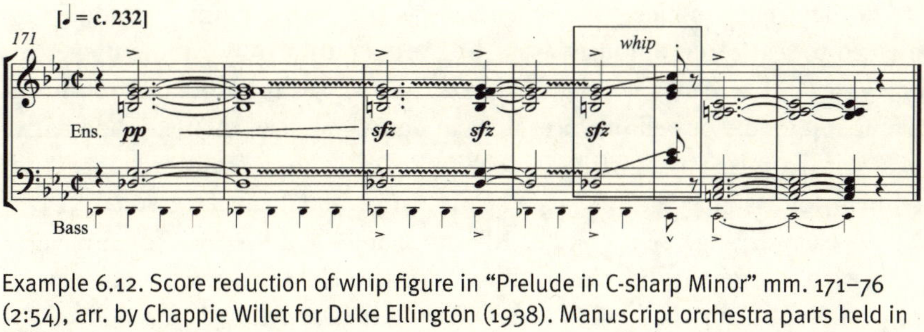

Example 6.12. Score reduction of whip figure in "Prelude in C-sharp Minor" mm. 171–76 (2:54), arr. by Chappie Willet for Duke Ellington (1938). Manuscript orchestra parts held in DEC.

Example 6.13: Score reduction of rip figure in "Blue Skies" mm. 81–84 (2:14), arr. by Chappie Willet for Red Norvo (1938). Manuscript orchestra parts held in RNP. Chord symbols provided by the author.

"ripped" note played open (without the mute) to accentuate the effect. Section or ensemble rips can also be heard in "Harlem Stomp" (1:02) and "Washington and Lee Swing" (1:38). "Chant of the Weed" again offers a precedent (see example 6.7, m. 67).

In contrast to idiomatic swing eighth-note phrasing, the scoring of quarter-note triplet rhythm could serve as a trope of "legit" concert music.[49] This effect suggests a rubato slowing down of the forward momentum associated with popular dance music (an interruption of MacDonald's "unbroken rhythm" principal). As a caricature of *pomposo* symphonic grandiosity, string section scoring often features quarter-note triplet phrasing among other symphonic-related devices, as in Margie Gibson's "Deuces Wild" (see example 4.5).[50] Predictably enough, quarter-note triplet phrases are prevalent in Willet's European classical arrangements like "Prelude in C-sharp Minor" (Barnet, 1:48), "Sonata Pathétique" (2:13, 2:52), and "Rustle of Spring" (1:53). But a number of Willet's nonclassical arrangements used this dramatic device as well, including climactic break passages in "Blue Skies" (2:31) and bass run fills in "Hallelujah" (example 6.14).[51]

Another "legit" concert music effect was the piano "chime" (sometimes referred to less ceremoniously as a "ding"). As outlined by Archie Bleyer in a 1933 issue of *Metronome*, the piano could be scored to mimic the sound of percussion chime or bell sets prevalent in dance bands of the 1920s and early 1930s—instruments that carried associations of symphonic orchestration.[52] Don Redman, for example, included scoring for chimes in "Chant of the Weed" (1:32); Willet's early arrangement of "Blue Rhythm Fantasy" for Armstrong indicates percussion scoring for "bells"; and chimes are heard in Armstrong's 1935 recording of "I Hope Gabriel Likes My Music" (0:38). In later arrangements, however,

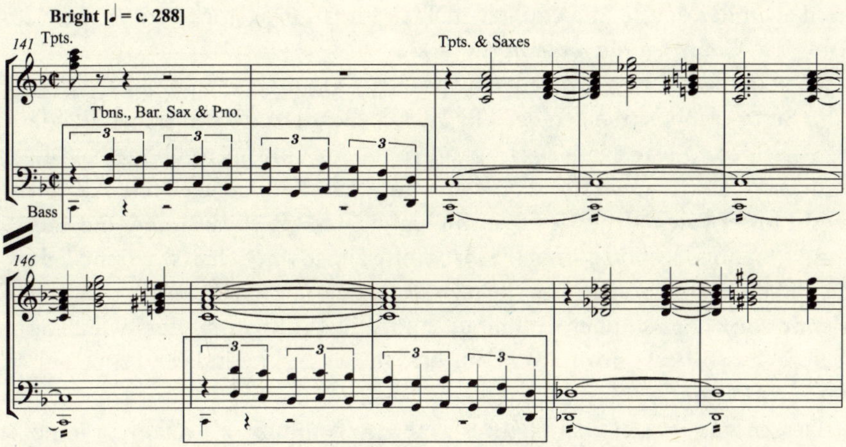

Example 6.14. Score reduction of triplet figure in "Hallelujah" mm. 141–50 (1:56), arr. by Chappie Willet for Jimmie Lunceford (1942). Partial manuscript orchestra parts held in FDCJLO.

Willet followed the Bleyer recipe in assigning this effect to the piano—usually in upper-register three-octave-unison voicings—as heard in "Jungle Madness" (Mills, 2:55); "Washington and Lee Swing" (2:16), or "Jump Jump's Here" (example 6.15).

An "accordion" accompaniment effect, described by Bleyer in connection with the Ted Weems orchestra, could be produced "either by clarinet and tenor sax in octaves; or better still, clarinet, alto and tenor in three octaves."[53] Willet

Example 6.15. Score reduction of piano chime figure in "Jump Jump's Here" mm. 4–6 (0:03), arr. by Chappie Willet for Red Norvo (1938). Manuscript orchestra parts held in RNP.

used a similar device in a counter-melody for his 1939 stock arrangement of "You Can Count on Me" (example 6.16).[54]

The popular success of arrangements like "Christopher Columbus"—a 1936 Chu Berry composition arranged by Horace Henderson for Fletcher Henderson—helped to usher in a swing band vogue for unison trombone bass-line figures or counter-melodies scored in a two-beat rhythmic feel, often doubled by the lower saxes.[55] This device again highlighted the expansion of the dance band trombone section during the 1930s (often up to three chairs), a trend led by Don Redman's orchestra. A 1937 *Down Beat* review noted the relation between Henderson's "Christopher Columbus" and Willet's "Rhythm Jam," which also features a two-beat unison trombone bass line as an interlude and supporting riff (example 6.17).[56]

Descending bass ostinato figures were also common, especially in minor-keyed pieces like Fields and McHugh's 1928 song "Diga Diga Doo," which helped to popularize the device in the form of a repeating two-bar phrase. Swing Era composers and arrangers expanded this concept through various harmonic adaptations: the bass line opening Ellington's 1932 "It Don't Mean a Thing"

Example 6.16. Score reduction of clarinet and tenor sax "accordion" effect in "You Can Count on Me" mm. 75–78, arr. by Chappie Willet for Exclusive Music (1939).

Example 6.17. Score reduction of unison trombone two-beat figures in "Rhythm Jam" mm. 85–90 (1:27), arr. by Chappie Willet for Lucky Millinder with Mills Blue Rhythm Band (1937). Transcription by the author.

was particularly popular; other variants include Edgar Battle and Eddie Durham's "Topsy" and Don Redman's "Down, Down, Down" (both recorded by Count Basie). Willet implemented a version of this device in rhythm section scoring behind Louis Armstrong's vocal patter in "I Hope Gabriel Likes My Music" (0:53); in "What Is This Thing Called Swing," a similar rhythm section vamp device leads into a descending bass line reinforced by unison trombones (example 6.18).[57]

The insertion of a "tricky" ensemble passage was another favorite jazz device that Willet drew upon. While the "tricky" label is fairly subjective, it may be applied more specifically to interlocking hocket scoring between individuals or sections, or breaks (passages where the rhythm section briefly stops playing) featuring intricate ensemble scoring. Necessarily dependent upon the skills of the client orchestra, this type of scoring tends to appear less often in stock arrangements. Willet's hocket interlude in "Hallelujah" (1:22), and multiple break passages in "Washington and Lee Swing" (chapter 9) and "Uptown Rhapsody" (example 6.19)—a whole-tone-infused piece that sounds to have been inspired by Coleman Hawkins's "Queer Notions"—celebrate the client

Example 6.18. Score reduction of descending unison trombone figures in "What Is This Thing Called Swing" reh. I (1:56), arr. by Chappie Willet for Louis Armstrong (1939). Transcription by the author; manuscript trombone part held in LAHM.

Example 6.19. Score reduction of ensemble break passage in "Uptown Rhapsody" mm. 153–56 (2:33), arr. by Chappie Willet for Teddy Hill (1936). Transcription by the author.

ensembles' rhythmic precision.[58] Note the sudden change of rhythmic pattern in the last bar of the descending sax phrase in "Uptown" (m. 156).

As with his use of episodic form or harmonic chromaticism, Willet could not claim ownership of any of the big band jazz arranging techniques outlined previously, no matter how regular their appearance in his work may have been. Benny Carter's 1940 "Fish Fry," for example, utilizes the trombone two-beat concept in combination with fourth-beat holds, as well as parallel chromatic half-step motion (or perhaps "side-slips") in the trumpet section (see example 6.20). Don Redman effectively combined elements of the tricky break, three-against-four rhythm, and parallel chromatic voicings in an interlude passage of "Chant of the Weed" (example 6.21).[59]

The fact that so many of Willet's tools outlined in this chapter have precedents in the work of Don Redman—whose floor-show-backing big band broadcast regularly from the Harlem Connie's Inn during Willet's college years—is probably no accident.[60] As recalled by Willet's Greystone Ballroom Orchestra side-musician Chico Hicks, it was understood that Willet "wanted to copy after Don Redman" professionally; that aspiration appears to have been musical as well.[61] Musicologist Jeffrey Magee identifies Redman's early-career idiolect to be marked by "inside the strain" textural contrast and intricate rhythmic phrasing,

Example 6.20. Score reduction of ensemble theme passage in "Fish Fry" mm. 9–12 (0:09), arr. by Benny Carter (1940). Manuscript parts held in BCC.

Example 6.21. Score reduction of ensemble break passage in "Chant of the Weed" mm. 83–86 (2:10), arr. by Don Redman (1931). Transcription by the author, also referencing manuscript parts for versions held in DRP.

strategies variably critiqued as exercises in "variety and contrast" or "baroque doodling."[62] Similar to Redman, Willet tends to leave relatively few rests for the performers—as compared to leaner arrangements like Carter's "Fish Fry"—and creates tightly packed scores that intensify the frequency of orchestration effects and sudden stylistic juxtapositions. Nevertheless, Redman's style can be differentiated from what Hicks described as Willet's "clean-cut" approach to ensemble scoring—even in passages employing comparably intricate orchestration.[63] Willet's attraction to consistently voiced textures and ensemble rhythmic-unison reinforcement of chromatic harmony passages—perhaps reflecting a broader 1930s arranging ideal of "flow and cohesion"—can be heard to offer a streamlined updating of Redman's proto–Swing Era style.[64]

But while identifying a collection of recurring techniques helps to establish the components of Willet's idiolect—perhaps even point up his artistic influences—it does not necessarily communicate the effective manner in which Willet combines these devices into a musical whole. Despite his reliance on

Arranger-bandleader Don Redman, ca. 1932. Redman arranged music for Count Basie, Jimmy Dorsey, and Harry James. Courtesy of the Institute of Jazz Studies, Rutgers University Libraries.

widely used gestures, the aural traces of Willet's hand in his arrangements can be striking. If Swing Era audiences were indeed "more arrangement conscious," as Dicky Wells claimed, dance band *musicians* of the period would have certainly recognized the focused—and demanding—style of an arranger like Willet. "Prelude in C-sharp Minor," for example, combines ensemble rips (Barnet version 0:06), sax trills (0:35), piano chimes (0:42), trombone bass runs (1:17), fourth-beat holds (2:03), and pedal whole-tone chords with ensemble slurs (2:44).[65] The insistent recurrence of Willet's favored devices in "Alexander's Ragtime Band"—including *pomposo* triplets scored against portamento trombones (0:01), stop-time parallel chromatic voicings (0:13), tricky ensemble breaks (0:50), fourth-beat holds (1:37), piano chimes (2:15), and a stop-time vamp coda (2:19)—leaves little doubt as to the identity of the arranger, even in the absence of surviving manuscript notation.[66]

Willet's work as staff arranger for Louis Armstrong's orchestra may be particularly instructive because a long-term relationship provided more opportunities to define a client ensemble's style. Despite many critics' perfunctory oversight of Armstrong's Swing Era big band, aural evidence suggests that the orchestra provided its leader with a musical identity as consistent and nuanced as any ensemble of the period.[67] By the height of the Swing Era, the trumpeter's legendary status offered motivation to celebrate his musical past as well as the present; swing big band updates of ragtime and New Orleans or Chicago jazz repertoire like "Alexander's Ragtime Band," "Sugar Foot Stomp," "Washington and Lee Swing," and "Struttin' with Some Barbecue" offered not only a discourse between big band swing and preceding popular music styles, but also with the bandleader's own life story—a project made explicit with the publication of his autobiography in 1936.[68] Beyond simply setting old repertoire into new arrangements, Willet embraced the power of dramatic stage orchestration to frame the performer within a programmatic continuum of musical development, even progress.

One example occurs near the end of "Alexander's Ragtime Band," where Willet reinterprets composer Irving Berlin's 1911 interpolation of Stephen Foster's 1851 "Swanee River" melody. The passage highlights Willet's reputation for creating challenging arrangements and demands a virtuosic performance on the part of the bandleader. A solo trumpet presentation of the "Swanee" melody, backed by upper-register chime-style piano and sustained saxes in "straight" rhythm (example 6.22, mm. 127–30), serves as a dramatic foil for the following passage of hard-swinging, close-position soli scoring for the full trumpet section—Armstrong joins and leads—over a tension-building stop-time vamp (mm. 130–34). Willet's juxtaposition of "Swanee" as a "legit" texture against this virtuosic "swing" coda—complete with "rips" and chromatic parallel voicings

Example 6.22. Score reduction of "Swanee River" interpolation and stop-time vamp passage in "Alexander's Ragtime Band" mm. 127–34 (2:15), arr. by Chappie Willet for Louis Armstrong (1937). Transcription by the author.

(as in m. 133)—both acknowledges and expands on Berlin's original ragtime-versus-sentimental imagery through the application of stage entertainment signifiers that had developed during the intervening decades of the 1920s and '30s.

Similarly intensive scoring is found in the introduction to "Struttin' with Some Barbecue" (example 6.23).[69] Willet opens with an ascending ensemble fanfare in triple-meter phrasing (mm. 1–4); in a swing big band context, the absence of rhythm section accompaniment contributes to a temporary rhythmic disorientation. This opening is answered by percussive ensemble figures voiced as altered chords (mm. 5–6) and a descending, chromatic solo trumpet break (mm. 6–9)—scored by the arranger—that delivers a dramatic image of sophisticated virtuosity. Armstrong's break is answered by a sequence of parallel flatted-fifth dominant chords (mm. 9–10) descending by half-step. Finally, the rhythm section enters as the listener is hit with the familiar "Barbecue" melody in straight ("legit") quarter-note rhythm and diatonic harmony (m. 11). A tailgate trombone figure (mm. 13–14) responds, recalling the sounds of a New Orleans ragtime band, while an ornate unison-sax counterline completes the regional polyphonic imagery. Performed in the space of fifteen seconds, this opening sequence is a powerful exercise in musical modernism, efficiently juxtaposing signifiers of present and past, urbane and provincial.

Example 6.23. Score reduction of introduction to "Struttin' with Some Barbecue" mm. 1–14 (0:01), arr. by Chappie Willet for Louis Armstrong (1938). Manuscript orchestra parts held in LAHM. (Armstrong plays a concert A-flat instead of the B-flat scored in m. 7 [see the note marked by an asterisk].)

Additional solo break opportunities for Armstrong arrive in "Barbecue"'s later interlude (0:44), transition (1:34), and coda passages (2:41), providing an effective showcase for the trumpeter's prowess. Willet's employment of "serious" concert music signifiers in short-form popular song frameworks like "Barbecue"—arguably even including such ubiquitous Swing Era devices as wind scoring in rhythmic unison or multiple changes of key—contribute to an overall "production number" (or "show" or "Broadway") sound. Another Broadway trope is Willet's preservation of the composition's original melodic phrasing in straight quarter-notes (as in m. 11)—a subtle tactic of "nonarrangement" through declamatory, on-the-beat rhythm that sets a triumphant mood suggestive of grand spectacle. The fact that many Tin Pan Alley compositions receiving similar "production" orchestrations happen to lie in a major key may be another inherent ingredient of this sound, carrying associations with bright expectation and good times.[70]

Similar to vocal features like "Alexander's Ragtime Band," or "I Ain't Gettin' Nowhere Fast" for Cab Calloway, the tricky breaks for the trumpet section (0:26), sax trills (2:15), and stop-time vamp coda (2:41) for "Barbecue" contribute to the imagery of a celebratory overture. Even as some of these strategies have seen decades of stylized parody (as in the theme song from television's *Family Guy*), Willet's production-style scores for Armstrong—"Satchel Mouth Swing" (1940) offers another example—deliver an infectious and upbeat "strutting" quality. Audiences receiving this music at a dance hall, or even at home over the radio, could easily imagine themselves in the audience of a Broadway stage spectacle.[71]

* * *

Writing for *Metronome* magazine in 1936, arranger Harold Rubenstein informed his readers:

> Too much stress cannot be laid on the advisability of styling your band. . . . Once you set your style, make all your arrangements in the same groove. Don't be afraid of repeating yourself because anything good bears repeating. If tune A happens to be the same type of tune as tune B, then arrange it the same way. Cut up your stocks in a certain definite pattern, do the same things in the same spots. And both you and your public will be pleased with the results.[72]

Three years later, Duke Ellington declared in *Down Beat*: "The most significant thing that can be said about swing music today is that it has become stagnant."[73] Was the continual return of Willet and other arrangers to the same orchestration techniques and formal devices indicative of the artistic stagnation that Ellington warned of? Willet's personal style emphasized an efficient execution of established musical signifiers and basic requirements of entertainment function; his arrangements stood out by sounding powerfully and immediately familiar. While the consistency of an arranger's cultivated idiolect might be criticized as "stagnant," Willet's impressive clientele suggests that it was also a prized attribute in a competitive marketplace.

Indeed, a stable idiolect could be considered the cornerstone of style. Jimmy Mundy arrangements of novelty songs like "Nagasaki" and "Bolero at the Savoy" (for Krupa) or jazz concertos like "Fiesta in Blue" (for Goodman and Basie) readily display Mundy's own arranging idiolect of the period—the scoring of unison trombone or low sax half-step figures in counterpoint against the rest of the ensemble, unison brass melodies over rhythm section stop-time or vamp passages, and sax section figures that temporarily break away from the brass section during full-ensemble scoring.[74] While Mundy's favored techniques can also be found scattered throughout the work of other Swing Era arrangers, none of them were particularly embraced by, for example, Chappie Willet. And similar to Willet's arranging idiolect, the *combined* use of these recurring devices is virtually unique to Mundy's writing. Even these two arrangers' shared use of parallel chromatic voicings may be differentiated by idiolect; Willet favored rhythmic-unison stop-time figures, whereas Mundy favored a counter-melody approach (as heard in "Fiesta in Blue" or his later "Black Velvet").

Willet's voice as an arranger is heard in other ways as well, including his subtle transformations of melody often found in introductory passages, like "Blue Skies" for Norvo or "Yesterdays" for Lunceford. Interestingly, the 1940s saw Willet abandon many of the ragtime references of his earlier idiolect in favor of harmonic substitutions or other "concert music" signifiers, as heard in "Hallelujah" for Lunceford or "Stardust" for Armstrong (chapter 7). This may have reflected a change in Willet's style, broader developments in popular practice, or simply client need. But throughout his Swing Era career, Willet's arrangements reveal a conscious engagement in programmatic arranging strategies that extend beyond the mere replication of idiomatic dance band conventions, even as he drew upon them. The following chapters consider how an arranger might use personalized approaches to rhythm, harmony, form, and orchestration to frame performer identity in popular entertainment genres.

7

Heavy Stuff

Classics and Concertos

"[Jimmie Lunceford's] showmanship is superb, and his constantly changing style keeps one's eyes glued on the podium. Swingeroos, ballads, novelty numbers follow one another in rapid-fire succession, executed with the finesse that only first-rate swing musicians can bring to current musical modes."[1]

—Daniel Richman, *Billboard*, 1938

The next three chapters explore Swing Era concerns of performer identity, arranging style, and popular entertainment genres. Whether the venue was a dance hall, radio studio, or theater stage, well-paced Swing Era music programs required readily identifiable changes in tempo, mood, or formal design. As suggested by the review of New York's midtown Kit Kat Club, Jimmie Lunceford's orchestra enjoyed a masterful command of idiomatic format (like big band swing), genre ("swingeroos, ballads, novelty numbers"), and performer identity ("first rate . . . finesse"), maximizing public appeal in a competitive market. For freelance arrangers like Chappie Willet, commercial and artistic success depended on a musical fluency across a range of genres, including classics, jazz concertos, novelty songs, vocal ballads, jazz dance instrumentals, and exotic numbers. These genres framed an array of musical devices referencing modernism, high art, drama, virtuosity, exoticism, or visual spectacle.

Commentaries disparaging of this genre-based variety—for example, pitting "vapid pop ballad" against "swinging jazz"—often suggest a friction between artistic integrity and entertainment requirements that might trouble a performer's critical reception or popular appeal.[2] However, audience expectations of style and genre could also work to the performer or arranger's advantage. For example, the late-1930s Count Basie orchestra's use of unwritten, collectively orchestrated "head" arrangements comprising successive choruses of solo improvisation ("One O'clock Jump" is a popular example) has been suggested by historians to represent a geographic, Kansas City–based (or "Southwestern") foil to the relatively intricate ensemble-focused arrangements of a New York (or "Eastern") show band sound—even heard as a "brave departure from established norms."[3] While such broadly sweeping assessments are often tenuous, their currency does acknowledge recognition of accepted conventions in period dance band performance.[4]

Swing Era arrangers took full advantage of these expectations in variety programs where multiple genres functioned as the "established norm." Of course, arrangers also responded to the individual needs or requests of their clients. A ballroom dance number might call for a fixed-meter, single-tempo arrangement with passages that could be repeated for an extended duration, while a concerto might call for the inclusion of multiple solo cadenzas or sudden meter and tempo shifts designed to frame solo or ensemble virtuosity.[5] Arrangers developed objective and reproducible harmonic, rhythmic, or formal techniques to satisfy expectations of a popular idiom and genre, while also manipulating those expectations—creating what Jeffrey Magee describes as "savvy, playful parodies of popular song and dance styles"—to highlight the musical identity of the performer, or even the arrangers themselves.[6]

The following case studies explore the communicative power behind these negotiations of genre, performer identity, and arranging style. In addition to the celebration of artistic versatility, Chappie Willet's legacy as a commercially successful black musician working in a segregated entertainment industry that often invoked racialized conceptions of style and creativity suggests additional motivations behind some of these Swing Era arranging strategies. His work for the Jimmie Lunceford orchestra offers an example of "jazzing the classics" that highlights some of the commercial, political, and artistic forces at work behind these hybrid creations.

Classics

Johnny Burke and James Monaco's "The Trumpet Player's Lament" pines: "I wish that I could play like José Iturbi, instead of blowing notes into a derby. Someone who knows art takes something from Mozart to sing, instead of swing."[7] Envisioned as a Hollywood film vehicle for Willet's frequent client Louis Armstrong, the song lightheartedly depicts the frustrations of a swing band trumpet player who aspires to play European classical music.[8] But the tongue-in-cheek references to European classical repertoire (including Mozart, Debussy, and "Vesti la giubba"), its opposition to popular swing music, and even the naming of virtuoso classical pianist José Iturbi (programmatically accompanied by solo piano) reflected significant aspects of Willet's own career. Willet was one of many Swing Era musicians who partook in "jazzing the classics," a tradition that has long suffered the stigma of commercialism and artistic inauthenticity within American culture's highbrow/lowbrow discourse, despite—or perhaps due to—its consistent popularity.[9]

"Jazzing"—or, in Swing Era parlance, "swinging"—the classics can be defined as the musical arrangement or other explicit musical referencing of European concert music repertoire in combination with syncopated dance rhythms, jazz instrumentation, or popular song forms.[10] In its manipulation of venerated classic texts, jazzing the classics has been read as either an irreverent poke at the establishment or a genuine adulation of high-art repertoire manifested through efforts to present the music to a wider (popular) audience; sometimes, it appears to have involved a little of both.[11] David Stowe notes that Swing Era bandleaders were also drawn to swinging the classics "because those classics were in the public domain and could be performed without paying royalties" (an aspect highlighted by the 1941 ASCAP strike/boycott, which limited the use of ASCAP-represented material), but the tradition is not dependent on this factor alone.[12] The hybrid tactic reflects a strategy integral to many modes of entertainment designed for broad popular audiences: the juxtaposition of cultural symbols perceived as oppositional or contradictory. John Howland examines similar strategies within the American popular music "symphonic jazz" tradition, arguing that "during the 1930s and 1940s, most contemporary critics damned this miscegenation of concert hall culture, entertainment intent, jazz, dance band arranging, Tin Pan Alley tunes, and quasi-symphonic instrumentation as mongrel, middlebrow culture for the masses."[13] Although the practice of jazzing the classics may differ from symphonic jazz in musical approach and intent—the label *symphonic jazz* is often applied to original composition, like Gershwin's *Rhapsody in Blue*—it has resided in the same "middlebrow" battle zone separating high and low art. Gunther Schuller, for example, critiques Swing Era "jazzing the classics" efforts in provocative rhetoric, dismissing them as "pitiful and naïve . . . attempts at bridging the two [classical and jazz] fields" and "falling ineptly between jazz and classical music."[14]

Yet it is difficult to identify any broad Swing Era musical commitment to "bridge" jazz and classical music, as compared to the artistic—and, yes, commercial—motivation to create material capitalizing on established cultural dichotomies like classic/popular, black/white, urban/rural, or old/new. The performance of celebrated European concert repertoire by jazz big bands would emerge as an immediately recognizable (and therefore effective) tool in variety programming. For example, Count Basie's saxophonist Earle Warren recalled: "It was essential—certainly when you played theaters—for the drummer to play an extended, interesting solo. . . . [Basie drummer Jo Jones's] vehicle was 'Prelude in C-sharp Minor,' a Rachmaninoff thing. Jimmy Mundy made an arrangement of it for him."[15] Archival logs of dance band radio broadcasts during 1937 reflect performances of contemporary hits alongside warhorse European classics like

Strauss's "Blue Danube Waltz" (Tommy Dorsey's orchestra), Rimsky-Korsakov's "Song of India" (Horace Henderson's orchestra), and Mendelssohn's "Spring Song" (Paul Whiteman's orchestra).[16]

"SONATA PATHÉTIQUE"

Period Swing Era media provide plentiful examples of criticism surrounding jazzed classics; as Scott DeVeaux points out, much of the ink spilled was clearly aimed to "boost circulation by fanning enthusiasms and controversies."[17] Media responses to Chappie Willet's arrangement of the first movement of Beethoven's Piano Sonata No. 8, op. 13 ("Pathétique"), recorded by Jimmie Lunceford in February 1940, included some revealingly mixed (if predictably dogmatic) reactions that reflected the high/low discourse surrounding crossings of European classics and jazz.[18] A writer for the *New York Times* commented, "Department of bad taste: Jimmie Lunceford has perfected a swing arrangement of Beethoven's 'Sonata Pathétique' which 'storms down the house whenever he plays it,' according to his representative."[19] In the black press, a *Chicago Defender* columnist wrote that "[Pathétique] doesn't fit the Lunceford aggregation, which may or may not suggest that he stick to swing and hot stuff."[20] Another black paper, the *New York Amsterdam News*, appears to have taken the Lunceford "representative" at his word, running a brief article titled "Jimmie Lunceford Knows His Musical History": "[Lunceford] knows his swing, but he knows the classics too. During a recent air interview, a music commentator mispronounced the name of Beethoven's 'Sonata Pathetitique.' Jimmie politely corrected the abashed 'expert.' . . . Lunceford has perfected a swing arrangement of this famous classic which storms down the house whenever he plays it."[21] The tone of these criticisms presumes an implicit understanding on the reader's part regarding the cultural boundaries of swing and classical domains; exactly why the piece "doesn't fit," was in "bad taste," or why Lunceford's knowledge of "the classics" or Beethoven would be newsworthy apparently needed no explanation. In fact, the commentators may never have even heard the arrangement, as Lunceford's management was clearly hyping the piece as a publicity tool to advertise the variety of his repertoire—or even to fan the media controversy themselves.

Decades later, Gunther Schuller derides Lunceford's recording of "Pathétique" as a key turning point in the fall of Lunceford's musical fortunes: "As if to underscore [Lunceford's] by now almost obsessive insistence on variety . . . the band descends to the absolute depths in an unspeakable arrangement (*derangement* would be a better term) of bits and pieces of Beethoven's *Sonata Pathétique*, a truly pathetic offering. From now on the band flounders erratically towards its ultimate decline."[22] Because Schuller does not identify the arranger—elsewhere he praises Willet's work for Armstrong and Gene Krupa—the attack appears to indicate less of a distaste for Willet's individual skills than for the broader practice of "jazzing the classics," and even the entire middlebrow variety stage-entertainment tradition.[23]

The identity of the Lunceford orchestra as an exceptionally virtuosic "hot" black dance band is critical in exploring the context of Willet's "Pathétique," elements of which were clearly designed to appeal to American audiences' fascination with technical showmanship associated with the European classical tradition.[24] As described by Albert McCarthy, Lunceford's ensemble enjoyed a reputation for presenting "virtuoso showcase[s]" through arrangements that featured contrasting, unpredictable orchestral textures and ensemble dynamics.[25] European critics and American jazz musicians alike responded that "everything was played with the utmost precision," or that "not many bands shared that precision."[26] Patrick Burke argues that efforts by black "precision" Swing Era ensembles like the John Kirby sextet worked to subvert racial stereotypes by demonstrating "to a large and diverse audience that black musicians were capable of 'musicianly and versatile' performances that involved ingenious arrangements and disciplined ensembles as well as inspired improvisation."[27] Just how consciously such strategies might have applied to an individual work like "Pathétique"—issued on disc as "Sonata by L. van Beethoven"—is difficult to assess without explicit testimony from Lunceford or Willet. But any reading of this performance requires a consideration of the style, techniques, and motivations of the musicians that created it.

Trumpeter-arranger Gerald Wilson, who performed on Lunceford's "Pathétique" recording, immediately recalled the piece when asked about Willet's work for the band:

> It was a classical number, and he [Willet] had done a wonderful job with it. I have the recording. . . . It was great, I loved the little trumpet trio thing they had. . . . It was so neat, 'cause you hear all of that . . . in the classical version, of course. And it was nice playing, and it was a difficult arrangement—I mean, you had to be really on your toes. . . . We played it very fast, too. I was very interested in knowing this person [Willet]. . . . I was thrilled to death to play his music.[28]

Pianist Edwin Wilcox, the featured soloist in "Pathétique," provided an anecdote relating to one of the band's live performances:

> I remember once when we were playing our concert arrangement of "Sonata Pathétique" in the Oriental Theater, Chicago. I didn't know our light man . . . was going to give the cue when I came in so that a pinpoint light hit me. . . . It shocked me so bad, I don't think I played five notes out of that first run. I felt so ashamed, but the band was tied up in knots. I had a brandy between shows and was ready the next time. It taught me a lesson, that you always had to be prepared.[29]

The testimony of these side-musicians reveals great pride in the technical performance of the arrangement. Lunceford himself had trained the core members of his band while teaching music in Memphis during the late 1920s. Lead saxophonist and clarinetist Willie Smith recalled the band's routines of daylong sectional rehearsals, with additional preparations for bandstand choreography and a variety of curtain bows cued by number; the group was sometimes referred to as "the trained seals."[30] Lunceford's "trained seals" were a perfect fit for Willet's niche of the dance band arranging market in New York. Swing Era musicians have testified to Willet's reputation for creating difficult scores designed to show off a client group's technical prowess. Trumpeter Harry "Sweets" Edison, describing his 1937 tenure with the Mills Blue Rhythm Band, remembered that "it took a lot of rehearsals to get what you wanted to get. And they had one guy, Chappie Willet, he used to write such hard arrangements it would take so long to get these guys together. And musicians could read in those days."[31] Drummer David "Panama" Francis cited a 1942 "band battle" at the Savoy Ballroom, where the Millinder band "opened with one of our big flag-wavers, 'Prelude in C-sharp Minor,' a great arrangement by Chappie Willet, to show off our musicianship."[32] A 1941 Apollo Theater review in *Variety* similarly celebrated "Prelude in C-sharp Minor" as "possibly [Millinder's] slickest orchestration."[33]

Willet's arrangement of Rachmaninoff's prelude was originally created for Duke Ellington's 1938 Cotton Club residency, and later was featured during Ellington's 1939 European tour.[34] One of Willet's more popular works, it was also performed by the orchestras of Charlie Barnet and Louis Armstrong; a stock publication of Willet's arrangement, scored by Spud Murphy, was distributed by Robbins Music in 1939.[35] The favorable public reception of technical display vehicles like the prelude likely reflected a continuing fascination with European classical virtuosity that emerged in America during the late nineteenth century, when the establishment of the home parlor piano as a socioeconomic status symbol created a demand for publications by so-called light-classical European composers.[36] Amateur aspirations to technical proficiency, presumably linked with notions of upward mobility, resulted in large concert audiences and commercial success for touring European piano virtuosos like Rachmaninoff, Arthur Rubinstein, or José Iturbi, whose 1930 Carnegie Hall performance of Balakirev's "Islamey" (op. 18) was celebrated for its display of "breath-taking speed, clarity and virtuosity rampant."[37] In fact, Iturbi's winter 1930–31 American tour repertoire may have influenced Willet's 1933 college recital programming of Alexandre Tansman's relatively obscure *Sonatine Transatlantique*; Willet even selected the same "Spiritual and Blues" movement that Iturbi had featured.[38]

Among more established light-classical fare, Frederic Chopin's publications in particular provided short-length works attractive for amateur piano performance; they were also relatively easy for arrangers to expand into repeating time-cycle forms for dance band arrangements.[39] From 1939 to 1941, for example, the John Kirby sextet's trumpeter-arranger Charlie Shavers, along with arranger Evan Young, added to a repertoire of Schubert, Grieg, and Beethoven Chopin's "Revolutionary Etude" (op. 10, no. 12), "Prelude in E Minor" (op. 28, no. 4; retitled "Prelude for Trumpet"), "Minute Waltz" (op. 64, no. 1), "Fantasy Impromptu" (op. 66), and a loose interpretation of "Opus 5" ("Rondo à la Mazur").[40] Kirby band arrangements like "Prelude for Trumpet" and "Opus 5" are typical in their extraction of one or two of the source work's themes; the themes are then modified as necessary to produce the eight-bar phrase units comprising popular song forms. Billy Moore Jr.'s arrangement of Chopin's Prelude No. 7 (op. 28; issued on disc as "Chopin's Prelude #7") for Lunceford (example 7.1) and Lloyd "Skip" Martin's arrangement of Paganini's "Caprice XXIV Paganini" for Benny Goodman (example 7.2) likewise transform the original compositions' waltz or two-beat meters into swing dance rhythms, with melodies rescored for syncopated solo expositions (Moore) or voiced for section soli (Martin).[41]

Vocalist Fran Warren and arranger Billy Moore Jr., ca. August 1946. Moore arranged music for Charlie Barnet, Tommy Dorsey, and Jimmie Lunceford. Courtesy of the Frank Driggs Collection at Jazz at Lincoln Center.

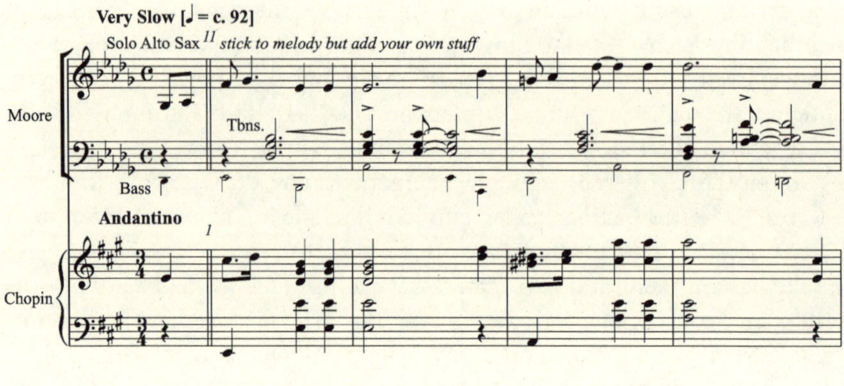

Example 7.1. Comparison of "Chopin's Prelude No. 7" mm. 11–14 (0:27), arr. by Billy Moore Jr. for Jimmie Lunceford (1940), and Chopin's solo piano score. Moore's manuscript orchestra parts held in FDCJLO.

Example 7.2. Comparison of "Caprice XXIV Paganini" mm. 5–8 (0:05), arr. by Skip Martin for Benny Goodman (1941), and Paganini's solo violin score. Martin's manuscript score held in BGP.

By contrast, Willet's "classic" arrangements identified to date—including a version of Sinding's "Rustle of Spring" for Millinder—tend to reflect a relatively completist approach to the original repertoire, maintaining much of the formal layout of the source works. Indeed, the substantial presentation of an eighteenth-century sonata-form movement in "Pathétique" may be unique to Swing Era dance band repertoire. If one allows for the jazz syncopations and embellishments Willet adds (discussed later) as not straying from the essential melodic and harmonic design of the original composition, the arrangement represents roughly two-thirds of Beethoven's sonata movement, in sequence.[42] (Admittedly, the exposition is not repeated.) This reflects a significant effort on the part of the arranger, considering that the movement's potential eight-and-a-half-minute duration (as performed by Vladimir Horowitz, for example) had to be cut down to under three-and-a-half minutes for ten-inch disc release.

"Pathétique" also demonstrates Willet's modernist swing-arranging style, juxtaposing tonal chromaticism with scoring techniques of ragtime marching bands and other vernacular idioms (not to mention Beethoven's original piano sonata). Ragtime references include the addition of trombone and baritone sax counterlines recalling brass band "bass run" fills (example 7.3, mm. 125–28) that respond to more contemporary soli voicings (in open-position "drop-two" formation) in the saxophones (mm. 123–25).[43] In one of the interlude passages that serves to replace part of the original sonata-form recapitulation, a bass run that recalls Lew Pollack's ragtime melody "That's a Plenty" is immediately followed by a sequence of parallel chromatic dominant-ninth voicings (example 7.4, mm. 176–80). During a tenor sax solo, a passage of rapid open-and-closed brass mute scoring (mm. 97–102) that recalls a "do-wa" effect outlined

Example 7.3. Comparison of "Sonata Pathétique" mm. 123–30 (2:10), arr. by Chappie Willet for Jimmie Lunceford (1940), and Beethoven's solo piano score. Willet's manuscript orchestra parts held in FDCJLO.

Example 7.4. Score reduction of break passage in "Sonata Pathétique" mm. 176–80 (2:50), arr. by Chappie Willet for Jimmie Lunceford (1940). Manuscript orchestra parts held in FDCJLO.

by Lange—Willet in fact specifies the syllables "do wa" in his own manuscript parts—reflects jazz dance orchestra conventions established in the 1920s.[44]

Willet's sonata "development" section arrives with a repeated, percussive ensemble whole-tone chord scored over a static pedal bass (example 7.5), building dramatic tension toward a climactic piano break that references Beethoven's original scoring. As noted earlier, Willet was not alone in invoking whole-tone harmony to grab the listener's attention, but the specific chord that arrives at the close of this passage (mm. 140–41) may be regarded as something of a personal

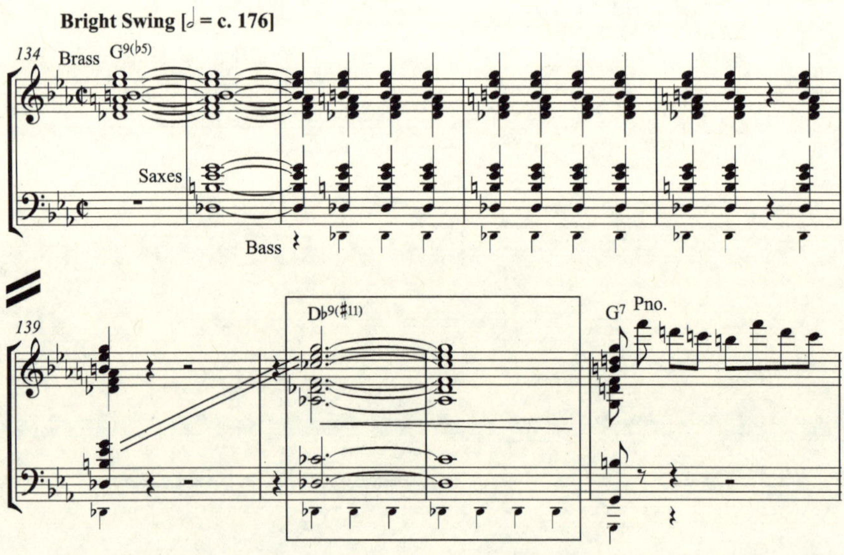

Example 7.5. Score reduction of interlude passage in "Sonata Pathétique" mm. 134–42 (2:23), arr. by Chappie Willet for Jimmie Lunceford (1940). Manuscript orchestra parts held in FDCJLO; chord symbols provided by the author.

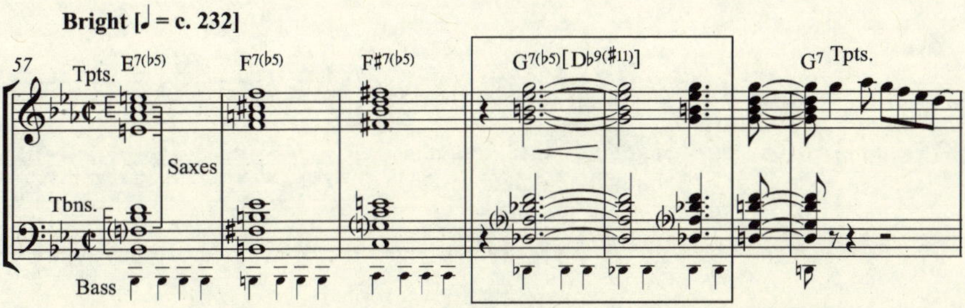

Example 7.6. Score reduction of interlude passage in "Prelude in C-sharp Minor" mm. 57–62 (0:54), arr. by Chappie Willet for Duke Ellington (1938). Manuscript orchestra parts held in DEC; chord symbols reflect the manuscript guitar part.

signature.[45] A similar chord appears in both his 1938 "Prelude in C-sharp Minor" (example 7.6, mm. 60–61) and 1942 "Rustle of Spring" (example 7.7, mm. 49–50) arrangements; in all three instances, this chord emerges in climactic ensemble scoring over a pedal bass and preceding rhythm section breaks in up-tempo "classic" numbers.[46] These voicings might be labeled as a dominant-ninth with an augmented eleventh chord tone, but in the guitar part for the Prelude, Willet provides a spelling of G dominant–seventh flat-five—essentially ignoring the dissonant A-flat (the flatted-ninth degree, using Willet's G root spelling) and emphasizing the flatted-fifth voice setting in the bass (there is also an augmented fifth included in the upper voices, similar to "After You've Gone," example 5.5).[47] It seems likely that Willet's reference to this "almost"-whole-tone voicing in "Prelude" as a flatted-fifth dominant chord reflects the arranger's broader attraction to the modernist whole-tone effect, and further connects these three passages as extensions of that device.

While certainly not the only precedent, a tantalizingly relevant model for Willet's pet sonority can be found in the bluesy final measure of his graduation recital repertoire: Tansman's "Spiritual and Blues" (example 7.8).

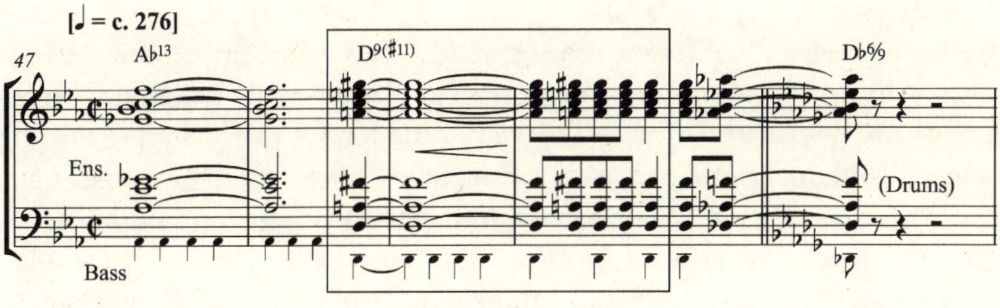

Example 7.7. Score reduction of interlude passage in "Rustle of Spring" mm. 47–51 (0:47), arr. by Chappie Willet for Lucky Millinder (ca. 1942). Transcription by the author.

Example 7.8. Closing of *Sonatine Transatlantique*: "Spiritual and Blues" m. 80, by Alexandre Tansman (1930).

Willet's insertion of his personal (or perhaps simply "bluesy") twist on the whole-tone effect as a substitution for Beethoven's sonata-form development might be heard to serve: (1) the necessity of shortening the piece's duration; (2) as an energy-building dissonance to frame the virtuosic solo piano run that immediately follows; (3) as an exercise in the modernist juxtaposition of European concert music signifiers against vernacular jazz dance music tropes and *other* European concert music signifiers (including Beethoven piano sonatas); (4) as a practical harmonic substitution for the long-range dominant function of classical sonata-form developments (especially if one privileges a "G" chord spelling in the key of C minor); (5) as the portion of the arrangement where Willet veers most significantly from Beethoven's original score, perhaps highlighting a conceptual parallel between the sonata-form development and the dance band "arranger's chorus"; and/or (6) as a personal tie-in to his own past and future efforts in "jazzing the classics," stylistically uniting the freelancer's work across several years and for different clients.

Willet also introduces a combination of devices to ensure the reception of "Pathétique" as a rendition of a classical work, independent of the audience's identification of the source text. Aside from replacing the development, one of his more conspicuous alterations is the addition of a fanfare introduction that precedes Beethoven's *Grave* piano theme. Harmonically, this passage serves to introduce a version of the whole-tone chord (example 7.9, m. 8) heard later on; rhythmically, the opening drum roll and rubato-inducing fermatas invoke theatrical drama, immediately alerting the listener that they are about to receive something spectacular. By following this preparatory fanfare with Beethoven's original solo piano scoring of the *Grave* theme (m. 9), Willet caricatures the erudite atmosphere of a classical piano recital. A tempo change and rescoring for solo clarinet in the *Grave* variation (m. 17), including rubato cadenzas with orchestral recitative accompaniment closing the passage (e.g., mm. 37–40), suggest a symphonic concerto setting.[48] The initial phrase of Beethoven's *Allegro* exposition, performed by Lunceford's orchestra at a tempo clocking over 300 quarter-notes per minute, is answered by Willet's own rapid-fire chromatic eighth-note embellishment (example 7.10, mm. 46–49) recalling the "virtuosity rampant" prized at Carnegie Hall concerts. And in contrast

Example 7.9. Score reduction of introduction to "Sonata Pathétique" mm. 1–40 (0:01), arr. by Chappie Willet for Jimmie Lunceford (1940). Manuscript orchestra parts held in FDCJLO.

Example 7.10. Comparison of "Sonata Pathétique" mm. 45–49 (1:19), arr. by Chappie Willet for Jimmie Lunceford (1940), and Beethoven's solo piano score. Willet's manuscript orchestra parts held in FDCJLO.

to the prevailing rhythmic idiom of swung eighth-notes, ensemble phrasing in quarter-note triplets injects a "legit" *pomposo* effect (example 7.3, m. 129; example 7.4, mm. 179–80). Further ties to the symphonic orchestra tradition are provided in Willet's designation of climactic timpani drum rolls at the close of the piece.

The theatrical aspect of "Pathétique's" function was specific; Lunceford did not consider the piece as part of his standard dance repertoire. A *Chicago Defender* report titled "Kirby, Lunceford Turn to 'Heavy' Stuff on Discs" explains that "Pathétique" was presented by the band "in their theatre engagements and on occasions of intermissions at dance engagements."[49] Wilcox's description of "Pathétique" as a "concert arrangement" also indicates the piece's role in the band book. Audiences would presumably be seated (or at least not dancing) and focused on the performance area, perhaps observing the choreographed lighting described by Wilcox. As recorded for Columbia, Lunceford's soloists did not improvise, but played their solo parts as written.

Although popular music arrangers have generally left us with few explicit verbal or written explanations regarding their work, there are some exceptions. In *Arranging for the Modern Dance Orchestra*, Arthur Lange offers his opinions regarding the practice of "paraphrasing classics":

> The art of transcribing classical works for the modern dance orchestra requires more thought and *technique* in scoring than popular music. Therefore, the arranger must first be proficient in scoring popular dance arrangements before attempting to score classical fox-trot paraphrases.
>
> Such works, if well constructed and well scored, may be considered works of art, but if distorted and poorly scored, they will invite unpleasant criticism. The original thought of the composer should always be respected and kept in mind when constructing and scoring.
>
> When selecting material for classical paraphrases, the composition selected . . . should be one with which the public is familiar. . . .
>
> The arranger should secure the orchestral score and . . . should be thoroughly familiar with every detail of the original work.[50]

For Lange, the division between popular and classical is clearly retained within the practice of dance band arranging. His emphasis on "thought and technique" (which he apparently believes popular repertoire to require less of) and the "original thought of the composer" (also apparently less of a concern in Lange's pop arranging) perhaps belies elitist notions regarding the art of "classical" composition and attendant perceptions of musical training. Lange would not have been alone in these beliefs; Willet's regular citing of his own educational pedigree in his early publicity could be read as an effort to legitimize the artistic status of his work as a commercial arranger.[51] In any case, Willet's arrangement clearly reflects Lange's concern in demonstrating familiarity with Beethoven's original *Pathétique* score.

Given that school music programs prior to World War II were much more likely to provide a traditional classical music curriculum than popular music studies (see chapter 4), it is little surprise that popular music of that era includes so many references to European repertoire, especially as represented in the output of formally trained musicians like Willet. The fascination of arranging classical works for dance band formats—or even dance band works for symphonic formats—continued throughout the Swing Era. White bandleader Freddy Martin, for example, had a lasting hit with Ray Austin's 1941 arrangement of the first movement from Tchaikovsky's Piano Concerto No. 1 (op. 23), prompting the addition of lyrics for vocal ballad performances.[52] In 1944, Willet reportedly provided arrangements for a jazz-meets-classical concert presented by Lucky Millinder at the Apollo Theater; publicity describes an augmented thirty-piece orchestra (including oboe, flute, and a "concert" pianist) and a thirty-voice choir performing "swing versions" of excerpts from Dvořák's *New World Symphony* and (presumably Gounod's) *Faust*, in addition to expanded symphonic orchestrations of popular repertoire.[53]

It seems that one of the problems that critics have had with arrangements designed to pit different cultural idioms against one another is that these efforts set the otherwise veiled task of arranging front and center. In Swing Era music, this transparency troubles ideologies regarding the relationship between jazz performers and their subject texts. Expectations of black popular music treatments of white industry-driven commercial idioms could only be sustained by racializing selected components of the written arrangements. At the same time, efforts to privilege the hot-jazz legacy of black bands like Lunceford's or black arrangers like Willet appear to have only further fueled endeavors to play off of established expectations with European-identified art works like "Pathétique." Contemporary critical responses to these efforts only made the divisions between entertainment and art more pronounced, as against-the-grain acts were identified as exceptions that simply reinforced the perceived hierarchy. Popular band arrangements of canonic repertoire simultaneously challenged and perpetuated the assumption that—as José Iturbi quipped—"only Beethoven is worthy to match Beethoven."[54]

Similar to its offspring "rocking the classics," "swinging the classics" would not have remained so prevalent a practice without audience appreciation.[55] The continual return of dance bands to this genre demonstrates how the invention of Swing Era popular music arranging—whether as a means of subverting stereotypes or accentuating them—thrived on the interplay between and among cultural binaries.[56] But this is only part of the story. "Pathétique" is not merely an exercise in hybridity, nor merely a vehicle to showcase the performer's technical virtuosity. It also represents the arranger's conscious assertion of musical identity, whether as one installment in a series of self-styled pieces celebrating musical education, influences, and professional experience, or—depending on how far one wishes to take the available evidence concerning the influence of Tansman or Iturbi—a personal homage to inspirations of formative years.

Jazzing the classics represents a broad conflation of influences, motivations, and efforts that reach well beyond the epithet "commercial."

Jazz Concertos

The jazz concerto is another Swing Era genre that carries associations with the European classical and symphonic jazz traditions. While some Jazz Age performances of the 1920s focused on a single soloist, the characteristics of the emergent big band format—framing a soloist within a large ensemble—offered obvious parallels with the symphonic concerto genre. By the mid-1930s, Duke Ellington had begun to use the concerto strategy—and title—to feature individuals in his orchestra, as in his 1936 "Clarinet Lament (Barney's Concerto)" and "Echoes of Harlem (Cootie's Concerto)." In later efforts, strategies of textural contrast were combined with formal designs that further reinforced parallels with concert music genres. Jazz historian André Hodeir, for example, heard Ellington's 1940 "Concerto for Cootie"—designed with a two-theme "exposition," a "middle section" set in a new key, and a "re-exposition and coda" returning to the original key—as "the furthest thing from being customary in jazz."[57] The success of "Concerto for Cootie" appears to have inspired similarly designed arrangements like Jimmy Mundy's "Fiesta in Blue" (1941).[58]

These classical-inspired strategies also reflect a broader "glorified" or episodic approach to arranging form that emerged with the modernist symphonic jazz vogue of the 1920s (chapter 5). Another jazz concerto vehicle featuring Cootie Williams was Eddie Sauter's extended (four-and-a-half-minute) composition "Superman," recorded by Benny Goodman's orchestra in 1940.[59] In a parallel with "Concerto for Cootie," Sauter occasionally strays from the expected eight-bar phrase groupings of popular song forms (table 8; see reh. A and D); an otherwise innocuous move to the relative minor key in mid-chorus (the last eight bars of rehearsal letter C1) injects even more contrast and variety. Combined with episodic interludes, modulations, and tempo changes, the resulting formal structure is effectively unpredictable.

Bandleader Harry James, whose addition of a string section offered further visual and aural association with classical concert music, presented multitempo concerto renditions of Tin Pan Alley standards like "Tea for Two," a Jack Matthias arrangement featuring saxophonist Willie Smith (1945).[60] The characteristics of the concerto genre offered obvious attractions to freelance arrangers like Chappie Willet, providing dramatic qualities that could be applied to a range of vocal, instrumental, theater stage, or radio broadcast needs. During the 1940s, Willet's client Jimmie Lunceford showed similar interest in exploiting the variety-entertainment possibilities of the jazz concerto.

Table 8. Formal structure of "Superman," arr. by Eddie Sauter for Benny Goodman (1940). Manuscript orchestra parts held in BGP.

Section	Bars	Scoring	Key
[Intro cut for recording]	18	Clarinet and trumpet solo	F major
Chorus 1 (reh. A)	46 (14+14+8+8)	Solo trumpet and ensemble theme	
Chorus 2 (reh. B)	32 (8+8+8+8)	Trumpet solo, ensemble background	
Interlude (reh. C)	12	Clarinet and trumpet solo, modulation	
Chorus 3 (reh. C1)	32 (8+8+8+8)	Tenor sax solo, ensemble background	B-flat major; last 8 bars in G minor
Chorus 4 (reh. D)	42 (22 + 20)	Trumpet over ensemble, chromatic interlude	G major
Interlude (reh. E)	4	Transition to half-time tempo in 4/4 meter, modulation	
Chorus 5 (reh. F)	18 (8+4+6)	Trumpet solo over ensemble, tag ending	B-flat major

"ESTRELLITA" AND "YESTERDAYS"

During 1942 and 1943, Willet arranged extended instrumental features for soloists in the Lunceford orchestra—"Estrellita" and "Yesterdays." Theater shows or radio broadcasts appear to have been the intended presentation format; multiple shifts in tempo and meter make unlikely ballroom vehicles, though staged choreography would certainly be possible. The length of the arrangements—each runs over five minutes—precluded recording to ten-inch disc without extensive editing (options of twelve-inch or double-sided recording were rarely made available to big bands). Performances of both arrangements, however, are documented in radio transcription recordings, as was a similar concerto treatment of "Alone Together" attributed to Ed Wilcox.[61]

"Estrellita" ("Little Star") was designed as a feature for solo trombone (possibly Fernando Arbello); orchestra parts reflect Willet's 1943 stamp, and the recording probably dates from the same period.[62] The 1912 Manuel Ponce composition had received a rumba treatment by Xavier Cugat's dance band in 1937, but the association of "Estrellita" with violin virtuoso Jascha Heifetz via Hollywood film provided a more overtly "concert" context; indeed, Willet's scoring appears to reference Heifetz's own arrangement of the song published in 1928.[63] Willet fulfilled the episodic-form concerto genre requirements by adding his own

Chappie Willet's score of "Estrellita" (p. 1), arranged for the Jimmie Lunceford orchestra (ca. 1943). Used by permission of the University of Missouri–Kansas City Libraries, Dr. Kenneth J. LaBudde Department of Special Collections.

introduction, interlude, coda, tempo changes, meter shifts, and solo cadenzas (see table 9); extensive scoring for arco bass likewise reinforces the piece's programmatic function.

As might be expected, Willet also incorporates the whole-tone effect; a descending sequence of whole-tone phrases for solo trombone (0:40) bridges the introduction and the initial theme statement (reh. A). Following the theme and an eight-bar interlude (reh. C), the soloist is framed in a series of contrasting orchestral textures (reh. D–G). Multiple pauses and transitions in meter and tempo, including quick-step and waltz rhythms (reh. D and F; examples 7.11 and 7.12), also provide an active role for Lunceford as conductor-bandleader. The climactic "swing" passage (4:00; reh. G) is appropriately reinforced by the assignment of ad lib solo improvisation, and indicates Willet's favorite out-chorus ensemble directive: "ride it." But similar to other multicultural dance band arrangements of the period—such as Frank Comstock's 1943 rumba/swing

Table 9. Formal structure of "Estrellita," arr. by Chappie Willet for Jimmie Lunceford (1943). Manuscript score held in JTC; partial manuscript orchestra parts held in FDCJLO.

Section	Bars	Scoring	Tempo and Meter	Key
Intro	12 (4+8)	Ensemble fanfare and trombone solo, transition to slow tempo	[Rubato], cut-time, ritardando	F major
Theme (reh. A)	16 (8+8)	Ensemble and solo trombone theme	Slow [ca. 69 bpm]	
Theme (reh. B)	16 (8+8)	Ensemble and solo theme		
Interlude (reh. C)	8	Ensemble interlude, trombone solo break		
Variation (reh. D)	12	Quick-step/polka ensemble, trombone solo	[Up-tempo ca. 176 bpm]	
Variation (reh. E)	5	Marcato stop-time ensemble, trombone solo	[Slow ca. 69 bpm]	
Variation (reh. F)	10	Waltz ensemble, trombone solo, transition to slow tempo	[Up-tempo ca. 189 bpm], 3/4, ritardando	
Variation (reh. G)	18 (12+6)	Swing ensemble, trombone solo, transition to slow tempo	"Ride It" [cut-time ca. 184 bpm]	
Theme (reh. H)	11	Ensemble theme, trombone solo cadenza, ensemble tag	Slower [ca. 92 bpm], 4/4	E-flat major

Example 7.11. Score reduction of quick-step passage (reh. D) in "Estrellita" mm. 57–60 (3:18), arr. by Chappie Willet for Jimmie Lunceford (1943). Manuscript score held in JTC.

Example 7.12. Score reduction of waltz passage (reh. F) in "Estrellita" mm. 70–74 (3:45), arr. by Chappie Willet for Jimmie Lunceford (1943). Manuscript score held in JTC.

rendition of "Poinciana" for Benny Carter—jazz is merely one of the musical references in the parade of popular styles found in "Estrellita."[64]

"Yesterdays" reflects a similarly glorified treatment of the 1933 Tin Pan Alley standard. A January 1943 press release from Lunceford's management, capitalizing on a recent residency at the Apollo, was published in the *New York Amsterdam News* as "Lunceford Answers Host of Queries on Arrangers of Music":

> Jimmie Lunceford's New Year's week engagement at the Apollo in Harlem, the orchestra's most successful run at the famous theater, scored such a sensation that the management was flooded with inquiries regarding the writers of the arrangements of the band's new numbers. Harold F. Oxley, Lunceford's manager and amanuensis, supplies the following information: Chappie Willet, former Gene Krupa staff arranger and stage production specialist, penned the Lunceford versions of "Hallelujah" and "Yesterdays," the latter featuring trumpeter Freddy [*sic*] Webster.[65]

Set in a slow, dirgelike tempo, the episodic routine of "Yesterdays" comprises an ensemble and solo introduction, thirty-two-bar theme chorus, interlude and modulation, a thirty-two-bar arranger's chorus featuring passages of triple-meter waltz (3:31) and up-tempo swing (3:49), a coda, solo cadenza, and ensemble tag ending.[66] Despite approaching six minutes in duration, Willet's application of contrasting tempos, meters, and orchestration textures—including Spanish *paso doble* rhythms (3:12) as well as *pomposo* quarter-note triplets (4:55)—provides for a well-paced performance, again supported by Lunceford's conducting. In its function as a solo showcase, the piece is something of a holy grail for fans of the little-recorded Freddie Webster; jazz trumpeter Art Farmer celebrated "Yesterdays" as "a complete showcase for [Webster's] incredible tone [that] featured him throughout. . . . Some of the most phenomenal trumpet playing I've ever heard."[67] Such accolades also tacitly acknowledge the arranger's successful framing of solo virtuosity.

"STARDUST"

An arrangement of "Stardust" for Louis Armstrong, probably dating from the trumpeter's fall 1944 residency at the Café Zanzibar, combines jazz concerto with vocal ballad.[68] The length of the arrangement—presumably running at least six minutes—suggests that the piece was conceived to support episodic stage ensemble choreography. An introductory ensemble fanfare with ornamental quintuplet phrases and dramatic *pomposo* triplet figures, supported by arco bass, provides a delicious example of theater-inspired, "glorified" dance band orchestration (example 7.13).

Following this melodramatic opening, Willet's "Stardust" score embarks on a marathon routine consisting of two thirty-two-bar choruses for ensemble and alto sax solo, a four-bar transition, a fifteen-bar verse, an eleven-bar whole-tone interlude and modulation, a thirty-two-bar vocal chorus, another six-bar interlude and modulation (including chromatic diminished and whole-tone passages), an eight-bar trumpet solo, an eight-bar sax section soli, and another

Example 7.13. Score reduction of ensemble introduction to "Stardust" mm. 1–8 (0:01), arr. by Chappie Willet for Louis Armstrong (1944). Manuscript orchestra parts held in LAHM.

modulation leading to a sixteen-bar ensemble closing. Unlike the Lunceford concertos, the tempo and meter of "Stardust" appear to remain constant throughout (one possible exception being the introduction), although the rhythm section rests at various points during transitions. It is a potentially exhausting workout for the orchestra—a factor that may have contributed to alterations made following Armstrong's Zanzibar residency. An August 1945 aircheck recording reveals a much leaner version of "Stardust" featuring solo trombone over a sax section background; the introductory fanfare is the only portion of Willet's original orchestration retained.[69]

* * *

The jazz concerto has enjoyed a life extending well beyond the Swing Era. A growing emphasis on solo virtuosity in jazz that paralleled the emergence of bebop resulted in regular returns to this genre, especially prominent in the 1950s and '60s repertoire of the Duke Ellington and Stan Kenton orchestras. Introduction of the LP-album format likewise encouraged extended showcases for individual players, a strategy that lent itself to suite-form concept albums like those created by Ellington, Francy Boland, or Maria Schneider. As researcher Alex Stewart suggests, mid-performance transitions in meter, tempo, and rhythmic texture (swing, Latin, rock, etc.) remain a hallmark of big band jazz arranging as the discipline enters the twenty-first century.[70] Given historical attempts to distance "authentic" jazz from stage entertainment, it is perhaps ironic—though certainly appropriate—that this glorified, theatrical, episodic-form strategy continues to be embraced as an indicator of "sophisticated" artistry in jazz performance.

8

Give Me Some Skin

Novelty Songs and Ballads

Novelty song wanted for immediate publication. It must be a novelty song—with a new idea and a catchy tune. Don't waste time by sending in a ballad or patriotic song.[1]

—Beacon Music advertisement, *Billboard*, 1941

The pitch above indicates the thirst of some publishers for the potentially quick-selling, if usually short-lived, "novelty song" compositions that permeated the Swing Era market. Period novelty songs typically present a simple or familiar melody, a standard thirty-two-bar form with few excursions from the tonic key (chord progressions are rarely more complex than "I Got Rhythm"), and—most importantly—lyrics featuring a phrase linked to contemporary popular culture.[2] Within these basic parameters, however, the genre reflected a range of strategies. Along with ballad love songs, novelties represented an important artistic as well as commercial component of Swing Era big band music.

Novelty Songs

Programs for nightclub and theater productions, for example, often featured novelty songs that described a real or imagined new dance craze, like "The Flat Foot Floogee" or "Push Out." These dance-themed numbers—ideal material for vaudeville song-and-dance acts, as well as an important ingredient of variety in dance band repertoire—typically incorporated rhythmic patterns identified with popular dance styles, like "boogie woogie" (as in "Beat Me Daddy, Eight to the Bar") or Latin rumba (as in "Six Lessons from Madame La Zonga"). Chappie Willet's 1938 arrangement of "The Flat Foot Floogee" for Red Norvo employs an additional tactic: assigning ensemble vocals to the band instrumentalists, sometimes referred to as a "glee-club" effect.[3] Here the arranger also capitalized on popular music's cult of personality, adding a "patter" vocal passage calling out the bandleader's name: "Alright Red, we've swung a mess for you, so now you've got to beat us out a riff or two. Lay it Red, you mustn't let us down, now grab a bunch of sticks and go to town!"[4] Similar ensemble vocals referencing the bandleader can be heard in a 1939 arrangement of Horace Gerlach's "What Is This Thing Called Swing" for Louis Armstrong: "Take your horn, Pops, beat it out. Show the world what swing's about."[5] "This Thing" also features an introduce-the-band concept—announcing a representative from each section of the orchestra—similar to Armstrong's earlier "I Hope Gabriel Likes My Music" (1935) or Ed Wilcox's arrangement of "Rhythm Is Our Business" for Jimmie Lunceford (1934).

Another novelty formula was the adaptation of familiar children's songs or nursery-rhyme themes into swing rhythm. This strategy intensified following Ella Fitzgerald's 1938 hit on Van Alexander's arrangement of "A-Tisket, A-Tasket"; competing versions of the same song included arrangements by Edgar Sampson (for Benny Goodman) and Willet (for Norvo).[6] Follow-up efforts like "Swingin' the Nursery Rhymes"—a stock publication scored by Jimmy Mundy—featured lyrics citing the characters Mother Hubbard and Cinderella amid "jitterbugs" and the swing dance "Truckin'."[7] Other novelty efforts invoked geohistorical references—Raymond Scott's 1937 "Twilight in Turkey" referenced the 1890s hit "Streets of Cairo" to novelty effect.[8] In 1938, Willet scored arrangements of Henry Work's 1875 "Grandfather's Clock" (for Gene Krupa)—featuring a mimetic woodblock "clockwork" solo—and Duke Ellington and Henry Nemo's "Swingtime in Honolulu" (for Ellington)—interpolating the familiar Hawaiian melodic trope of Lili'uokalani's 1878 "Aloha 'Oe."

"TOY-TOWN JAMBOREE"

"Toy-Town Jamboree," a 1938 novelty song by Major Hurwitz, John Redmond, and Mary Schaeffer, combined references to traditional nursery figures—like Jack Horner and Red Riding Hood—with the currency of Walt Disney's 1937 film *Snow White*. Disney characters including the Seven Dwarfs, Donald Duck, and Mickey Mouse are cited in the lyrics and depicted on the cover of the printed leadsheet.[9] Willet's arrangement of this piece for Red Norvo's orchestra may date from the band's August 1938 residency at New York's Pennsylvania Hotel.[10]

The published leadsheet introduction for "Toy-Town" fulfills the requisite nursery-room imagery with a triadic staccato phrase mimicking the sound of a wind-up toy mechanism. Willet scored his own intro with a similarly articulated effect, but instead quotes the melody of "Parade of the Wooden Soldiers," a familiar children's trope and a favorite musical reference in the Broadway tap-dance world.[11] Willet's "Wooden Soldiers" quotation is framed in a stark juxtaposition of orchestration textures, as staccato "straight" eighth-notes scored for muted trumpet, unison low saxes, and percussion woodblocks—representing the sound of the toy soldiers—are suddenly overtaken by a syncopated version of the same melody, scored for the full band with open brass and an indication for a "swing" feel (example 8.1). At this point, jazzier dominant-seventh chords replace the opening triads (compare m. 5 with m. 1), followed by a chromatic harmony substitution descending by half-step (compare m. 6 with m. 2). The dramatic and efficient contrast—pitting hip against square—demonstrates Willet's stylistic fluency in creating clear and unambiguous programmatic imagery.

For an instrumental theme chorus, Willet scored the piano in a manner recalling the "music-box" orchestration effect outlined in Lange's *Arranging for the Modern Dance Orchestra,* where it is prescribed as "effective in an arrangement of a dainty composition."[12] Willet utilizes a right-hand broken-chord pattern perhaps more suggestive of a pipe organ, reinforcing the imagery of children's mechanized entertainment (example 8.2). The piano's half-note counterline is

Example 8.1. Score reduction of "Toy-Town Jamboree" mm. 1–6, arr. by Chappie Willet for Red Norvo (1938). Manuscript orchestra parts held in RNP.

Example 8.2. Piano part for "Toy-Town Jamboree" mm. 9–12, arr. by Chappie Willet for Red Norvo (1938). Manuscript orchestra parts held in RNP.

later taken up by unison saxes; following the vocal chorus, subsequent orchestration includes Willet's favorite ensemble "whip" figures, and chord voicings descending in parallel half-step motion.

In addition to dance band arranging assignments like "Toy-Town," Willet collaborated with stage acts to compose original material. At least two of these works—"The Hicky Ricky" and "Eh! Now"—employed another crucial Swing Era novelty formula: the representation of African American culture in the form of "Harlem jive" slang. Similar to songs like "Harlem Stomp" (1940), "I Dreamt I Dwelt in Harlem" (1941), or "Let Me Off Uptown" (1941), these compositions reflect the complexity of musical and cultural borrowings in the novelty genre and the broader American entertainment industry. Surviving music manuscripts also reveal parallels between techniques of Swing Era popular song composition and big band scoring.

"THE HICKY RICKY"

Willet's relationship with "The Hicky Ricky" and its performers demonstrates multiple facets of the Swing Era music business. A tracing of the song's origins, publicity, and reception reveals not only trends in popular music arranging, composing, marketing, and performance, but also the racial segregation of American entertainment, the business structures that maintained those barriers, and the available options of response for black artists. It also reflects new approaches to audio-recording technology, and the rising power of the film medium as it replaced traditions of live stage performance. The tale begins in 1940, with a notice printed in the *Chicago Defender*: "NEW DANCE: As Usual It Started in Harlem and Is Called the Hicky Ricky."[13]

"The Hicky Ricky" was designed as a vehicle for the comedy-dance trio the Three Chocolateers. The lyrics were written by ensemble members Paul Black and Albert Gibson, with music composed by Esvan Mosby and "ace Broadway Race arranger" Chappie Willet.[14] By 1940, the Chocolateers were a veteran act, having worked their way up from vaudeville tours to Hollywood films and top-tier nightclub floor shows. The group's leader and manager, Kansas City native Esvan Scott Mosby (ca. 1910–86), is credited for appearances in Hollywood films with his older brother Curtis as early as 1929.[15] Curtis Mosby was a California-based bandleader and nightclub owner known as the "mayor of Central Avenue"—the black entertainment district of Swing Era Los Angeles—although Esvan occasionally shared this title as well.[16] Albert "Gip" (or "Gyp") Gibson (ca. 1913–90), from Atlanta, had grown up performing with his family's vaudeville act prior to joining the *Olsen and Johnson* show on the Orpheum theater circuit; trumpeter-bandleader Buck Clayton remembered Gibson as "one of the best street corner dancers in Los Angeles."[17] Paul Black was known for doing a "Chinese" walking splits stunt; he left the Chocolateers at the end of 1940 (joining the group Paul, Slim & Eddie—later Paul, Dinky & Eddie), although he apparently returned at some point later in the decade.[18] Subsequent editions of the Chocolateers included Albert Gibson's brother Duke, Eddie "Half Pint" West, James "Buster" Brown, and James "Chuckles" Walker.[19]

The Three Chocolateers had received their first national—and international—publicity in the fall of 1934, after arriving in China to be featured with Buck Clayton's orchestra at Shanghai's Canidrome Ballroom.[20] Their steamship journey demonstrates the lengths that Depression-era vaudeville acts might take for a shot at commercial success; Clayton recalled the trio's condition upon arrival as "so ragged and tattered that if the wind had blown on them they would have whistled like a peanut stand."[21] In 1935, the trio returned to California to capitalize on the growing trend of Hollywood film comedies featuring a black musical number, usually framed within an otherwise white production.[22] This included a brief but uncredited appearance in the Jane Withers feature *Can This Be Dixie?* (Twentieth Century Fox, 1936)—where the trio danced on a cotton field as part of the "Pick, Pick, Pickaninny" sequence—and a contracted appearance in the Marx Brothers' *A Day at the Races* (MGM, 1937)—presumably for the "All God's Chillun Got Rhythm" sequence, featuring the Marx brothers in blackface—though the Chocolateers's bit was apparently unused or never filmed.[23] Finally, the trio landed a featured slot in RKO's *New Faces of 1937*, starring Milton Berle.[24] Their dance routine titled "Peckin'" kicked off the film's climactic production number, resulting in a novelty hit that would remain the Chocolateers's primary stage vehicle through the end of the decade.[25]

Albert Gibson later recalled his *New Faces* scene at a videotaped event hosted by dance instructor–historian Jane Goldberg: "I jumped up in the tree and pecked with the chickens . . . it was a fun picture."[26] A 1937 *Pittsburgh Courier* review explained that the Chocolateers's number involved "their heads weaving and bobbing in the same manner a barnyard fowl pecks at his dinner"; historians Marshall and Jean Stearns later criticized that the "clowning was emphasized as [the Chocolateers] ran all over the stage and up the walls, and it obscured the excellent dancing."[27] In the wake of their film success, the Chocolateers traveled to New York to present "Peckin'" at the Apollo Theater and the Broadway Cotton Club, where they probably met Willet.[28] Meanwhile, the music that accompanied the Chocolateers's performance—a melody derived from trumpeter Cootie Williams's solo on Duke Ellington's "Rockin' in Rhythm" (1930)—went on to enjoy a successful life of its own, published by impresario Irving Mills and recorded by Cab Calloway, Johnny Hodges (with Duke Ellington), Benny Goodman, and Bing Crosby (with Jimmy Dorsey); a stock arrangement was scored by Jimmy Mundy.[29] White bandleader Ben Pollack and trumpeter Harry James shared composer credits for the music, although Esvan Mosby later claimed, "I wrote the music and lyrics for 'Peckin'' with Harry James."[30]

Regardless of the "Peckin'" song's origins, it appears that the Chocolateers were interested in the music publishing royalties relating to the success of their act. The new "Hicky Ricky" routine was reportedly developed at the Apollo during the summer of 1940.[31] In early September—*after* the song was registered for copyright—the Chocolateers unveiled their new vehicle as part of a Cab Calloway–led *Cotton Club Revue* at Broadway's Paramount Theater.[32] The Paramount's management claimed that this program was viewed by 192,000 patrons in two weeks, breaking summer-season attendance records.[33] Furthering the hype, the *Pittsburgh Courier* boasted: "Jimmie Lunceford, Cab Calloway, Tommy Dorsey, and the Three Peppers will record the ["Hicky Ricky"] number which will be released late this month [September]."[34] Any such recordings or publications, if planned, were never issued. But even bigger ambitions for the song emerged the following spring. On April 5, 1941, the *Chicago Defender* announced "Chocolateers' Tune Used in Navy Film":

> When the Andrews Sisters appear on the screen in their latest film "We're in the Navy Now" . . . they'll be seen singing the Hickory Rickory [*sic*], composed and introduced by the Three Chocolateers a few months ago at the Apollo theatre. In addition to the tune appearing in the Universal film it was also announced that the dance, also created by the originators of the popular dance and song, pecking [*sic*], will be executed. The popular singing sisters left the city last week for Hollywood to start work on the picture. For usage of their brainchild the Chocolateers will be paid a sum said to exceed $5,000. It was said that previous commitments prevented them from going West to appear in the "Navy" film.[35]

A few days later, *Amsterdam News* columnist (and perennial Willet advocate) Dan Burley noted that "the Chocolateers' new song, 'Hicky Ricky,' recorded at Chappie Willet's studio, got into the hands of the publishers via the waxed disc which was submitted to Leeds Music Co. In turn, the Andrews Sisters will sing and record it!"[36] The establishment of Willet's recording services had previously been celebrated in an article titled "Ace Arranger Turns to Recording Field"; Willet claimed that his studio "not only enables the sponsor to get a perfect idea of how the auditioner will actually sound on the air or on records, but it also gives the applicant a chance to hear himself and to correct certain little faults that he little dreams he had."[37] In September 1940—just after the Chocolateers's Paramount stand—a *Pittsburgh Courier* feature announced an additional attraction of Willet's services: "Broadway's only Negro recording studio" had "been of invaluable aid to composers and song writers who use this new means of presenting their songs to publishers."[38]

A solo vocal recording of "The Hicky Ricky," performed by Esvan Mosby on a privately recorded disc probably dating to between 1940 and 1942, was issued in 1998.[39] While apparently not the disc sent to Leeds Music, this artifact may be similar to the "demo" recorded by Willet.[40] Additional verse lyrics—announced by Mosby as "second stanza"—reflect those provided in a second "Hicky Ricky" copyright registered in November 1941 and listing publisher Kaycee Music, a company whose "sole selling agent" was Leeds Music.[41] At the close of the unaccompanied performance, a second voice announces: "Ladies and gentleman, that was 'The Hicky Ricky' by the one and only, Central Avenue's Mayor, Esvan Mosby. Thank you, Mr. Mosby."

A paragon of swing novelty, "The Hicky Ricky" features a thirty-two-bar AABA-form chorus with an indication for "jump tempo"; lyrics describe an accompanying dance and incorporate Harlemese jive slang. Similar to stage numbers like "Peckin'" or "Skrontch"—which the Chocolateers had performed with Duke Ellington at the Cotton Club—the "Ricky" lyrics also reference the names of other popular dances. Outdoing the "Peckin'" citation of "Truckin'" and "Susi-Q," or even "Skrontch's" citation of "Truckin'," "Susi-Q," and "Peckin'," "The Hicky Ricky" cites the "LaConga," "Susi-Q," "Ballin' the Jack," "Peckin'," and "Skrontch."[42] In addition, references to the jive "vout" language popularized by Slim Gaillard—creator of the "The Flat Foot Floogee"—emerge, as names like "Susi-Q" and "Skrontch" are transformed into "Susi-ma-Q" and "Scronch-a-ma-roo."[43] The "Ricky" bridge closes with some fashionable Harlem slang: "Swing into the Peckin' or the Scronch-a-ma-roo, very simple and easy to do. / Work'a your shoulders up and down, then you stand back and grin, say give me some skin."[44]

The piano accompaniment for "The Hicky Ricky" chorus is built on familiar ii7—V7—I progressions in the tonic key; a dominant-cycle bridge recalls that of "I Got Rhythm" (except that the third and fourth measures are set in minor vi instead of major VI7). A fourth-beat hold rhythm device similar to "Skrontch"—and also familiar to Willet (chapter 6)—arrives at the end of the "Ricky" verse, where it is combined with another of Willet's favorite devices: a sequence of flatted-fifth dominant chords voiced in parallel half-step motion (example 8.3).[45] The same passage (mm. 15–16) also closes with a descending half-step bass line (D—D-flat—C), suggesting a "tri-tone substitution" (see chapter 5).[46]

Example 8.3. Verse sendoff passage in "The Hicky Ricky" mm. 9–16, copyright leadsheet arr. by Chappie Willet (1941).

Willet's leadsheet arrangement for "The Hicky Ricky" further reflects his big band arranging style by juxtaposing harmonic chromaticism with signifiers of ragtime marching bands. "Rockin' in Rhythm"–like tailgate figures—retained in Mosby's vocal performance a cappella—provide "fill-in" endings for the chorus A sections (example 8.4, m. 24); eighth-note "secondary rag" syncopation (see chapter 6) is woven into the repetitions of the title phrase (example 8.4, mm. 21–22), as well as the line beginning "stand back and grin . . ." at the end of the bridge (example 8.5). An augmented dominant chord punctuates the last word of the invitation "give me some skin" (example 8.5, m. 40), with a percussive response provided by the following octave-drop bass note. Similarly syncopated rhythm breaks—often in combination with augmented dominant chords—frequently appear at the end of the bridge in period novelty songs, building dramatic tension prior to the return of the final A section.

Judging from newspaper accounts, the phrase *gimme* or *give me some skin* appears to have hit Harlem around the summer of 1940.[47] By the following year, the phrase had become a hot commodity. The Delta Rhythm Boys vocal ensemble recorded a song titled "Gimme Some Skin" in December 1940 and released the following March; their performance closed with the line "my friend, gimme some skin!"[48] Lionel Hampton waxed Tiny Parham's "Give Me Some

Example 8.4. Secondary rag and tailgate figures (end of chorus A section) in "The Hicky Ricky" mm. 21–24, copyright leadsheet arr. by Chappie Willet (1941).

Example 8.5. Secondary rag rhythm break figure (end of bridge) in "The Hicky Ricky" mm. 39–40, copyright leadsheet arr. by Chappie Willet (1941).

Skin" in April 1941.[49] The following September, Willet's associate Porter Grainger included a "Gimme Some Skin" number in his *Rhythm Bound* stage revue at Harlem's Club Mimo.[50] The Three Chocolateers, of course, had been in on the ground floor of this jive line, and *In the Navy*—a well-publicized Abbott and Costello feature—may have appeared to be the perfect opportunity to position "The Hicky Ricky" as their next "Peckin'."

But it wasn't going to happen in a mainstream military propaganda production. Certainly the announcement of the Chocolateers's unavailability for filming due to "previous commitments" was overly optimistic, as the only nonwhite character depicted in the final cut of *In the Navy* served as the butt of an Asian slur. But "The Hicky Ricky" song itself is absent from the film: the Andrews Sisters filled *In the Navy*'s black culture slot with a different Harlem jive song.[51] Registered for copyright on March 13, 1941, as "Gimme Some Skin," and reregistered in April—following the release of the Delta Rhythm Boys disc—as "Gimme Some Skin, My Friend," the sisters' vehicle delivers the lines "skin me, papa, skin me" and "like they do it in Harlem."[52] Following novelty convention, an augmented dominant chord reinforces a syncopated rhythm break at the end of the bridge (see example 8.6, m. 36).[53] The creation of this new song was credited to white composers Don Raye and Gene de Paul, and—in its initial copyright filing—black Los Angeles trumpeter Red Mack.[54] The publisher was Leeds Music, which had turned out hits including "Rhumboogie," another Andrews Sisters vehicle with lyrics by Don Raye, and again citing Harlem.[55]

In Goldberg's documentary videotape, Gibson demonstrates brief excerpts of the Chocolateers's dance routines for "Peckin'," "Skrontch," and "The Hicky Ricky," explaining that the latter served as "the Apollo [theater] theme song [for] taking amateurs off [stage]."[56] His steps for "Ricky" appear to reflect the choreography described in the second eight-bar section of the chorus: his ankles and knees move in and out as if to "get way back and ball the jacky," and his right foot advances forward to pat time while his shoulders pull back for "right foot front and shoulders backy."[57] During the Andrews Sisters' "Gimme Some Skin" sequence for *In the Navy*—toward the end of a "camp meeting" ensemble handclap passage—Patty Andrews executes similar novelty dance steps.[58] Parallels between Gibson's "Ballin' the Jack" motions and the sisters' film performance (possibly under the direction of Hollywood choreographer Nick Castle) may be a coincidence, but Patty Andrews's steps stand out fairly distinctly against of the rest of the group's routine.[59]

The manuscript collection of Willet's colleague Tom Whaley includes a thirty-three-bar dance band score for "The Hicky Ricky."[60] As with much of Whaley's surviving music, this artifact—scored for a stock format of five brass, four saxes, and rhythm section—suggests intended use in a nightclub or stage revue production, although it is unclear whether Whaley's single-chorus arrangement was intended as an introduction, a brief transitional entr'acte, or was complete as is.[61] His orchestration prominently highlights the Willet leadsheet's tailgate figures (example 8.7, m. 16), and adds additional ensemble fourth-beat hold figures in the bridge—appropriately following the lyrics "Scronch-a-ma-roo"

Example 8.6. Rhythm break figure (end of bridge) in "Gimme Some Skin, My Friend" published leadsheet mm. 35–37, by Don Raye, Red Mack, and Gene de Paul (1941).

Example 8.7. Score reduction of tailgate and fourth-beat hold figures (bridge) in "The Hicky Ricky" mm. 16–19, arr. by Tom Whaley. Manuscript score held in DEC.

(m. 18). As noted earlier, neither orchestration device is unique to Willet's or Whaley's writing; indeed, this sort of musical borrowing—like Harry James's use of Cootie Williams's lick in "Peckin'"—defines the novelty genre. Nevertheless, it is notable that while neither device is directly reflected in the "Gimme Some Skin" leadsheet published by Leeds Music, versions of *both* devices appear in Vic Schoen's arrangement of "Gimme Some Skin" as heard on film and as recorded by the Andrews Sisters for Decca on May 29, 1941.[62] Ensemble fourth-beat holds are heard in the introductory verse (0:13), and again closing the first two A sections of the AABA-form chorus (0:27); trombones execute a descending tailgate figure during an instrumental chorus (example 8.8, m. 116).[63]

As *In the Navy* was being completed, the Chocolateers (with Duke Gibson replacing Paul Black) toured their way to Los Angeles; the *Defender* explained that "a film contract remains to be fulfilled by the trio, following their chores at the Paramount theatre."[64] The group returned to California again in early 1942, when they reportedly filmed their "Hicky Ricky" routine for a low-budget Republic Pictures release titled *Moonlight Masquerade*.[65] However, surviving copies of *Moonlight* reflect a version of the film in which "The Hicky Ricky" is—again—absent. Instead, Albert Gibson (in the role of a train porter) delivers

Example 8.8. Score reduction of tailgate figure (instrumental chorus) in "Gimme Some Skin, My Friend" mm. 115–17 (2:18), arr. by Vic Schoen for the Andrews Sisters (1941). Transcription by the author.

an acrobatic solo performance to an uncredited big band arrangement, segregated from his white dance "partner" in the number (Betty Kean, who inhabits a separate compartment of the train) by an actual wall. Only a single, brief shot of the complete Chocolateers trio—what appears to be the unintentional remnant of sloppy editing—remains.

Leeds Music's piano and vocal leadsheet for "The Hicky Ricky" was also published in 1942; a heading on the interior page belatedly announced "the new dance sensation created by The 3 Chocolateers."[66] The publisher's involvement in the music production decisions for either *In the Navy* or *Moonlight Masquerade* is unclear, but the Leeds-filed copyright for "Ricky" was not registered until July 20, 1942—after the release of *Moonlight Masquerade*, and over a year after the release of *In the Navy*.[67] Although Cab Calloway would have been an attractive choice for the cover-page photo endorsement—his orchestra had appeared with the Chocolateers on tour—the Leeds publication advertised its contents as "featured by Harry James and his orchestra." The "Ricky" cover's modest, single-color stock design offers stark contrast to the lavish, multicolor "Gimme Some Skin" publication, which featured a depiction of the Andrews Sisters and tie-in artwork from *In the Navy*.

Although the Chocolateers had clearly hoped that "The Hicky Ricky" would "be as great as 'Peckin','" their new song never achieved the hit status they were aiming for.[68] Despite extended exposure as theme material at the Apollo, record-breaking theater tours, representation by a mainstream publisher, Willet flexing his connections in the black press, and repeated claims of a Hollywood film appearance, concern surrounding the number eventually faded. By the time the Three Chocolateers appeared in a "soundie" film short at the end of 1942, they had retreated to a boogie-woogie-styled update of their 1930s warhorse "Peckin'."[69]

"The Hicky Ricky" represents one story from an industry that published hundreds of similar tunes competing for hit status.[70] As the Hollywood film industry offered an increasingly lucrative music market, the transfer of cultural products from sources like Harlem became a major avenue of commerce.[71] Original material was a valued commodity, especially in an era when sound recordings and films served to publicize an act's live engagements; the potential loss of marketable identity through the distribution of recordings appears to have been, in the case of the Chocolateers, a very real threat. At the same time, any number of pop-culture music and lyric references were tapped in manufacturing a song's "novelty" character, including citations of other popular songs, dances, or recognizable rhythmic devices and arranging techniques. Even if Leeds Music and Universal Pictures did pilfer the Chocolateers's material, the creators of "Ricky" borrowed from their competitors just as much as the writers

Table 10. Chronology of copyright registrations, publicity, and performances of "The Hicky Ricky" and "Gimme Some Skin, My Friend."

August 15, 1940	Composers' copyright registration for "The Hicky Ricky."
September 1940	Chocolateers present "The Hicky Ricky" on Cab Calloway tour.
December 16, 1940	Delta Rhythm Boys record title "Gimme Some Skin" in NYC.
March 13, 1941	Leeds copyright registration for "Gimme Some Skin," crediting Raye, Mack, and de Paul.
April 5, 1941	*Chicago Defender* announces "The Hicky Ricky" to be performed by the Andrews Sisters in *In the Navy*.
April 8, 1941	Leeds copyright registration for "Gimme Some Skin, My Friend," crediting Raye and de Paul.
April 8, 1941	Lionel Hampton records title "Give Me Some Skin" in Chicago.
April 8–mid-May, 1941	Universal Pictures' *In the Navy* produced in Hollywood.
April 12, 1941	*New York Amsterdam News* reports plans for Andrews Sisters to record "The Hicky Ricky" resulted from Willet's demonstration disc sent to Leeds.
May 29, 1941	Andrews Sisters record "Gimme Some Skin, My Friend" for Decca.
May 30, 1941	Universal Pictures' *In the Navy* released.
November 7, 1941	Kaycee copyright registration for "The Hicky Ricky."
June 1942	Republic Pictures *Moonlight Masquerade* released.
July 20, 1942	Leeds copyright registration for "The Hicky Ricky."
Ca. 1946?	Red Mack records "Gimme Some Skin—Mah Friend," crediting Mack as sole composer.

of "Gimme Some Skin" did. The chronology of copyright registrations and disc recordings allows for any number of theories regarding a trail of relationships and borrowings (see table 10); "Gimme Some Skin" cocomposer Red Mack even reentered the fray a few years later with a recording titled "Give Me Some Skin—Mah Friend," crediting Mack as sole composer.[72]

Yet, as musicologist Ingrid Monson observes, "the history of twentieth-century American popular music . . . is the history of an interracial encounter through music under asymmetrical economic, aesthetic, and political circumstances."[73] While Swing Era Harlem was embraced as a vibrant source of marketable cultural product, that product would be sold to mainstream audiences primarily by white performers like Harry James and the Andrews Sisters. Aside from the question of whether the Chocolateers ever received their $5,000—perhaps, after all, simply a buyout to keep competition off the market—Leeds Music apparently sat on their song for at least fifteen months. Limitations in publishing, recording, or film opportunities for the Chocolateers to market "The Hicky Ricky" were endemic of a segregated entertainment business that also defined an act's live performance opportunities—which might include destinations as distant as Shanghai.[74]

Even as ambitious figures like Willet positioned themselves to move into new mediums like film or capitalize on new technologies like private recording gear, racial barriers remained a constant concern. It was following Willet's experiences with Robbins Music and Leeds Music that he created his own publishing company in 1944, an event celebrated by the *Chicago Defender* as a venture into "Negro-owned" enterprise.[75] Willet's publication "A Rainy Sunday" would be featured in Cab Calloway's 1947 film musical *Hi-De-Ho*, produced by the black-owned media company All-American News.[76] Of course, even if a black act survived the scissors of racist film censors or turned to a black economy for distribution, a vast array of other market factors still needed to fall into alignment to achieve mainstream success—the fickle elements of timing and public taste among them. Despite considerable efforts, the novelty lightning of "Peckin'" struck only once for the Three Chocolateers.

"EH! NOW"

Another entry in the "gimme some skin" chronicle is Willet's 1941 composition "Eh! Now," with lyrics by choreographer and stage personality Lew Crawford.[77] "Eh! Now" follows a lyric formula similar to "The Hicky Ricky" and "Gimme Some Skin," including the lyrics "gimme some skin"; additional jive references include "au reet now" and a repetitive emphasis of the dance-inspired line "splank the plank."[78] The latter phrase enjoyed some currency in the black press during 1942 and 1943, but never caught on to the degree of "gimme some skin."[79]

"Eh! Now" also employs similar novelty form. A sixteen-bar chromatic-flavored verse introduction—invoking sequences of chords with root motion shifting by whole-step (G—F—E-flat—F—G, A—G—F—G—A, etc.)—closes with a flatted-fifth dominant-seventh chord *pomposo* triplet break; the subsequent thirty-two-bar AABA-form chorus presents the title lyric phrase (this time set to "Charleston" rhythm; see example 8.9, mm. 31 and 37) no less than seven times.[80] The chord progression for "Eh! Now's" chorus is a bit more involved than "Ricky"—including some chromatic diminished chords (mm. 31 and 35)—but the end of the bridge uses the familiar augmented dominant chord and rhythm break device (on the word *say*; see m. 33) leading into the last A section.

During the fall of 1941, "Eh! Now" was publicized as a stage vehicle for two song-and-dance trios: the Peters Sisters and the Bye Sisters.[81] The Peters Sisters reportedly performed the song for a Warner Brothers film short, although no such artifact has been discovered to date.[82] The Bye Sisters act was managed by

Example 8.9. Interpolation of copyright deposit leadsheet and manuscript piano part of "Eh! Now" mm. 30–37 (end of bridge and beginning of last A section), arr. by Chappie Willet (1941). Manuscript piano part held in DEC. Chord symbols provided by the author, also referencing Tom Whaley manuscript score held in DEC.

Willet and received an impressive plug (undoubtedly publicity material from Willet's office) in the *Baltimore Afro-American*:

> Sisters all, Doris, Henrietta, and Frances were born and reared in New York. . . . Little did they realize in winning a singing contest at the Elks' Rendezvous in '38 that three years later they would be back there as the stars of the show. . . . Last December, Broadway's topflight sepia arranger and talent agent, Chappie Willet, heard them and realizing the heights to which they could ascend, took them under his personal management. Rehearsing diligently with them in the art of showmanship, Willet secured several Broadway night club engagements for them. . . . Now back at the Elks' Rendezvous, they will soon leave for Detroit to headline a four weeks' show at the Congo Club. Unlike the majority of swing trios, they feature popular ballads treated in their unique, sweet-swing type of voices. However, on the jump tunes, they swing and dance their way into a groove loved by all jitterbugs.[83]

Relationships crossing among the Bye Sisters, Lew Crawford, the Elks' Rendezvous Club, and Willet's 1941 Indigo Room production (chapter 2) provide a number of opportunities for the creation and performance of "Eh! Now." In mid-1942, however, Willet apparently had a falling out with the Bye Sisters over the group's contract for a revue tour with Lionel Hampton. A *Chicago Defender* columnist reported: "Intimates of the arranger and talent scout Chappie Willet are saying that his singing finds, the Bye sisters, didn't do right by him when they joined with Lionel Hampton and his crew. He had them under contract and they didn't consult him at all."[84]

"Eh! Now" also made its way into the repertoire of Ella Fitzgerald's orchestra, as documented in an aircheck recording from early 1942.[85] Fitzgerald presents the song at a relaxed tempo that allows her to take some personalized liberties with the melody, though the complete lyrics are clearly delivered. The band arrangement features numerous orchestration devices favored by Willet, including ensemble fourth-beat holds (added to the introductory verse, eight-bar instrumental interlude, and chorus reprise), a two-beat bass line for unison trombones and low saxes (during the interlude), and a coda ending with ensemble stop-time breaks and a portamento trombone figure.

A Tom Whaley–scored manuscript arrangement of "Eh! Now" survives as well. Orchestra parts reflect a more extensive rendition than the Fitzgerald version, with penciled markings indicating use in an unspecified stage revue program.[86] Written for four saxes, three trumpets, three trombones, and rhythm section, Whaley's arrangement includes an introduction, verse, chorus, transitional modulation, an eight-bar "dance chorus" vamp (marked on the parts to be repeated six times), and a complete out-chorus; the parts also reflect directions for an additional sixteen-bar tag (and to continue to a piece indicated only as "Horse").

The brief lifespan of Willet's novelty songs is not entirely surprising. As in other periods, the Swing Era novelty market seems to have focused on quantity and fast turnover, with hopes of playing the statistical odds in finding a hit.[87] As early as 1935, some music publishers reportedly discussed curtailing the number of songs being published in order to reduce costs of arranging and other "incidentals"; according to *Billboard* magazine, the publishers hoped that with fewer publications, "the life of an average number will be much longer than at present . . . the [current] duration of a hit is about three months at best."[88] To compound difficulties for "Eh! Now," media coverage of the Bye Sisters immediately ceased following the Hampton tour dustup; no commercial recording of "Eh! Now" has been discovered to date. Not long after its creation, however, a number of novelty songs using similarly phrased titles did find their way onto disc, including Henry Nemo's "'Ay Now" (1942) and Cab Calloway and Elton Hill's "Hey Now, Hey Now" (1946). As with "The Hicky Ricky," Willet and his colleagues appear to have been ahead of the curve, but unable to score a hit.

Vocal Ballads

In addition to representations of novelty slang, period vocal arrangements often drew upon "standard" love song repertoire of Broadway stage or Hollywood film musicals. The ubiquitous "fox-trot" designation—sometimes indicated on disc as simply "F.T."—was applied loosely. Fox-trot vehicles comprised not only medium or up-tempo jazz dance material, but also ballads associated with "sweet" or "society" bandleaders, including jukebox hits by Xavier Cugat, Eddy Duchin, and Paul Whiteman.[89] Jeffrey Magee identifies the typical dance band "fox-trot with vocal refrain" routine as comprising "a single vocal chorus framed by at least two instrumental choruses" and featuring the services of "intimate male crooners" or "peppy, vaudevillian" singers.[90] During the Swing Era, the role of this romantic singer expanded to include female vocalists; despite the presence of female orchestra musicians, the "girl singer" was often portrayed as many big bands' "lone female participant."[91]

Whether the setting was hot or sweet, or the singer male or female, the proportion of vocal performances in big band swing recordings appears to have steadily increased throughout the 1940s.[92] Chappie Willet's early Swing Era (mid-1930s) compositions and publications tend to reflect an emphasis on instrumental dance numbers—Willet's first four documented compositions are instrumentals—while almost all of his original works composed or published after 1940 emphasized songwriting. A brief overview of some of his vocal ballad arrangements and compositions reveals many of the same big band scoring techniques discussed earlier, while also applying necessary genre characteristics.

"MEMORIES OF YOU"

For a double-threat vocalist and instrumental virtuoso like Louis Armstrong, the "fox-trot with vocal refrain" format was ideal for establishing musical identity. This design was the focus of Armstrong's studio recordings during the 1930s, but also featured in radio broadcast programming like the 1937 *Fleischmann's Yeast* show. The latter included Willet's arrangement of Eubie Blake and Andy Razaf's "Memories of You": a mid-tempo ballad vehicle comprising a six-bar intro, thirty-two-bar vocal chorus, six-bar interlude, thirty-two-bar trumpet solo chorus, and a solo cadenza ending. Similar to ballad arrangements like Jimmy Mundy's 1936 "These Foolish Things" for Benny Goodman (featuring Helen Ward), or Sammy Lowe's 1940 "Song of the Wanderer" for Erskine Hawkins (featuring Jimmy Mitchelle), consistency of orchestration is generated through sustained wind voicings and repeated background riffs, reinforcing programmatic imagery of romance through stability of form and balance of texture.[93]

For "Memories," sustained sax voicings support the vocal refrain in legato phrasing on the A sections of the AABA-form chorus, but staccato on the bridge (0:51), providing a simple but effective reinforcement of the form. Staccato muted brass figures maintain rhythmic momentum and provide textural contrast against Armstrong's vocal pitch bends and held-note vibrato. For the solo trumpet chorus, the background energy intensifies by alternating legato and staccato ensemble phrases within the eight-bar A and B sections (1:38). "Memories" also incorporates subtle similarities to other Willet arrangements in the orchestra's book, including "legit" quarter-note triplet phrasing in the ensemble fanfare introduction (0:13), an ensemble whole-tone interlude separating the vocal and instrumental choruses (1:25), and climactic sax section trills (2:17). More than just a pandering to Tin Pan Alley commerce, "Memories" was conceived to hone the Armstrong brand.

"EAST OF THE SUN"

In 1942, Willet created a ballad arrangement of "East of the Sun (and West of the Moon)" for Jimmie Lunceford's popular crooner-vocalist Dan Grissom. Composed by Brooks Bowman in 1934, "East of the Sun" was a musical theater piece that had only gradually established itself as standard repertoire, largely through the success of Frank Sinatra's 1940 recording with Tommy Dorsey.[94] Although the length of Willet's arrangement precluded release on the ten-inch disc format (without alterations), "East of the Sun" is not as extreme in duration as Armstrong's concerto-like "Stardust" (chapter 7), and focuses much more exclusively on the vocalist. In this thirty-two-bar ABAC-form song, the eight-bar A sections are scored with sustained wind voicings in consistent half-note rhythm (example 8.10, mm. 25–28), followed by a recurring syncopated ostinato

Example 8.10. Score reduction of vocal chorus background passage in "East of the Sun" mm. 25–32, arr. by Chappie Willet for Jimmie Lunceford (1942). Manuscript orchestra parts held in FDCJLO. Chord symbols provided by the author.

figure in the bass and piano (mm. 29–32).[95] This bass figure highlights the chromatic shift of the song's chord changes while suggesting a "Latin" rhythmic flavor; a similar figure ties together the introduction and coda. A clarinet and alto sax unison obbligato countermelody in the second half of the first chorus (mm. 25–32) might be heard as an extension of the "accordion" effect (although scored in unison instead of octaves) found in Willet's ballad arrangement of "You Can Count on Me" (chapter 6).

Willet's "East of the Sun" also presents the song's verse (often omitted entirely in ballad arrangements, as in Sinatra's recording) as an interlude between choruses. At the end of the verse, dramatic *pomposo* triplet figures (example 8.11, m. 60) create a fanfare-like build into a four-bar climax that briefly slows in tempo (orchestra parts indicate "slower"), highlighted by half-note drum accents and an ensemble quarter-note triplet figure (m. 61). Probably conceived as an opportunity to highlight Lunceford's role as conductor, this dramatic rubato passage ends with a rhythm section break and chromatic parallel voicings (mm. 63–64) that transition back into the original tempo and a return of the syncopated bass line.

Example 8.11. Score reduction of tempo change (end of verse interlude) in "East of the Sun" mm. 59–65, arr. by Chappie Willet for Jimmie Lunceford (1942). Manuscript orchestra parts held in FDCJLO. Chord symbols provided by the author.

"NOTHIN' TO DO BUT LOVE"

Willet's 1938 ballad composition "Nothin' to Do but Love" features lyrics penned by his Broadway Music Clinic colleague Porter Grainger.[96] Their song follows standard Tin Pan Alley ballad format, with an eight-bar verse, a thirty-two-bar AABA chorus, and a tempo designation of "slowly." Indeed, the piano leadsheet arrangement (copied in Grainger's hand) embodies numerous period characteristics identified in Allen Forte's study of the genre—some of which also reflect prevalent Swing Era big band arranging practices. Characteristics applicable

Example 8.12. Second A section of "Nothin' to Do but Love" mm. 17–24, by Porter Grainger and Chappie Willet (1938). Copyright deposit leadsheet held in LOC. Chord symbols provided by the author.

to "Nothin' to Do" include the assimilation of decorative notes in the form of sixth chords (example 8.12, m. 23), frequent use of half-diminished chords (mm. 17–18), parallel chord embellishment (especially m. 24), harmonic chains of fifths (especially mm. 17–19), an underlying Charleston dance rhythm in the melody (mm. 17–18, 21–23), and short "cellular" motives throughout the song (see brackets 1 and 2).[97]

These recurring melodic cells—combined with multiple instances of chromatic half-step descent in the piano accompaniment arrangement (mm. 21–24)—unify the song rhythmically and melodically. Similar to Willet's approach in big band vehicles like "Blue Rhythm Fantasy" (chapter 9), the emphasis on descending half-step motion throughout "Nothin' to Do" reveals a chromatic idiolect that extends beyond the application of isolated effect passages. Grainger's lyrics are also representative of the ballad genre, including the element of "text painting."[98] Poetic imagery of ascent suggested in the lines "the heaven above," "I picked up your glove," and "sweet as a dove" is set to a melodic phrase ascending the compass of a ninth (see m. 19), arguably the most outstanding feature of the composition. It appears that this song was never distributed in print—perhaps the title was too similar to Phil Harris's 1933 hit "I've Got Nothing to Do but Love"—but it demonstrates solid craft by the Music Clinic crew.

* * *

As Peter Townsend argues, Swing Era "big-band performance . . . was more thoroughly characterized by singers than jazz writers have acknowledged."[99] William Bauer has also challenged the "remarkable lack of curiosity about jazz singers" within musicology, highlighting jazz historians' habitual dismissal of Louis Armstrong's influential vocal repertoire.[100] Popular vocal harmony groups featured with Swing Era big bands (like the Dandridge Sisters, the Modernaires, or the Pied Pipers)—and the orchestral arrangements that backed them—have similarly received little scholarly attention. Traditional emphasis on the accomplishments of male instrumentalists is problematic in other ways as well; as Jessica Bissett Perea observes, a broader legacy of female exclusion from jazz in part reflects "tendencies of conventional jazz narratives to marginalize or exclude dance bands, vocalists, and women as 'mere' entertainment."[101] Consideration of jazz as popular music requires an acknowledgment of the music's gendered documentation. Whether male or female, sweet or hot, more inclusive and comprehensive studies of vocal arrangements from the Swing Era remain to be undertaken.

9

Jungle Madness

Jazz Dance and Exotic Numbers

Joe Garland wrote and arranged many of the numbers including "In the Mood" that [Edgar] Hayes recorded in 1938. That piece was heavy music—had four big manuscript pages just for the trombone parts. We called it his Black Symphony.[1]

—Trombonist-vocalist Clyde Bernhardt

Arranger Joe Garland's instrumental composition "In the Mood"—recorded in its definitive version by Glenn Miller in 1939 (as arranged by Eddie Durham and edited by Miller), and further immortalized in the film *The Glenn Miller Story* (Universal, 1954)—stood as the archetypal Swing Era dance vehicle in the decades following World War II. "In the Mood" is built around the "riff" device: a brief, insistently repeated melodic phrase generating rhythmic momentum ideal for dancing. But while riffs were emblematic of the swing dance idiom, they were just one tool arrangers drew upon in their musical representations of drama, virtuosity, exoticism, or visual spectacle.

Jazz Dance Instrumentals

Miller's version of "In the Mood" is deceptively simple in its textural division of sax and brass sections, while its fanfare introduction, interludes (1:32; 2:01), and closing passages (3:18) frame a more adventurous formal design that transitions from a twelve-bar blues chorus (featuring ensemble riffs) into a sixteen-bar chorus (featuring sax and trumpet solos), then returns to another series of twelve-bar (and even fourteen-bar) blues riff choruses (see table 11). This coupling of simple texture with "sophisticated" form proved a successful formula for many Swing Era dance band instrumentals. Hits like Jerry Gray's "String of Pearls" (which also alternates twelve-bar and sixteen-bar choruses) or Garland's "Leap Frog" (a sort of AABBA chorus form that never quite repeats) similarly avoided conventional repetitions of Tin Pan Alley song form. Interestingly, Gray's arrangement of Cole Porter's unusually long-form (108-bar)

Table 11. Formal structure of "In the Mood," arr. by Eddie Durham for Glenn Miller (1939). Transcription by the author.

Section	Bars	Scoring
Intro	8	Saxes and ensemble
Chorus 1	12	Sax riff with brass fill-in
Chorus 2	12	Sax riff with brass fill-in
Chorus 3	16 (8+8)	Sax riff with brass fill-in
Chorus 4	16 (8+8)	Sax solos with brass fill-in
Interlude	4	Ensemble
Chorus 5	16 (8+8)	Trumpet solo, sax background
Interlude	2	Ensemble
Chorus 6	14 (12+2)	Sax riff with brass fill-in
Chorus 7	14 (12+2)	Sax riff with brass fill-in
Chorus 8	12	Sax riff with brass fill-in
Chorus 9	10	Sax riff with brass fill-in (shout)
Coda	8	Ensemble

composition "Begin the Beguine"—described by Gray's employer Artie Shaw as "a very strange song"—enjoyed similar success as an instrumental dance number during this period.[2]

Joel Dinerstein suggests that big band swing can be heard as "a synthesis of the rhythmic drive of New Orleans music with Paul Whiteman's 'symphonic jazz' of the 1920s."[3] Swing Era efforts to minimize chorus repetitions or disguise customary thirty-two-bar and twelve-bar forms allowed dance band arrangers to create their own "symphonies"—subversions of form so frequently undertaken as to arguably become standard practice. Supporting devices designed to conjure European concert music and Broadway stage spectacles were applied across a range of popular genres, as swing dance arrangements paralleled the concerto or classical genres in their inclusion of introductory fanfare, transition, modulation, and coda passages. For example, Chappie Willet's 1942 instrumental arrangement of Vincent Youmans's "Hallelujah" for Jimmie Lunceford included an eight-bar introduction, twenty-four-bar interlude (0:32), six-bar transition (1:16), sixteen-bar expansion on the chorus-form (1:21), and a twenty-one-bar coda (1:55)—passages that in combination (seventy-five bars) rival the time allotted to the source composition (eighty-eight bars).[4]

Another popular strategy in variety programming was the dance medley format, usually comprising an episodic sequence of recognizable Broadway standards or traditional songs. Clyde Bernhardt recalled the talents of bandleader Vernon

Arranger-bandleader Jerry Gray, ca. 1946. Gray arranged music for Glenn Miller and Artie Shaw. Photo by William P. Gottlieb. Music Division, Library of Congress.

Andrade, who "knew how to call a set: usually four songs, different tempos, maybe a waltz, then a sweet number, a calypso, then a hot number. Sometimes we did a beautiful twenty-minute waltz medley from *Tales from the Vienna Woods* and the people just loved it."[5] The Lunceford orchestra had a waltz medley that included "Till We Meet Again, "Danny Boy," and "Together"; the Shaw and Barnet orchestras performed medleys of Duke Ellington ballads, as well as Broadway standards like "Ghost of a Chance," "You're Mine, You," and "Embraceable You" (as arranged for Barnet by Bud Estes). Medleys designed for stage show productions grouped pieces like "Tea for Two," "Moonlight on the Ganges," and "Cherokee" (as in a Barnet medley arranged by George Siravo); the Armstrong Museum holds a mid-1940s medley (possibly arranged by Willet) comprising "Jeepers Creepers," "Old Man Mose," "Rockin' Chair," and "When You're Smiling."[6]

Following historical narratives on big band jazz icons like Count Basie and Duke Ellington, instrumental dance numbers tend to be the swing genre most closely associated with jazz improvisation. But arrangements designed for dancing audiences at venues like the Roseland or Savoy Ballrooms still drew upon many of the same theatrical music signifiers and variety entertainment strategies that marked classics, concertos, or vocal features. This chapter considers some of Chappie Willet's approaches to instrumental dance music, including the framing of solo or ensemble virtuosity, the setting of new melodies over familiar chord progressions, and the stylized representation of performer identity or "exotic" variety.

"I KNOW THAT YOU KNOW"

Willet created two arrangements of the 1926 Broadway standard "I Know That You Know" for his staff-arranging clients Louis Armstrong and Gene Krupa. Armstrong's version is documented in a May 1937 *Fleischmann's Yeast* radio program aircheck; the Krupa version was recorded for Brunswick in April 1938. These arrangements are fundamentally similar in scoring and routine, although the Krupa recording lacks the Armstrong version's second chorus (featuring trombone and trumpet solos)—possibly a cut made by Krupa himself. Both arrangements open with an ensemble rhythmic-unison stop-time figure (scored in altered chord voicings) before presenting the melody in familiar close-position, five-part voicings for brass.

This opening brass melody is set against a sinuous unison sax counter-melody, but the sax figures in the two versions differ significantly. Krupa's sax parts alternate linear eighth-note phrases with half-notes and whole-notes, staying out of the way of the brass melody and functioning in a true counter-melody—or even background—role. In the Armstrong version, the sax scoring is more adventurous, bobbing and weaving in syncopated ascending and descending phrases to provide its own call-and-response texture; a recurring chromatic half-step figure (in the form of a "passing" or "neighbor" tone) catches the ear and unifies the passage (see example 9.1; the recurring half-step figure is in brackets). In this context, the simple brass melody may even be heard as subservient to the active sax line, which could well stand on its own as a new melody over the standard chord changes. The subordinate role of the standard melody is texturally reinforced in Willet's subsequent chorus, where the melody returns in close-position sax voicings as a background for improvised brass solos.

Both "I Know" arrangements also include a middle chorus reflecting a concept Jeffrey Magee describes as "inside the strain" scoring: sudden changes in orchestration texture within the usual eight-bar or twelve-bar phrase groupings of popular song forms.[7] Willet recasts the melody in "legit" straight-rhythm texture—four-bar passages of piano in close-position "block-chord" voicings over a sustained sax background (Armstrong, 1:20; Krupa, 0:40)—immediately followed by four bars of swinging sax solo and tricky ensemble unison breaks. These sudden contrasts in dynamics (soft to loud), texture (piano to brass), and rhythm (straight to syncopated) offer an element of surprise while highlighting the precision capabilities of the client orchestras. A sax section whip (Armstrong, 0:41), tailgate trombone fill (Armstrong, 1:53; Krupa, 1:05), interlude comprising altered dominant chords in parallel half-step motion (Armstrong, 2:18; Krupa, 1:32), climactic sax section trills (Armstrong, 2:26; Krupa, 1:40), and a brief

Example 9.1. Unison sax counter-melody in "I Know That You Know" mm. 5–36 (0:14), arr. by Chappie Willet for Louis Armstrong (1937). Transcription by the author.

chromatic harmony substitution supported by fourth-beat holds (Armstrong, 2:48; Krupa, 2:01) contribute to Willet's recognizable idiolect.

"RHYTHM JAM"

The setting of new melodic themes over familiar chord progressions was not uncommon among dance band arrangers. Jeffrey Magee discusses similar strategies in Benny Carter's 1929 arrangement of "The Wang Wang Blues" for Fletcher Henderson; David Schiff outlines Duke Ellington's series of compositions set to the chord changes of "Tiger Rag," which eventually included "Braggin' in Brass"—the orchestra's feature on the spring 1938 Cotton Club program.[8] Another favorite harmonic framework for new melodies (sometimes referred to as *contrafacts*) was George and Ira Gershwin's 1930 "I Got Rhythm."[9] Willet provided an explicit demonstration with a pair of arrangements documented in Armstrong's 1937 *Fleischmann's* airchecks.[10] Multiple passages of scoring from "I Got Rhythm" are carried over into "Rhythm Jam," including the ensemble background figures behind the sax solo ("I Got Rhythm," 1:11; "Rhythm Jam," 0:50), a trombone transition passage and sax backgrounds behind the trumpet solo (1:48; 1:23), and a subsequent chorus of full-ensemble backgrounds (2:24; 1:59). But in "Rhythm Jam," Willet replaced the Gershwin-composed "head" with an original melody created—and copyrighted—by the arranger. A stop-time interlude with whole-tone voicings in parallel half-step descent ("Rhythm Jam," 0:41) provides an additional personal touch.

A few months prior to Armstrong's broadcast, Lucky Millinder with Mills Blue Rhythm Band had recorded a nearly identical version of Willet's "Rhythm Jam" arrangement. Because most of Armstrong's studio recordings during this period are vocal features, it seems that the Mills band may have simply been the first ensemble to record Willet-arranged instrumentals that had been in Armstrong's book for some time (including "Jungle Madness" and possibly "Prelude to a Stomp").[11] The Mills Band trumpet soloist's high B-flat wails over the shout chorus of "Rhythm Jam" (2:02) are replicated in Armstrong's solo (1:59); a similar trumpet solo in Gene Krupa's 1938 recording of the same piece (2:04) suggests that this bravura figure was written into all three versions. Another notable dramatic device in "Rhythm Jam" is the chord substitutions in the bridge of the last solo chorus (example 9.2)—a climactic, chromatically ascending ensemble buildup that catapults the soloist into the last eight bars of the song form.

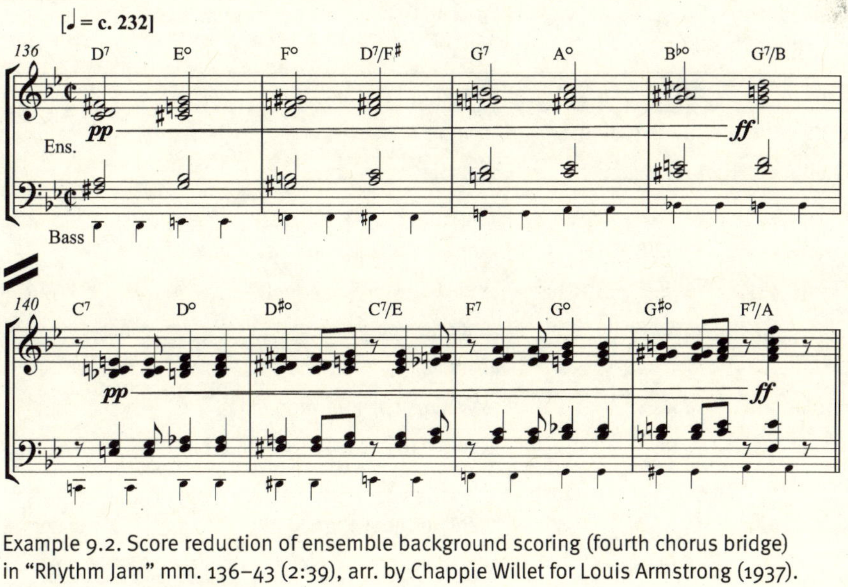

Example 9.2. Score reduction of ensemble background scoring (fourth chorus bridge) in "Rhythm Jam" mm. 136–43 (2:39), arr. by Chappie Willet for Louis Armstrong (1937). Transcription by the author.

"WASHINGTON AND LEE SWING"

In contrast to his stock-like treatment of "Rhythm Jam," Willet's varied conceptions of "Washington and Lee Swing" for Louis Armstrong and Red Norvo display clear efforts to address the specialized needs of different clients. The "Washington and Lee" college fight song was already a venerable standard, having made inroads into the dance band world during the 1920s (including recordings by Jan Garber and Snooks Friedman); the similarity of the song's chord progression to the final strain of "Tiger Rag" ensured a position in Dixieland repertoire for decades to come.[12] Willet may have been aware of "Washington" since his own college days, when he reportedly composed a school cheer for West Virginia State College.[13]

As documented in a 1937 *Fleishmann's* aircheck, Willet's arrangement for Armstrong features the orchestra as much as the bandleader. The initial thirty-two-bar ABAC-form theme is cast for ensemble close-position five-part voicings and straight, unsyncopated quarter-note and half-note rhythms, but suddenly cut short by a tricky, syncopated ensemble break (0:25), the first event in a barrage of surprise ensemble interlude, stop-time, and break passages (see table 12). Subsequent choruses feature solo clarinet, solo trumpet, soli sax section, solo trombone, solo bass, and solo sax.

As might be expected, Willet's arsenal of favored orchestration devices (chapter 6) also emerges in "Washington," including "Rockin' in Rhythm" tailgate figures (0:30), "secondary rag" phrasing (1:23), sax soli "whips" (1:28), downbeat

Table 12. Formal structure of "Washington and Lee Swing," arr. by Chappie Willet for Louis Armstrong (1937). Transcription by the author.

Section	Bars	Scoring	Key
Chorus 1	30 (8+8+8+6)	Ensemble theme	C major
Interlude	8	Ensemble "tricky" break	
Chorus 2	32 (8+8+8+8)	Clarinet solo	
Chorus 3	32 (8+8+8+8)	Trumpet solo, ensemble stop-time	
Chorus 4	16 (8+8)	Sax section soli	
	14 (8+6)	Trombone solo	
Interlude	4	Ensemble	
Chorus 5	16 (8+8)	Bass solo, ensemble stop-time	
	12 (8+4)	Ensemble theme, sax solo stop-time	
Interlude	8	Ensemble break, modulation	
Chorus 6	16 (8+8)	Ensemble shout chorus	F major
	16 (8+8)	Trumpet solo over ensemble theme	

lip slurs (1:28, 1:32), and isolated short-note "rips" (1:39). The arrangement climaxes with a dramatic transition and modulation (example 9.3) leading into the shout chorus.[14] This stunning ensemble passage ascends, descends, then ascends again, featuring stop-time solo breaks (mm. 161–64), parallel chromatic voicings (mm. 165–68), a piano "chime" effect (m. 169), and another chromatic ensemble break (mm. 170–72). Armstrong's orchestra rises to the occasion, swinging hard and—in light of the intricate scoring—fearlessly.

Surviving manuscript orchestra parts for the 1938 Norvo version may coincide with that band's summer residency at the Pennsylvania Hotel. Willet's new "Washington" opens with a close-position five-voice ensemble scoring nearly identical to the Armstrong version's first chorus, but forgoes the ensuing ensemble break. Norvo's version is more streamlined overall, with no additional interlude passages or "tricky" breaks (see table 13). A relative scarcity of eighth-notes throughout, as well as the presence of two additional choruses, suggests a tempo even faster than the Armstrong version (surviving manuscript parts

Example 9.3. Score reduction of interlude passage in "Washington and Lee Swing" mm. 161–72 (2:09), arr. by Chappie Willet for Louis Armstrong (1937). Transcription by the author.

Table 13. Formal structure of "Washington and Lee Swing," arr. by Chappie Willet for Red Norvo (1938). Manuscript orchestra parts held in RNP.

Section	Bars	Scoring	Key
Chorus 1 (reh. A)	32 (8+8+8+8)	Ensemble theme	C major
Chorus 2 (reh. B)	32 (8+8+8+8)	Clarinet solo	E-flat major
Chorus 3 (reh. C)	32 (8+8+8+8)	Trumpet section soli	
Chorus 4 (reh. D)	32 (8+8+8+8)	Trumpet section soli cont'd.	
Chorus 5 (reh. E)	32 (8+8+8+8)	Tenor sax solo	
Chorus 6 (reh. F)	32 (8+8+8+8)	Xylophone solo	D-flat major
Chorus 7 (repeat reh. F)	32 (8+8+8+8)	Xylophone solo cont'd.	
Chorus 8 (reh. G)	16 (8+8)	Ensemble theme	D major
	8	Stop-time bass solo	
	6	Ensemble	
Tag ("Slower")	4	Tag ensemble ending	

simply indicate "fast"), perhaps comparable to the blistering tempo of Willet's "Tiger Rag" for Armstrong (also documented in a 1937 aircheck). Extreme tempos like this—a test of the rhythm section's discipline and physical stamina, among other factors—may have been intended for not just dance hall or ballroom engagements, but also for backing specialty stage acts or displaying the orchestra's virtuosity in a theater, nightclub, or radio broadcast setting.

The Norvo band solo choruses also begin with clarinet, but in place of Armstrong's trumpet solo, Willet scored a trumpet section soli over two consecutive thirty-two-bar choruses (backed by saxes accenting fourth-beat hold figures). A fairly bold move in Swing Era arranging, this extended soli statement recalls showcase specialty numbers like Ellington's "Braggin' in Brass," similarly built on "Tiger Rag" chord changes. Perhaps the soli was offered in lieu of a soloist the caliber of Armstrong (or, for that matter, trumpeter Red Allen, who was featured in the Mills Blue Rhythm Band's "Tiger Rag"–based "Ride Red Ride"); the measured pacing and gradual buildup of Willet's soli scoring (example 9.4) even suggests a conscious tribute to Armstrong's solo trumpet style. Nevertheless, the arranger's vision may not have been to the Norvo band's taste; in lieu of the intended soli, indication for an improvised "hot solo" was penciled into the second trumpet part.

Willet's trumpet soli is followed by a tenor sax solo, and a modulation that leads into two choruses featuring Norvo on xylophone. A closing ensemble shout chorus follows the pattern of Willet's other arrangements for Norvo (chapter 5)—the insertion of a brief passage of reharmonization with chromatic parallel voicings (example 9.5, mm. 229–31). A stop-time bass solo is also included;

Example 9.4. Second chorus of trumpet soli (reh. D) of "Washington and Lee Swing" mm. 95–128, arr. by Chappie Willet for Red Norvo (1938). Manuscript orchestra parts held in RNP.

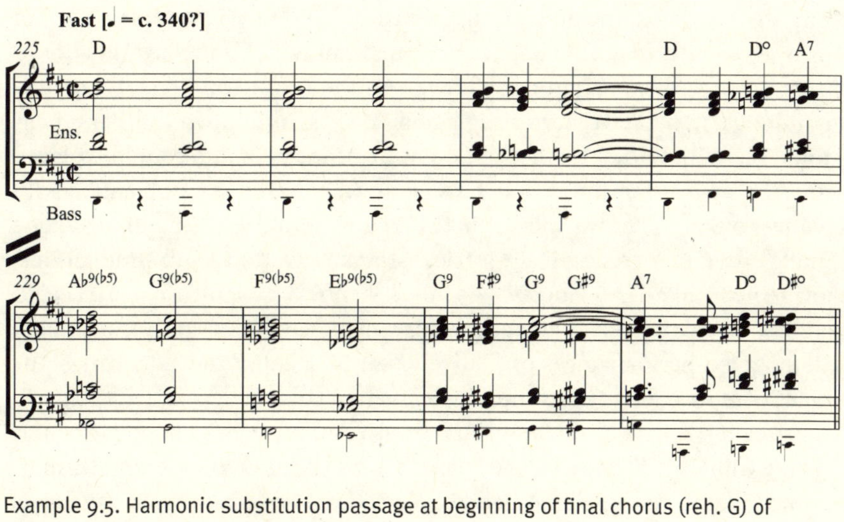

Example 9.5. Harmonic substitution passage at beginning of final chorus (reh. G) of "Washington and Lee Swing" mm. 225–32, arr. by Chappie Willet for Red Norvo (1938). Manuscript orchestra parts held in RNP.

following a return of the ensemble pitting brass against saxes, a tag ending designated as suddenly "slower"—probably half-time tempo—further accentuates the virtuosic speed of the preceding performance.

Exotic Numbers

In Swing Era variety entertainment, programmatic themes of geographic or cultural exoticism could be represented by individual arrangements or even entire orchestras. "Rumba"- or "tango"-style dance bands led by Xavier Cugat or Alberto Socarrás were paired opposite swing-style orchestras in revue stage shows like those at the Cotton Club, or in multiple-orchestra radio programs like NBC's *Let's Dance* series—where sweet, hot, "Latin," or other dance ensembles could be programmed in sequence for stylistic contrast.[15] But even in productions with only one orchestra, the exotic genre remained integral. Exotic scoring effects were frequently applied to instrumental jazz dance arrangements, extending a tradition of exotic themes in popular music dating back to the nineteenth century.[16]

As musicologist Ralph Locke notes, twentieth century "composers, songwriters, popular-music singers, and jazz musicians . . . concerned with broad audience appeal used a limited but familiar collection of exotic styles, and in a wide range of ways."[17] Swing Era arrangers similarly relied on a fairly small and insistent collection of orchestration devices, expanding on strategies outlined by Arthur Lange in the 1920s—"tom tom" drums and "a slow moving melody."[18] Rhythm section ostinato figures, including references to "Latin" dance music patterns like the rumba, offered a contrast against traditional fox-trot swing rhythm. Long melodic lines emphasized held notes, in contrast to Tin Pan Alley's preference for short, syncopated phrases. Minor-key tonality or chromatic melodies (including references to the whole-tone-scale) provided an ominous, non-Western, or simply non-"pop" sound (open fifths and pentatonic scales provided further options). Brass instruments could be played with a throat growl or flutter-tongue technique, typically in combination with a plunger or hat mute "wa" effect. Duke Ellington found success with his exotic "jungle" style in stereotypically African-themed Cotton Club productions; arrangements like "The Mooche" (1928) or "Echoes of the Jungle" (1931) could reinforce visual stage show imagery of foreign or "savage" narratives that often accompanied performances of "native" (that is, scantily clad) dancers.[19] The exotic formula could also exploit instrumental colors considered foreign to mainstream swing's dominant sax and brass textures, such as bass clarinet (as in Larry Clinton's "Strictly for the Persians"), violin (as in Ellington's "Bakiff"), or flute (as featured by flutist-bandleader Alberto Socarrás, billed as "Cuba's Duke Ellington").[20]

Broadway standards likewise lent themselves to exotic treatment. Willet's arrangement of "East of the Sun" for Jimmie Lunceford employed syncopated, Latin-style figures for the bass (chapter 8). The supernatural lyrics and minor-key tonality of "You've Got Me Voodoo'd," as recorded by Louis Armstrong for Decca in 1940, prompted the scoring of tom drums and a whole-tone interlude (1:44); Willet's favored fourth-beat holds (0:37) and downbeat lip slurs (1:07) appear as well, with a closing trumpet cadenza even adding a "concerto" component. In addition to the interpretation of Tin Pan Alley material, Willet referenced the exotic genre in two original instrumentals: "Jungle Madness" and "Blue Rhythm Fantasy."

"JUNGLE MADNESS"

While exotic orchestration devices might reference tropes of Asia, the Middle Eastern "Orient," or Latin America—including novelty vocals like "Six Lessons from Madame La Zonga" (recorded by Jimmy Dorsey and Charlie Barnet) or "Chinese Rhythm" (recorded by Cab Calloway)—"jungle" effects arguably reigned as the primary exotic trope of the Swing Era, especially in instrumental arrangements. Willet's version of "Jungle Madness" for the Mills Blue Rhythm Band opens with a stark ostinato passage scored for rhythm section and unison trombones—a pattern notably similar to that found in the minor-key verse-interlude passage of Gene Gifford's arrangement of "Chant of the Jungle" for the Casa Loma Orchestra (1935).[21] In "Jungle Madness," Willet continues the ostinato underneath the thirty-two-bar AABA-form theme chorus (set in the key of C minor), which pits growling downbeat-slur brass figures against serpentine unison sax lines in chromatic half-step motion (example 9.6).[22] An eight-bar bridge features a tricky sax section soli (0:24) before the growling brass reenter with a chromatic half-step descent (0:31) back to the A-section theme. This

Example 9.6. Score reduction of ensemble theme passage in "Jungle Madness" mm. 5–8 (0:04), arr. by Chappie Willet for the Mills Blue Rhythm Band (1937). Transcription by the author.

overtly "jungle" head is followed by a sudden shift to major-key tonality (0:42) and swing dance rhythm for the duration of the performance, suggesting some ironic humor in the piece's "madness."

Gene Krupa's 1939 recording of "Jungle Madness" embraces Willet's tom-tom opening to introduce an extended dialogue between tom drums and solo clarinet; this routine was further expanded upon in a short film production, released as *America's Ace Drummer* (UM&M TV Corporation, ca. 1940). Krupa traced his own association with tom drums back to a 1929 Paramount Theater stage revue and a "Samoan number" he performed with the house band.[23] But the "Madness" duet sequences were undoubtedly aimed at recalling the drummer's tom drum spots with clarinetist Benny Goodman on Jimmy Mundy's arrangement of "Sing, Sing, Sing," popularized through the film *Hollywood Hotel* (First National, 1937), a double-sided disc recording for Bluebird, and Goodman's celebrated Carnegie Hall concert in January 1938.[24] Comparable duet performances in "Jungle Madness"—Krupa's studio recording includes a twenty-bar introduction passage prior to the trombones' entry, and a later thirty-bar interlude—may have been arranged to personal specifications, or even edited into Willet's arrangement by the bandleader himself (omitting the Mills version's piano and woodwind solos to allow time for the clarinet spots). In both Krupa performances, a return to the exotic minor-key ensemble theme at the close of the arrangement suggests a more earnest interpretation of the title than the earlier Mills band version. "Madness" also featured the Krupa orchestra's signature spectacle of choreographed ensemble drumming performed by his side-musicians, each of which had a small tom drum attached to their music stands.

"BLUE RHYTHM FANTASY"

Along with "Prelude in C-sharp Minor" (chapter 7), Willet's best-known work during the Swing Era appears to have been his original composition "Blue Rhythm Fantasy." Arrangements of "Fantasy" were recorded by three different orchestras, broadcast by at least two others, and published as a stock arrangement. Willet's musical influences and personal style are highlighted in the song's combination of whole-tone voicings and half-step chromaticism, while various adaptations reflect the differing requirements of his clients. In addition to documentation in period audio recordings and archival manuscripts, "Fantasy" also carries a modest reception history that parallels broader trends in jazz historiography.

The exact chronology of the earliest versions of "Blue Rhythm Fantasy" is difficult to verify. In January 1936, the *Chicago Defender* cited the piece in connection with Louis Armstrong and Luis Russell's concurrent residency at Connie's Inn.[25] Surviving Armstrong orchestra manuscript parts include Willet's (preunion-membership) arranging stamp, but no explicit composer credits to indicate whether Teddy Hill—the cocomposer eventually listed on the October 1936 copyright registration—was involved. Regardless of whether Hill made any creative contribution or simply commissioned an arrangement (a more likely scenario), the musical evolution of "Fantasy" suggests that Hill's version of the piece—first recorded in May 1936—was in fact created prior to the unrecorded

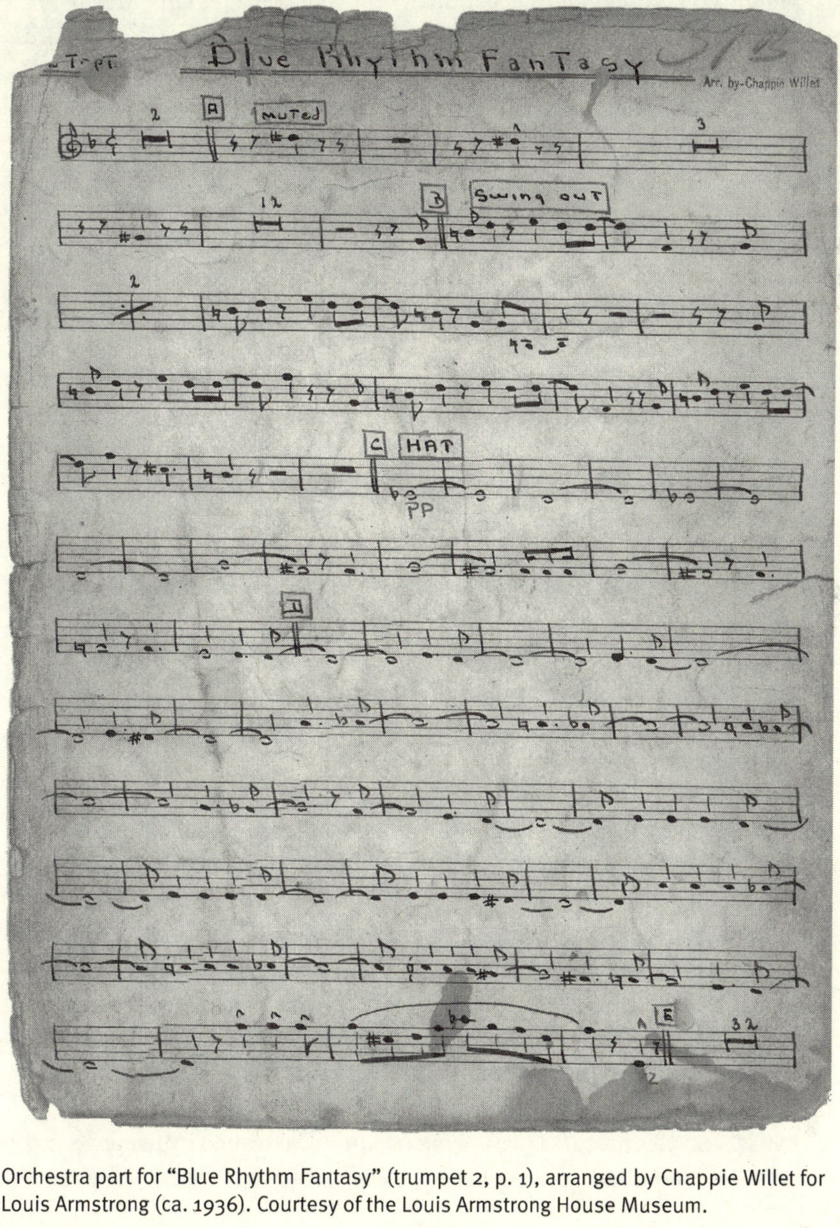

Orchestra part for "Blue Rhythm Fantasy" (trumpet 2, p. 1), arranged by Chappie Willet for Louis Armstrong (ca. 1936). Courtesy of the Louis Armstrong House Museum.

Armstrong version.[26] Following this presumption, the piece may date from the Hill band's October 1935 residency at the Apollo Theater.[27] Radio logs cite Hill performing the piece at the Savoy Ballroom through 1936 and into spring 1937, when—in something of a Swing Era oddity—Hill recorded the same arrangement a second time (though for a different record label and featuring new soloists).[28] "Fantasy" may have even been presented in Europe that summer, as the Hill band accompanied an internationally touring stage revue.[29] Meanwhile, the Mills Blue Rhythm Band recorded a third version of "Fantasy" in February 1937 (the "Blue Rhythm" title seems to have been a happy coincidence); radio logs indicate that Willie Bryant's orchestra also performed "Fantasy" as a radio theme song in broadcasts from the Savoy Ballroom that same year.[30] The piece probably entered Gene Krupa's repertory in spring 1938 (along with the other Mills-recorded Willet originals commissioned by Krupa); the drummer-bandleader recorded an extended version of "Fantasy"—released across two sides of a ten-inch disc—in 1940, and continued to perform it as late as 1943.[31]

In addition to Willet's special arrangements, Exclusive Publications (a subsidiary of publisher Irving Mills) published a stock arrangement of "Fantasy" that reflects the copyright date of 1936, but was probably printed in 1937.[32] Scored by Edgar Battle, this fifteen-piece arrangement—including a three-violin string section—offers an exciting rendition of the piece, but deviates significantly from all known versions created by Willet. This is especially the case regarding the formal routine, which (among other alterations) repositions the "head" riff-theme as the concluding shout chorus. A corresponding piano leadsheet publication—apparently scored by Battle as well—designates a tempo of "Mod[erato] to Jig Tempo," in style "Quasi Misterioso," indications that may have reflected Mills's recent success with Juan Tizol's "Caravan," which carried the same tempo and style directives.[33] Built on the requisite signifiers of tom drums, long melodic lines, and minor-key tonality, "Caravan" would go on to become the definitive Swing Era exotic number.[34]

"Blue Rhythm Fantasy" follows the exotic formula as well—including a tom drum intro—but features passages of whole-tone chromaticism and a more episodic formal design. Indeed, Willet's piece stands as an explicit exploration of tonal chromaticism, fusing melodic theme and harmonic structure through an insistent combination of whole-tone sonorities and descending half-step motion. In this regard, the title is worth consideration: "Blue Rhythm Fantasy" could have been a reference to Ferde Grofé's symphonic-jazz composition *Metropolis: A Blue Fantasie* (also billed as "a Fantasie in Blue").[35] Grofé's piece had been premiered by Paul Whiteman's orchestra at Carnegie Hall in 1928, on a program of modernist works that included Bix Beiderbecke's whole-tone infused "In a Mist" and George Gershwin's *Concerto in F.* Described by contemporary critics as "entirely modern in conception and treatment" and "following no traditional form," *Metropolis* swims through a sea of chromatic scoring effects, including a series of descending half-step figures that rise sequentially by whole-step (example 9.7).[36] Willet's fantasy-like introduction to "Blue Rhythm Fantasy" features a similar repetition of descending half-step phrases that rise sequentially by whole-step in parallel voicings (example 9.8).[37] While "Fantasy" does not quote any of Grofé's material directly, Willet's long-standing attraction to combinations of whole-tone and half-step chromaticism suggests the possibility of familiarity with the earlier piece, available in a solo piano arrangement published by Robbins Music.[38]

Another potential model for "Blue Rhythm Fantasy" is Don Redman's 1931 "Chant of the Weed," recorded and released while Willet was studying at West Virginia State College. Redman's West Virginia roots likely encouraged an enthusiastic local reception, and the publication of a ten-piece stock arrangement might have further influenced a budding arranger.[39] In addition to Redman's and Willet's shared attraction to combining whole-tone melodies with

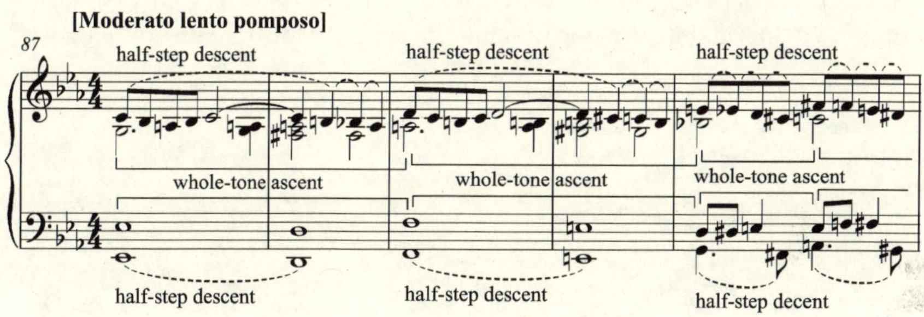

Example 9.7. Chromatic voicing sequence in *Metropolis: A Blue Fantasie* (solo piano arrangement) mm. 87–91, by Ferde Grofé (1928). Whole-tone motion is indicated by brackets; half-step motion is indicated by dashed lines.

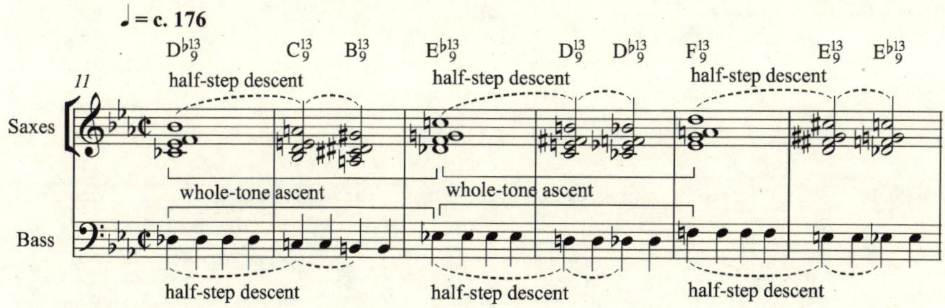

Example 9.8. Score reduction of chromatic voicing sequence (reh. A) in "Blue Rhythm Fantasy" mm. 11–16 (0:13), arr. by Chappie Willet for Teddy Hill (1936, 1937). Transcription by the author, also referencing manuscript parts of version held in LAHM. Whole-tone motion is indicated by brackets; half-step motion is indicated by dashed lines.

chord voicings in parallel half-step motion, the orchestration of the opening of "Fantasy" can be heard as sly homage to the bridge of "Chant." Both pieces set muted, open-voiced brass punctuations against three-note sax figures scored in short-short-long rhythm and half-step motion, and are built around the tonality of an A dominant chord (as per the Hill, Armstrong, and stock versions of "Fantasy")—even as "Fantasy" and "Chant" are set in different keys (examples 9.9, 9.10).[40]

Willet's later "Fantasy" renditions for Mills and Krupa recast this opening on a B chord (instead of A). The change may have been motivated by a desire for more consistent whole-tone sequencing (B9—Db9—Eb9 instead of A9—C9—Eb9) leading into the following *Metropolis*-like passage, which also saw the addition of "legit" arco bass scoring in the later arrangements (Mills, 0:15; Krupa, 0:42). Following this introductory material, however, all recorded performances of "Fantasy" share essentially the same routine established on the Hill recording (see table 14). As with "Jungle Madness" and "Prelude to a Stomp," Willet's two-theme strategy—arguably a throwback to jazz arranging forms of the 1920s (chapter 5)—stands apart from the thirty-two-bar AABA chorus structures associated with Swing Era popular song. The two themes of "Fantasy"

Example 9.9. Score reduction of first chorus bridge in "Chant of the Weed" (stock arrangement) mm. 22–24 (comparable to 0:34), arr. by Don Redman for Gotham Music (1932). Chord symbols reflect the published guitar part.

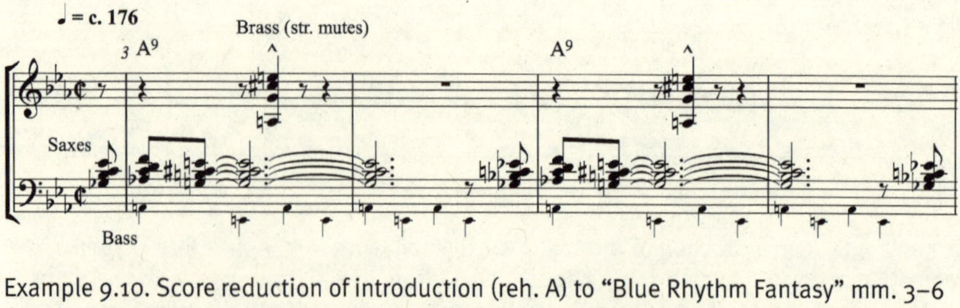

Example 9.10. Score reduction of introduction (reh. A) to "Blue Rhythm Fantasy" mm. 3–6 (0:03), arr. by Chappie Willet for Teddy Hill (1936, 1937). Transcription by the author, also referencing manuscript orchestra parts of version held in LAHM.

Table 14. Formal structure of "Blue Rhythm Fantasy," arr. by Chappie Willet for Teddy Hill (1936). Transcription by the author; rehearsal letters and solo chorus lengths reference manuscript orchestra parts held in LAHM.

Section/Theme	Bars	Scoring	Key
Intro	2	Tom drums, bass	A9
Fantasy (reh. A)	16	Trombone solo over chromatic ensemble background	A9, etc.
	4	Riff transition	C minor
Theme 1 (reh. B)	16 (8+8)	Riff-theme ensemble, brass versus reeds	
Interlude (reh. C)	8	Solo sax and clarinet over ensemble	
	8	Unison reed whole-tone melody with brass background, modulation	
Theme 2 (reh. D)	16 (or 16+16)	Clarinet solo	E-flat major
Theme 2 (reh. E)	16 (or 16+16)	Trumpet solo	
Theme 2 (reh. F)	16	Sax solo	
	16	Sax solo cont'd. over shout chorus	
Theme 1 variation (reh. G)	4	Riff-theme ensemble, brass versus reeds	C minor
	4	Unison ensemble tag	

are set in related but contrasting tonalities (C minor and its relative major key, E-flat), framed by episodic passages including the extensive introduction (reh. A), a sixteen-bar interlude (reh. C), and a concluding return to the first theme (reh. G).

The interlude (reh. C) of "Fantasy" comprises two parts. The first eight-bar, bridge-like passage (Hill, 0:51) features a written alto sax solo alternating with ad lib clarinet; these solos are supported by ensemble background chords alternating via half-step voice-leading (while percussive fourth-beat hold figures for the trombone inject rhythmic imperative). A subsequent eight-bar passage sets a whole-tone-inflected unison woodwind melody over sustained brass chords, alternating between augmented-fifth and unaltered dominant-chord voicings (example 9.11). This ear-catching, harmonically unstable passage again recalls Redman's scoring in the first chorus of "Chant of the Weed" (0:06), where sequences of altered dominant chords descend in parallel half-step motion.[41] The interlude of "Fantasy" culminates with an additional parallel chromatic descent (example 9.11, mm. 52–54) and modulation to E-flat major; chromatic half-step motion is maintained in background scoring voice-leading (lead trumpet F-sharp to F) behind the emergent clarinet solo (repeating the "wa-wa" figure introduced in m. 54).

Example 9.11: Score reduction of interlude passage (second half of reh. C) in "Blue Rhythm Fantasy" mm. 47–54 (1:02), arr. by Chappie Willet for Teddy Hill (1937 [two-trombone version]). Transcription by the author, also referencing manuscript orchestra parts of version held in LAHM.

The descending half-step concept of "Fantasy" is further reinforced by voice-leading through the chord sequences that close each sixteen-bar solo chorus (reh. D, E, and the first half of reh. F; example 9.12). An augmented-fifth dominant-chord triplet figure (example 9.12, m. 102) announces the ensemble shout chorus (the second half of reh. F). This shout chorus climaxes with an ensemble quarter-note-triplet figure, voiced in parallel dominant-ninth chords descending by half-step (example 9.13, m. 112).

Following the shout chorus, an ensemble break and another augmented-fifth dominant chord (2:38) lead back to the key of C minor. The subsequent variation of the first theme riff ends with a four-bar unison ensemble melody that outlines a series of minor and diminished chords connected by half-step motion (example 9.14). This "tricky break" ending arguably conjures the angular unison arpeggios associated with 1940s bebop jazz, including Dizzy Gillespie's 1945 composition "Bebop" (example 9.15).[42] Although the conceptual similarities may be coincidental, Gillespie was certainly familiar with Willet's work; the trumpeter's debut recording sessions with both Teddy Hill ("Blue Rhythm Fantasy") and

Example 9.12. Score reduction of chromatic ensemble background passage (reh. F) in "Blue Rhythm Fantasy" mm. 100–103 (2:13), arr. by Chappie Willet for Teddy Hill (1937 [two-trombone version]). Transcription by the author, also referencing manuscript orchestra parts of version held in LAHM.

Example 9.13. Score reduction of triplet ensemble figure (reh. F) in "Blue Rhythm Fantasy" mm. 111–14 (2:28), arr. by Chappie Willet for Teddy Hill (1937 [two-trombone version]). Transcription by the author, also referencing manuscript orchestra parts of version held in LAHM.

Example 9.14. Closing unison tag (reh. G) in "Blue Rhythm Fantasy" mm. 123–26 (2:44), arr. by Chappie Willet for Teddy Hill (1936, 1937). Transcription by the author, also referencing manuscript orchestra parts of version held in LAHM.

Example 9.15. Excerpt of unison break in "Bebop" mm. 5–8 (0:03), arr. by Dizzy Gillespie (1945). Transcription by the author

Cab Calloway ("I Ain't Gettin' Nowhere Fast") featured Willet arrangements, and Gillespie was a member of Lucky Millinder's orchestra around the time they performed Willet's "Prelude in C-sharp Minor" (chapter 7).[43]

Although the overall form of "Fantasy" remained fairly fixed in its later versions, some alterations can be traced through the years, reflecting either changes in the arranger's conception or the needs of different clients. In addition to his adaptations to the introduction, Willet replaced the Hill version's eighth-note-triplet entry into the shout chorus with a more dramatic, rhythmic-unison *pomposo* quarter-note-triplet figure in subsequent versions (Mills, 2:38; Krupa pt. 2, 0:26); the triplet figure of the shout chorus climax was also reinforced by comparable rhythm section scoring (Mills, 2:53; Krupa pt. 2, 0:43).[44] Solo assignments also changed, depending on the client ensemble's featured side-musicians. Surviving Armstrong band parts indicate that the first two solo choruses (reh. D and E) were to be played twice for each soloist (for a total of thirty-two bars each), suggesting that these solos may have been truncated in all studio-recorded versions. There was also a brass send-off figure (separating the clarinet and trumpet solos) added to both the Armstrong and Mills (1:45) versions, but subsequently omitted from the Krupa arrangement. Perhaps the most notable alteration, however, is the Krupa version's extended solo drum cadenza and replacement of the unison tag ending with a more generically symphonic-styled fanfare figure (pt. 2, 2:35), adaptations that turn "Fantasy" into a more concerto-like vehicle, and perhaps reinforce a symphonic-jazz ancestry.

Despite Willet's stature in the black press during the Swing Era, media responses to "Fantasy" were fairly scarce and tend to emerge only in white press coverage of the Krupa band. Similar to the "Jungle Madness" routine featured in the *America's Ace Drummer* film short, Krupa's version of "Fantasy" incorporated the spectacle of ensemble tom drumming; as described in a *Billboard* theater review, "the band goes to town on a congo rhythm . . . with the entire band beating drums in a frenzy and Krupa's own hide-beating a spectacular standout. Great jitterbug stuff, and a very flashy number."[45] A scene in the Bob Hope film *Some Like It Hot* (Universal, 1939; reissued as *Rhythm Romance*) documents part of the ensemble drum routine of "Fantasy," but the main body of the arrangement is not included.

There was little other critical notice of "Blue Rhythm Fantasy" until decades later, with the rising interest in the origins of bebop jazz. Early LP reissues of the title presented the second Hill recording, celebrating Gillespie's debut recording session. In this context, the work was portrayed as an anomaly of the Swing Era; David Himmelstein's 1966 liner notes lauded Willet's "Fantasy" score as "forward-looking," and Albert McCarthy's 1974 *Big Band Jazz* described the arrangement as "advanced for the period"—presumably in response to the prominent chromaticism and intricate formal routine.[46] As noted earlier, however, the strategies invoked in "Fantasy" were not unique among Swing Era big band arrangements; a couple of relevant precedents might include Russ Morgan's chromatic "Phantom Fantasie" for Fletcher Henderson (1934) or Joe Garland's quasi-exotic "Congo Caravan" for the Mills Blue Rhythm Band (1935). The fact that some post-bebop jazz commentators still found Willet's piece "advanced" may well attest to the lasting powers of the exotic and modernist signifiers invoked and their convincing execution by the arranger. Willet's dramatic approach to "glorified" form and effective combination of whole-tone sonorities with descending half-step chromaticism serve to unify the different melodic themes and contrasting episodes of "Fantasy" into a cohesive and entertaining piece, regardless of period or style.

* * *

Willet's arrangements for multiple clients across a range of genres testify to the influence of theatrical devices in Swing Era jazz and popular music. Although successful swing bands and their arrangers may have initially embraced these strategies to meet the requirements of live stage productions, competing mediums of disc, radio, and film were also quick to embrace orchestral signifiers of dramatic virtuosity, exoticism, and visual spectacle. During the early 1940s, efforts by bandleaders like Gene Krupa and Earl Hines to add string sections—a trend spearheaded by the popular success of Artie Shaw, Tommy Dorsey, and Harry James—can be viewed as further attempts to compete with the programmatic power of theater, film, and radio studio arrangements. Indeed, the popular emergence and financial viability of the big band format was closely tied to that of live stage entertainment—perhaps too closely to survive without it. Alongside factors including suburban migration and the advent of television, the economic collapse of the big bands following World War II paralleled a broader decline of live stage entertainment across America. Activities at Willet's Broadway Music Clinic offer further testimony; the midtown offices are reported to have quietly closed around June 1950.[47]

Conclusion

Show bands . . . needed dramatic qualities that the dance band could ignore. . . . The show-band style died with the Depression . . . and had no wide influence [in jazz].[1]

—Hsio Wen Shih, "The Spread of Jazz and the Big Bands," 1959

Make them [arrangements of "Time on My Hands" and "I Cover the Waterfront"] so I could play them on stage as well as at dances.[2]

—Louis Armstrong, correspondence to arranger Don Redman, 1939

The creative and commercial versatility of jazz and popular music arrangers remains a largely unexplored topic in American music studies. Twentieth-century critics often disparaged the artistic value of music accompanied by visual entertainment, whether Broadway staging or music video. But the practice of jazz musicians turning to the stage as inspiration or setting for their creations is more representative than exceptional. This was especially true during the Swing Era, when jazz musicians were stage performers, and the big band format provided an enticing range of orchestral resources for arrangers to frame visual presentations or invoke programmatic imagery. Jazz dance bands frequently drew upon variety entertainment genres and "show band" orchestration techniques—to say nothing of the actual stage, film, or radio program material produced by prolific jazz arrangers like Andy Gibson, Jimmy Mundy, Sy Oliver, or Eddie Sauter. While figures like Chappie Willet or Tom Whaley may have been exceptional in the degree to which their reputations derived from work in vaudeville formats, a closer examination of Swing Era music and its creators reveals strong ties between theater, dance, and jazz. This relationship demands the consideration of stage entertainment as a central component of American popular music, jazz included.

Swing Era jazz arrangements often capitalized on representations of European classical forms or American vernacular blues and folk styles. Indeed, the wide range of musical influences comprising jazz itself offered a cultural foil to popular conceptions of a homogenous mainstream (typically Euro-American) identity.[3] Performers, composers, and arrangers further reinforced these representations of difference—or perhaps simply "variety"—with explicitly new musical techniques and sounds. In addition to modernist orchestration devices or episodic formal structures, tools like brass mutes, drum kits, electric-powered instruments, slang lyrics, and exotic dance rhythms all provided a crucial signifier of novelty (a strategy that remains central to popular music, as witnessed by digital drum machines, auto-tune, and so on). Another important novelty device not addressed in this study is jazz improvisation; Swing Era big bands incorporated jazz solos not only as individualized expressions of modernity, but also as an exercise in dramatic stage presentation.[4] Jazz's continuing emphasis on live performance may be the clearest expression of its stage entertainment roots.

Considering jazz historians' frequent preoccupation with notions of linear progress, the obscurity of Chappie Willet may be puzzling. It is true that most working musicians—and certainly most arrangers—can expect to work in anonymity; it is also possible that Willet's alliances with established musicians of an older generation added to the challenges of a post–Swing Era career transition. But given Willet's esteemed position in the music community and unusually prominent media presence, his subsequently low profile in most (or any) histories still begs some explanation. Indeed, the sheer volume of his media publicity efforts—even if largely self-generated—only further indicates the severity of his exclusion from jazz narratives. Willet enjoyed professional relationships not only with popular icons like Armstrong, Calloway, Ellington, and Krupa, but also critically celebrated innovators like pianist-composers Herbie Nichols and Mary Lou Williams. His music demonstrated impressive technical skills, exercising fluency across multiple genres. His personal arranging style was recognizable and in demand, while his compositions reflected the stylistic evolutions of his era, from instrumental dance numbers to vocal ballads, novelty songs, and rhythm and blues. In addition to his "commercial" endeavors, original compositions like "Blue Rhythm Fantasy" have been embraced under more conservative frameworks of jazz authenticity; as a black musician, Willet even possessed that "native attribute" celebrated by the *Baltimore Afro-American*. His career was explicitly progressive for the period, politically and professionally.

It may be simply a matter of luck—there is not enough space to document *everyone*—but Willet's obscurity also seems to highlight the consequences of post–Swing Era efforts to separate jazz from popular entertainment. As Peter Townsend has noted, the phenomenon of jazz purification in music histories has tended to weigh disproportionately against black contributions to American popular (commercial) music.[5] And Willet's work for nightclub floor shows, vaudeville stage acts, rhythm and blues singers, and even Louis Armstrong's big band committed almost every sin available in post–Swing Era assessments of jazz authenticity. In critical responses to arrangements like "Sonata Pathétique," Willet is caught in the crossfire of the very cultural discourses that had inspired his musical invention; the arranger's background in European classical music and theater idioms is highlighted—perhaps even celebrated in its reflection of a modernist aesthetic—yet ultimately deemed less authentic, and therefore commercial. Although Willet's Swing Era career thrived uptown and downtown, his legacy (along with that of his clients Armstrong and Lunceford) later ran the risk of being relegated by jazz critics to a monolithic trash heap of "variety" or "show band" music—precisely the mainstream commercial market that was often denied to black musicians under segregation.

Some of the motivations behind these historical judgments are understandable. Racism in America has been largely based on appearances, and the theater medium's emphasis on visual representation made stage entertainment especially susceptible to the propagation of racist attitudes and imagery. Jazz's young history—documented in the nonvisual medium of audio recordings—seems to have provided an irresistible temptation to the music's proponents: an opportunity to intercede in the machinations of popular culture and to formulate a history that might free the music (and perhaps, by extension, its performers) from racial prejudice. But the idea that passing over the artistic accomplishments of representative figures—history by omission—could compensate for past offenses has also proved problematic. Attempts to establish a standard of content or a reliable cutoff date to mark the birth of American entertainment deemed politically appropriate for public consumption remain—for worse or for better—unfulfilled.

But perhaps these past judgments of historiography may also be instructive. If the "Harlem antics" presented by stage entertainers like the Three Chocolateers (or, for that matter, the Andrews Sisters) were eventually dismissed as dated stereotypes, the story behind the "Hicky Ricky" novelty song demonstrates the frustrations that accompanied the successes in a highly competitive, fast-paced, and racist entertainment industry.[6] These stories need not compete against the subsequent political rhetoric of the civil rights era; rather, they explain those later efforts' emergence and insistency. Independent business efforts by post–Swing Era black musicians like Charles Mingus—who initiated his own booking, recording, and publishing enterprises during the 1950s and '60s—have found an important role in recent jazz histories.[7] It might be worth considering whether the strategies taken by musicians like Willet to carve out their own voice in society—including such "commercial" efforts as establishing and publicizing their own businesses or attempting to find financial prosperity under segregation by taking on white clients as well as black—should (or could) be isolated from their artistic legacy.

Removal of commercial music arrangers from the politically empowered narrative of the "jazz tradition" requires still further contortions of history. Although some commentators have suggested that developments in post–Swing Era jazz idioms were made *despite* the industrial versatility of musicians like Willet, any tracing of a jazz lineage from pre- to post–Swing Era requires an acknowledgment of stage entertainment practices. Not only is it the only way to fit canonic figures like Bessie Smith or Duke Ellington into the story, but programmatic conceptions of difference have consistently defined American music. In postwar "modern jazz," holdovers of Swing Era variety included exotic numbers (from "A Night in Tunisia" to John Coltrane's "India"), novelties (from "Salt Peanuts" to "Watermelon Man"), and ballad love songs (from "'Round Midnight" to Jeanne Lee's rendition of "Night and Day"). And it was precisely the Swing Era's most dramatic theatrical devices—modernist chromaticism, rhythmic and harmonic surprise, and a growing emphasis on individual virtuosity—that would carry over as the essential hallmarks of the new styles. Even the "third-stream" genre, which aimed to integrate the idioms of African American jazz and European classical music, typically relied on the programmatic arranging strategies of contrasting form and texture that had long lay at the core of urban modernism, symphonic jazz, the avant-garde, and a hefty portion of Swing Era dance band music.[8]

Big band jazz arrangers continued to invoke tropes of theatrical drama well beyond the Swing Era. Kimberly Hannon Teal traces the rhetorical evolution of exotic orchestration effects from Ellington's "jungle" stage show music of the 1920s—historically dismissed as inauthentic, commercially driven formula—into the 1950s and '60s, when the same orchestration effects could be "recast" as a trope of jazz authenticity.[9] Todd Decker's study of dancer and vocalist Fred Astaire highlights the central role that big band jazz arrangers like Skip Martin maintained in Hollywood film spectacles through the "long" Swing Era of the 1950s.[10] Donald Bogle presents the story of black arranger Phil Moore, who forged a career in Hollywood film music along with Benny Carter and J. J. Johnson, arrangers whose pioneering efforts remain largely untold.[11] Recording-studio arrangers like Nelson Riddle extended swing dance band scoring techniques through the 1960s, as popular Swing Era vocalists like Nat "King" Cole, Ella Fitzgerald, and Frank Sinatra hit new peaks of popularity.[12] Alex Stewart explores the twenty-first-century big band jazz scene in New York, tracing the evolution of Swing Era arranging styles into contemporary ideologies of "jazz composition."[13] In the popular music realm, arrangers like Quincy Jones extended arranging into the realm of studio production.[14] "Commercial" music producers continue to take an active role in work formerly executed by arrangers, whether via live orchestral accompaniment or its contemporary counterpart in digital programming.

All of this indicates that the popular embrace of jazz dance bands during the 1930s was not an isolated aberration of crossover taste. Throughout the twentieth century, strategies of creating and presenting vernacular or exotic (still often "black") tropes against some form of established mainstream (still often "white") idiom continued to shape American popular music. Chappie Willet engaged in this dialogue by combining arranging techniques associated with—among other popular and classical traditions—ragtime (e.g., rhythmic displacement), the 1920s Jazz Age (e.g., harmonic chromaticism), and the 1930s Swing Era (e.g., section-based soli scoring and riff-based call-and-response). These deliberately calculated cultural mash-ups, as heard in arrangements like "Alexander's Ragtime Band," "Estrellita," or "I Know That You Know," offer one possible reason that arranging has been so controversial for jazz historians. Whether listening to a "commercial" stock or an "inspired" special arrangement, the audience receives significant social commentary from an unidentified source—the arranger—who may not relate to that audience in the same way that the identified performer does (or at least pretends to). The uncertainties surrounding an unidentified source perhaps explain why idiom, genre, and style play such integral roles in popular music; the more efficiently Swing Era arrangers and performers could codify their representations of genre and style, the more effectively their artistic statements could be transmitted through nonvisual formats like radio and phonograph.

Andrew Berish suggests that "music creates meaning through the arrangement of . . . recognizable materials that can echo nonmusical behavior or signify through association. . . . Big band jazz of the 1930s and '40s helped shape Americans' perception of the spaces of their lives and . . . provided listeners and musicians with new maps of their reality."[15] In their musical negotiations of genre, performer identity, and personal style, Swing Era arrangers documented their rapidly evolving social environments—integration versus segregation, rich versus poor, urban versus rural—through the tools of harmony, rhythm, orchestration, and form. A consideration of freelancers' work for multiple clients helps to bring these artistic efforts into focus, as Willet and his music regularly crossed boundaries of cultural identity and landscape. His big band arrangements for Louis Armstrong set tropes of urban modernism (like the whole-tone scale) against quaint rustic imagery (like tailgate trombone) that complemented the trumpeter's biographical status as one of jazz's founding figures. For Jimmie Lunceford, dramatic episodic-form vehicles for solo and ensemble virtuosity delivered class branding for both conductor and arranger. In arrangements for Red Norvo, brief harmonic substitutions reinforced an urbane, "sophisticated" musical style. And for Gene Krupa, the performance of hot dance repertoire recorded by black bands and created by black arrangers highlighted the bandleader's jazz-inspired identity. As Albert Murray argues, "What counts in a work of art . . . is . . . how adequately it fulfills the requirements of the circumstances for which it was created. . . . Art is nothing if not stylized statement."[16]

Dismissal of arrangers as "commercial" also risks overlooking another important aspect of the job: the day-to-day pleasure of creating music. Careers are rarely built for the convenience of historical representation, and closer examination of these musical legacies reminds us that arrangers are very much individuals. Acknowledgment of Willet's formal music studies, experience touring with territory dance bands, perceptions of his own role in the African American community, ambitions in the mainstream entertainment industry, and dedication to producing work of high quality counters historical narratives that dismiss arrangers as merely components of industry. Accounts of arranged music would benefit from a consideration of arrangers' personal backgrounds, the musical tools and techniques available to them, and the client performers' arranging needs. Benny Goodman recognized that "the art of making an arrangement a band can play with swing—and I am convinced it is an art—one that really helps a solo player get off, and gives him the right background to work against—that's something that very few musicians can do."[17] As artistic creations, arrangements can tell us much about their time and place, including information about the performers, their audiences, and—just as important—the arrangers themselves.

Acknowledgments and Credits

This publication is generously supported by a Society for American Music publishing subvention award. Research was supported by an American Musicological Society Ora Frishberg Saloman travel award. This project began as a City University of New York (CUNY) doctoral dissertation supported by a Martin E. Segal Dissertation Fellowship, and a Barry S. Brook Dissertation Award; additional funding for research and travel was provided by the CUNY Baisley Powell Elebash Fund and Franziska Dorner Fund. Initial research was supported by a grant from the Institute of Jazz Studies Morroe Berger–Benny Carter Jazz Research Fund.

Many people have contributed to this project over many years. Thanks are due foremost to the extraordinarily patient people who published it: editor Laurie Matheson, along with Marika Christofides, Jennifer Clark, Roger Cunningham, and Amanda Wicks at the University of Illinois Press. Anne Rogers contributed copyediting of inspirational vision and skill. Jeeyun Lee, Ben Bierman at CUNY John Jay College, and Ben Young provided valuable feedback and ideas on my book manuscript. Earlier manuscripts and publications of this material benefited from the insightful editing and peer reviews of Patrick Burke, Mark Katz, Evan Spring, and Chris Wilkinson. At the Rutgers University Jazz History and Research program, my research efforts were aided by Lewis Porter, Henry Martin, and John Howland. At the CUNY Graduate Center, my dissertation benefited from the input of Ben Bierman, Stephen Blum, John Graziano, John Howland, Jeff Taylor, and Salim Washington; vital logistical support was provided by Allan Atlas, Norman Carey, David Olan, and Peg Rivers. Special thanks are due to bandleader-historian Vince Giordano, whose Nighthawk orchestra performed concerts of Chappie Willet's unrecorded music at the CUNY Graduate Center, and to Graduate Center president William P. Kelly for his support.

Phil Schaap at radio station WKCR-FM New York contributed valuable advice, contacts, and encouragement throughout this project. Additional scholars, librarians, arrangers, performers, and colleagues who have helped me to access research materials or locate sources include: Ed Berger, John Clement, Tad Hershorn, Annie Kuebler, Dan Morgenstern, Vincent Pelote, Joe Peterson, and Elizabeth Surles at the Institute of Jazz Studies; Michael Cogswell and Ricky Riccardi at the Louis Armstrong House Museum, Queens College; Ryan Maloney at the National Jazz Museum in Harlem; Ellen Ressmeyer at the Drain-Jordan Library of West Virginia State College; Peggy Turnbull at the Bluefield State College Archives; Richard Boursey and Suzanne Lovejoy at the Irving S. Gilmore Music Library of Yale University; Arturo Ortega at the University of North Texas Music Library; Keith Pawlak at the University of Arizona School of Music; Michelle Romero at the Northeastern University Libraries; Phil Greene at the Columbia University Law School Library; Warren Adams at the Lummis Library of the Cumberland County Historical Society, New Jersey; Kay Peterson and Susan Strange at the Smithsonian National Museum of American History; Mark Horowitz at the Music Division of the Library of Congress; Kimberly Lamb at the University of Southern California Doheny Library; Kelly McEniry at the University of Missouri–Kansas City Miller Nichols Library; historians Bree Benton, Franklin Bruno, Brenda Bufalino, John Chilton, Jane Goldberg, Catherine Goode, Michael Heller, Aaron Johnson, Carlos Kase, Barry Kernfeld, Brian Linde, Paul Munson, Arnold Rampersad, Howard Rye, David Schiff, Alyn Shipton, and Michael Steinman; arrangers Van Alexander, Hart Leavitt, Lyle "Spud" Murphy, and Gerald Wilson; and performers Harold Cromer, Cleo Hayes, Chico Hicks, and Brooks Kerr. There are undoubtedly others I have missed, but you all deserve my sincerest thanks.

Portions of this research have previously appeared in the following publications:

"Chappie Willet, Frank Fairfax, and Phil Edwards' Collegians: From West Virginia to Philadelphia." *Black Music Research Journal* 27, no. 1 (Spring 2007): 1–22.

"Chappie Willet: A Jazz Arranger in Swing Era New York." *Annual Review of Jazz Studies* 14 (2009): 101–88.

"Jazzing the Classics: Race, Modernism, and the Career of Arranger Chappie Willet." *Journal of the Society for American Music* 6, no. 2 (May 2012): 175–209.

* * *

Every effort has been made to locate and contact copyright holders of music examples included in this work. Permission to use notated excerpts of the following compositions is hereby acknowledged:

A-Tisket A-Tasket
Words and Music by Ella Fitzgerald and Van Alexander
© 1938 (Renewed) EMI ROBBINS CATALOG INC.
Exclusive Print Rights Controlled and Administered by ALFRED MUSIC.
All Rights Reserved.

Alexander's Ragtime Band
Words and Music by Irving Berlin
© Copyright 1911 by Irving Berlin.
© Arrangement Copyright 1938 by Irving Berlin.
Copyright Renewed.
This arrangement © Copyright 2014 by the Estate of Irving Berlin.
International Copyright Secured. All Rights Reserved.
Reprinted by Permission of Hal Leonard Corporation.

Be-Bop
By John "Dizzy" Gillespie
Copyright © 1944, 1945 UNIVERSAL MUSIC CORP.
Copyright Renewed.
This arrangement Copyright © 2014 UNIVERSAL MUSIC CORP.
All Rights Reserved. Used by Permission.
Reprinted by Permission of Hal Leonard Corporation.

Blue Skies
Words and Music by Irving Berlin
© Copyright 1927 by Irving Berlin.
Copyright Renewed.
This arrangement © Copyright 2014 by the Estate of Irving Berlin.
International Copyright Secured. All Rights Reserved.
Reprinted by Permission of Hal Leonard Corporation.

Chant of the Weed
By Don Redman
© 1932 GOTHAM MUSIC SERVICE, INC.
© Renewed 1960 EDWIN H. MORRIS & COMPANY, A Division of MPL Music Publishing, Inc.
This arrangement © 2014 EDWIN H. MORRIS & COMPANY, A Division of MPL Music Publishing, Inc. All Rights Reserved.
Reprinted by Permission of Hal Leonard Corporation.

Deuces Wild
By Margie Gibson
Copyright © 1942 Administered by Sinless Music Publishing.
International Copyright Secured. All Rights Reserved. Reprinted by Permission.

East of the Sun (and West of the Moon)
Words and Music by Brooks Bowman
© 1934 (Renewed) CHAPPELL & CO., INC.
All Rights Reserved.

Fish Fry
Words and Music by Benny Carter
Copyright © 1943 Sony/ATV Music Publishing LLC.
Copyright Renewed.
This arrangement Copyright © 2014 Sony/ATV Music Publishing LLC.
All Rights Administered by Sony/ATV Music Publishing LLC, 424 Church Street, Suite 1200, Nashville, TN 37219.
International Copyright Secured. All Rights Reserved.
Reprinted by Permission of Hal Leonard Corporation.

Gimme Some Skin [My] Friend
Words and Music by Don Raye, Gene de Paul, and Red Mack
Copyright © 1941 UNIVERSAL MUSIC CORP.
Copyright Renewed.
This arrangement Copyright © 2014 UNIVERSAL MUSIC CORP.
All Rights Reserved. Used by Permission.
Reprinted by Permission of Hal Leonard Corporation.

Hallelujah (from *Hit the Deck*)
Words by Leo Robin and Clifford Grey
Music by M. Vincent Youmans
Copyright © 1927 (Renewed) by Leo Robin Music Co., Warner Bros. Publications, Range Road Music and Quartet Music.
This arrangement © 2009 by Leo Robin Music Co., Warner Bros. Publications, Range Road Music and Quartet Music.
All rights for Leo Robin Music Co. administered by Music Sales Corporation (ASCAP). International Copyright Secured. All Rights Reserved.
Reprinted by Permission.

Hicky Ricky
Words and Music by Esvan Mosby, Chappy [*sic*] Willet, and Albert Gibson
Copyright © 1942 UNIVERSAL MUSIC CORP.
Copyright Renewed.
This arrangement Copyright © 2014 UNIVERSAL MUSIC CORP.
All Rights Reserved. Used by Permission.
Reprinted by Permission of Hal Leonard Corporation.

I Ain't Gettin' Nowhere Fast
By Porter Grainger, Cab Calloway, and Chappie Willet
Copyright © 1939 Music Sales Corporation.
International Copyright Secured. All Rights Reserved. Reprinted by Permission.

I Know That You Know
Words by Anne Caldwell
Music by Vincent Youmans

Jubilee
Words by Stanley Adams
Music by Hoagy Carmichael and Stanley Adams

Metropolis
By Ferde Grofé

Paganini Caprice XXIV
By Benny Goodman [*sic*]

Persian Rug
Music by Neil Moret
Lyrics by Gus Kahn

Sonatine Transatlantique
By Alexandre Tansman

Stardust
Words by Mitchell Parish
Music by Hoagy Carmichael

Struttin' with Some Barbecue
Words and Music by Lillian Hardin Armstrong and Don Raye

Swingtime in Honolulu
Words and Music by Duke Ellington, Henry Nemo, and Irving Mills

What Is This Thing Called Swing
By Louis Armstrong and Horace Gerlach

Appendix: The Music of Chappie Willet

Selected Discography

Some of the Chappie Willet arrangements cited in the text are available on the following CD and LP releases:

Louis Armstrong, *The Complete Louis Armstrong Decca Sessions 1935–1946* (Mosaic Records 7CD-243, 2009). Includes "Alexander's Ragtime Band," "I Hope Gabriel Likes My Music," "I've Got My Fingers Crossed," "Jubilee," "The Music Goes 'Round and Around," "Struttin' with Some Barbecue," "What Is This Thing Called Swing," "Wolverine Blues," and "You've Got Me Voodoo'd."

Louis Armstrong, *Fleischmann's Yeast Show and Louis' Home-Recorded Tapes* (Jazz Heritage Society CD 5289147, 2008). Includes "After You've Gone," "I Got Rhythm," "I Know That You Know," "Memories of You," "Prelude to a Stomp," "Rhythm Jam," "Them There Eyes," "Tiger Rag," "Sugar Foot Stomp," and "Washington and Lee Swing."

Teddy Hill, *Uptown Rhapsody* (Hep CD-1033, 1992). Includes "Blue Rhythm Fantasy" (1936 and 1937 recordings) and "Uptown Rhapsody."

Gene Krupa and His Orchestra 1935–1938 (Classics CD-754, 1994). Includes "Grandfather's Clock," "I Know That You Know," "The Madam Swings It," and "Prelude to a Stomp."

Gene Krupa and His Orchestra 1938 (Classics CD-767, 1994). Includes "Apurksody" and "Rhythm Jam."

Jimmie Lunceford and His Orchestra 1939–1940 (Classics CD-565, 1996). Includes "Sonata Pathétique."

Jimmie Lunceford at His Rare of All Rarest Performances Vol. 1 (Kings of Jazz LP-20016, n.d.). Includes "Estrellita," "Hallelujah," and "Yesterdays."

Mills Blue Rhythm Band 1936–1937 (Classics CD-731, 1993). Includes "Blue Rhythm Fantasy," "Jungle Madness," "Prelude to a Stomp," and "Rhythm Jam."

Red Norvo 1938: Red and Mildred (Circle LP-3/CD-3, 1991). Includes "A-Tisket, A-Tasket," "Blue Skies," "I'd Climb the Highest Mountain," and "Jump Jump's Here."

Chappie Willet Arrangements and Compositions

The following entries identify Chappie Willet arrangements, compositions, and copyrights discovered to date. Section 1 lists copyright deposits and archival manuscript or print music arranged or composed by Willet. Copyright deposit materials are registered with the U.S. Library of Congress; archival collections are designated per the list of abbreviations. Dates prefaced by "Willet AFM" reflect the date of Willet's American Federation of Musicians Local 802 stamp displayed on manuscript music. Corresponding period audio recordings and additional copyist identifications are cited when available. Section 2 selectively cites forensically unconfirmed attributions to Willet provided by contemporary media reports, primary participants, or other commentators (including this author); some disputed attributions are also noted. Section 3 cites additional copyright registrations filed by Willet or Duo Music.

1. WILLET ARRANGEMENTS OR COMPOSITIONS IN ARCHIVAL COLLECTIONS

Apurksody
(Gene Krupa and Chappie Willet)
Copyright Deposit: May 7, 1938 [E unp. 165955], registered by Robbins Music.
Recordings: Gene Krupa, NJMH Savory 19 [aircheck] (ca. 1938), Brunswick 8296 (December 12, 1938).
Note: Numerous aircheck recordings present a truncated version listed as "Theme"; the Savory 19 recording includes an extended trumpet solo passage not reflected in the Brunswick recording.

A-Tisket, A-Tasket
(Van Alexander and Ella Fitzgerald)
RNP: Parts (xylophone, sax 1–4, trumpet 1–3, trombone 1–2, guitar, piano, bass, drums), Willet AFM 1938.
Recording: Red Norvo, Hep CD-1050 [take 1] (July 28, 1938), Columbia CD-53424 [take 2] (July 28, 1938), Circle LP-3 [transcription, alias "Russ Norman"] (September 9, 1938).

Blue Rhythm Fantasy
(Teddy Hill and Chappie Willet)
Copyright deposit: October 16, 1936 [E pub. 57971], registered by Exclusive Publications.
Leadsheet publication: Exclusive Publications, 1936.
Stock arrangement: Exclusive Publications, 1936, arranged by Edgar Battle.
LAHM: Parts (sax 3, trumpet 2, trombone 2–3, guitar), second trumpet and drums stamped "arr. by—Chappie Willet," remaining parts recopied (no stamp).
Recording: Teddy Hill, Vocalion 3247 (May 4, 1936), Bluebird 6989 (May 17, 1937); Mills Blue Rhythm Band, Variety 503 (February 11, 1937); Gene Krupa, Okeh 5627 (January 2, 1940).
Note: Some variations between the stock arrangement and recorded versions.

Blue Room
(Lorenz Hart and Richard Rodgers)
RNP: Parts (bass, drums), Willet AFM 1938.

Blue Skies
(Irving Berlin)
RNP: Parts (sax 1–4, trumpet 1–3, trombone 1–2, piano, bass, drums), Willet AFM 1938; some parts in duplicate recopied by Lyman Vunk (including additional fifth sax and third trombone).
Recording: Red Norvo, Circle LP-3 [transcription, alias "Russ Norman"] (September 9, 1938).

Cherry Tree
(Rudolph Toombs, Claude Demetrius, and Chappie Willet)
Copyright deposit: November 11, 1945 [EU 446427], registered by the composers.
Recording: Johnny Moore [featuring Charles Brown], Exclusive 704 (ca. 1946).
Note: Moore recording issued as "Way Over There by the Cherry Tree."

Darling, Will You?
(Carroll Tate and Chappie Willet)
Copyright deposit: August 5, 1941 [E unp. 266028], registered by the composers.

East of the Sun (and West of the Moon)
(Brooks Bowman)
FDCJLO: Part (conductor), Willet AFM 1943; parts (sax 1–4; trumpet 1–2, 4; trombone 1–2; piano; bass; drums), Willet AFM 1942, copied by Tom Whaley.

Eh! Now
(Lew Crawford and Chappie Willet)
Copyright deposit: September 3, 1941 [E unp. 268863], registered by Chappie Willet.
DEC: Piano leadsheet, arranged by Chappie Willet (no stamp); score, arranged by Tom Whaley (no stamp); parts (sax 1–4, trumpet 1–3, trombone 1–3, piano, guitar, bass, drums), copied by Tom Whaley (no stamp).
Recording: Ella Fitzgerald, collection of Ben Young [aircheck] (ca. April 1942).
Note: Fitzgerald version differs from Whaley arrangement; Whaley's orchestra parts include additional material not reflected in the Whaley score.

Estrellita (Little Star)
(Manuel Ponce)
FDCJLO: Parts (piano, drums), Willet AFM 1943.
JTC: Score, arranged by Chappie Willet (no stamp).
Recording: Jimmie Lunceford, Kings of Jazz LP-20016 [transcription] (ca. 1943–44).
Note: Issued recording runs a half-step flat (slow).

The Flat Foot Floogee
(Slim Gaillard, Bud Green, and Slam Stewart)
RNP: Parts (sax 1–4, trumpet 1–3, trombone 1–2, guitar, bass, drums), Willet AFM 1938.

Good Night Now
(Evelyn Morris)
Copyright deposit: May 12, 1942 [E unp. 295764], "arranged by Chappie Willet," registered by Evelyn Morris.

Grandfather's Clock
(Henry Work)
Stock arrangement: Robbins Music, February 28, 1939 [E pub. 75171], scored by Spud Murphy, "based on Chappie Willet's arr.".
Recording: Gene Krupa, Brunswick 8124 (April 14, 1938).
Note: Some variations between the stock arrangement and Krupa recording.

Hallelujah
(Clifford Grey, Leo Robin, and Vincent Youmans)
FDCJLO: Parts (trombone 1 [incomplete], piano), Willet AFM 1942.
Recording: Jimmie Lunceford, Kings of Jazz LP-20016 [transcription] (ca. July 1943), http://archive.org/details/AFRSJubilee [transcription] (ca. July 1944).

The Hicky Ricky [1]
(Paul Black, Albert Gibson, Esvan Mosby, and Chappie Willet)
Copyright deposit: August 15, 1940 [E unp. 228569], registered by the composers.

The Hicky Ricky [2]
(Albert Gibson, Esvan Mosby, and Chappie Willet)
Copyright deposit: November 7, 1941 [E unp. 274977], registered by Kaycee Music.
Published leadsheet: Leeds Music, July 20, 1942 [E pub. 106386].
DEC: Score [incomplete?], arranged by Tom Whaley (no stamp).
Recording: Esvan Mosby, Document CD-5601 [demonstration disc] (ca. 1940–42?).
Note: Mosby recording issued as performed by "Stanford Mosby, ca. 1938."

I Ain't Gettin' Nowhere Fast
(Cab Calloway, Porter Grainger, and Chappie Willet)
Copyright deposit: May 29, 1939 [E unp. 196815], registered by Lewis Music.
Recording: Cab Calloway, Vocalion 5195 (August 30, 1939).

I Wanted You So Bad Blues
(Jacqueline DeShazor and Chappie Willet)
Copyright deposit: June 17, 1947 [EU 80441], registered by Jacqueline DeShazor.

I'd Climb the Highest Mountain
(Lew Brown and Sidney Clare)
RNP: Parts (xylophone, saxes 1–4, trumpet 1–3, trombone 1–2, piano, bass, drums), Willet AFM 1938.
Recording: Red Norvo, Circle LP-3 [transcription, alias "Russ Norman"] (September 9, 1938).

I'm Tellin' You in Front (So You Won't Feel Hurt Behind)
(W. C. Handy, Andy Razaf, and Russell Wooding)
Stock arrangement: Handy Bros., September 15, 1937 [E pub. 64157], arranged by Russell Wooding and Chappie Willet.

In the Still of the Night
(Cole Porter)
LAHM: Parts (trumpet 1, trombone 3, guitar), Willet AFM 1937.

Isn't She a Honey
(Abe A. Sandler, Derniece Harris, and Chappie Willet)
Copyright deposit: August 25, 1941 [E unp. 272510], registered by the composers.

I've Just Begun to Live
(Betty Martina and Chappie Willet)
Copyright deposit: October 10, 1939 [E unp. 206565], registered by the composers.

Japan
(Andy Razaf and Chappie Willet)
Copyright deposit: October 19, 1944 [E unp. 394505], registered by the composers, copied by Maceo Jefferson.

Jump Jump's Here
(Mildred Bailey, Red Norvo, and Dick Kline)
RNP: Parts (xylophone, sax 1–4, trumpet 1–3, trombone 1–2, guitar, piano, bass, drums), Willet AFM 1938.
Stock arrangement: Robbins Music, October 5, 1938 [E pub. 71968], scored by Les Brown.
Recording: Red Norvo, Brunswick 8202 [takes 1 and 2] (July 28, 1938), Circle LP-3 [transcription, alias "Russ Norman"] (September 9, 1938), NJMH Savory 80 [aircheck] (ca. 1938).
Note: Stock publication reflects some elements of the Norvo version; sax and xylophone solos truncated in Brunswick recording.

Jungle Madness
(Chappie Willet)
Copyright deposit: May 25, 1937 [E pub. 62364], registered by Exclusive Publications.
Published leadsheet: Exclusive Publications, 1937.
Recording: Mills Blue Rhythm Band, Variety 503 (February 11, 1937); Gene Krupa, Brunswick 8400 (April 17, 1939), UM&M TV *America's Ace Drummer* [film short] (ca. 1940).
Note: Some variations between the Mills and Krupa versions; also performed by Louis Armstrong, per Allan McMillan, CD, January 11, 1936.

(I) Know How to Do It
(Leonard Feather)
DEC: Piano leadsheet ("Billie Hayes"), Willet AFM 1943.

"Let My People Go," Now!
(Langston Hughes and Chappie Willet)
Copyright deposit: September 7, 1944 [E unp. 389290], registered by Text Music.
Published leadsheet: Text Music, 1944.
Recording: Mary Lou Williams, MLWC Acetates and Sound Recordings 719 [aircheck] (June 17, 1945) and 749 [aircheck] (August 12, 1945).

Low Down Guy—High Class Girl
(Ted Murry and Irving Taylor?)
DEC: Part (trombone 3), Willet AFM 1945, copied by Maceo Jefferson.
Note: Arrangement possibly reflects medley including "Take a Plane, Take a Train, Take a Car to the Zanzibar."

The Madam Swings It
(Morry Olsen and Henry Russell)
RNP: Parts (trumpet 3, trombone 2, bass), Willet AFM 1938.
Recording: Gene Krupa, Classics CD-754 [unissued take] (April 14, 1938), Brunswick 8335 (February 26, 1939).
Note: Some variations between the Krupa and Norvo versions.

Not Now, but Soon
(Lucille Boone and Chappie Willet)
Copyright deposit: September 7, 1944 [E unp. 389216], registered by Duo Music.

Nothin' to Do but Love
(Porter Grainger and Chappie Willet)
Copyright deposit: April 28, 1938 [E unp. 165622], registered by Robbins Music, copied by Porter Grainger.

Opening
(Chappie Willet?)
FDCJLO: Part (piano), Willet AFM 1938 or 1939 (stamp smudged).

Persian Rug
(Charles Daniels and Gus Kahn)
RNP: Parts (xylophone, sax 1–4, trumpet 1–3, trombone 1–2, piano, bass, drums), Willet AFM 1938; also additional parts for fifth sax and third trombone (no stamp).
Recording: Red Norvo, NJMH Savory 57 [aircheck] (ca. 1938), NJMH Savory 68 [aircheck] (ca. 1938).

Prelude in C-sharp Minor
(Sergei Rachmaninoff)
Stock arrangement: Robbins Music, February 3, 1939 [E pub. 74635], scored by Spud Murphy, "based on Chappie Willet's arr."
DEC: Parts (sax 1–2, sax 4, trumpet 1, trombone 1–3, guitar [incomplete]), Willet AFM 1938, second trombone part recopied.
Recording: Charlie Barnet, Alamac QSR LP-2435 [transcription] (May 16, 1938); Duke Ellington, Jazz Archives LP-13 [aircheck] (May 29, 1938).
Note: Some variations between the stock arrangement and recorded versions.

Prelude to a Stomp
(Chappie Willet)
Copyright deposit: June 7, 1937 [E pub. 62542], registered by Exclusive Publications.
Published leadsheet: Exclusive Publications, 1937.
Recording: Lucky Millinder with Mills Blue Rhythm Band, Variety 546 (February 11, 1937); Louis Armstrong, Jazz Heritage Society CD-5289147 [aircheck] (May 28, 1937); Gene Krupa, Brunswick 8139 (April 14, 1938).
Note: Some variations between the Millinder, Armstrong, and Krupa versions; Armstrong recording issued as "Will You Do a Stomp."

Push Out (Te-Huey, Te-Huey, Te-Huey)
(Alex Lovejoy and Nat Reed)
Stock arrangement: Handy Bros., July 12, 1939 [E pub. 78571], arranged by Chappie Willet.

Put Your Brakes On, Papa [1]
(Lucille Boone and Chappie Willet)
Copyright deposit: March 13, 1946 [EU 14374], registered by Leeds Music.
Recording: Hal Mitchell, Regis 6001 (ca. 1946).

Put Your Brakes On, Papa [2]
(Sid Robin, Lucille Boone, and Chappie Willet)
Copyright deposit: December 26, 1947 [EU 111677], registered by Leeds Music.
Recording: Wini Beatty, Coast 8045 (ca. 1948).

A Rainy Sunday
(Art Franklin, Lucky Millinder, and "Blackie" Warren [Chappie Willet?])
Copyright deposit: May 23, 1944 [E unp. 376106], registered by Duo Music.
Published leadsheet: Duo Music, September 5, 1944 [E pub. 125215].
Recording: Luis Russell, Apollo 1139 (October 19, 1946); Cab Calloway, Storyville DVD-16053 [*Hi-De-Ho* film performance featuring the Peters Sisters] (ca. March 1947).
Note: Some variations between the Russell and Calloway versions.

Rhythm Jam
(Chappie Willet)
Copyright deposit: June 7, 1937 [E pub. 62540], registered by Exclusive Publications.
Published leadsheet: Exclusive Publications, 1937.
Recording: Lucky Millinder with Mills Blue Rhythm Band, Variety 546 (February 11, 1937); Louis Armstrong, Jazz Heritage Society CD-5289147 [aircheck] (May 7, 1937); Gene Krupa, Brunswick 8198 (July 19, 1938).
Note: Some variations between the Millinder, Armstrong, and Krupa versions.

Russian Lullaby
(Irving Berlin)
RNP: Parts (xylophone, trombone 2), Willet AFM 1938.

Sister to You
(unknown)
DEC: Piano leadsheet, Willet AFM 1945, copied by Maceo Jefferson.

Slide, Slide
(Sammy Martin [Lipton] and Chappie Willet)
Copyright deposit: March 3, 1941 [E unp. 249877], registered by Samuel Martin Lipton.

Sonata Pathétique
(Ludwig van Beethoven)
Copyright deposit: "Beethoven's Sonata Pathétique," January 26, 1940 [E unp. 215639], "arr. Jimmie Lunceford," registered by Harold Oxley.
FDCJLO: Parts (conductor, sax 1–4 [sax 2 incomplete], trumpet 1, trumpet 3 [incomplete], trombone 1, trombone 2 [incomplete], piano, bass, drums), Willet AFM 1939.
Recording: Jimmie Lunceford, Columbia 35453 (February 28, 1940).
Note: Lunceford recording issued as "Sonata by L. van Beethoven"; "arr: Willet."

(I Don't) Stand for That Jive
(William Campbell)
DEC: Piano leadsheet ("Billie Hayes"), Willet AFM 1943; score, arranged by Tom Whaley (no stamp).
Note: Score appears to be derived from Willet's leadsheet.

Stardust
(Hoagy Carmichael and Mitchell Parish)
LAHM: Parts (sax 1–5, trumpet 1–4, trombone 1–4 [trombone 2 incomplete], guitar, bass, drums), Willet AFM 1944, copied by Maceo Jefferson.
Recording: Louis Armstrong, Swing Mania CD-682470 [aircheck] (ca. August 1945).
Note: Armstrong aircheck reflects arrangement introduction only.

Struttin' with Some Barbecue

(Lil Hardin)

LAHM: Parts (solo trumpet, sax 1–4, trumpet 1–3, trombone 1–3, bass, drums), solo trumpet part stamped "arr. by—Chappie Willet," remaining parts appear to have been recopied (no stamp).

Recording: Louis Armstrong, Decca 1661 (January 12, 1938), Ambassador CD-1907 [aircheck] (April 15, 1940).

Swingtime in Honolulu

(Duke Ellington, Henry Nemo, and Irving Mills)

DEC: Parts (sax 1, trumpet 1–3, trombone 1, bass 1–2), Willet AFM 1938.

Recording: Duke Ellington, Brunswick 8131 (April 11, 1938).

Note: Parts labeled and filed under "Hawaii"; parts reflect last half of recorded performance only.

Toy-Town Jamboree

(Major Hurwitz, John Redmond, and Mary Shaeffer)

RNP: Parts (xylophone, sax 1–4, trumpet 1–3, trombone 1–2, guitar, piano, bass, drums), Willet AFM 1938.

Unlucky Woman

(Carol Feather and Leonard Feather)

DEC: Piano leadsheet ("Billie Hayes"), Willet AFM 1943; score, arranged by Tom Whaley (no stamp).

Note: Score appears to be derived from Willet's leadsheet.

Washington and Lee Swing

(Thornton Allen, Clarence Robbins, and Mark Sheafe)

RNP: Parts (xylophone, sax 1–4, trumpet 1–3, trombone 1–2, guitar, piano, bass, drums), Willet AFM 1938.

Recording: Louis Armstrong, Jazz Heritage Society CD-5289147 [aircheck] (May 14, 1937).

Note: Some variations between the Armstrong and Norvo versions.

What Is This Thing Called Swing

(Louis Armstrong and Horace Gerlach)

LAHM: Parts (sax 3, trombone 3).

Recording: Louis Armstrong, Decca 2267 (January 18, 1939), NJMH Savory 7 [aircheck] (February 19, 1939), Ambassador CD-1906 [aircheck] (October 6, 1939).

Note: Parts labeled and filed under "This Thing Called Swing."

You Can Count on Me

(Robert Maxwell and Josef Myrow)

Stock arrangement: Exclusive Publications, July 20, 1939 [E pub. 78334], arranged by Chappie Willet.

2. ADDITIONAL SELECTED WILLET ARRANGEMENT ATTRIBUTIONS

After You've Gone
(Henry Creamer and Turner Layton)
Attribution: Bill Chase, NYAN, July 10, 1937.*
Recording: Louis Armstrong, Jazz Heritage Society CD-5289147 [aircheck] (April 30, 1937).

Alexander's Ragtime Band
(Irving Berlin)
Attribution: Dan Morgenstern, liner notes to *Greatest Jazz Recordings of All Time Volume 2* (Franklin Mint Record Society, 1982).
Recording: Louis Armstrong, Decca 1408 (July 7, 1937).

Harlem Stomp
(Buddy Feyne, Irene Higginbotham, and Jay C. Higginbotham)
Attribution: John Wriggle.
Stock arrangement: Lewis Music, 1940 (no arranger cited).
Recording: Louis Armstrong, Ambassador CD-1906 [aircheck] (December 18, 1939), Decca 3092 (March 14, 1940), Ambassador CD-1910 [aircheck] (April 22, 1942).

I Got Rhythm
(George Gershwin and Ira Gershwin)
Attribution: Bill Chase, NYAN, July 10, 1937.*
Recording: Louis Armstrong, Jazz Heritage Society CD-5289147 [aircheck] (May 21, 1937).

I Hope Gabriel Likes My Music
(Dave Franklin)
Attribution: Allan McMillan, CD, February 8, 1936.
Recording: Louis Armstrong, Decca 672 [takes A, B, and C?] (December 19, 1935).

I Know That You Know
(Otto Harbach, Anne O'Dea, and Vincent Youmans)
Attribution: Bill Chase, NYAN, July 10, 1937*; Gene Krupa, liner notes to *Drummin' Man* (Columbia C2L-29, 1963).
Recording: Louis Armstrong, Jazz Heritage Society CD-5289147 [aircheck] (May 21, 1937); Gene Krupa, Brunswick 8124 (April 15, 1938).
Note: Some variations between the Armstrong and Krupa versions.

I'll Be Yours (J'attendrai)
(Dino Oliveri, Louis Poterat, and Anna Sosenko)
Attribution: John Wriggle.
Recording: Cootie Williams, "Let's Go Nightclubbing: Café Zanzibar" www.oldtimeradiodownloads.com [aircheck] (January 21, 1946).

I'm Slappin' Seventh Avenue (with the Sole of My Shoe)
(Duke Ellington, Henry Nemo, and Irving Mills)
Attribution: Brooks Kerr (per conversation with Ray Nance), interview November 8, 2004.
Recording: Duke Ellington, Brunswick 8131 (April 11, 1938).
Note: Surviving DEC orchestra parts stamped by Kaye Parker.

I've Got My Fingers Crossed
(Ted Koehler and Jimmy McHugh)
Attribution: NYAN, March 12, 1936.
Recording: Louis Armstrong, Decca 623 [take A] (November 21, 1935), Meritt LP-19 [take D] (November 21, 1935).

Jubilee
(Stanley Adams and Hoagy Carmichael)
Attribution: Dan Morgenstern, liner notes to Louis Armstrong, *Rare Items 1935–1944* (Decca DL-9225, 1967).
Recording: Louis Armstrong, Alamac LP-2401 [film soundtrack *Every Day's a Holiday*] (ca. 1937), Decca 1635 (January 12, 1938).
Note: Soundtrack recording is a truncated version of the arrangement recorded for Decca, with additional instruments added.

A Lesson in C
(Duke Ellington, Henry Nemo, and Irving Mills)
Attribution: Klaus Stratemann, *Duke Ellington: Day by Day and Film by Film* (Copenhagen: JazzMedia, 2002), 152.
Recording: Cootie Williams, Vocalion 4086 (April 4, 1938).
Note: Stratemann's cited source contains no mention of this title; surviving DEC orchestra parts stamped by Jacinto Chabania (a.k.a. Jerry Blake).

Memories of You
(Eubie Blake and Andy Razaf)
Attribution: Bill Chase, NYAN, July 10, 1937.*
Recording: Louis Armstrong, Jazz Heritage Society CD-5289147 [aircheck] (May 7, 1937).

The Music Goes 'Round and Around
(Edward Farley, William Hodgson, and Mike Riley)
Attribution: Allan McMillan, CD, February 8, 1936.
Recording: Louis Armstrong, Decca 685 (January 18, 1936).

One Alone
(Oscar Hammerstein, Otto Harbach, and Sigmund Romberg)
Attribution: Bill Chase, NYAN, December 17, 1938; performance by Cab Calloway.

Pluckin' the Bass
(Roy Eldridge and Joe Eldridge)
Attribution: Alyn Shipton, *Hi-De-Ho: The Life of Cab Calloway* (New York: Oxford University Press, 2010), 142.
Recording: Cab Calloway, Vocalion 5406 [take 1] (August 30, 1939), Merritt LP-12 [take 2] (August 30, 1939).

Quiet and Roll 'Em
(Ray Biondi, Sam Donahue, Gene Krupa, and [?] Richards)
Attribution: Bruce Klauber, *World of Gene Krupa: That Legendary Drummin' Man* (Ventura, CA: Pathfinder, 1990), 47.
Recording: Gene Krupa, Brunswick 8335 (February 26, 1939).
Note: Sam Donahue is credited as arranger in Gene Krupa, liner notes to *Drummin' Man* (Columbia C2L-29, 1963).

Rustle of Spring
(Christian Sinding)
Attribution: John Wriggle.
Recording: Lucky Millinder, Hindsight LP-233 [transcription] (ca. 1942).

Satchel Mouth Swing
(Louis Armstrong, Lillian Armstrong, and Clarence Williams)
Attribution: Alain Gerber, liner notes to *Louis Armstrong 7: Satchmo's Discoveries 1936–38* (MCA LP-1326, 1980).
Recording: Louis Armstrong, Decca 1636 (January 12, 1938).

Sugar Foot Stomp
(Walter Melrose and Joseph Oliver)
Attribution: Bill Chase, NYAN, July 10, 1937.*
Recording: Louis Armstrong, Jazz Heritage Society CD-5289147 [aircheck] (May 21, 1937), Dr. Jazz CD-oIoI-II [aircheck] (December 11, 1939).

Swing That Music
(Louis Armstrong and Horace Gerlach)
Attribution: Michael Cogswell, *Louis Armstrong: The Offstage Story of Satchmo* (Portland, OR: Collector's Press, 2003), 94.
Recording: Louis Armstrong, Decca 866 (May 18, 1936); Louis Armstrong with Jimmy Dorsey, Decca 3105 (August 7, 1936).

Them There Eyes
(Maceo Pinkard, Doris Tauber, and William Tracey)
Attribution: Bill Chase, NYAN, July 10, 1937.*
Recording: Louis Armstrong, Jazz Heritage Society CD-5289147 [aircheck] (April 9, 1937).

There's a Lull in My Life
(Mack Gordon, Mort Howard, Harry Revel, and Frank Skinner)
Attribution: Allan McMillan, CD, July 10, 1937 (no performer cited).

Tiger Rag
(Harry DeCosta, Edwin Edwards, James LaRocca, Henry Ragas, Anthony Sbarbaro, and Larry Shields)
Attribution: Allan McMillan, CD, January 11, 1936; Bill Chase, NYAN, July 10, 1937.*
Recording: Louis Armstrong, Jazz Heritage Society CD-5289147 [aircheck] (April 9, 1937).

Uptown Rhapsody
(Leon Berry and Teddy Hill)
Attribution: Leonard Feather, liner notes to *The Jazz Arranger, Vol. 1* (Columbia LP-45143, 1989).
Recording: Teddy Hill, Vocalion 3294 (April 1, 1936).

Wolverine Blues
(Jelly Roll Morton, Benjamin Spikes, and John Spikes)
Attribution: Dan Morgenstern, liner notes to *Complete Louis Armstrong Decca Sessions 1935–1946* (Mosaic 243, 2009).
Recording: Louis Armstrong, Decca 3105 (March 14, 1940).

Yesterdays
(Otto Harbach and Jerome Kern)
Attribution: "Lunceford Answers," NYAN, January 16, 1943.
Recording: Jimmie Lunceford, Kings of Jazz LP-20016 [transcription] (ca. 1943).

You've Got Me Voodoo'd
(Louis Armstrong, Cornelius Lawrence, and Luis Russell)
Attribution: John Wriggle.
Recording: Louis Armstrong, Decca 3092 (March 14, 1940).

* In the July 10, 1937, edition of NYAN, Bill Chase attributed "all of the music [arrangements] heard on the recent [Louis Armstrong] *Fleischmann's* program on NBC" to Willet. I believe Chase's claim to be accurate regarding these titles citing this source. Other potential Willet arrangements documented in Armstrong's *Fleischmann's* airchecks and issued on JHS CD-5289147 include: "Bugle Blues," "Chinatown, My Chinatown," "Darling Nellie Gray," "Hustlin' and Bustlin' for Baby," "(I've Got) A Heart Full of Rhythm," "Ida," "The Love Bug Will Bite You," "Pennies from Heaven," "Rockin' Chair," "Shoe Shine Boy," "Sunny Side of the Street," "That's What I Like," and "You Rascal You." Unfortunately, much of Armstrong's big band repertoire—including a number of potential Willet arrangements—is not represented in LAHM manuscript holdings.

3. ADDITIONAL COPYRIGHTS REGISTERED BY WILLET OR DUO MUSIC

Baigian Gal
(Tosh Hammed)
Copyright deposit: January 5, 1945 [E unp. 403606], registered by Duo Music.

Barbados
(Tosh Hammed)
Copyright deposit: January 5, 1945 [E unp. 403604], registered by Duo Music.

Bomgailia Blues
(Tosh Hammed)
Copyright deposit: January 5, 1945 [E unp. 403608], registered by Duo Music.

Bradshaw's Bounce
(Tiny Bradshaw, Dick Boone, and Ben Bart)
Copyright deposit: July 20, 1944 [E unp. 383357], registered by Duo Music.
Recording: Tiny Bradshaw, Regis 1010 (ca. 1944).
Note: Bradshaw recording issued as "Bradshaw Bounce."

Darlin'
(Frances Kraft Reckling and Lucky Millinder)
Copyright deposit: May 27, 1944 [E unp. 377881], registered by Duo Music.
Recording: Lucky Millinder, Decca 18779 (May 25, 1944).
Note: Original copyright September 8, 1942 [E unp. 308207], registered by Frances Kraft Reckling as sole composer, with leadsheet published by Douglas Music, 1943.

Hurry with My Come On
(Al Moss)
Copyright deposit: February 26, 1941 [E unp. 248881], registered by Chappie Willet.

Jamaica
(Tosh Hammed)
Copyright deposit: January 5, 1945 [E unp. 403607], registered by Duo Music.

John Baker
(Tosh Hammed)
Copyright deposit: January 5, 1945 [E unp. 403603], registered by Duo Music.

Mango Stew
(Tosh Hammed)
Copyright deposit: January 5, 1945 [E unp. 403605], registered by Duo Music.

Pealing Thee Mango
(Tosh Hammed)
Copyright deposit: January 5, 1945 [E unp. 403602], registered by Duo Music.

List of Abbreviations

Archival Collections

AMPAS	Academy of Motion Picture Arts and Sciences, Margaret Herrick Library.
ASC	Artie Shaw Collection MSS5, University of Arizona School of Music.
BCC	Benny Carter Collection, Smithsonian National Museum of American History. (Includes the John Kirby Band Book Collection.)
BGP	Benny Goodman Papers MSS53, Irving S. Gilmore Library, Yale University.
CBC	Charlie Barnet Collection of Big Band Arrangements, Library of Congress.
DEC	Duke Ellington Collection, Smithsonian National Museum of American History. (Includes material relating to TWC.)
DRP	Don Redman Papers, Schomberg Center for Research in Black Culture, New York Public Library.
FDCJLO	Frank Driggs Collection of Jimmie Lunceford Orchestrations, Smithsonian National Museum of American History.
FSATC	Frank Schiffman Apollo Theater Collection, Smithsonian National Museum of American History.
GGC	Glen Gray and the Casa Loma Orchestra Collection M31, Northeastern University Libraries.
HFHC	Horace and Fletcher Henderson Music and Photographs Collection, Smithsonian National Museum of American History.
HJC	Harry James Collection, Doheny Library, University of Southern California.
IJS	Institute of Jazz Studies, Rutgers University–Newark.
JOHP	Jazz Oral History Project, Smithsonian Institution of Performing Arts. Transcripts on file at IJS.
JTC	Joe Thomas Collection MS14, Dr. Kenneth J. LaBudde Department of Special Collections, University of Missouri–Kansas City Miller Nichols Library.
LAHM	Louis Armstrong House Museum.
LOC	Library of Congress, Music Division.

MLWC	Mary Lou Williams Collection, IJS.
NJMH	National Jazz Museum of Harlem.
NYPL	New York Public Library, Library for the Performing Arts.
RNP	Red Norvo Papers MSS48, Irving S. Gilmore Library, Yale University.
TWC	Tom Whaley Collection, Smithsonian National Museum of American History.
UNT	University of North Texas Music Library.

Newspapers

ADW	*Atlanta Daily World*
BAA	*Baltimore Afro-American*
CDT	*Chicago Daily Tribune*
CD	*Chicago Defender*
NJG	*New Journal and Guide* [Norfolk]
NYAge	*New York Age*
NYAN	*New York Amsterdam News*
NYPost	*New York Post*
NYSun	*New York Sun*
NYT	*New York Times*
PC	*Pittsburgh Courier*
PT	*Philadelphia Tribune*

(Additional newspaper sources cited by full title.)

Notes

Introduction

1. Tucker, "In Search of Will Vodery," 123, 171.

2. Ibid., 143.

3. For further definitions of *arranger*, see Wriggle, "Arranger."

4. For a Swing Era description of "production-line" arranging work in the music industry, see "The Boys That Make the Noise," *Time*, July 5, 1943, 65.

5. For a critique of the Kirby band's arranging style, see Schuller, *Swing Era*, 814–15.

6. Accounts vary as to the exact dates comprising the Swing Era. This study focuses on the mid-1930s through mid-1940s as the apex of a broader jazz-dance big band era extending from the mid-1920s through the 1950s.

7. See Erenberg, *Swingin' the Dream*; Stowe, *Swing Changes*.

8. For statistics on Goodman's repertoire, see Allen, *Hendersonia*, 319.

9. Although the terms *arranging* and *scoring* are used more or less interchangeably throughout this book, *scoring* is sometimes defined more narrowly as *orchestration*; historical examples of such differentiated credits can be found in the appendix.

10. A definition of *re-composition* versus *arrangement* is offered in Lajoie, *Miles Davis and Gil Evans*, 19–23. See also Sturm, *Changes over Time*, 15.

11. Ake, "Crossing the Street," 251.

12. Stewart, *Making the Scene*, 6.

13. Regarding conceptions of jazz identity in jazz historiography, see Eric Porter, "Incorporation and Distinction," 13–30.

14. DeVeaux, *Birth of Bebop*, 134.

15. Willet's name, occupation, and office address are printed on the bottom of manuscript orchestra parts, including "Blue Skies," held in RNP.

16. For example, acknowledging the racial identity of (black) arranger Andy Gibson illuminates (white) bandleader Charlie Barnet's anecdote relating how prankster friends "scared Andy into thinking they were Ku Klux Klanners" during a tour of the South;

Barnet, *Those Swinging Years*, 101. In period press, *black* denoted African American as well as any nonwhite heritage; thus, arrangers like Margie Gibson—described to be of "Hindu" or "East Indian" descent—were celebrated in the *Baltimore Afro-American* alongside their African American peers. See Nell Dodson, "Margie Gibson BG's New Arranging Find," BAA, January 7, 1941.

17. The description of Willet's music as "advanced" is offered in McCarthy, *Big Band Jazz*, 286. For an example of canonized Redman and Strayhorn, see DeVeaux and Giddins, *Jazz*, 121–22, 220–23.

18. Tom Whaley, interviews by Milt Hinton, 1979–80, JOHP.

19. See Dance's *World of Count Basie*, *World of Duke Ellington*, *World of Earl Hines*, and *World of Swing*.

20. Lees, *Arranging the Score*.

21. Bernhardt with Harris, *I Remember*; Alexander with Fratallone, *From Harlem to Hollywood*.

22. Schuller, *Swing Era*.

23. Wald, "Louis Armstrong Loves Guy Lombardo," 46.

24. Magee, *Uncrowned King of Swing*, 8. Max Harrison, for example, posits audio recordings against cultural and social histories as "our sole reliable witnesses" to the development of 1930s jazz music; Harrison, "Swing Era Big Bands," 277.

25. For example, the absence of musical analysis in some Swing Era cultural studies is noted in DeVeaux, "Review of *Swing Changes: Big-Band Jazz in New Deal America*, by David Stowe," 90.

26. Regarding the controversies of the jazz canon in academia, see Kenneth E. Prouty, "Toward Jazz's 'Official' History: The Debates and Discourses of Jazz History Textbooks," *Journal of Music History Pedagogy* 1, no. 1 (2010): 19–43.

27. Hugues Panassié's 1956 *Guide to Jazz*, perhaps the only reference source to include an entry devoted to Willet, is notable for its prescient claim that "his best arrangements have not been recorded"; Panassié and Gautier, *Guide to Jazz*, 295.

28. Swing Era manuscript scores and orchestra parts typically include rhythm section guitar parts with chord symbol notation (a practice discussed in chapter 4). Period guitar parts—along with the piano and bass parts—often incorporate enharmonic spellings of the corresponding orchestra wind and string parts, and rarely reflect chord extensions above the ninth degree (elevenths, thirteenths, etc.), regardless of the full ensemble voicing content. While these chord symbol spellings are perfectly functional for rhythm section performance, they may or may not reflect the arranger's "theoretical" harmonic conception. In the chord symbols accompanying my own transcriptions of period recordings—where the exact rhythm section guitar and piano voicings are often difficult to ascertain anyway—I generally attempt to reflect the full ensemble voicing. Exceptions are noted as they arise.

29. Bill Chase, "Arrangers Are Real Originators of Swing," *NYAN*, July 10, 1937.

30. Regarding the "false choice" of jazz improvisation versus arrangement, see Decker, *Music Makes Me*, 129–30.

31. For definitions of arrangement as improvisation, see Benson, *Improvisation of Musical Dialogue*, 26–30.

32. Gushee, *Pioneers of Jazz*, 33–38, 165–66.

33. Ibid., 9.

34. Regarding Europe's career and the introduction of "jazz" in New York, see Howland, *Ellington Uptown*, 17–22, 27. See also Badger, *Life in Ragtime*, 53–69.

35. Nelson, *All about Jazz*, 63–70, see also 39–41; Panassié, *Hot Jazz*, 192–220.

36. Nelson, *All about Jazz*, 70, see also 39–41, 63–69.

37. Panassié, *Hot Jazz*, 192.

38. Ibid., 193.

39. For example, see Coker, *Jazz Idiom*, 73–81; Stewart, *African American Music*, 119–32.

40. Simon, *Big Bands*, 44–45.

41. Sudhalter, *Lost Chords*, 601; McCarthy, *Big Band Jazz*, 193. McCarthy's survey features more than 350 pages of writing on swing dance bands, much of which is aimed at establishing (or questioning) the "jazz" credentials of the orchestras under discussion.

42. Townsend, *Pearl Harbor Jazz*, 128.

43. For more on criticism surrounding large-ensemble jazz from the Swing Era to the present, see Stewart, *Making the Scene*, 4–7.

44. Blesh, *Shining Trumpets*, 13.

45. Ibid., 7, 13, 20. See also DeVeaux, "Constructing the Jazz Tradition," 529.

46. Mezzrow and Wolfe, *Really the Blues*, 124–25.

47. Russell, "Bebop," 202. See also DeVeaux, "Constructing the Jazz Tradition," 529.

48. Schuller, "Arrangement," 37–38.

49. See also Townsend, *Pearl Harbor Jazz*, 135–36.

50. Baraka, *Blues People*, 160, 163. For an example of an alternative analysis of black "middle-class values" and the emergence of arranged dance band jazz, see Hennessey, *From Jazz to Swing*, 82–83, 95.

51. Baraka, *Blues People*, 164–65.

52. Ibid., 162. Also regarding Ellington's middle-class background, see Tucker, *Ellington*, 24–25.

53. As one jazz history textbook attempts to explain: "Though big bands went hand in hand with the swing era, big band style did not necessarily mean swing style. There were also jazz-oriented big bands before and after the swing era. Many of these sounded very different from swing bands. Big band style doesn't necessarily mean jazz style, either"; Gridley, *Concise Guide to Jazz*, 94.

54. For example, see the discussion of "jazz" versus "commercial" repertoire in Firestone, *Swing, Swing, Swing*, 129.

55. Harrison, "Swing Era Big Bands," 280.

56. Schuller, *Swing Era*, 202.

57. Ibid., 203–4. For example, Earl Stewart's textbook on African American music describes Whiteman's performances as "generally rigid, rhythmically and harmonically dull, and not oriented towards improvisation"; Stewart, *African American Music*, 120. Schuller's own critique of Whiteman's Swing Era orchestra can be found in Schuller, *Swing Era*, 660–61.

58. Schuller, *Swing Era*, 222.

59. Dance, *World of Count Basie*, 3–4. See also Shih, "Spread of Jazz and the Big Bands," 181–82.

60. Patterns of criticism regarding jazz's relationship with vaudeville, for example, are noted in Harker, "Louis Armstrong, Eccentric Dance, and the Evolution of Jazz," 67–70.

61. DeVeaux, "Constructing the Jazz Tradition," 553.

62. Berish, *Lonesome Roads*; Howland, *Ellington Uptown*; Magee, *Uncrowned King*; Tackley, *Benny Goodman's Famous*; van de Leur, *Something to Live For*.

63. Bindas, *Swing, That Modern Sound*; Burke, *Come In and Hear the Truth*; Decker, *Music Makes Me*; Dinerstein, *Swinging the Machine*; Erenberg, *Swingin' the Dream*; Stowe, *Swing Changes*; Townsend, *Pearl Harbor Jazz*; Tucker, *Swing Shift*; Wilkinson, *Big Band Jazz in Black West Virginia*.

Chapter 1. Business and Politics

1. Spud Murphy, interview by the author, February 12, 2004.

2. Erenberg, *Swingin' the Dream*, 153.

3. "Gala Opening: Harlem on Broadway," Ubangi Club invitation, 1941, *The Eubie Blake Collection*, Maryland Historical Society, accessed January 16, 2005, http://www.mdhs.org/.

4. Stowe, *Swing Changes*, 10.

5. Listings of Swing Era bands represented by these booking agencies are provided in "The Booking of Bands," *Metronome*, October 1945, 18–21.

6. Dance, *World of Swing*, 235, see also 236–39. Norman did not accept the job offered him by Rockwell-O'Keefe, but turned to freelance arranging in 1938.

7. For an overview of radio's importance to Swing Era dance bands, see Stowe, *Swing Changes*, 107–12.

8. Allen, *Hendersonia*, 319.

9. Erenberg, *Swingin' the Dream*, 165.

10. Richard B. Gilbert, "$2,000,000 Theft of Orchestrations," *Metronome*, March 1934, 18, 21; Leo Edwards, "Evolution of Song Plugging," *Metronome*, December 1932, 38.

11. Harold Rubenstein, "Seeing a Song through the Mill," *Metronome*, March 1936, 63.

12. Chappell and Company correspondence to Select Operating Corporation, July 8, 1935, "At Home Abroad," Shubert Archives, New York. The Federal Reserve Bank Consumer Price Index cites a historical conversion rate of approximately seventeen 2015 dollars to one 1935 dollar. This and subsequent historical currency conversion rates are provided per the *Federal Reserve Bank of Minneapolis* website, accessed June 28, 2015, www.minneapolisfed.org.

13. "Music Publishers Ask Strike Parley," NYT, March 31, 1936.

14. "Radio Musicians Win Pay Increase," NYT, March 27, 1936. By comparison, current fee schedules for AFM Locals 802 (New York) and 47 (Los Angeles) still reflect wage scales roughly equivalent to the 1936 rates after historical currency conversion: approximately twenty-five dollars per hour for copyists, and between thirty-three and fifty-eight dollars per hour for orchestrators and proofreaders, depending on the venue

and medium. *Local 802 AFM*, accessed December 26, 2010, http://www.local802afm.org; *Professional Musicians Local 47*, accessed December 26, 2010, http://www.promusic47.org/.

15. "Music Strike Ends; Contract Signed," NYT, May 6, 1936.

16. Ibid.

17. "Increase Your Income by Studying Arranging," advertisement, *Billboard*, April 12, 1941, 7; "Learn Right at Home," advertisement, *Metronome*, December 1932, 37; "Beihoff Music Co.," advertisement, *Down Beat*, February 1937, 12.

18. "Arranging," advertisement, *Metronome*, March 1934, 42.

19. [American Federation of Musicians Local 802], *Directory and Instrumentation*, 1938, 1941, 1947.

20. "Duke Ellington, Inc. pay role [*sic*] for week ending Sept. 23, 1943," held in DEC.

21. Dance, *World of Swing*, 127.

22. Firestone, *Swing, Swing, Swing*, 114. By comparison, Don Redman claimed to have received over $100 per arrangement from Paul Whiteman during the late 1920s—at that time probably one of the highest-paying bandleaders in the business; ibid. Driggs, "Don Redman," 97.

23. Hinton and Berger, *Bass Line*, 88.

24. ASC, Series II (Business Records 1945–55), California Bank checks 1601, 1602 (dated March 23, 1945). The part-copying fee was paid to Jack Collins, though surviving manuscript parts suggest that other copyists did the labor.

25. Qtd. in Jones, *Talking Jazz*, 196.

26. Spud Murphy, interview by the author, February 12, 2004.

27. Alexander with Fratallone, *From Harlem to Hollywood*, 25.

28. Lees, *Arranging the Score*, 169, 225.

29. Spud Murphy, interview by the author, February 12, 2004.

30. DeVeaux, *Birth of Bebop*, 52.

31. Irving Spiegel, "Spotlight Wanted: Paul Baron Laments the Obscurity of the Arrangers Who 'Fix' Tunes for Radio," NYT, June 15, 1941.

32. Ibid.

33. For example, see "Your Arranger This Month [Fred Norman]," *Metronome*, February 1938, 28; "Your Arranger This Month [Joe Lipman]," *Metronome*, August 1938, 19.

34. Barry Ulanov, "Thanks, Mr. Redman, for Modern Style," *Metronome*, June 1941, 20–21, 25.

35. For example, see Leonard Feather, "Men behind the Bands [Jiggs Noble]," *Down Beat*, October 15, 1940, 7; [William Moore Jr.], *Down Beat*, February 15, 1941, 12.

36. Bill Chase, "Arrangers Are Real Originators of Swing," NYAN, July 10, 1937; "Unsung Heroes of Swing," NYAN, April 9, 1938; "Munday's [*sic*] Not Blue," NYAN, November 26, 1938.

37. During the Swing Era, integration in big bands tended to be either well-publicized events or secrets. For example, see *Variety* magazine's notice "Barnet's Negro—Ofay Band for Pk. Central," reprinted in Mather, *Charlie Barnet*, 79. See also "Lionel Stars White Ace on All Dates," PC, March 24, 1945. An account of black trumpeter-vocalist Hot Lips Page's tenure with Artie Shaw is provided in Weeks, *Luck's in My Corner*, 148–53. Stories

of saxophonist Willie Smith's "passing" while in Harry James's orchestra are included in Levinson, *Trumpet Blues*, 155–56.

38. For example, see the space afforded Hammond in the *New York Times* to explain the strategy behind his 1938 *From Spirituals to Swing* presentation of black folk and jazz performers. John Hammond, "From Spirituals to Swing," NYT, December 18, 1938. For contemporary accounts of perceptions of race, booking agencies, and white promoters, see Jack Gould, "News of Night Clubs: Debut of a Band Leads to Some Notes on the Negro Musician in the Cabaret," NYT, July 17, 1938; Leonard Feather, "Retrospect of the Year in Jazz," NYT, December 21, 1941. Black bandleaders' hiring of white arrangers is discussed in Edgar T. Rouzeau, "Stardust: Arrangers Really Make Dance Bands," NJG, August 2, 1941.

39. Regarding Swing Era efforts to equate swing music with "Americanism," see Stowe, *Swing Changes*, 73–80.

40. Phil Moore, "Jim Crow on the Bandstand," reprinted in Porter, *Jazz*, 161–62.

41. For example, it is suggested that Swing Era competition "became so intense that racial 'segregation' among arrangers [and client bandleaders] fell easily" in Berger, Berger, and Patrick, *Benny Carter*, 174.

42. Major Robinson, "Harlem's Music Arrangers Make Broadway's Tops [*sic*] Leaders," CD, February 14, 1941.

43. For example, see the discussion of Fletcher Henderson's career in Trezzvant W. Anderson, "Made Goodman but His Color Stood in His Own Way," BAA, May 16, 1942.

44. Lillian Johnson, "Light and Shadow," BAA, November 4, 1939.

45. "Chappie Willet May Arrange for Krupa's New Band," PC, April 2, 1938.

46. Stowe, *Swing Changes*, 123–24.

47. Ibid., 124.

48. Berish, *Lonesome Roads*, 44.

49. Lucky Millinder, as narrated to Dan Burley, "Negro Bands Are Not Doomed Says Millinder," NYAN, December 21, 1940.

50. Ronald Radano, for example, discusses the "exalted hotness" of African American music that "supplied the creative and economic basis of an emerging urban subculture of black professional musicians"; Radano, "Hot Fantasies," 459.

51. Paul Secon, "On the Stand: Claude Hopkins," *Billboard*, November 11, 1944, 18.

52. "Top Arrangers and Arrangements," *Billboard*, April 12, 1941.

53. To cite just a couple of examples, publisher Leo Feist advertised stock arrangements by white arrangers Spud Murphy, Charlie Hathaway, Red Bone, Carmen Mastren, Dean Kincaide, and Bob Haggart in "Leo Feist, Inc.," advertisement, *Metronome*, June 1938, 36, 37; arrangements by Spud Murphy, Larry Clinton, and Gordon Jenkins were advertised in "Miller Music, Inc.," advertisement, *Metronome*, April 1939, 48.

54. Fees for writing stock arrangements are cited per Archie Bleyer, "Arranging Questions," *Metronome*, May 1933, 38.

55. Willet's inscribed publicity photo is held in LAHM.

56. "Unsung Heroes of Swing," NYAN, April 9, 1938. Other exceptional photo spreads featuring Willet include "Chappie Willet, New Luminary in Field of Composition, Shows How He 'Goes to Town,'" PC, March 26, 1938; Bill Chase, "Ace Arranger Turns to

Recording Field," NYAN, July 22, 1939. The papers also printed individual portraits of Willet and publicity shots presenting him in the company of clients or entertainment celebrities.

57. "Visit the Garden Barber Shop," advertisement, NYAN, August 7, 1937.

58. Mundy, Sauter, and Williams performed with the bands of Earl Hines, Red Norvo, and Andy Kirk, respectively. Contemporary accounts of their careers are provided in "The Man behind the Band: Jimmy Mundy," *Tempo*, on file at IJS; Leonard Feather, "Men behind the Bands [Eddie Sauter]," *Down Beat*, March 1, 1940, 17; Sharon Pease, "Andy Kirk's Pianist also Brilliant Arranger," *Down Beat*, October 1937, 30.

59. Lees, *Arranging the Score*, 224.

60. Ibid., 225.

61. Dance, *World of Count Basie*, 67.

62. See Allen, *Hendersonia*, 371–406.

63. Duning, "What the Band Leader Means to the Arranger," *Billboard*, June 4, 1938, 13; Kay Kyser, "What the Arranger Means to the Orchestra Leader," *Billboard*, June 11, 1938, 13.

64. Duning, "What the Band Leader Means."

65. Kyser, "What the Arranger Means."

66. Sudhalter, *Lost Chords*, 564.

67. Firestone, *Swing, Swing, Swing*, 263.

68. Lees, *Arranging the Score*, 241.

69. Willard, liner notes to *Artie Shaw and His Orchestra 1938 Vol. 2*.

70. Firestone, *Swing, Swing, Swing*, 160.

71. Lees, *Arranging the Score*, 230.

72. Simon, *Glenn Miller*, 151.

73. Willard, liner notes to *Artie Shaw and His Orchestra 1938 Vol. 2*.

74. Magee, *Uncrowned King*, 231.

75. Manuscript orchestra parts for "Superman" are held in BGP.

76. van de Leur, *Something to Live For*, 70.

77. Gray's score for "It's a Long Way to Tipperary" is held in ASC. The cited ensemble passage is at rehearsal G.

78. The trumpet part for "Jump Jump's Here" is held in RNP.

79. Lees, *Arranging the Score*, 228.

80. Manuscript orchestra parts for "Jump Jump's Here" are held in RNP.

81. Note on manuscript score of "Picadilly," arranged by Jimmy Mundy, held in HJC.

82. Cohen, *Duke Ellington's America*, 158.

Chapter 2. Ace Race Arranger

1. Allan McMillan, "Chappie Willette [*sic*] Tells How Songs Are Made Popular," CD, February 8, 1936. This excerpt may reveal some public-relations maneuvering by the reporter or his subject; Armstrong had already recorded "I Hope Gabriel Likes My Music" on December 19, 1935, and the disc was probably released around the time this article was published. See Willems, *All of Me*, 96.

2. This theater is unrelated to the subsequent Loew's Mayfair Theater on West Forty-Seventh Street.

3. "Mayfair Theatre Opens," NYT, February 20, 1926; "Sammy Lee a Producer," NYT, June 13, 1928; "A. F. of A. Gets New Quarters," NYT, May 10, 1934; "To Weigh Theatre Strike," NYT, November 11, 1934; "New Theatre Magazine," advertisement, NYT, April 5, 1936; Louis Calta, "Fonda May Return in 'Mister Roberts,'" NYT, November 1, 1947; Christopher Gray, "Streetscapes," NYT, March 7, 1993; "George Keister," *Cinema Treasures*, accessed October 18, 2015, http://cinematreasures.org/architect/168.

4. "To Convert Old Theatre," NYT, May 29, 1928; "John the Barber Held," NYT, December 28, 1929; "Night Club Notes," NYT, April 17, 1937; "Jimmy Dwyer's Sawdust Trail," advertisement, NYT, May 19, 1937; "Jimmie Dwyer's Sawdust Trail," advertisement, NYT, August 27, 1938; [New York Telephone Company], *Manhattan Telephone Directory*, 1955. Folksinger Woody Guthrie was briefly among the featured performers at Jimmie (or Jimmy) Dwyer's; see Cray, *Ramblin' Man*, 195.

5. "Francis Robert Willet," application for Social Security, form SS-5, November 5, 1939; McMillan, "Chappie Willette."

6. Among other pursuits, Willet was a member of the vaunted Briscoe Athletic Club basketball team during 1928. See "Briscoe Passers Victors in Tilt with St. Cyprian," PT, January 26, 1928; "Chappie Willett" [*sic*], photo caption, PT, February 9, 1928; "Briscoe Takes Peerless into Camp," PT, March 22, 1928. See also "Southwest 'Y' Preparing for Sports Outing," PT, July 11, 1929; "W. Va. Open Tennis Meet July 28–30," BAA, July 23, 1932.

7. Regarding Willet's career with Edwards' Collegians, see Wriggle, "Chappie Willet, Frank Fairfax," 10–13.

8. According to stage entertainer Harold Cromer ("Stumpy" of the stage act Stump & Stumpy), Willet commuted from his hometown of Philadelphia during his early New York career, presumably circa 1934–35. The new midtown offices may have coincided with permanent settlement in New York, although Willet provided various "care of" entities (including the Harlem YMCA) as residence addresses through 1940. Harold Cromer, interview by author, May 7, 2004, New York City; [American Federation of Musicians Local No. 802], *Directory and Instrumentation*, 1939; "Francis Robert Willet," application for Social Security, form SS-5, November 5, 1939.

9. Willet's union membership is cited in Jack Oglesby, "'Ol' Satchmo' Is King, Says Mr. Winchell," CD, February 26, 1938. LAHM manuscript orchestra parts for "In the Still of the Night" reflect Willet's 1937 union stamp.

10. The Willets' son, Robert Fredrick Willet (1943–83), provided the same home address in 1958; Olena Willet remained listed at this location through at least 1974; "Olena Mariella Hunter," application for Social Security, form SS-5, September 28, 1939; "Robert Fredrick Willet," application for Social Security, form SS-5, June 11, 1958; New York voter registration records, 1974. Olena Hunter performed in theater productions, including *Dixie to Broadway* and *Swing It*, and also used the stage name "Olena Williams"; see "Big-Time Stars in N.Y. Project Play," CD, April 18, 1936; "The Play," NYT, July 23, 1937.

11. Regarding Willet's "exclusive services" for Armstrong, see McMillan, "Chappie Willette." Krupa's invitation to Willet was announced in Bill Chase, "All Ears," NYAN, April 9, 1938.

12. "Star Talks over New Song," CD, December 18, 1937; "Chappie Willet, New Luminary in Field of Composition," PC, March 26, 1938.

13. "Broadway Has All-Race Studios for Recording," CD, October 5, 1940; "Plea for Training," NYAN, February 4, 1939.

14. "Chappie Willet's Shoulders Broad Enough to Carry Load of Negro's in Showlife," NYAN, September 14, 1940. The same quote also appeared in "Chappie Willet Has Studio and Agency in Heart of Broadway," PC, September 21, 1940.

15. "Chappie Willet's Shoulders."

16. "Derniece Harris Joins Chappie Willette [*sic*] Staff," NYAN, April 6, 1940; Dan Burley, "Back Door Stuff," NYAN, November 29, 1941; Mary Elizabeth Cronin, "Unchanged Melody—Sharply Tuned Memories Span 65-Year Career of Jazz Pianist," *Seattle Times*, April 18, 1993; Mary Elizabeth Cronin, "Local Jazz Great 'Melody' Jones Is Dead," *Seattle Times*, August 16, 1996.

17. "Apollo," advertisement, NYAN, July 21, 1934; Dan Burley, "Back Door Stuff," NYAN, June 1, 1946.

18. "On Television," NYT, April 3, 1954; "Especially for Children," NYT, July 4, 1954; "Folk Music Program Offers Creative Fare," NYT, July 26, 1954; J. P. Shanley, "A Lesson from Charity," NYT, January 16, 1955; Axtell, "Hello, Ev'rybody, Yes Indeed."

19. "New Goodwill Tavern," advertisement, NYAN, September 28, 1940; "Harlem Defense Center Makes Annual Report," NYAN, February 28, 1942.

20. "Basie at Apollo," NYAN, January 28, 1939.

21. "Chappie Willet Booking Agency Seeks New Talent," NJG, November 9, 1946; "Willett [*sic*] Artists Bureau Newest Newsreel Feature," PC, February 1, 1947; Marguerite Cartwright, "People You Should Know," PC, December 11, 1954; "Requiem: Gerald Cook," *Allegro*, December 2006.

22. "Miss Susie Washington," NYAN, March 7, 1942; Tommy Watkins, "Escapading in Brooklyn," NYAN, November 24, 1945; "Sepia Outfit Makes History on B'way," PC, November 9, 1946. Some of Susie Mildred Washington's lyrics were published in Nelson, *Lyrics for Song Hits*, 442, 502.

23. "Chappie Willet," advertisement, NYAN, February 1, 1941.

24. "Powder Room Hit," *Ebony*, July 1946, 42–44.

25. "A. Russell Wooding Dies in New York City Fire," NJG, March 7, 1959. Wooding's 1891 birth year is provided on a World War I draft registration card, although a World War II draft registration card provides a date of 1892. "Alfred Russell Wooding," reg. number 7665 [June 1917]; "Russell Wooding," U.S. Selective Service Registration Card, D.S.S. form 1 [ca. 1945].

26. Lucien H. White, "Dramatic Music Notes," NYAge, June 22, 1916; "Fifteen Thousand Witness 369th Review," PC, September 19, 1936; "Jive in Barracks," *Time*, March 17, 1941, 52; "Distinguished Harlem Regiment Protects Residents of Hawaii," CD, August 15, 1942; "Russell Wooding," National Archives and Records Administration, NA form 13164, December 3, 2004.

27. Regarding Wooding's Broadway and conducting career, see Peterson, *Profiles*, 312; "Russell Wooding Continues Rise," PC, July 20, 1929; Bill Chase, "Arrangers Are Real Originators of Swing," NYAN, July 10, 1937.

28. "Unsung Heroes of Swing," NYAN, April 9, 1938.

29. "Porter Grainger," U.S. Selective Service Registration Card, D.S.S. form 1 [ca. 1942]; "Entertainment World," NYAN, June 19, 1937.

30. Regarding Grainger's earlier career, see Peterson, *Profiles*, 118, 296; "Rare Negro Songs Given," NYT, January 11, 1932; Alvin Moses, "Footlight Flickers," ADW, February 7, 1939.

31. "Panorama Friday Will Aid Nursery," CD, February 18, 1939.

32. Grainger and Wooding's "369th March" was registered for copyright by Handy Brothers on September 2, 1937 (E pub. 65425).

33. "Network Singer Plans Aid to Young Singers by Scholarship," CD, February 28, 1942. A WWII Selective Service card, citing Heywood's age as forty-five and providing Willet's office address as "place of employment," suggests a Music Clinic relationship extending as late as October 1943; "Donald Gerard Heywood," U.S. Selective Service Registration Card, D.S.S. form 1 [ca. 1943]. Willet also advertised three rooms of office space to rent in January 1943, although it is not clear who was leaving or arriving; "For Rent," advertisement, NYAN, January 23, 1943.

34. Regarding Heywood's earlier career, see Peterson, *Early Black American Playwrights*, 97–99; Buster Vodery, "Donald Heywood Dropped Knife for Baton," NYAN, November 19, 1938.

35. "'Harlem Moon' Prevue Shows Stars at Best," NYAN, May 27, 1939; "LeGon and Fletcher in Revue," NYAN, July 8, 1939; "Roosevelt Theatre," advertisement, PC, April 12, 1941; Dan Burley, "Heywood vs. Strauss in the 'Chocolate Soldier,'" NYAN, July 11, 1942.

36. "Heywood's Pet Musical Finally Hits Broadway," CD, May 4, 1940.

37. Goode, "Thomas Le Roy Whaley."

38. Examples of additional TWC/DEC artifacts reflecting Music Clinic ties include a leadsheet of "Moanin' Low" stamped by Russell Wooding (1940) and a leadsheet of Porter Grainger's "Sepia Sorrow Song (A Negro Lament)" in Grainger's hand. In his JOHP interview, Whaley cited work with Grainger and Heywood, apparently at the Apollo or its basement nightclub; Whaley, interview, reel 2, transcript p. 52.

39. For example, Willet and Billy Moore Jr. reportedly hosted a meeting of the "Jeffersonian Cultural League," convened "for the purpose of improving the Harlem press"; Layle Lane, "Land of the Noble Free," NYAge, November 25, 1944.

40. Bill Chase, "All Ears," NYAN, November 12, 1938.

41. Bill Chase, "Ace Arranger Turns to Recording Field," NYAN, July 22, 1939, 17.

42. Ibid.

43. Ibid. For example, Willet airchecks of the Andy Kirk orchestra at the Cotton Club are held in MLWC; airchecks of the Roy Eldridge and Cab Calloway orchestras were held in the collection of Roy Eldridge.

44. Chase, "Ace Arranger Turns."

45. Dan Burley, "Back Door Stuff," NYAN, May 24, 1941, and July 19, 1941; "Willet Is Host," NYAN, August 16, 1941. Chase's attendance at the July 1941 event is specifically cited; Burley's attendance at a party for Cab Calloway's band is surmised from Burley's description of the event as "roacheous." For a jive translation of *roach*, see Burley, *Dan Burley's Original Handbook of Harlem Jive*, 146.

46. "Handy Gives Congratulations," PC, September 21, 1940.

47. "Chappie Willet's Shoulders."

48. "Wax Letters Latest Fad for Soldiers," NYAN, March 7, 1942.

49. "Network Singer Plans Aid."

50. The "Enterprizes" with a *z* designation appears in a series of advertisements printed in NYAN from November 23, 1946, through May 31, 1947.

51. Alvin Moses, "Alvin Moses Says," CD, March 28, 1942; Billy Jones, "Star Twinkles," CD, June 20, 1942; Major Robinson, "Through Harlem," CD, July 11, 1942. Regarding Willet's association with Carrie Belle Powell (no relation to Adam Clayton Powell Jr.'s wife, Isabel "Belle" Washington Powell, also a stage performer), see Allan McMillan, "Hi-Hattin' in Harlem," CD, November 27, 1937; January 8, 1938; "Star Talks over New Song," CD, December 18, 1937; "Singing Find," PC, January 8, 1938; "'Oh, Willie' New Fan Cry," CD, May 14, 1938; Rollo S. Vest, "Detroit Topics," CD, October 24, 1942; "Swingin' the Dream," *Internet Broadway Database*, accessed October 18, 2015, http://www.ibdb.com/Production/View/13212. Regarding the Bye Sisters, see "New Singing Sensations," NYAN, September 20, 1941; "They're Small's Paradise Stars," NYAN, January 10, 1942; "Cootie Williams, Bye Sisters at Apollo," NYAN, November 27, 1943.

52. "Donald Heywood's Musical, 'Tropicana,' at the Apollo," NYAN, March 1, 1941; Maurice Dancer, "Tan Manhattan," CD, December 20, 1941.

53. Al Moses, "Alvin Moses Says," CD, January 3, 1941.

54. "Chappie Willet Named Manager of New Rochelle 'Indigo Room,'" PT, December 27, 1941.

55. "Chappie Willet Takes Over Spot in Westchester for New Talent," NYAN, December 6, 1941.

56. "Indigo Room," advertisement, CD, December 27, 1941.

57. "Willet Restores New Rochelle Nitelife," NYAN, December 20, 1941; Maurice Dancer, "Tan Manhattan," CD, December 27, 1941.

58. "Armstrong Triumphs at the Apollo Theatre," NYAN, September 7, 1935; *The Duke Is Tops* (Million Dollar, 1938), reissued on Classic Musicals DVD (Mill Creek Entertainment, 2005).

59. "22 New Shorts for Soundies Completed," NYAN, August 21, 1943. See also "Ollie Mae Morris," NYAN, December 21, 1946.

60. Inez Washingon recorded "Soldier Man Blues" and "That Ain't Right," backed by the Four Kings of Rhythm; see Lord, *Jazz Discography*, W204.

61. Howard Taubman, "Records: New Contract," NYT, May 30, 1943; Billy Rowe, "Sepia Talent Flourishing on Broadway and in Harlem," PC, July 10, 1943; "Latest Find," CD, July 17, 1943. The Willet-affiliated Billie Hayes is no relation to the 1950s television actress of the same name.

62. The presence of Grainger on piano—under the pseudonym "Peter Pan"—is suggested by Joe Davis biographer Bruce Bastin; two of the recorded compositions are credited to "Leslie Beacon," a pseudonym for Davis. Bastin, *Never Sell a Copyright*, 99, 108. See also Dixon, Godrich, and Rye, *Blues and Gospel Records*, 366.

63. Willet's piano leadsheet arrangements designated for Hayes—"Know How to Do It," "Stand for That Jive," and "Unlucky Woman"—are held in DEC.

64. Gary Lambert "Pete" Nugent toured with Count Basie in 1947; he was also featured in the 1943 Irving Berlin musical, *This Is the Army*. See Atkins and Malone, *Class Act*, 78–80; Stearns and Stearns, *Jazz Dance*, 298. For a description of a Calloway revue including the Miller Brothers & Lois, see Don Marshall, "Vaudeville Reviews: Strand, New York," *Billboard*, April 12, 1947, 42.

65. For an example of personnel changes in Harold Norton's act, see Al Monroe, "Swingin' the News," CD, February 14, 1942. One of Norton's longest-running partnerships was with Margot Webb, whose career is examined in Dixon Gottschild, *Waltzing in the Dark*.

66. "Back on Broadway," CD, December 7, 1946; "Talented Beauty," CD, January 25, 1947; Billy Rowe, "Billy . . . Rowe's Notebook," PC, April 19, 1947.

67. "Vulcan Bowl Classic in All American News," NJG, January 18, 1947.

68. "Willett [*sic*] Artists Bureau Newest Newsreel Feature," PC, February 1, 1947. The *Courier* article describes Willet's staff as including "Berniece" [*sic*—Derniece] Harris, who was serving overseas during 1945 and 1946 (see "'Jive' Units Back from USO Tours," CD, March 23, 1946), but was apparently back in New York in October 1946 (per "USAT Zebulon B. Vance," Passenger List, October 12, 1946); the references to Willet's short-lived Duo Music and Text Music publishing companies might suggest an earlier production date altogether, circa 1944. Regardless of the film's date of creation, the 1947 notice probably indicated the newsreel's first appearance in theaters; it is difficult to imagine Willet not inserting some notice of it in his publicity had it been released earlier. Although some All-American Newsreel films circa 1944 to 1946 survive at the Schomberg Center for Research in Black Culture, a copy of the Willet segment has yet to be found.

69. "Willett [*sic*] Heads Music Firm," CD, July 29, 1944; Charley Cherokee, "National Grapevine," CD, November 25, 1944.

70. Frances Kraft Reckling, "Darlin'," publisher leadsheet (New York: Douglas Publishing, 1943).

71. Blackie Warren, Lucky Millinder, and Art Franklin, "A Rainy Sunday," publisher leadsheet (New York: Duo Music Publishing, 1944).

72. "Willett [*sic*] Heads Music Firm"; "Songwriter Congratulates Peters Sisters for Harmonizing His Tune," NYAge, October 21, 1944. The photo includes a caption stating that "the tune is *also* [emphasis added] published by a concern of which Mr. Willet is president"—wording that further intimates Willet as the songwriter in question. "Warren" is credited for both words and music.

73. "'Rainy Sunday' New Hit Tune," CD, September 30, 1944.

74. "U.S. Orders 250,000 Records of 'A Rainy Sunday' for Overseas," NYAN, September 30, 1944. See also "'Rainy Sunday' New Hit Tune."

75. Russell and Richardson's performance of "A Rainy Sunday" was recorded on October 19, 1946, and issued on Apollo 1139; see Lord, *Jazz Discography*, R763. It is possible that the disc itself was not marketed until some time later; see "Lee Richardson Triumphs Again," CD, November 20, 1948.

76. *Hi-De-Ho*, Classic Musicals DVD (Mill Creek Entertainment, 2005).

77. V. C. Bevenue, "Milwaukee, Wisc.," CD, October 23, 1944.

78. Langston Hughes and Chappie Willet, "'Let My People Go'—Now!," publisher leadsheet (New York: Text Music Publishing, 1944).

79. Regarding the work of Langston Hughes and civil rights political movements in Swing Era New York, see Bakan, "Jazz and the 'Popular Front,'" 35–56.

80. A later (1955) alternative set of lyrics—with some verses reordered and others rewritten—has been published in Hughes, *Collected Works of Langston Hughes*, 633–35.

81. Ted Yates, "New York Show Whirl," BAA, June 30, 1945; Al Monroe, "Swinging the News," CD, May 26, 1945. Williams's performances are documented on aircheck recordings held in MLWC.

82. Andy Razaf and Chappie Willet, "Japan: An American Battle Song," copyright deposit, October 19, 1944 (E unpub. 394505), U.S. Library of Congress.

83. The committee's efforts reportedly culminated in a recording and radio broadcast program in November 1944; "Songs by Razaf, Johnson to Open War Loan Drive," BAA, November 18, 1944. See also Singer, *Black and Blue*, 313–14.

84. Chase, "Arrangers Are Real Originators."

85. "(Way Over There by the) Cherry Tree" was recorded by Johnny Moore's Three Blazers, featuring vocalist Charles Brown; the copyright registration credits words by Toombs and Willet, and music by Demetrius and Willet, though only Toombs's name appeared on the issued disc (Exclusive 704). Vinson's crediting of Willet is cited per Eddie Vinson, interview, Jazz FM91 Toronto, March 17, 1981, accessed October 27, 2013, http://www.canadianjazzarchive.org/en/interviews.

Chapter 3. Harlem on Broadway

1. Robert Dana, "Tips on Tables," *New York World Telegram and Sun*, October 15, 1945.

2. "Big New York Clubs Struggle, Hope to Stick Thru Summer," *Billboard*, June 11, 1938, 16. Tax fraud was commonly cited in connection with nightclubs; for example, see "Tax Frauds Laid to 9 Nightclubs," NYT, December 24, 1940. Historical currency conversions are calculated per rates cited by the *Federal Reserve Bank of Minneapolis* website, accessed June 28, 2015, www.minneapolisfed.org.

3. Dana, "Tips on Tables"; Bernhardt with Harris, *I Remember*, 169.

4. Dance, *World of Duke Ellington*, 48. In his interview with Stanley Dance, Whaley cited the Hurricane Club as the venue providing him $400 per week, but identified his employer as Joe Howard; Howard ran the Café Zanzibar, which moved into the Hurricane site in 1944. Duke Ellington, whom Whaley's testimony centers on, performed at both establishments.

5. The chorus-line wages are those cited for Leon & Eddie's nightclub as negotiated by the American Guild of Variety Artists; see "Entertainers Get Rise," NYT, April 2, 1943.

6. Louis Armstrong, correspondence to Don Redman, January 2, 1945, DRP.

7. "Duke Ellington, Inc. pay role [*sic*] for week ending Sept. 23, 1943"; "Receipts, Hurricane Restaurant," DEC.

8. For example, 1938 touring performances by Benny Goodman in Pittsburgh and Gene Krupa in Virginia Beach reportedly grossed $1,800 and $1,490, respectively, with

the latter cited by *Billboard* as a "heavy money-maker for all concerned." "6,000 Gaze at Goodman but Only 2,000 Dancing," *Billboard*, September 3, 1938, 13; "Krupa's 15C Plenty Gravy," *Billboard*, September 3, 1938, 13.

9. "Calloway's 10 Grand," *Billboard*, November 2, 1935, 15; "New Mark Set by Calloway at Paramount," PC, September 7, 1940.

10. Stearns and Stearns, *Jazz Dance*, 299.

11. Dixon-Stowell, "Between Two Eras," 14.

12. Ibid.

13. Ibid., 16.

14. Robert Russell Bennett, "Orchestrating for Broadway," in Bennett, *Broadway Sound*, 281.

15. Simon, liner notes to *Gene Krupa: Drummin' Man*. This Krupa quote previously appeared in truncated form in Simon's liner notes to *Gene Krupa's Sidekicks* (Columbia CL-641, 1955). See also Klauber, *World of Gene Krupa*, 46.

16. Leonard Reed, interview by Fred Strickler, (ca. 1997), transcript p. 71, Oral History Project, Dance Collection, New York Public Library; see also Howland, *Ellington Uptown*, 118.

17. Reed, interview by Strickler, transcript pp. 37–38.

18. "Cotton Club Presents," programs, March 1937 and March 1938, reprinted in Strateman, *Duke Ellington*, 694–97; Reed, interview by Strickler, transcript p. 71; see also Howland, *Ellington Uptown*, 118.

19. "Joe Howard Presents the International Laugh-Lease Revue," Café Zanzibar program ca. December 1945–February 1946. Portions of this program, including the Ink Spots performance of "I'd Climb the Highest Mountain," are included in a *March of Time* newsreel "Night Club Boom" (vol. 12, episode 8), distributed ca. March 1946; *YouTube*, accessed October 18, 2015, https://www.youtube.com/watch?v=B_fG2DEFa_o. Outtakes for this newsreel include additional footage of the Zanzibar's floor-show program; *YouTube*, accessed October 18, 2015, https://www.youtube.com/watch?v=XCooy5BXMgQ.

20. Heywood's "Halloween" material is held in DEC.

21. Precedents for the "Mysterioso" theme include the popular silent-film accompaniment publication by Zamecnik, *Sam Fox Moving Picture Music*, 16.

22. Watkins, "That Vaudeville Style."

23. Howland, *Ellington Uptown*, 117.

24. *The Duke Is Tops*, Classic Musicals DVD (Mill Creek Entertainment, 2005). Other relevant Swing Era film musicals include *Swing Hostess* (PRC, 1944), *Trocadero* (Republic, 1944), and *Killer Diller* (All-American, 1948), available in the same collection. A cultural analysis of *The Duke Is Tops* is offered in Knight, *Disintegrating the Musical*, 169–94.

25. Stearns and Stearns, *Jazz Dance*, 51, 147.

26. The arranger of "Harmony Is Harlem" is unknown; Lena Horne's musical director Phil Moore is the only arranger listed in the film's credits.

27. Dance, *World of Duke Ellington*, 48.

28. While some of Whaley's surviving production scores in DEC include informative titles like "Opening Zanzibar November 24 '43," others are unlabeled or simply indicate "Opening" or "Finale." Most of the scores reflect a stock big band instrumentation.

29. Green and Laurie, *Show Biz*, 442. Despite their association with Harlem entertainment, the Kit Kat and Harlem Uproar House were located in midtown; the Black Cat was in Greenwich Village. See also "8 More N.Y. Spots Open," *Billboard*, November 2, 1935, 11.

30. Herbert H. Nichols, "The Jazz Life," NYAge, August 9, 1941.

31. "Youth Creates for Armstrong," NYAN, March 12, 1936.

32. "Apollo," advertisement, NYAN, December 1, 1934, and December 29, 1934.

33. Dance, *World of Duke Ellington*, 48–49.

34. The Apollo Theater payments are cited from financial records held in folders 2–3, box 4, FSATC.

35. For example, see the program lineups listed in "Apollo," advertisement, NYAN, March 14, 1936; "Basie's Band, Billie Holiday on Apollo Bill," NYAN, November 6, 1937; "Waller at Apollo in Hot Show," NYAN, July 8, 1939; "Lunceford and Peters Sisters Apollo Stars," PC, November 16, 1940; "Donald Heywood's Musical, 'Tropicana,' at the Apollo," NYAN, March 1, 1941. Regarding the Apollo's weekly program policy, see bandleader Andy Kirk's testimony in Malone, *Steppin' on the Blues*, 99.

36. Harold Cromer, interview by author, May 7, 2004, New York City.

37. Both Whaley scores are held in DEC.

38. Grainger's "Miss High Brow" material is held in DEC. Cooper and Markham appeared together regularly at the Apollo and on tour; see "Apollo," advertisement, NYAN, October 26, 1935; "Over 1500 Fans Hear Jam 'Sesh,'" NYAN, June 22, 1940; Dan Burley, "Back Door Stuff," NYAN, August 24, 1940; "Apollo," advertisement, NYAN, September 20, 1940; "Elks' Rendezvous," advertisement, NYAN, September 16, 1944.

39. Heywood's "Pigmeat" music is held in DEC.

40. "Lunceford Answers Host of Queries on Arrangers of Music," NYAN, January 16, 1943; "Earl Hines, after Losing Men to Army, Forms Sensational Mixed Band," NYAN, September 11, 1943. Orchestra parts for "East of the Sun," dated 1942 and 1943, reside in FDCJLO.

41. "Millinder to Open with 'Panorama of Jazz,'" BAA, June 24, 1944.

42. Stearns and Stearns, *Jazz Dance*, 299.

43. For examples of Leonard Harper credits, see "Claude Hopkins on Stage Again," NYAN, March 12, 1936; "Basie's Band, Billie Holiday on Apollo Bill," NYAN, November 6, 1937; "Waller at Apollo in Hot Show," NYAN, July 8, 1939; "Leonard Harper's Death Recalls His Place in Showlife," NYAN, February 13, 1943.

44. For example, see "Russell Band Heads Apollo Theatre Revue," NYAN, June 15, 1935; "Duke Ellington to Top Apollo Theatre Show," NYAN, October 5, 1935. Regarding the career of Clarence Robinson, see Billy Rowe, "Clarence Robinson Dead at 79," NYAN, September 8, 1979.

45. Stearns and Stearns, *Jazz Dance*, 299.

46. Atkins and Malone, *Class Act*, 80.

47. Leonard Reed, telephone interview by author, December 2, 2002.

48. "Louis Jordan Next in Apollo," NYAN, April 19, 1958; "Apollo," advertisement, NYAN, December 13, 1958.

49. "Night Club Notes," NYT, April 13, 1935; "Connie's Inn Opens on Broadway with Hot Show," CD, November 9, 1935.

50. "Chocolates Cast Opens for Easter," CD, April 20, 1935. See also Allan McMillan, "Broadway Sees and Likes 'Hot Chocolates' Show," CD, May 4, 1935.

51. "Youth Creates for Armstrong."

52. Love [Jackson], "Black and Tan Clubs," 122.

53. "Places to Dine: Connie's," advertisement, NYT, January 1, 1936.

54. A brief history of the *Connie's Hot Chocolates* touring productions is provided in Morgenstern, "Hot Chocolates," 605–16. Regarding Powell, see "Three Melody Girls of Connie's," CD, January 23, 1937.

55. The last mention of a Connie's Inn production in the NYT "News of Stage" column was on June 25, 1936.

56. "Night Club Notes," NYT, July 4, 1936, and September 26, 1936.

57. A May 1940 Cotton Club production opening that marked "the second time in its entertainment history that the sepian emporium has been open for the Summer" appeared in "News of Night Clubs," NYT, May 12, 1940.

58. See Isadora Smith, "Cab Calloway, Nicholas Brothers Reach Peak in the Cotton Club's Latest Broadway Offering," PC, October 22, 1938; Reed, telephone interview by author; Jack Gould, "Night Club Notes," NYT, March 13, 1938; "Cotton Club Parade: World's Fair Edition," spring 1939 program, reprinted in Haskins, *Cotton Club*, 150; "Cotton Club Closes," NYAN, June 22, 1940.

59. Bill Chase, "Arrangers Are Real Originators of Swing," NYAN, July 10, 1937.

60. Reed, telephone interview by author.

61. Quentin Jackson, interview by Milt Hinton, June 1976, tape 3, transcript p. 38, JOHP.

62. Hill, *Brotherhood in Rhythm*, 139–40. The rehearsal is described by Hill to have taken place "with Willett [*sic*] in his Harlem studio"—the only suggestion I have ever found of Willet maintaining a working studio in Harlem (unless Nicholas meant Willet's apartment, which appears to have been obtained only after the Cotton Club folded). The Broadway Music Clinic, four blocks from the Cotton Club, seems a more likely location.

63. "Night Club Notes," NYT, March 20, 1937; "Cotton Club," spring 1937 program, reprinted in Bergmeier and Lotz, liner notes to *Live from the Cotton Club*, 93.

64. "Plea for Training," NYAN, February 4, 1939.

65. M. H. Orodenker, "Orchestra Notes," *Billboard*, March 26,1938, 12.

66. "Cotton Club Show Primed for Opening," NYAN, March 5, 1938. Willet's orchestra parts for "Swingtime in Honolulu" are held in DEC (filed under "Hawaii"). Brooks Kerr (in a telephone interview by author, November 8, 2004) suggests "I'm Slappin' Seventh Avenue" as another Willet arrangement from this production, per testimony from trumpeter Ray Nance, who claimed to have occasionally substituted with the Ellington orchestra during this period. However, the only surviving manuscript music for this number discovered to date identifies arranger Kaye Parker.

67. Isadora Smith, "Cab Calloway, Nicholas Brothers Reach Peak in the Cotton Club's Latest Broadway Offering," PC, October 22, 1938.

68. "Places to Dine: Harlem Uproar House," advertisement, NYT, September 22, 1937; Smith, "Cab Calloway, Nicholas Brothers Reach Peak"; "Cotton Club," spring 1937 program, reprinted in Bergmeier and Lotz, liner notes to *Live from the Cotton Club*, 93; "Cotton Club Parade," spring 1939 program, reprinted in Haskins, *Cotton Club*, 150.

69. Radio aircheck recordings of these titles have been issued on *Louis Armstrong Vol. 7* (Ambassador CD-1907, 1995), and Duke Ellington, *Cotton Club 1938 Vol. 2* (Jazz Archives LP-13, 1973).

70. "Chappie Willet Has Agency and Studio in Heart of Broadway," PC, September 21, 1940.

71. "No Cotton Club?," CD, June 15, 1940; "Cotton Club Closes," NYAN, June 22, 1940.

72. Regarding nightclub bookkeeping practices, it is probably no coincidence that Willet reported his occupation to the government in 1939 as "unemployed"; "Francis Robert Willet," application for Social Security, form SS-5, November 5, 1939.

73. "Elks Rendezvous," advertisement, NYAN, November 20, 1937; Charles T. Magill, "In the Fraternal World," NYAN, July 12, 1933. Advertisements in early 1940 cite the Elks' Rendezvous as "remodeled and enlarged"; see "Elks Rendezvous," advertisement, NYAN, March 9, 1940.

74. "Hello and Goodbye," CD, October 11, 1941; Dan Burley, "Back Door Stuff," NYAN, November 29, 1941; "Llewellyn Crawford," NYAN, April 17, 1943; "Elk's Rendezvous," advertisement, NYAN, May 27, 1944.

75. Stan Stanley, "For Here the Blues Must 'Jump,'" NYAN, September 23, 1944. Another Grainger leadsheet, "Sexegenarian," appears to be related to the "One Hour Mama" project.

76. Dan Burley, "Elks Rendezvous Show Stars Ralph Cooper," NYAN, March 7, 1942; "Elk's Rendezvous," advertisement, NYAN, May 27, 1944.

77. Alvin Webb, "Footlights and Sidelights," NYAN, January 23, 1954; [New York Telephone Company], *Manhattan Telephone Directory*, 1955; George Palmer, "Tavern Topics," NYAN, July 6, 1957.

78. "Night Club Notes," NYT, October 26, 1935; "Auction Sales," NYT, September 11, 1942; Louis Calta, "News of Night Clubs," NYT, November 8, 1942.

79. Cromer, interview by author; "Chappie Willet, New Luminary in Field of Composition," PC, March 26, 1938.

80. Panassié, *Cinq Mois à New York*, 76; Panassié and Gautier, *Guide to Jazz*, 295. See also "'Old Gray Bonnet' at the Kit Kat," BAA, November 5, 1938.

81. Daniel Richman, "Night Club Reviews: Kit Kat Club, New York," *Billboard*, November 5, 1938, 21.

82. Louis Calta, "News of Night Clubs," NYT, April 4, 1943.

83. See "Actual Ownership of Nightclubs Is Goal of Investigation by City," NYT, September 8, 1944; "Jules Podell, Showman, Dead; Owned Copacabana since '40," NYT, September 28, 1973.

84. Romeo L. Dougherty, "Things Theatrical," NYAN, September 7, 1935; "Duke Ellington Here; Tops Loew's Stage Bill," NYAN, October 26, 1935; "Stage . . . Screen . . . Radio," NYAN, March 27, 1937; Allan McMillan, "High-Hattin' in Harlem," NYAN, July 10, 1937; Lou Layne, "Moon over Harlem," NYAN, March 12, 1938; Vail, *Swing Era Scrapbook*, 238.

85. McMillan, "High-Hattin' in Harlem"; Vail, *Swing Era Scrapbook*, 238. Cab Calloway is also reported to have performed an arrangement of "There's a Lull in My Life" in an August 1937 radio broadcast; Vail, *Swing Era Scrapbook*, 233.

86. Bill Chase, "All Ears," NYAN, December 17, 1938. In addition to Gene Krupa's testimony cited earlier, Chick Webb was cited as a Willet client in "Chappie Willet, New Luminary."

87. For example, see "News of the Stage," NYT, January 9, 1937; "Fats Waller at Loew's State," NYT, April 30, 1943.

88. Paul Ross, "Vaudeville Reviews: State, New York," *Billboard*, February 5, 1944, 26; John Sippel, "Vaudeville Reviews: Chicago, Chicago," *Billboard*, February 24, 1945, 35. The Three Hearts included dancer Beverly Becker; see Ray Lynch, "Beverly Puckett, Dancer, Toured with Big Bands," *Fort Lauderdale Sun-Sentinel*, March 20, 1990.

89. Dan Burley, "Back Door Stuff," NYAN, March 19, 1938.

90. "Bill's Busiest Day Closes at Breakfast at Mimo Club," NYAN, June 3, 1939.

91. "Mimo Show Friday," NYAN, January 25, 1941; "Apollo," advertisement, NYAN, June 21, 1941; Maurice Dancer, "Harlem Goes Broadway for Reopening of Mimo Club," CD, September 27, 1941. It is not clear if Nugent and Norton were part of the spring 1941 revue prior to its theater tour.

92. Grainger's "Slaves de Orient" script is held in DEC.

93. "Harlem's Famed Club Mimo . . .," NYAN, January 31, 1942. Grainger's "When You're at Murrain's" leadsheet is held in DEC.

94. "Dine and Dance: Murrain's," advertisement, NYAN, April 18, 1942; "Sandra, Lakeeta Starred in New Harlem Cabaret," CD, May 30, 1942; Cleon Wilson, "Through Harlem," CD, June 13, 1942.

95. Dan Burley, "Newest Murrain Revue Sensational," NYAN, February 27, 1943; "New Revue at Murrain's," NYAN, April 17, 1943.

96. A. B. Spellman, "Herbie Nichols," *Jazz*, October 1964, 12. The Dennis band is advertised as performing at Murrain's in the "Where to Wine and Dine" section of the NYAN from October 23, 1943, through March 18, 1944.

97. Burley, "Elks Rendezvous Show"; "Currently Starring at Murrain's Cabaret Opening," NYAN, July 12, 1947; "Where to Wine and Dine: Murrain's," advertisement, NYAN, July 12, 1947.

98. See "Murrain's," advertisement, NYAN, May 28, 1949. This advertisement lists both the Harlem and Bronx locations.

99. "More Swing," *Wall Street Journal*, June 17, 1938; "Paramount," advertisement, NYT, July 1, 1939.

100. "Cab Calloway's Tour Takes Him into the West," CD, September 14, 1940.

101. "Willet Is Host," NYAN, August 16, 1941.

102. "Night Club Notes," NYT, May 30, 1936.

103. "Night Club Notes," NYT, May 30, 1936, and May 8, 1937.

104. "Depict Takeoff of 'Well of Loneliness,'" PC, April 10, 1937; Dan Burley, "'One More Dip Will Get It' Hit Song of New Revue at Plantation Club," NYAN, May 13, 1939; Dan Burley, "Cubans, Chorines, Singers Pace Plantation Revue," NYAN, May 13, 1939.

105. Dan Burley, "Barrington Guy, Valda Top Plantation Revue: Called Hottest Show in Town," NYAN, November 5, 1938; "It's Girls . . . Girls . . . Girls as Harlem's Plantation Opens with Snappy Revue," PC, November 12, 1938.

106. Earl J. Morris, "Pete Nugent New Headliner at the Club Plantation," PC, March 12, 1938.

107. "Chappie Willet, New Luminary"; "Cotton Club Show Primed for Opening," NYAN, March 5, 1938.

108. Dan Burley, "Back Door Stuff," NYAN, August 12, 1939.

109. "Smart Show at Small's Club," NYAN, October 24, 1936; "It's 'Scronching' [*sic*] Now at Small's: Novel Dance Is Featured at Paradise," NYAN, April 10, 1937; "Small's Paradise," advertisement, NYAN, December 11, 1943.

110. Dan Burley, "Small's Paradise Features Edna Mae Holly, Ray Sneed," NYAN, February 14, 1942; "Dine and Dance: The New Small's Paradise," advertisement, NYAN, April 11, 1942; "Star Twinkles," CD, April 18, 1942; "Small's Paradise Stage Set for 25th Year Celebration," NYAN, November 25, 1950. The "new Small's" probably refers to the club's renovations, announced in late 1941, per "Building Plans Files," NYT, November 1, 1941.

111. "Smart Show at Small's Club"; "Say Harlem Is Home of Dance Craze, 'Susie-Q,'" CD, December 12, 1936; "Where to Dine and Dance: Small's Paradise," advertisement, NYAN, December 11, 1943.

112. "It's 'Scronching' [*sic*] Now at Small's."

113. "Places to Go: The New Small's Paradise" [advertisement], NYAN, November 7, 1942.

114. "Say Harlem Is Home of Dance Craze, 'Susie-Q'"; "It's 'Scronching' [*sic*] Now at Small's."

115. Gould, "Night Club Notes." Notated music or recordings representing Grainger's "Bowling Green Skronch" remain elusive as of this writing.

116. The "Small's"-labeled material is held in TWC. The stock arrangement of "Zigeuner" appears to be the 1929 Chappell Music publication scored by Walter Paul. Noel Coward, "Zigeuner" [stock arrangement], arranged by Walter Paul (New York: Chappell, 1929).

117. Maurice Dancer, "Tan Manhattan," CD, December 20, 1941; "Cab Celebrates," NYAN, July 19, 1941; Dan Burley, "Back Door Stuff," NYAN, July 19, 1941, and June 12, 1943.

118. Don Marshall, "Vaudeville Reviews: Strand, New York," *Billboard*, April 12, 1947, 42.

119. Roi Ottley, "This Hectic Harlem," NYAN, April 21, 1934.

120. "Pearl Baines Has New Song Hit for Show," CD, November 2, 1935; "Chappie Willet, New Luminary"; "Ubangi Club," advertisement, NYT, January 29, 1935; "Before and after Theatre: Ubangi Club," advertisement, NYT, March 7, 1936; "Night Club Notes," NYT, May 8, 1937.

121. "Armstrong Triumphs at the Apollo Theatre," NYAN, September 7, 1935.

122. Billy Rowe, "Billy Rowe Goes into a Rave over New Musical at the Ubangi Club," PC, April 30, 1937; "Gala Opening: Harlem on Broadway," Ubangi Club invitation, 1941, *The Eubie Blake Collection*, Maryland Historical Society, accessed January 16, 2005, http://www.mdhs.org/; Louis Calta, "Night Clubs," NYT, January 16, 1944.

123. "Gala Opening: Harlem on Broadway."

124. "Ubangi Club," postcard, ca. 1941–44.

125. Bernhardt with Harris, *I Remember*, 162–63.

126. Louis Calta, "Night Clubs," NYT, January 16, 1944.

127. James E. Powers, "Tax on Night Clubs Costs 5,000 Jobs of Entertainers," NYT, April 22, 1944.

128. The Cocoanut Grove nightclub also closed at the end of May, citing the cabaret tax; "We Regret to Announce," advertisement, NYT, May 29, 1944. Regarding the reduction of the tax, see "Night Club Business Back at Peak, with Spenders Less Aware of Tax," NYT, October 6, 1944.

129. Jerome Robinson, "News Notes of the Night Clubs," NYT, April 14, 1940; Louis Calta, "News of Night Clubs," NYT, June 27, 1943, and January 9, 1944; Al Monroe, "Swinging the News," CD, September 23, 1944; "Levine-White Deal in Making for Old Zanzibar Location," *Billboard*, June 30, 1945, 30; "Zanzibar Location Goes Ruby Foo," *Billboard*, August 18, 1945, 27; "Mills Brothers, Eddie Heywood Zanzibar Picks," NYAN, February 22, 1947; Rob Roy, "Zanzibar's Closing Is Proof That 'Broadway Ain't What It Used to Be,'" CD, February 22, 1947; Frank Gill, "Nightclub Reviews: Zanzibar, New York," *Billboard*, March 1, 1947, 38; Alvin Moses, "Nightlife in Harlem," CD, May 24, 1947.

130. "Former Zanzibar Chorines to Be Featured in Club 845," NYAN, February 22, 1947.

131. Louis Calta, "News of Night Clubs," NYT, June 27, 1943; Bill Smith, "Nightclub Reviews: Zanzibar, New York," *Billboard*, December 9, 1944, 28. Some 1943 advertising for the Zanzibar cites admission of $2.00; see "Hotels and Restaurants: Café Zanzibar," advertisement, NYT, September 16, 1943.

132. Bernhardt with Harris, *I Remember*, 168–69.

133. "Sepia Talent Flourishing on Broadway and in Harlem," PC, July 10, 1943; Izzy [Isadora Smith], "Duke Tops Jordan in Billing Row at Zanzibar," PC, September 22, 1945.

134. Bill Chase, "Ace Arranger Turns to Recording Field," NYAN, July 22, 1939, 17. The photo of Curtis in Willet's studios was reprinted in "Comeback, Maybe," CD, November 1, 1941.

135. Cleo Hayes, telephone interview by author, November 14, 2006.

136. Hayes, interview by author.

137. Louis Calta, "News of Night Clubs," NYT, July 4, 1943; "Café Zanzibar," advertisement, NYT, September 16, 1943.

138. "Hotels and Restaurants: Café Zanzibar," advertisement, NYT, September 16, 1943; Joe Cohen, "Nightclub Reviews: Zanzibar, New York," *Billboard*, November 13, 1943, 20.

139. Whaley's and Redman's Zanzibar scores are held in TWC.

140. Willet's work on the fall 1944 Zanzibar show was also cited in Bernhardt with Harris, *I Remember*, 168–69. The "Stardust" manuscript orchestra parts are held in LAHM.

141. Izzy [Rowe], "New Café Zanzibar Show Top-Heavy with Name Stars," PC, December 9, 1944; "Café Zanzibar," advertisement, NYT, December 19, 1944; Dan Burley, "The

Show of Shows: What Performers Did," NYAN, December 23, 1944; "Notes Pertaining to Stage, Movie, Radio," NYAN, February 3, 1945.

142. Virginia Forbes, "Café Life in New York," NYSun, September 5, 1945; "Duke Tops Jordan in Billing Row at Zanzibar," PC, September 22, 1945.

143. "Joe Howard Presents the International Laugh-Lease Revue," Café Zanzibar program, ca. December 1945; Fritts and Vail, *Ella Fitzgerald*, 73–74. In 1941, Willet cited both Snead and Bowser along with other acts that Willet booked at that time, including the Bye Sisters and the Miller Brothers & Lois. See E. Billingsworth, "Encores and Echoes," BAA, September 27, 1941.

144. "Nightclub Reviews: Zanzibar, New York," *Billboard*, March 16, 1946, 43, 49; "Joe Howard Presents the New Spring Edition of 'Zanzibarabian Nights,'" Café Zanzibar program, ca. spring 1946, reprinted in Waggoner, *Nightclub Nights*, 61.

145. Izzy, "Billy Rowe's Notebook," PC, April 20, 1946; "Zanzibar," advertisement, NYPost, June 25, 1946; "Joe Howard Presents the Fall Edition of 'Zanzibarabian Nights,'" Café Zanzibar program, ca. November 1946.

146. Roy, "Zanzibar's Closing Is Proof."

147. Bill Chase, "All Ears," NYAN, February 15, 1947.

148. "Mills Brothers, Eddie Heywood Zanzibar Picks," NYAN, February 1, 1947.

149. Al Monroe, "Cocktail Bars Replace Cabarets in Many Cities," CD, October 25, 1947; "Business Records," NYT, January 14, 1948.

150. Chase, "Arrangers Are Real Originators of Swing"; "Chappie Willet, New Luminary"; "LeGon and Fletcher in Revue," NYAN, July 8, 1939; "The World," advertisement, CD, January 4, 1941; "Sandra, Lakeeta Starred in New Harlem Cabaret," CD, May 30, 1942. Regarding the lifespan of the Harlem Uproar House, see "Night Club Notes," NYT, January 2, 1937; "Night Club Fails to Open," NYT, December 1, 1937. Regarding Ben Marden's Riviera, see "Fight Jersey Dry Raiders," NYT, September 19, 1932; Louis Calta, "Night Clubs Here and There," NYT, June 2, 1944; "Gossip of the Rialto," NYT, September 10, 1944. Regarding the Sky Club, see Archie Seale, "Around Harlem," NYAN, November 6, 1937; Dan Burley, "Back Door Stuff," NYAN, January 13, 1940. Regarding the World, see "300 at Nifty Dinner-Dance," NYAN, May 4, 1940; "World Restaurant Presents Top Show," NYAN, April 11, 1942; "Tavern Topics," NYAN, March 13, 1943.

151. "Night Club Notes," NYT, January 2, 1937.

152. "Night Clubs Told to Clean Up Shows," NYT, May 25, 1937.

153. "Night Club Notes," NYT, May 8, 1937.

154. "Cabarets Warned to Change Shows," NYT, June 2, 1937.

155. "Night Club Notes," NYT, September 18, 1937.

156. "Business Records," NYT, November 10, 1937; "Night Club Fails to Open," NYT, December 1, 1937. An account of the Uproar House's closing is also provided in Mezzrow and Wolfe, *Really the Blues*, 289–90.

Chapter 4. Theory and Practice

1. Steve Kemp, "Jimmy Dale Joins Met. Staff," *Metronome*, November 1933, 45.

2. Kay Kyser, "What the Arranger Means to the Orchestra Leader," *Billboard*, June 11, 1938, 13.

3. DeVeaux, *Birth of Bebop*, 66–67.

4. See Lees, *Arranging the Score*, 151; Dance, *World of Earl Hines*, 198.

5. Dance, *World of Swing*, 111.

6. Ibid., 215.

7. Ibid., 138.

8. Ibid., 233.

9. Murphy, *Spud Murphy's Swing Arranging*, 3.

10. Jones, *Talking Jazz*, 188.

11. Challis cites Forsythe in Lees, *Arranging the Score*, 159–60. See also Miller, *Glenn Miller's Method*, 8; Riddle, *Arranged by Nelson Riddle*, 82, 116. Exceptionally, Henry Mancini did cite Frank Skinner's instructional arranging book among his education; see Mancini, *Did They Mention*, 21.

12. Jones, *Talking Jazz*, 188. Williams's scores for later versions of "Messa Stomp" are held in MLWC.

13. Berliner, *Thinking in Jazz*, 290.

14. Gerald Wilson, telephone interview by author, April 15, 2004.

15. "Don Redman Dead; Leader of Band, 64," NYT, December 2, 1964.

16. Feather, *Encyclopedia of Jazz*, 301.

17. Eddie Sauter, interview by Bill Kirchner, August 11, 1980, JOHP, transcript pp. 64–65, 187–88. See also Clarkson, "Stefan Wolpe in Conversation," 388–89.

18. Dance, *World of Duke Ellington*, 47–48.

19. David Hajdu, *Lush Life: A Biography of Billy Strayhorn* (New York: North Point Press, 1997), 31–33.

20. Dance, *World of Earl Hines*, 199.

21. Berliner, *Thinking in Jazz*, 290–91.

22. Henderson, interview by Tom McClusky, April 9–12, 1975, JOHP, transcript pp. 20–22.

23. Hart Leavitt, telephone interview by author, January 7, 2004.

24. Mancini, *Did They Mention*, 21.

25. "Your Arranger" [Edgar Sampson]," *Metronome*, September 1938, 14.

26. Firestone, *Swing, Swing, Swing*, 160; Dance, *The World of Earl Hines*, 200.

27. Alexander with Fratallone, *From Harlem to Hollywood*, 13–14; see also Levin, "Reminiscing with Van Alexander," 25. Otto Cesana advertised private arranging lessons at his Fifth Avenue Aeolian Hall studios in *Metronome*; see "Otto Cesana," advertisement, *Metronome*, December 1935, 50. Regarding additional Cesana students, see "Study Arranging with Otta Cesana," advertisement, *Metronome*, June 1942, 39. Regarding Camarata, see Sauter, interview by Bill Kirchner, August 1980, JOHP, transcript p. 65.

28. Lees, *Arranging the Score*, 186.

29. Ibid., 160; Simon, *Big Bands*, 356; Nauert, "Theory and Practice in 'Porgy and Bess,'" 9–10. A number of other Swing Era musicians are also reported to have studied with Schillinger, including Will Bradley, Tommy Dorsey, Benny Goodman, Hal Kemp, Red Norvo, and Alvino Rey. See Brodsky, "Joseph Schillinger," 69 n. 20.

30. Brodsky, "Joseph Schillinger," 49–50.

31. Horace Henderson, interview by Tom McClusky, April 9–12, 1975, part 1, JOHP, transcript p. 34.

32. Simon, *Glenn Miller*, 152.

33. Schillinger, *Schillinger System of Musical Composition*.

34. On the emergence of jazz orchestra programs in higher education, see Luty, "Jazz Education's Struggle," 38–39, 53; Williams, "Wilfred C. Bain," 2; Prouty, "History of Jazz Education," 79–100.

35. Allan McMillan, "Chappie Willette [*sic*] Tells How Songs Are Made Popular," CD, February 8, 1936. Regarding the career of Clarence Cameron White, see Edwards and Mark, "In Retrospect: Clarence Cameron White," 60; Southern, *Music of Black Americans*, 277.

36. Performances by Willet's instructors Theodore Phillips and Joseph W. Grider are documented in "Recital to Be Held," *Charleston Daily Mail*, October 4, 1930; "Piano Recital to Be Given at Institute," *Charleston Daily Mail*, March 22, 1932; "Recital at Institute," *Charleston Daily Mail*, February 18, 1934.

37. *Program of National Music Week, West Virginia State College, Institute, West Virginia, May 7th to May 12th, 1933* ["Conducted under the auspices of the Music Department"].

38. "Joint Recital," [West Virginia State College] *Yellow Jacket*, May 15, 1933.

39. "W.V. State Band Clicks on Air," BAA, February 6, 1932. The Revelers did not travel far outside the Charleston area, but did broadcast regularly over long-range radio station WOBU. See Morrison Ryder, "'Chappie' and Band Score Hit at Daniel Boone Hotel," [West Virginia State College] *Yellow Jacket*, November 1, 1932; Al Baillou Jr., "Mixing Radio Mortar," PT, February 23, 1933.

40. Regarding swing and mass production, see DeVeaux, *Birth of Bebop*, 8–17.

41. Lange, *Arranging*. On Lange's influence, see Howland, *Ellington Uptown*, 119–20, 126, 153, 189.

42. Weirick, *Dance Arranging*; Skinner, *New Method*; Lapham, *Scoring*.

43. Ellis, *Instrumentation and Arranging*; Miller, *Glenn Miller's Method*. Miller's relatively lavish publication is notable for including two complete arrangements in full score.

44. "Robbins Presents," advertisement, on the back cover of Skinner, *New Method*. In this printing (ca. 1937–41), Spud Murphy's *Swing Arranging Method* and Xavier Cugat's *Latin-American Rhythms* were priced at one dollar; reprints of Lange's (hardcover) book cost five dollars.

45. Murphy, *Spud Murphy's Swing Arranging*; Van Alexander, *First Arrangement* (New York: Criterion Music, 1947). Regarding additional publications, see Jimmy Dale, "Arranging Questions," *Metronome*, July 1936, 36, and November 1937, 48; Jimmy Dale, "Jimmy Dale Explains Voicing for Eight Brass," *Metronome*, January 1940, 48. Compilations of Otto Cesana's *Metronome* columns, *Course in Modern Dance Arranging* and *Course in Modern Harmony*, were eventually made available for separate purchase direct from the author. See "Study Arranging with Otto Cesana," advertisement, *Metronome*, April 1942, 39.

46. Eddie MacDonald, "It Must Have That Swing," *Metronome*, August 1933, 28.

47. In MacDonald's original published example of the "ride" rhythm, the banjo is assigned an alternating quarter-note and eighth-note/sixteenth-note pattern (similar to the drum part) that is not explicitly referenced in any of the other texts cited in this chapter. The "slash" shorthand notation for banjo and separate bass part have been

added to MacDonald's examples for the present demonstration. For earlier examples of these patterns, see Lange, *Arranging*, 90–95. Duke Ellington also discusses similar rhythm section patterns in his 1931 article "The Duke Steps Out," reprinted in Tucker, *Duke Ellington Reader*, 47–48.

48. MacDonald, "It Must Have."

49. See Lange, *Arranging*, 90–91; Weirick, *Dance Arranging*, 18–20, 37; Murphy, *Spud Murphy's Swing Arranging*, 24–25; Lapham, *Scoring*, 45. Notably, neither Ellis nor Miller specify the differentiation between two-beat and four-beat rhythmic patterns. For further discussion of period rhythm section scoring, see Spring, "Swing and the Lindy Hop," 195–97.

50. Lange, *Arranging*, 90; see also Skinner, *New Method*, 109. Mark Tucker refers to 1920s dance band "oom-pah" piano scoring as period "standard accompaniment"; see Tucker, "Count Basie and the Piano," 48.

51. Spring, "Swing and the Lindy Hop," 187. Examples of four-beat scoring include Lange, *Arranging*, 94–95; Lapham, *Scoring*, 45.

52. Hudson advocates the "pleasing rhythmic effect . . . produced by the constant variation of 2–4 and 4–4 style" in "Will Hudson Answers Your Modern Arranging Problems," *Down Beat*, December 1937, 29.

53. Will Hudson, "Arranging," *Down Beat*, April 1939, 24.

54. Henderson, interview, transcript p. 66. See also Lange, *Arranging*, 34; Skinner, *New Method*, 67; Weirick, *Dance Arranging*, 18–19.

55. Perhaps reflecting a transition in performance practice, Miller advocates the addition of chord symbols to fully notated piano and bass parts, and suggests that the bass player "should improvise freely except where it is marked to play as written"; Miller, *Glenn Miller's Method*, 56.

56. See Spring, "Swing and the Lindy Hop," 193–94.

57. Murphy, for example, uses slash notation exclusively for his guitar part examples. Murphy, *Spud Murphy's Swing Arranging*, 25.

58. For a brief description of the drum kit's evolution during this period, see Korall, "Jazz Drumming," 684–85.

59. Krupa, *Gene Krupa Drum Method*. Regarding notation for press roll pattern and hi-hat cymbals, see 56–58, 72.

60. See Skinner, *New Method*, 58.

61. Miller, *Glenn Miller's Method*, 56. Regarding the terms *fake* and *ad lib* in jazz parlance, see Gushee, "Improvisation and Related Terms," 263–80.

62. Lange, *Arranging*, 13; Skinner, *New Method*, 110–11; Lapham, *Scoring*, 121–23. Examples of Latin dance rhythms are also provided in magazine articles including [Jerry Shelton], "Conga Is Cuban with the Sugar Scraped Off," *Down Beat*, August 1937, 24. See also Ronald Hunt, "Rhumba Rhythm as She Is Played," *Metronome*, March 1938, 19.

63. Fernett, *Swing Out*, 37.

64. Regarding the rhythmic and textural elements of the Swing Era dance band, see Spring, "Swing and the Lindy Hop," 185–86, 191–93.

65. Giddins, liner notes to American Jazz Orchestra—Benny Carter, *Central City Sketches*. See also Magee, *Uncrowned King*, 160–61.

66. Archie Bleyer, "Business in F" [stock arrangement], arranged by Archie Bleyer (New York: Southern Music, 1931). Specifically, see the "3rd Alto Sax" and "2nd Trumpet" parts. See also Jimmy Dale, "Arranging Questions," *Metronome*, October 1935, 47. A study of "Business in F" is provided in Clark, "Archie Bleyer and the Lost Influence," 138–79.

67. Archie Bleyer, "Arranging Questions," *Metronome*, January 1933, 42.

68. Russell Procope, interview by Chris Albertson, March 1979, reel 2, JOHP, transcript p. 11.

69. Benny Goodman, for example, noted that "you could do a lot more, in the way of voicing and variety of effects, with four saxes than you could with two or three"; Goodman and Kolodin, *Kingdom of Swing*, 128.

70. On sixth-chords and popular song publications, see Forte, *American Popular Ballad*, 7–8. Music theorist Philip Tagg goes so far as to identify minor triads with added sixths as "the 'jazz' minor six" chord, a "genre synecdoche for a semantic field including such phenomena as seedy US urban locations, African-American subculture, night, danger and crime"; see Philip Tagg, "Musical Meanings, Classical and Popular: The Case of Anguish" [English version], accessed October 18, 2015, http://www.tagg.org/articles/xpdfs/musemeuse.pdf.

71. See Lange, *Arranging*, 8; Weirick, *Dance Arranging*, 56–66; Skinner, *New Method*, 20–21. See also Otto Cesana, "Course in Modern Harmony," *Metronome*, January 1937, 30.

72. Will Hudson, "Will Hudson Answers Your Modern Arranging Problems," *Down Beat*, June 1937, 18. See also Jimmy Dale, "Arranging Questions," *Metronome*, March 1935, 39.

73. For example, the bridge of Will Hudson's 1936 "Sophisticated Swing" prominently features a melody built on a succession of dominant-ninth chord voicings. Will Hudson and Mitchell Parish, "Sophisticated Swing" [stock arrangement], arranged by Will Hudson (New York: Mills Music, 1936). The root or fifth degree of the dominant-seventh chord could be omitted in a three- or four-part voicing of a dominant-ninth chord. For example, see Jimmy Dale, "Arranging Questions," *Metronome*, November 1935, 50.

74. For example, see Weirick, *Dance Arranging*, 123; Skinner, *New Method*, 91–97, 127–31; Ellis, *Instrumentation and Arranging*, 79; Murphy, *Spud Murphy's Swing Arranging*, 21; Lapham, *Scoring*, 98.

75. On scoring for five brass, or five brass and four reeds, see Ellis, *Instrumentation and Arranging*, 93; Archie Bleyer, "Arranging Questions," *Metronome*, May 1933, 38; Will Hudson, "Will Hudson to Answer Your Modern Arranging Problems," *Down Beat*, March 1937, 16; Jimmy Dale, "Arranging Questions," *Metronome*, June 1937, 53; Otto Cessana, "Course in Modern Dance Arranging," *Metronome*, June 1938, 32; Miller, *Glenn Miller's Method*, 112.

76. See Hudson, "Will Hudson to Answer Your Modern Arranging Problems"; Will Hudson, "Arranging," *Down Beat*, February 1, 1940, 17, and March 1, 1940, 17.

77. Murphy suggests that "the Brass seems to be the most important section" in regard to "swing arranging"; Will Hudson suggests scoring "the five brass first" in ensemble voicings. Murphy, *Spud Murphy's Swing Arranging*, 36–37; Will Hudson, "Will Hudson

Answers Your Modern Arranging Problems," *Down Beat,* September 1937, 30. See also Otto Cesana, "Course in Modern Dance Arranging," *Metronome,* June 1938, 32.

78. In some contexts, close-position voicings are also referred to as "block chords" or "block voicing" texture, though the term *block* does not appear to have been prevalent during the Swing Era. Later texts provide other labels for these techniques, such as "five-way close doubled lead"; see Boras, *Jazz Composition,* 159. In scoring ensemble melody passages, passing tones are typically harmonized with dominant-seventh chords, sixth chords, or diminished chords. See Will Hudson, "Will Hudson Solves Problems Submitted to Him by Arrangers," *Down Beat,* January 1939, 22.

79. Decisions regarding "open" or "close" voicing also depend on instrument range. See Archie Bleyer, "Arranging Questions," *Metronome,* December 1932, 36; Jimmy Dale, "Arranging Questions," *Metronome,* August 1934, 28; Will Hudson, "Arranging," *Down Beat,* November 15, 1939, 17.

80. Otto Cesana refers to this method as a "fill-in"; Otto Cesana, "Course in Modern Dance Arranging," *Metronome,* November 1937, 21. See also Will Hudson, "Your Arranging Problems," *Down Beat,* February 1939, 20.

81. Skinner, *New Method,* 27 (ex. 97). A similar technique is outlined in Miller, *Glenn Miller's Method,* 41. Later texts designating "semi-open" or "drop two" include Sebesky, *Contemporary Arranger,* 49; Boras, *Jazz Composition,* 160.

82. For example, see DeVeaux and Giddins, *Jazz,* 175.

83. Murphy, *Spud Murphy's Swing Arranging,* 26–27. Magee similarly describes Henderson's strategy as "chains of syncopation"; Magee, *Uncrowned King,* 195.

84. Murphy, 34.

85. Dance, *World of Count Basie,* 66.

86. For example, Elton Hill's manuscript score for "Pyramid" held in ASC reflects additional scoring for strings provided by a second, unidentified arranger.

87. Skinner's text is somewhat exceptional in including a number of examples of mixed reed and brass scoring. See Skinner, *New Method,* 116–26, 135, 137–38.

88. Regarding Ellington and Strayhorn, for example, see Schuller, *Swing Era,* 123–26; van de Leur, *Something to Live For,* 76.

89. Teddy Hill and Chappie Willet, "Blue Rhythm Fantasy" [stock arrangement], arranged by Edgar Battle (New York: Exclusive Publications, 1936).

90. Skinner, *New Method,* 82–83; Otto Cesana, "Cesana Analyzes Use of Strings in Dance Band," *Metronome* April 1942, 39; Otto Cesana, "Further Analysis of Strings in Dance Band," *Metronome* May 1942, 39.

91. Intersections of string scoring and jazz are examined in Howland, "Jazz with Strings," 111–47.

92. Still's "Frenesi" score is held in ASC.

93. Regarding Margie Gibson's career, see "A Sight for Jitterbug Eyes," NYPost, June 27, 1941.

94. Robert Maxwell and Josef Myrow, "You Can Count on Me" [stock arrangement], arranged by Chappie Willet (New York: Exclusive Publications, 1939).

95. A similar counterline string strategy is outlined in Cesana, "Further Analysis."

96. Weirick, *Dance Arranging,* 105–6.

97. Ellis, *Instrumentation and Arranging*, 156–57.

98. Lange, *Arranging*, 207–14.

99. See Weirick, *Dance Arranging*, 86–87; Ellis, *Instrumentation and Arranging*, 153–83; Lapham, *Scoring*, 132–38.

100. Lange, *Arranging*, 210.

101. Weirick, *Dance Arranging*, 88; Ellis, *Instrumentation and Arranging*, 163.

102. Lapham, *Scoring*, 132; Lange, *Arranging*, 210.

103. Lange, *Arranging*, 211.

104. Lapham, *Scoring*, 136. See also Weirick, *Dance Arranging*, 112–24; Ellis, *Instrumentation and Arranging*, 177; Otto Cesana, "Course in Modern Dance Arranging," *Metronome*, January 1938, 30. Skinner does not refer explicitly to an "arranger's" or "special" chorus, but his sample routine only consists of two sixteen-bar choruses (plus an introduction, modulation, and ending). See Skinner, *New Method*, 144–45.

105. Otto Cesana, "Course in Modern Dance Arranging," *Metronome*, June 1938, 32.

106. Lange, *Arranging*, 212.

107. Ellis, *Instrumentation and Arranging*, 167.

108. Otto Cesana, "Course in Modern Dance Arranging," *Metronome*, February 1938, 28.

109. Cesana, "Course in Modern Dance Arranging," *Metronome*, March 1938, 28.

110. Cesana, "Course in Modern Dance Arranging," *Metronome*, January 1937, 30; Lange, *Arranging*, 200–203. See also Weirick, *Dance Arranging*, 139; Otto Cesana, "Parallel Harmony Produces Many a Refreshing Effect," *Metronome*, June 1942, 39.

111. Lapham, *Scoring*, 124; Murphy, *Spud Murphy's Swing Arranging*, 32.

112. Lange, *Arranging*, 212.

113. Ellis, *Instrumentation and Arranging*, 159.

114. Ibid.

115. On the emergence of American marching band and ragtime stock arrangements, see Hagert, "Band and Orchestral Ragtime," 268–84.

116. Earlier stock arrangements of the late 1920s and early '30s typically included parts for only three brass, three saxes, and four rhythm.

117. Prices are quoted in "Get an Earful from These Eyefuls," advertisement, *Metronome*, October 1937, 7; "Swing with Feist," advertisement, *Metronome*, November 1938, 46; "These Titles Belong in Your Books," advertisement, *Metronome*, April 1939, 48.

118. Tom Herrick, "Orchestration Review of the Month," *Down Beat*, October 1937, 24; Tom Herrick, "'Stocks' Take the Band Spotlight in 1940 . . .," *Down Beat*, June 15, 1940, 21.

119. Stock arrangement advertisements featuring female models include Exclusive Publications' full-page spread "Get an Earful from These Eyefuls."

120. The songs "Push Out" and "You Can Count on Me" were recorded by a number of performers; none of the recordings discovered to date reflects any clear parallels to Willet's stock arrangements. The more obscure "I'm Tellin' You in Front" may not have been recorded in any form.

121. Lange, *Arranging*, 208–12. Commercial arrangements are also referred to as "print arrangements" in Ellis, *Instrumentation and Arranging*, 94–95, 169–73.

122. Alex Lovejoy and Nat Reed, "Push Out (Te-Huey, Te-Huey, Te-Huey)" [stock arrangement], arranged by Chappie Willet (New York: Handy Brothers Music, 1939). Whaley's manuscript orchestra parts for "Push Out" are held in DEC.

123. Ellis, *Instrumentation and Arranging*, 181–82. In discussing arranging practices for his 1930s dance band, Artie Shaw offers an exception to the rule in claiming that he and arranger Jerry Gray "didn't believe in modulations before vocals. [The singer] comes in just like a horn"; Willard, liner notes to *Artie Shaw and His Orchestra 1938*.

124. Mildred Bailey, "Dick Kline" [Henry Nemo], and Red Norvo, "Jump Jump's Here" [stock arrangement], orchestrated by Les Brown (New York: Robbins Music, 1938).

125. By comparison, an entirely different arrangement of "Jump Jump's Here"—scored by Benny Carter—is available on *Charlie Barnet: Make Believe Ballroom 1935–1939* (Giants of Jazz CD-53274, 1997).

126. Billy Rowe, "Chappie Willet Signed," PC, April 30, 1938.

127. The "Grandfather's Clock" stock arrangement includes a sax soli passage not heard in Krupa's recording; the passage may have been an addition by Spud Murphy or a portion of Willet's original score that Krupa had cut. To date, the only known period recordings of Willet's "Prelude in C-sharp Minor" comprise an aircheck of a Duke Ellington performance and a radio transcription made by Charlie Barnet; neither was issued commercially until the LP era. When asked about the arrangement more than six decades later, Murphy did not recall having Willet's "Prelude in C-sharp Minor" score to work from, noting that such an occurrence was rare. But there is little other explanation for that stock publication's reflection of an arrangement that had not yet been commercially issued on disc. Murphy, telephone interview by author.

128. Ellis, *Instrumentation and Arranging*, 181–83; Weirick, *Dance Arranging*, 141–42.

129. Archie Bleyer, "Arranging Questions," *Metronome*, June 1933, 30. See also Jimmy Dale, "Arranging Questions," *Metronome*, August 1934, 28; Harold Rubenstein, "Making Specials for [*sic*] Stocks," *Metronome*, November 1936, 47.

130. See Magee, *Uncrowned King*, 41–46.

131. Larry Clinton, "A Study in Brown" [stock arrangement], arranged by Larry Clinton (New York: Lincoln Music, 1937). Teddy Hill's recording is available on *Uptown Rhapsody* (Hep CD 1033, 1992).

132. Bob Crosby, *Dixieland Shuffle (1935–1939)* (Naxos Jazz 8.120652, 2003); Edward Ory, "Muskat [*sic*] Ramble" [stock arrangement], arranged by Bob Haggart (New York: Melrose Music, 1936); Roy Eldridge, *The Varsity Sessions Vol. 1* (Storyville SLP-701, n.d.).

133. Ellis, *Instrumentation and Arranging*, 192.

134. MacDonald, "It Must Have."

Chapter 5. Episode and Interlude

1. Robert Russell Bennett, "Orchestration of Theatre and Dance Music," in Bennett, *Broadway Sound*, 288, 291.

2. On the various classes of music performers, see Howland, *Ellington Uptown*, 29–31.

3. Regarding Bennett's reputation, see "The Boys That Make the Noise," *Time*, July 5, 1943, 65.

4. Fox, *Showtime at the Apollo*, 81 (emphasis in original). Count Basie offers a more complex view regarding issues of band style and stage show music in Basie and Murray, *Good Morning Blues*, 126–27, 181–82.

5. Dance, *World of Swing*, 218–19.

6. Regarding Ellington's hiring of Whaley, see Dance, *World of Duke Ellington*, 48. On Strayhorn, see van de Leur, *Something to Live For*, 23–25.

7. Barry Ulanov, "Ellington's Carnegie Hall Concert a Glorified Stage Show," *Metronome*, January 1944, 8, 48. Within the body of this article itself, Ulanov merely calls the program a "glorified one-nighter." Gunther Schuller similarly criticized selected Ellington works dating from the bandleader's Cotton Club residencies as "slick trying-to-be-modern show music"; Schuller, *Early Jazz*, 330. Harvey Cohen's 2010 biography of Ellington, *Duke Ellington's America*, does not even mention the bandleader's extended stage show residencies at the Broadway Hurricane Club and Café Zanzibar.

8. See Howland, "Jazz with Strings," 115–16.

9. See Howland, *Ellington Uptown*, 117–18.

10. Ibid., 103.

11. Ibid., 103–4, 119.

12. Ibid., 2.

13. Regarding the reception of *Rhapsody in Blue*, see Oja, *Making Music Modern*, 319.

14. Magee, *Uncrowned King*, 194.

15. Magee, *Uncrowned King*, 193.

16. Lange classified modulation passages beginning prior to the end of the chorus form as "premature" modulations; Lange, *Arranging*, 205–6.

17. Berish, *Lonesome Roads*, 53.

18. Van de Leur, *Something to Live For*, 67.

19. Lees, *Arranging the Score*, 158.

20. "Prelude to a Stomp" is issued on *Mills Blue Rhythm Band 1936–1937* (Classics CD-731, 1993).

21. Regarding the arranger attribution and formal design of "The Stampede," see Magee, *Uncrowned King*, 111–14. Regarding "East St. Louis Toodle-Oo," see Baumgartner, "Duke Ellington's 'East St. Louis Toodle-Oo' Revisited," 30.

22. Oja, *Making Music Modern*, 46–47, 19.

23. Ibid., 319. Guthrie Ramsey posits a parallel "Afro-modernist" tendency that emerged in urban America from the 1920s through the 1940s as a result of the Great Migration, reflecting "historical actors' self-conscious attitudes about and their responses to the relationship among the past, the present, and the future"; Ramsey, *Race Music*, 97.

24. Oja, *Making Music Modern*, 324–34. George Gershwin's 1925 *Concerto in F* is similarly described as fusing "a standard three-movement form with African American traditions" and "rife with unorthodox juxtapositions" with "expectations for a [European] concerto . . . realized at the same time as gestures of American popular music were delivered in various guises"; Oja, *Making Music Modern*, 319–25.

25. Floyd, *Power of Black Music*, 255–56.

26. Howland, *Ellington Uptown*, 6.

27. On the blending of jazz orchestra and concert music traditions that emerged during the 1920s, see Howland, *Ellington Uptown*, 29–45; Oja, *Making Music Modern*, 318–29.

28. "Traditional" elements of African American jazz and popular music relevant to this discussion include musical "features such as blue notes, slurring, bent notes, growls, and . . . a loosening of the melodic line from the ground beat"; Collier, "Jazz (i); §II, 5: The Emergence of Hot Music," 582. See also Floyd, "African Roots of Jazz," 13.

29. Original in French: "De transcrire 'la réaction' d'un musicien européen au contact des rhythmes de danse d'outre-mer"; Tansman, notes to *Sonatine Transatlantique*, n.p. Translation by the author.

30. Tansman, notes to *Sonatine Transatlantique*.

31. "Joint Recital," [West Virginia State College] *Yellow Jacket*, May 15, 1933.

32. See Oja, *Making Music Modern*, 320–24.

33. Ragtime-novelty piano composers, for example, had incorporated the whole-tone sound by the early 1920s; for example, Rube Bloom's "That Futuristic Rag" (New York: Jack Mills, 1923).

34. Ray Heindorf's manuscript orchestra scores for *Whoopee!* and *Palmy Days* are held in AMPAS.

35. Some related discourses surrounding the emergence of "jazz composition" are discussed in Harrison, "Swing Era Big Bands," 285–86.

36. DeVeaux, *Birth of Bebop*, 107. Similar references are offered in Teachout, "Jazz and Classical Music," 345; Youngren, "European Roots of Jazz," 22; van de Leur, *Something to Live For*, 29.

37. Rattenbury, *Duke Ellington, Jazz Composer*, 141.

38. Kart, "Avant-Garde," 449. Kart cites dance band works of the 1920s and 1930s as precedents for the later artistic movement discussed in the article.

39. For theme song identifications, see Simon, *Big Bands*, 588–90; Vail, *Swing Era Scrapbook*, 65, 223, 232. Regarding the attribution of "Uptown Rhapsody" and other arrangements to Willet, see Appendix.

40. Cook's letter to Johnson is reprinted in Howland, *Ellington Uptown*, 43–44.

41. Sayre Hillerson, "Krupa Shaping Outmoded Style," *Metronome*, July 1938, 30; Edgar Jackson, "Swing Music: Gene Krupa, Apurksody," *Gramophone*, April 1939, 28.

42. Schuller, *Swing Era*, 211, 370.

43. Ibid., 437.

44. Regarding the 1920s arranging work of Will Vodery, Mark Tucker observes: "When chromaticism [in Vodery's music] does occur, it is usually in introductions . . . nodding in the direction of Paul Whiteman's 'symphonic' jazz. Once past the introductions, though, the 'chromatic tendencies' disappear and diatonicism reigns"; Tucker, "In Search of Will Vodery," 168. For further discussion of Tucker's analysis of Vodery, see Howland, *Ellington Uptown*, 40–43. Regarding Confrey, see the introduction and interlude passages of his 1921 "Kitten on the Keys," in *Jazz, Blues, Boogie and Swing for Piano*, ed. Ronny S. Schiff (Milwaukee: MCA Music, 1977), 12–15.

45. Lange, *Arranging*, 8.

46. Ibid., 202.

47. On the application of instrumental effects to "forms and routines," see ibid., 207–12.

48. "Stratosphere" is issued on *Jimmie Lunceford and His Orchestra 1930–1934* (Classics CD-501, 1990). A brief discussion of "Stratosphere's" "startling modernisms" is provided in Schuller, *Swing Era*, 208–9.

49. Will Hudson, for example, recommended that augmented chord voicings in four-part harmony include "the seventh or the ninth" scale degree; Husdon, "Arranging," *Down Beat*, March 1939, 27.

50. Among Swing Era arrangers, there appears to be little theoretical differentiation between augmented or flatted-fifth nomenclature in chord symbols accompanying whole-tone passages; guitar parts may reflect one or the other, regardless of the chord tone (or tones) provided in corresponding ensemble voicings.

51. "After You've Gone" is issued on Louis Armstrong, *Fleischmann's Yeast Show and Louis' Home-Recorded Tapes* (Jazz Heritage Society CD-5289147, 2008). Regarding the chord spellings provided, Willet frequently voiced altered-fifth chords assigning the flat-fifth degree to the bass part; to judge from surviving orchestra rhythm section parts for other arrangements, Willet might have spelled the first chord in this "After You've Gone" sequence as C7(b5), despite the additional presence of a raised fifth. Referencing the common addition of the ninth degree is another option, offering a possible spelling of the first chord as Gb9(b5).

52. Schuller, *Swing Era*, 207.

53. Jazz composers and performers of the 1920s had also explored the possibilities of similar rhythmic-harmonic relationships. For example, pianist James P. Johnson's 1929 "Riffs" introduces a passage of parallel chromatic voicings in half-note rhythm that disrupts the prevailing quarter-note stride pattern. See mm. 79–82 in James P. Johnson, "Riffs," in Schiff, *Jazz, Blues, Boogie and Swing for Piano*, 28–33. A comparable passage can be heard in Johnson's 1929 recording for Okeh (2:55).

54. Dinerstein, *Swinging the Machine*, 165.

55. Willet's union stamp on the manuscript piano part for "Opening" reflects a date of either 1938 or 1939 (the stamp is smudged). Following a fall 1938 residency at the Kit Kat Club, Lunceford performed at the Apollo in January, May, August, and December of 1939. See "Lunceford at Apollo," NYAN, December 31, 1938; "Apollo," NYT, May 20, 1939; Dance, *World of Swing*, 410–13.

56. "Apurksody" is issued on *Gene Krupa and His Orchestra 1938* (Classics CD-767, 1994).

57. Regarding Red Norvo's Swing Era reputation, see Burke, *Come In and Hear the Truth*, 106. See also [George T. Simon], "Pick-Ups: Roasts and Toasts," *Metronome*, February 1936, 23. Norvo was similarly tagged as "soft, subtle, suave, sophisticated" in M. E. Lee, "Air Dance Fare," *Metronome*, October 1937, 30.

58. Aircheck recordings of "Persian Rug" performed by Red Norvo's orchestra are held in the NJMH.

59. "Rhythm Jam" is issued on *Mills Blue Rhythm Band 1936–1937* (Classics CD-731, 1993). The corresponding passage in the 1937 Exclusive Publications piano leadsheet for "Rhythm Jam" reflects an Eb9 voicing instead of Eb7.

60. Skinner's use of this device (labeled as "dominant-seventh forward [progression] . . . flatted-fifth in the bass") is outlined in Skinner, *New Method*, 32 (ex. 115). Musicians and historians have frequently identified the "tri-tone substitution" as a modernist hallmark of 1940s bebop jazz improvisers; the tri-tone substitution and its role in jazz history is discussed in DeVeaux, *Birth of Bebop*, 104–10. On the "flatted-fifth" as "fetish" in jazz history, see Townsend, *Pearl Harbor Jazz*, 138–45.

61. "I Ain't Gettin' Nowhere Fast" is issued on *Cab Calloway and His Orchestra 1939–1940* (Classics CD-595, 1991).

62. As bebop pioneer Dizzy Gillespie asserted, "[ca. 1938] we always looked on that [tri-tone substitution] as simply a half-step, not as a 'flatted fifth';" Gillespie, *To Be or Not . . . to Bop*, 92. See also DeVeaux, *Birth of Bebop*, 109. A similar concept is suggested in Gillespie's references to "the chord progression A-minor seventh to D seventh to D-flat"; see Dizzy Gillsepie and Gene Lees, "The Years with Yard," reprinted in Woideck, *Charlie Parker Companion*, 163. Regarding related improvisational approaches to the tri-tone substitution, see the discussion of Charlie Parker's "Donna Lee" (take 2) in Woideck, *Charlie Parker: His Music and His Life*, 146.

Chapter 6. Futuristic Ragtime

1. Korall, *Drummin' Men*, 71–72.

2. Louis Armstrong, *Fleischmann's Yeast Show and Louis' Home-Recorded Tapes* (Jazz Heritage Society CD 5289147, 2008); Vail, *Swing Era Scrapbook*, 65, 150, 223.

3. Variations between the different versions of "Rhythm Jam" include the insertion of a piano solo on the bridge of the third chorus in the Mills and Krupa recordings; the Krupa arrangement also omits the tricky, high-register unison brass introduction of the previous versions. Regarding the Krupa alteration, George Simon related: "This arrangement [of "Rhythm Jam"] by Chappy [*sic*] Willet originally had a different introduction, but it was too high for the trumpets, so, after 31 false starts, as Gene [Krupa] recalls it, Sam Donahue came up with this sax intro from an old Earl Hines record that Jimmy Mundy (also a Krupa arranger) had written"; Simon, liner notes to *Gene Krupa: Dummin' Man*. The sax intro that Donohue plays on the Krupa recording is a quote from the end of Jimmy Mundy's sax solo on Hines's 1934 recording of "Copenhagen."

4. For a discussion of issues in Swing Era dance band "personality" marketing, see DeVeaux, *Birth of Bebop*, 128–29.

5. Dicky Wells, as told to Stanley Dance, *The Night People: The Jazz Life of Dicky Wells* (Washington, DC: Smithsonian Institution Press, 1991), 41.

6. Townsend, liner notes to *Artie Shaw and His Orchestra 1939 Vol. 4*.

7. For example, see the discussion of arrangers in Simon, *Big Bands*, 41 ff.

8. Regarding the Henderson repertoire performed by Goodman, see Allen, *Hendersonia*, 319–21. Regarding the Henderson repertoire and alterations made by Goodman, see Magee, *Uncrowned King*, 231, 245–71.

9. Mancini, *Did They Mention*, 23.

10. Bernhardt, *I Remember*, 120.

11. Williams's score and orchestra parts for "Riffs" are held in BGP.

12. Mundy's "Rank Frank" score is held in HJC.

13. Hart Leavitt, telephone interview by author, January 7, 2004. Leavitt's arrangement of "And Then Your Lips Met Mine" was recorded by the Yale Collegians in 1930, and reissued on *Stew Pletcher 1929–1937* (Harrison Records LP-X, 1985).

14. Glenn Miller, as quoted in [George T. Simon], "Band Styles Are Great—If They Don't Limit You!," *Metronome*, May 1939, 12, 39. See also Jimmy Dale, "Background Arranging Varies According to Soloists," *Metronome*, February 1940, 40; Schuller, *Swing Era*, 672–73.

15. Regarding Kemp's style (as heard in "Love for Sale"), see Maher, liner notes to *Hal Kemp and His Orchestra*. Regarding the styles of Lunceford (as heard in "My Blue Heaven"), Miller (as heard in "Moonlight Serenade"), and Savitt (as heard in "And the Angels Sing"), see Schuller, *Swing Era*, 207, 211–12, 765.

16. In 1941, for example, the *Pittsburgh Courier* honored Krupa with an award named for black jazz saxophonist Chu Berry following Krupa's arrest in a dispute over performing with black trumpeter Roy Eldridge in a segregated venue; "Contest Takes on True American Aspect," PC, December 20, 1941. See also Erenberg, *Swingin' the Dream*, 130.

17. Korall, *Drummin' Men*, 56 (emphasis in original).

18. Berish, *Lonesome Roads*, 109–10. Association of "Let Me Off Uptown" with Harlem is discussed in Anita O'Day and George Eells, *High Times, Hard Times* (New York: Limelight Editions, 1989), 105. The song was also recorded by black bandleader Lucky Millinder and white bandleader Larry Clinton; the Clinton version lyrics reassigned "uptown" to "52nd Street."

19. A cultural study of the Barnet orchestra's musical identity is offered in Berish, *Lonesome Roads*, 73–118.

20. Allan McMillan, "Hi-Hattin' in Harlem," CD, January 11, 1936.

21. Schuller criticizes the antiphonal "riff cum call-and-response formulas" of Swing Era arrangers as indicative of stylistic stagnation and representing the "Henderson formula's Achilles' heel"; Schuller, *Swing Era*, 19, 10. As Magee notes, Henderson was certainly not the only arranger using antiphonal and block-chord scoring devices, although his high-profile work for Goodman did help to popularize the approach. Magee, *Uncrowned King*, 193.

22. See Moore and Ibrahim, "'Sounds Like Teen Spirit,'" 139–58, 140–41. For an introduction to the term *idiolect* in popular music studies, see Middleton, *Studying Popular Music*, 136–37, 174.

23. Van de Leur, *Something to Live For*, 67.

24. For examples of the "bass run" in the American marching band tradition, see van der Merwe, *Origins of the Popular Style*, 283–84. Adept Swing Era bass players like John Kirby frequently incorporated bass run or "tailgate" phrases in "fill-in" or "turnaround" passages, as heard in Edgar Sampson's "Blue Lou," recorded by Chick Webb in 1934. For an earlier dance orchestra example, hear Andy Kirk's 1929 bass saxophone performance on his orchestra's "Blue Clarinet Stomp."

25. A similar trombone phrase is referenced in the notated figure accompanying testimony from trombonist Trummy Young, as quoted in DeVeaux, *Birth of Bebop*, 57. Other big band precedents for this ubiquitous phrase include the introduction of

Fletcher Henderson's arrangement of "Remember" recorded by Benny Goodman in 1936—possibly a programmatic reference to the piece's title.

26. "Washington and Lee Swing" is issued on Louis Armstrong, *Fleischmann's Yeast Show and Louis' Home-Recorded Tapes* (Jazz Heritage Society CD 5289147, 2008).

27. "Jubilee" is issued on Louis Armstrong, *The Complete Louis Armstrong Decca Sessions 1935–1946* (Mosaic Records 7CD-243, 2009).

28. Matty Matlock and Bob Haggart, "Dixieland Arranging," *Metronome*, December 1937, 16.

29. Examples of similar chromatic bass lines in Scott Joplin's ragtime music are provided in Edward A. Berlin, *King of Ragtime: Scott Joplin and His Era* (New York: Oxford University Press, 1994), 112 (ex. 6—9a), 169–70 (ex. 10—1b).

30. "Prelude to a Stomp" is issued on *Mills Blue Rhythm Band 1936–1937* (Classics CD-731, 1993).

31. Matlock and Haggart, "Dixieland Arranging," 15, 54.

32. "Swingtime in Honolulu" is issued on Ivie Anderson, *Ivie and Duke Vol. 2* (Hep CD-1069, 2000).

33. For examples and discussions of the "Dixieland trio" effect, see Paul Weirick, "Dixieland Chorus of Rockin' Chair," *Metronome*, March 1935, 18; Matlock and Haggart, "Dixieland Arranging," 15; Murphy, *Spud Murphy's Swing Arranging*, 29.

34. A relevant example of "secondary rag" scoring can be found in the notated excerpt of Scott Joplin's 1908 "Pine Apple Rag" included in Berlin, *King of Ragtime*, 181 (ex. 10—4b).

35. For example, see the stride piano change-step pattern in mm. 29–32 of James P. Johnson's 1930 "Riffs," reprinted in *Jazz, Blues, Boogie and Swing for Piano*, ed. Ronny S. Schiff (Milwaukee: MCA Music, 1977), 28–33. A comparable passage can be heard in Johnson's 1929 recording for Okeh (0:30). Regarding stride piano "change-step" metric displacement, see Buehrer and Hodson, "Metric Dissonance in Jazz"; see also Schuller, *Early Jazz*, 218–21.

36. Aircheck recordings of "Persian Rug" performed by Norvo's orchestra are held in NJMH.

37. "I Know That You Know" is issued on Louis Armstrong, *Fleischmann's Yeast Show and Louis' Home-Recorded Tapes* (Jazz Heritage Society CD 5289147, 2008).

38. For example, Schuller identifies the repeated-note device in his discussion of arranger Gene Gifford's work for the Casa Loma Orchestra of the early 1930s. Schuller, *Swing Era*, 635–36.

39. "Chant of the Weed" is issued on Don Redman, *Shakin' the Africann* (Hep CD-1001, 2002).

40. Ellington's manuscript score for "Skrontch" is held in DEC.

41. "Rhythm Jam" is issued on *Mills Blue Rhythm Band 1936–1937* (Classics CD-731, 1993).

42. Regarding the relationship between stop-time and vaudeville dance, see Harker, "Louis Armstrong," 111–14.

43. "I've Got My Fingers Crossed" is issued on Louis Armstrong, *The Complete Louis Armstrong Decca Sessions 1935–1946* (Mosaic Records 7CD-243, 2009).

44. Related—but not identical—to the "lip slur" is the "smear," a popular jazz technique defined by arranger Jimmy Dale as playing "a said note a little flat, then this note is brought up to its correct pitch by lipwork"; Jimmy Dale, "Arranging Questions," *Metronome*, March 1934, 42.

45. "Grandfather's Clock" is issued on *Gene Krupa and His Orchestra 1935–1938* (Classics CD-754, 1994).

46. Some missing parts for "Prelude in C-sharp Minor" (including the second trumpet, third trumpet, and tenor sax) have been reconstructed by the author.

47. Incomplete manuscript orchestra parts for Willet's 1945 arrangement of "Low Down Guy" are held in the DEC.

48. This differentiation between *whip* and *rip* reflects their use in Willet's manuscript orchestra parts, but is not universal. Arranger Jimmy Dale, for example, describes a *rip* as a "quick glissando to the note and cut off short," and also as "a sort of fast glissando from one note to the actual note"; arranger Eddie Sauter appears to use the term *rip* for what Willet designates as a *whip*, moving from one distinct pitch to another. Jimmy Dale, "Arranging Questions," *Metronome*, March 1934, 42; Jimmy Dale, "Arranging Questions," *Metronome*, March 1938, 53; Eddie Sauter, "Heir to a Jersey Meadow," Special *Metronome* Orchestration, *Metronome*, April 1938, 34–36.

49. The "legitimate" or "legit" orchestra sound was generally associated with devices opposed to jazz and popular music, such as "saxless" instrumentation. See Robert Russell Bennett, "Orchestration of Theatre and Dance Music," in Bennett, *Broadway Sound*, 288–89.

50. I've borrowed the term *pomposo* from a "symphonic jazz" score written for Paul Whiteman's orchestra and analyzed by John Howland. See Ferde Grofé, *Metropolis* (New York: Robbins Music, 1928); Howland, *Ellington Uptown*, 154.

51. "Hallelujah" is issued on *Jimmie Lunceford at His Rare of All Rarest Performances Vol. 1* (Kings of Jazz LP-20016, n.d.).

52. Archie Bleyer, "Arranging Questions," *Metronome*, April 1933, 26. See also Lange, *Arranging*, 183–84.

53. Archie Bleyer, "Arranging Questions," *Metronome*, December 1932, 36, and July 1933, 34.

54. Robert Maxwell and Josef Myrow, "You Can Count on Me" [stock arrangement], arranged by Chappie Willet (New York: Exclusive Publications, 1939).

55. For a notated example of the Henderson "Christopher Columbus" trombone ostinato, see Magee, *Uncrowned King*, 237.

56. "Record Review: Blue Rhythm," *Down Beat*, June 1937, 16.

57. "What Is This Thing Called Swing" is issued on Louis Armstrong, *The Complete Louis Armstrong Decca Sessions 1935–1946* (Mosaic Records 7CD-243, 2009). In later recorded performances, Armstrong's pianist Luis Russell apparently simplified Willet's piano part to match the more common ("It Don't Mean a Thing"–like) descending bassline pattern.

58. "Uptown Rhapsody" is issued on Teddy Hill, *Uptown Rhapsody* (Hep CD-1033, 1992).

59. Gunther Schuller critiques this break passage of "Chant of the Weed" as a "modulation to nowhere"; Schuller, *Swing Era*, 370.

60. Some of Redman's Connie's Inn broadcast repertoire (ca. 1932) is documented in the bandleader's ledger books held in DRP.

61. Chico Hicks, telephone interview by the author, May 1, 2004.

62. Regarding Redman's 1920s arranging style, see Magee, *Uncrowned King*, 39–40, 195. The "baroque" label emanates from Giddens, *Satchmo*, 81.

63. The description of Willet's music as "clean-cut" is from Chico Hicks, telephone interview by the author, May 8, 2004.

64. Regarding Swing Era concepts of musical "flow and cohesion," see Magee, *Uncrowned King*, 130–31, 195; Eddie MacDonald, "It Must Have That Swing," *Metronome*, August 1933, 28.

65. Barnet's recording of "Prelude in C-sharp Minor" is issued on *Charlie Barnet and His Orchestra: Make Believe Ballroom 1935–1939* (Giants of Jazz CD-53274, 1997).

66. "Alexander's Ragtime Band" is issued on Louis Armstrong, *The Complete Louis Armstrong Decca Sessions 1935–1946* (Mosaic Records 7CD-243, 2009).

67. Armstrong has long been relegated to an irrationally low standing in narratives of Swing Era jazz; the orchestra he led from 1935 to 1947 is frequently belittled in critical commentary, if acknowledged at all. For example, George Simon claimed that Armstrong's orchestra "seldom achieved even mediocrity"; Albert McCarthy wrote that "the big bands with which Louis Armstrong worked for a decade and a half frequently included excellent musicians, but . . . contributed nothing of note to big band jazz as such." Even Armstrong biographer Terry Teachout, who allows that the Armstrong orchestra could sound "exciting in front of live audiences," somehow concludes that "Armstrong, who left the musical direction of his bands to other men, never pushed his arrangers to develop a distinctive style that would complement his own uniquely individual playing." Simon, *Big Bands*, 466; McCarthy, *Big Band Jazz*, 271; Teachout, *Pops*, 228, 251. Regarding the troubled reception of Armstrong's Swing Era big band in jazz histories, see Riccardi, *What a Wonderful World*, 5–6.

68. Armstrong, *Swing That Music*.

69. "Struttin' with Some Barbecue" is issued on Louis Armstrong, *The Complete Louis Armstrong Decca Sessions 1935–1946* (Mosaic Records 7CD-243, 2009). Willet's "Barbecue" arrangement was recorded in January 1938, but probably created the preceding year—although Willet had obtained his AFM union stamp prior to the close of 1937 (as reflected on parts for "In the Still of the Night" held in LAHM), the solo trumpet part for "Barbecue" displays the arranger's preunion-membership stamp.

70. Indeed, the *avoidance* of straight quarter-note phrasing or changes of key is arguably one of the defining qualities of post–World War II modern jazz styles, with the few exceptions typically taking the form of—predictably enough—"extended" compositions.

71. Trumpeter Harry James—a master of dramatic presentation with popular arrangements like "Flight of the Bumble-Bee"—was apparently impressed by Willet's "Barbecue" as well, commissioning a transcription of Willet's arrangement for his own orchestra in the 1950s; arranger Ray Conniff's manuscript score is held in HJC.

72. Harold Rubenstein, "Making Specials for [*sic*] Stocks," *Metronome*, November 1936, 47.

73. Duke Ellington, "Duke Says Swing Is Stagnant," *Down Beat*, February 1939, 2. Reprinted in Tucker, *Duke Ellington Reader*, 132.

74. Benny Goodman and Jimmy Mundy, "Fiesta in Blue" [stock arrangement], arranged by Jimmy Mundy (New York: Regent Music, 1941). "Nagasaki" and "Bolero at the Savoy" are issued on *Gene Krupa and His Orchestra 1938* (Classics CD-767, 1994). The out-chorus of "Nagasaki" also includes a favorite Mundy sax phrase that reappears in "Super Chief," recorded by Count Basie in 1940.

Chapter 7. Heavy Stuff

1. Daniel Richman, "Night Club Reviews: Kit Kat Club, New York," *Billboard*, November 5, 1938, 20.

2. For example, see the appraisal of arranger Skip Martin's work for the Count Basie orchestra in Schuller, *Swing Era*, 238.

3. Harrison, "Swing Era Big Bands," 284. For other examples of the Kansas City–versus–New York dichotomy, see Schuller, *Swing Era*, 222; Shih, "Spread of Jazz," 185–86; Stowe, "Jazz in the West," 55–56.

4. Alternative interpretations of the provenance of head arrangements are offered in Jeffrey Magee's discussion of the New York–based Fletcher Henderson orchestra. Magee, *Uncrowned King*, 131–35. A review of a December 1941 Count Basie–backed stage show perhaps offers an alternative reception of the Basie orchestra's performance practices; see George T. Simon, "Basie Band Provides Stage Thrill," *Metronome*, January 1942, 14.

5. For a discussion of the preferred musical qualities for the popular Swing Era Lindy Hop dance, including "no two-bar breaks to interrupt the momentum of the music" and "consistent four-beats-to-the-bar rhythm," see Spring, "Swing and the Lindy Hop," 186, 188.

6. Magee, *Uncrowned King*, 41. Magee's description is offered in the context of "signification": a theoretical framework that some musicologists have used to explain the aesthetics of jazz and its manipulation of established forms. Regarding the observation of musical manipulations as an extension of signification theories outlined by Henry Louis Gates Jr., see Floyd, *Power of Black Music*, 4–8.

7. Johnny Burke and James V. Monaco, "The Trumpet Player's Lament," copyright deposit, November 15, 1937 (E unp. 155540), U.S. Library of Congress.

8. "The Trumpet Player's Lament" was created as a vehicle for Armstrong to perform in the Bing Crosby film *Doctor Rhythm* (Paramount, 1938), but was cut from the production. Westerberg, *Boy from New Orleans*, 59.

9. An overview of pervasive "commercialism" and "authenticity" themes in Swing Era criticism is provided in Townsend, *Pearl Harbor Jazz*, 126–33. The emergence of America's highbrow/lowbrow cultural discourse is outlined in Savran, *Highbrow/Lowdown*, 44–51.

10. David Stowe extends his definition of "swinging the classics" to include folk song repertoire. Stowe, *Swing Changes*, 95. My personal preference is to place swing updates of vernacular vocal hits like "I Dream of Jeanie" or nursery rhymes like "A-Tisket, A-Tasket" under the "novelty song" banner.

11. For a discussion of the contemporary media debate surrounding "swinging the classics," see Stowe, *Swing Changes*, 94–98. See also Tanner, "Classic Swing," 64–66.

12. Stowe, *Swing Changes*, 98.

13. Howland, *Ellington Uptown*, 3.

14. Schuller, *Swing Era*, 815–16, 756. Treatments of Dvořák's "Humoresque" in particular seem to have struck a nerve with Schuller, who connected the title with the phrase "gullible public" *twice* in other chapters of *Swing Era* (485, 682). Schuller's unique partisanship in the jazz-meets-classical arena must be acknowledged, given his participation in (and naming of) the 1950s "third stream" movement—efforts to fuse "the improvisational spontaneity and rhythmic vitality of jazz with the compositional procedures and techniques acquired in Western music during 700 years of musical development"; Schuller, "Third Stream," 115.

15. Korall, *Drummin' Men*, 152.

16. Vail, *Swing Era Scrapbook*, 223, 232, 244.

17. DeVeaux, "Review of *Swing Changes*," 90.

18. "Sonata Pathétique" (originally issued on Columbia 35453) is issued on *Jimmie Lunceford and His Orchestra 1939–1940* (Classics CD-565, 1996).

19. "News of Night Clubs," NYT, February 4, 1940.

20. Al Monroe, "Swingin' the News," CD, May 25, 1940.

21. "Jimmie Lunceford Knows His Musical History," NYAN, March 9, 1940.

22. Schuller, *Swing Era*, 218–19 (emphasis in original). Similar criticism of "Pathétique" is offered in Dance, liner notes to Jimmie Lunceford, *The Complete Jimmie Lunceford 1939–40*.

23. In additional to being credited on the Columbia/CBS LP reissues, Willet had garnered public credit for the "Pathétique" arrangement two weeks before it was recorded. See Bill Chase, "All Ears," NYAN, February 10, 1940. Schuller's praise of Willet's work for Armstrong and Krupa can be found in Schuller, *Swing Era*, 193, 724. For additional Schuller criticism on "classic" repertoire, see his discussion of the John Kirby sextet in Schuller, *Swing Era*, 815. Regarding Schuller and middlebrow criticism, see Burke, *Come In and Hear the Truth*, 108.

24. Regarding the celebrated characteristics of the Lunceford orchestra and the context of African American "signification," see Berish, *Lonesome Roads*, 53–57.

25. McCarthy, liner notes to Jimmie Lunceford, *Harlem Express: Jimmie Lunceford and His Orchestra 1934–1936*. Curiously, an alternative analysis of Lunceford's style emerged in post–Swing Era efforts to highlight the important contributions of arranger Sy Oliver by fetishizing a "two-beat" rhythmic feel, an effect heard in a portion of Lunceford's repertoire (and a portion of Oliver's arrangements), but repeatedly emphasized in histories and reissue compilations. For example, see McCarthy, liner notes; Simon, *Big Bands*, 330; Shih, "Spread of Jazz," 185. Most of these "two-beat" pieces date from the mid-1930s, when many swing bands and arrangers shared a similar approach; the two-beat effect (as heard on Lunceford recordings like "On the Beach at Bali-Bali") often contrasts with passages of straight "four-beat" swing within the same arrangement, and can just as easily be heard as another ingredient toward textural variety. For example, see the discussion of Lunceford's 1935 recording of "Avalon" in Berish, *Lonesome Roads*, 54.

26. These descriptions by the Swedish *Orkester Journalen* and pianist Hank Jones are quoted in Determeyer, *Rhythm Is Our Business*, 135, 155.

27. Burke, *Come In and Hear the Truth*, 109.

28. Gerald Wilson, telephone interview by author, April 1, 2004.

29. Dance, *World of Swing*, 117.

30. Ibid., 102.

31. Harry "Sweets" Edison, interview by Stanley Dance, May 1981, cassette 2, transcript p, 18, JOHP.

32. Dance, *World of Swing*, 380.

33. "House Reviews: Apollo, N.Y.," *Variety*, May 7, 1941, 24.

34. Bill Chase, "All Ears," NYAN, April 9, 1938; Edgar A. Wiggins, "Duke Ellington's Band a Hit in France and Belgium," CD, April 22, 1939.

35. Sergei Rachmaninov, "Prelude in C-sharp Minor" [stock arrangement], "based on Chappie Willet's arr.," orchestrated by [Lyle] Spud Murphy (New York: Robbins Music, 1939). Armstrong's performance is cited in Vail, *Swing Era Scrapbook*, 337.

36. On the "light-classical" publishing phenomenon in America, see Krummel, "Printing and Publishing of Music §II, 4."

37. Olin Downes, "Music: José Iturbi Again Triumphs," NYT, November 1, 1930. H. Wiley Hitchcock discusses the American adulation of "technical brilliance" and European virtuosos in *Music in the United States*, 48–53. See also Lott, *From Paris to Peoria*, 289–94.

38. Olin Downes, "Music: José Iturbi Applauded by Throng," NYT, January 7, 1931. Iturbi's receptiveness to jazz influences is further exemplified by his later American premiere performance of Jean Wiener's "Franco-American Jazz Concerto"; see Olin Downes, "Music in Review: Iturbi and Musicians' Symphony Present Wiener's Franco-American Jazz Concerto," NYT, December 28, 1932.

39. As Iturbi himself declared in *Etude* magazine, Chopin's preludes and mazurkas represent "his greatest works . . . because they are short"; Florence Leonard, "Outline and Atmosphere in Piano Music: An Interview with José Iturbi," *Etude*, February 1932, 89. "Original" scores for all of the Willet-arranged classics identified to date were published in the monthly amateur music magazine *Etude*, as was most of the classical repertoire cited in this chapter. See Bomberger, *Index to Music*, 286, 376, 378, 397.

40. For example, Kirby also recorded versions of Schubert's "Serenade," Grieg's "Anitra's Dance," and Lou Singer's arrangement of Beethoven's seventh symphony (issued as "Beethoven Riffs On").

41. The score comparisons reference Frédéric Chopin, *Préludes Opus 28: An Authoritative Score, Historical Background, Analysis, Views, and Comments* [solo piano score], ed. Thomas Higgins (New York: Norton, 1973); Niccolò Paganini, *Caprice No. XXIV, Variations* [solo violin score] (New York: Carl Fischer, 1922).

42. Passages of Beethoven's first movement represented in Willet's arrangement include mm. 1–112, 187–220, 277–88, and 303–9. Ludwig van Beethoven, *Complete Piano Sonatas* [solo piano score], vol. 1 (1923; reprint, New York: Dover, 1975), 143–51.

43. The score comparisons reference Beethoven, *Complete Piano Sonatas*.

44. See Lange, *Arranging*, 52–54.

45. Regarding the voicings shown in these examples, it might be noted that although Lunceford carried a five-piece sax section at this time, Willet appears to have scored

"Pathétique" for only four (apparently omitting vocalist-saxophonist Dan Grissom from the section).

46. "Rustle of Spring" is issued on *Lucky Millinder and His Orchestra 1942* (Hindsight LP-233, 1986).

47. In the Ellington version of "Prelude," the "flatted-ninth" voice in mm. 57–61 is reflected in the baritone sax part. The Murphy-scored stock publication rescores the baritone sax part for a second tenor sax, but voices the minor-seventh degree of the dominant-seventh chord. In "Pathétique," the corresponding "flatted-ninth" voice at m. 141 is reflected in the second trombone part. The Murphy-scored stock publication of Willet's "Prelude in C-sharp Minor" arrangement reflects a guitar part chord spelling of "G7+" that more explicitly accounts for the presence of the augmented fifth. Willet also regularly used the augmented "+" nomenclature at this time (e.g., 1938 manuscript parts for "Washington and Lee Swing," held in RNP), perhaps making his choice of "flat-five" in "Prelude" all the more notable. Admittedly, referencing an orchestra part note spelling or guitar chord to extrapolate the arranger's theoretical intentions is problematic; dance band guitar parts of the period seldom reflect any chord extensions above the ninth degree, regardless of the corresponding ensemble voicing. It should also be noted that Willet's guitar part for "Pathétique" has not been located, and the notated excerpt of "Rustle of Spring" reflects an audio transcription.

48. As Evan Rapport notes, clarinets and flutes "have always been staples of jazz bands," but remain "strongly linked with the concert hall" in symphonic jazz contexts; Rapport, "Bill Finegan's Gershwin Arrangements," 522–23. Michael Broyles suggests that the clarinet solo in Willet's "Pathétique" arrangement is "reminiscent of the opening of Gershwin's *Rhapsody in Blue*"; Broyles, *Beethoven in America*, 299.

49. "Kirby, Lunceford Turn to 'Heavy' Stuff on Discs," CD, May 25, 1940.

50. Lange, *Arranging*, 212–13 (emphasis in original).

51. For example, see "Youth Creates for Armstrong: Willett [*sic*], Hot Tune Writer, Holds Music Degree—Russell Aided Him," NYAN, March 12, 1937.

52. The lyric version of Austin's arrangement was retitled "Tonight We Love"; see Simon, *Big Bands*, 338–39.

53. "Millinder to Open with 'Panorama of Jazz,'" BAA, June 24, 1944.

54. "Liszt Rejected by Iturbi, Pianist," NYT, August 10, 1933.

55. For additional examples of Swing Era renditions of classical repertoire, see Stowe, *Swing Changes*, 94–95. For examples of "rocking the classics," see Duxbury, *Rockin' the Classics*.

56. On concepts of "invention" in African American music, see Martin, "Review of *Lying Up a Nation*, by Ronald Radano," 761–64.

57. Hodeir, *Jazz*, 80–81. One might counter that Ellington's two-themed "exposition" is merely an AABA chorus form—the B theme being the bridge—although the chorus is not the typical thirty-two-bar Tin Pan Alley duration, and never repeats in its entirety.

58. Benny Goodman and Jimmy Mundy, "Fiesta in Blue" [stock arrangement], arranged by Jimmy Mundy (New York: Regent Music, 1941).

59. Goodman's recording reflects some of the cuts Goodman made to Sauter's arrangement, originally closer to five minutes in duration.

60. An aircheck recording of "Tea for Two" has been issued on Harry James, *King Porter Stomp* (Hep LP-31, 1984).

61. "Alone Together," "Estrellita," and "Yesterdays" are issued on *Jimmie Lunceford at His Rare of All Rarest Performances Vol. 1* (Kings of Jazz LP-20016, n.d.).

62. The identity of the trombonist featured on the issued "Estrellita" recording has not been confirmed; Willet's score assigns the solo to the first trombone chair of a three-trombone section. The dating of radio transcription recordings is complicated by aircheck recordings documenting broadcasts of the transcription recordings, often presented (falsely) as live performances; a single transcription recording may have been broadcast multiple times.

63. Manuel Ponce and Jascha Heifetz, "Estrellita (My Little Star)" (New York: Carl Fisher Music, 1928). Haifetz had performed "Estrellita" in the film *They Shall Have Music* (Samuel Goldwyn, 1939).

64. Frank Comstock's "Poinciana" score is held in BCC.

65. "Lunceford Answers Host of Queries on Arrangers of Music," NYAN, January 16, 1943. A similar presentation of the same press release was published as "Lunceford Makes Musical History," CD, January 30, 1943.

66. The "Yesterdays" recording may date to June–July 1943, as provided in Lotz and Neuert, *AFRS "Jubilee" Programs*, 33.

67. Art Farmer, as quoted in Miller, "Freddie Webster."

68. The "Stardust" orchestra parts held in LAHM display Willet's 1944 union stamp and are copied in the hand of Maceo Jefferson (1898–1974), who had been interned as a war prisoner in 1941 and repatriated in March 1944; Jefferson's copy work for Willet first appears in manuscripts dating to October 1944. Rye, "Maceo Jefferson."

69. "Stardust" is issued on Louis Armstrong, *Masters of Swing* (Swing Mania, 1995). The performance was reportedly broadcast around August 1945 from the Trianon Ballroom in South Gate, California; the trombone soloist is Russell "Big Chief" Moore; Willems, *All of Me*, 152.

70. Stewart, *Making the Scene*, 132–75.

Chapter 8. Give Me Some Skin

1. "Novelty Song Wanted for Immediate Publication," advertisement, *Billboard*, June 14, 1941, 13.

2. The Swing Era novelty song defined here differs somewhat from the "novelty ragtime" genre of the 1920s. See Howland, *Ellington Uptown*, 151–52.

3. For example, see "Lunceford Band Has Glee Club: Famous Cotton Club Orchestra Features Many Vocal Novelties," *Cornell Daily Sun*, February 4, 1936.

4. Willet's manuscript orchestra parts for "The Flat Foot Floogee" are held in RNP.

5. Willet's manuscript orchestra parts for "What Is This Thing Called Swing" are held in LAHM.

6. See "Sheet-Music Leaders," *Billboard*, September 10, 1938, 13. Sampson's score for "A-Tisket, A-Tasket"—one of (at least) two versions of the song commissioned by Goodman in 1938—is held in BGP; Willet's manuscript orchestra parts for Norvo are held in RNP.

7. Al Jacobs, Dave Oppenheim, and Jack Palmer, "Swingin' the Nursery Rhymes" [stock arrangement], arranged by Jimmy Mundy (New York: Stasny Music Corp., 1938).

8. Raymond Scott, "Twilight in Turkey" [stock arrangement], arranged by Jack Mason (New York: Circle Music, 1937).

9. Major Hurwitz, John Redmond, and Mary Schaeffer, "Toy-Town Jamboree" [publisher leadsheet] (New York: Red Star Songs, 1938).

10. The dating of "Toy-Town Jamboree" is in part based on the arrangement's numbering in the Norvo band book. The first recordings of "A-Tisket, A-Tasket" and "The Flat Foot Floogee" by their composers were released in June 1938. Willet's arrangement of "The Flat Foot Floogee" for Norvo is numbered "285" and "A-Tisket, A-Tasket," recorded by Norvo on July 28, is numbered "302"; "Toy-Town Jamboree" is numbered "330."

11. Regarding "Parade of the Wooden Soldiers" and tap-dancing, see Stearns and Stearns, *Jazz Dance*, 167, 187.

12. Lange, *Arranging*, 15. See also Weirick, *Dance Arranging*, 118.

13. "NEW DANCE," CD, September 14, 1940.

14. Ibid.

15. Esvan Mosby is credited with an appearance in *Hallelujah!* (MGM, 1929); see Frank, *Tap!*, 298. Mosby's cited birthplace and date reference a Seattle "Passenger and Crew List" of January 11, 1935, and the Social Security Death Index (both per AncestryLibrary.com).

16. Curtis Mosby was proprietor of the Apex Club and Club Alabam, among other venues. See Bakan, "Way Out West," 64–67; Eastman, "'Pitchin' Up a Boogie,'" 79–103, 82–83, 85–93. Trumpeter Clora Bryant clarified Esvan Mosby as "the second" mayor of Central Avenue in Bryant et al., *Central Avenue Sounds*, 358. Esvan was sufficiently involved in his brother's nightclub ventures to be implicated in a 1940 lawsuit concerning the Classic Café; see Major Robinson, "Mosby of Chocolateers Sued by California Firm," CD, September 7, 1940. Regarding Curtis Mosby's career, see Bakan, "Way Out West," 23–78, 65. Bakan states Curtis Mosby's year of birth as 1895; the 1900 *Twelfth Census of the United States* suggests the year 1890; the Social Security Death Index suggests a date of July 7, 1888; and World War I draft records suggest July 6, 1892.

17. Harry Levette, "Coast Codgings," CD, July 14, 1934; Clayton and Elliott, *Buck Clayton's Jazz World*, 73. Gibson's cited birthplace and date reference a Seattle "Passenger and Crew List" of January 11, 1935, and the Social Security Death Index (both per AncestryLibrary.com).

18. Billy Rowe, "Billy Rowe's Notebook," PC, December 7, 1940; "Detroit Finds a Set of Comic Jewels in Paul, Slim and Eddie," CD, March 21, 1942; Albert and Bleis, "Buster Brown Story," n.p. Paul Black's birth date and origins remain difficult to establish, although he was apparently still active as of 1982; see Jennifer Dunning, "A Tap Extravaganza in Brooklyn," NYT, February 19, 1982.

19. Albert and Bleis, "Buster Brown Story." The Chocolateers continued to perform into the 1950s, including a 1955–56 tour of Europe. See "'Smart Affairs of 1953' Now on Stage at Regal," *Chicago Daily Tribune*, November 23, 1952; "3 Chocolateers Triumph Abroad after Setback," CD, July 7, 1956.

20. Harry Levette, "The Three Chocolateers in China for Long Engagement," CD, September 1, 1934; "Chicago Defender Photo-Chart Shows Nationally Known Stage Celebrities," CD, July 10, 1937. The China-tour edition of the Chocolateers may have included one Guss Moore—who is listed in the 1935 return passenger list (cited in n. 17) alongside Mosby and Gibson—instead of Paul Black.

21. Clayton and Elliott, *Buck Clayton's Jazz World*, 73.

22. Publicity for the Chocolateers also claims that the group performed in the film *Murder at the Vanities* (Paramount, 1934), though this (uncredited) appearance remains unconfirmed; "3 Chocolateers Bring 'Peckin'' to Apollo Bill," NYAN, August 28, 1937.

23. "'Can This Be Dixie?' Will Open at Republic Friday," BAA, December 26, 1936; Contract 2208-C (MGM "A Day at the Races" Contract Office File Copy), "The Three Chocolateers," January 13, 1937, held in AMPAS. The MGM contract specified payment of $500 for the trio to be on call for one week; Esvan Mosby is listed as the group's contact.

24. "3 Chocolateers Bring 'Peckin'' to Apollo Bill"; Al Moses, "Blanche Calloway Scores at Apollo," BAA, September 11, 1937; "'Chocolateers' in Republic Picture," CD, June 6, 1942; "Chicago Defender Photo-Chart Shows Nationally Known Stage Celebrities."

25. See "Howard [Theater]," *Washington Post*, April 1, 1940.

26. [Goldberg], *By Word of Foot I*.

27. "'Duke Goes to Town' in His Latest Revue," PC, July 17, 1937; Stearns and Stearns, *Jazz Dance*, 246. Mark Knowles's *Tap Dance Dictionary* defines *peckin'* as "an eccentric dance move which consists of pushing the head forward and then back in place"; Knowles, *Tap Dance Dictionary*, 143. On the etymology of *eccentric dance*, see Harker, "Louis Armstrong," 70–82.

28. "3 Chocolateers Bring 'Peckin'' to Apollo Bill"; "Chocolateers, Dancing Demons, Cotton Club Hit," PC, January 29, 1938; M. H. Orodenker, "Orchestra Notes," *Billboard*, March 26, 1938, 12; "Cotton Club Show," NYAN, March 5, 1938; "Lunceford at Apollo," NYAN, December 31, 1938; "Cab Calloway Now on Tour of Country," CD, October 21, 1939; "Cab Calloway Opens Apollo for One Week," CD, December 23, 1939.

29. Levinson, *Trumpet Blues*, 25; Ben Pollack and Harry James, "Peckin'" [stock arrangement], arranged by James R. Mundy (New York: Mills Music, 1937).

30. Ben Pollack and Harry James, "Peckin'" [leadsheet] (New York: Mills Music, 1937); Cox, *Central Avenue*, 263. Cox's citation of Mosby's claim is excerpted from an interview of unspecified provenance, but probably dating from the 1970s or early '80s.

31. "Chocolateers' Tune Used in Navy Film," CD, April 5, 1941. Perhaps the piece was rehearsed while the Apollo was closed to the public during August 1940 for renovations and reorganization. See Dan Burley, "Apollo Theatre Closes Down," NYAN, July 27, 1940.

32. "The Hicky Ricky," copyright deposit, August 15, 1940 (E unp. 228569), U.S. Library of Congress; Nell Dodson, "Chocolateers' Manager Named in Suit," PC, September 7, 1940; "Cab Calloway's Tour Takes Him into the West," CD, September 14, 1940. Calloway's tours continued under the Cotton Club name beyond the lifespan of the club.

33. "New Mark Set by Calloway at Paramount," PC, September 7, 1940.

34. Dodson, "Chocolateers' Manager Named in Suit."

35. "Chocolateers' Tune Used in Navy Film." Also see Dan Burley, "Boston Footlite Flickers," CD, June 7, 1941.

36. Dan Burley, "Back Door Stuff," NYAN, April 12, 1941.

37. Bill Chase, "Ace Arranger Turns to Recording Field," NYAN, July 22, 1939, 17.

38. "Chappie Willet Has Studio and Agency in Heart of Broadway," PC, September 21, 1940.

39. Stanford [*sic*—Esvan] Mosby, "[The] Hicky Ricky," *Too Late, Too Late, Volume 10: 1926–1951* (Document Records CD-5601, 1998). This issue incorrectly lists the performer as "Stanford Mosby" and provides the less likely recording date of "ca. 1938."

40. According to the Document Records release, the Mosby recording derives from the West Coast; the opposite side of the disc presents a performance by the Camp Acton Jive Cats, presumably a reference to California's substance-abuse rehabilitation camp by that name.

41. "The Hicky Ricky," copyright deposit, November 7, 1941 (E unp. 274977), U.S. Library of Congress. As issued, Mosby sings "The Hicky Ricky" in the key of E-flat, a whole-step lower than the key of F reflected in copyright leadsheets. The 1941 leadsheet lists only Mosby, Gibson, and Willet as composers, likely reflecting Paul Black's exit from the group at the end of 1940; see Billy Rowe, "Billy Rowe's Notebook," PC, December 7, 1940. The 1941 leadsheet also reflects a change in the chorus lyrics from the original 1940 version: "tippy tippy tin wham" is replaced by "stand back and grin say." The Kaycee-Leeds relationship is noted in 1941 leadsheet publications, including "Fur Trapper's Ball" and "Sailboat in the Sky."

42. Cab Calloway, "Peckin'," *Cab Calloway and His Orchestra 1934–1937* (Classics CD-554, 1991); Duke Ellington, Irving Mills, and Henry Nemo, "Skrontch" [leadsheet] (New York: Mills Music, 1938).

43. Regarding Slim Gaillard's style, see "New Jive Talk Rage of Harlem," PC, June 25, 1938; Eugene Kinkead and Harold Ross, "The Talk of the Town: Jive Men," *New Yorker*, June 25, 1938, 9; Charles Herndon, "Slim Gaillard Coins New Jazz Language," NYAN, September 20, 1952.

44. On the bridge of the demo recording, Mosby repeats "Susi-ma-Q" instead of citing "Scronch-a-ma-roo."

45. The 1942 Leeds Music–published leadsheet for "Hicky Ricky" includes an additional four-bar piano introduction and awkwardly adds unaltered fifths to some of the left-hand voicings of the verse, obscuring the whole-tone quality of Willet's original parallel voicing effect.

46. Bars 19–20 present an altered II7—bII7—I7 sequence in the local tonality of C, with bII7 substituting for the expected V7 (G7).

47. Dan Burley cited the phrase "gimme some skin" as representative of recently emerging "Harlemese" in his column "Backdoor Stuff," NYAN, July 6, 1940. Additional sources date the phrase to the 1940s; see Major, *Juba to Jive*, 202.

48. The release of the Delta Rhythm Boys disc was noted in "Delta Rhythm for Downtown Theatre," NYAN, March 29, 1941.

49. Michel Ruppli, *The Eastern and Southern Sessions, 1934–1942*, vol. 2 of *The Decca Labels: A Discography*, 640; Hampton and Haskins, *Hamp*, 103.

50. Maurice Dancer, "Harlem Goes Broadway for Reopening of Mimo Club," CD, September 27, 1941.

51. *In the Navy* (MCA Universal [VHS], 1991). The film was in production from April 8 through mid-May 1941, and released on May 30, according to "In the Navy," *Turner Classic Movies*, accessed October 18, 2015, http://www.tcm.com/tcmdb/title/563965/In-the-Navy/.

52. "Gimme Some Skin," copyright deposit, March 13, 1941 (E unp. 251362), *U.S. Copyright Report*. "Gimme Some Skin, My Friend," was registered for copyright on April 8, 1941 (E unp. 254542), and again on June 17, 1941 (E pub. 95956). The potential for sexual innuendo in the Andrews Sisters' material was noted by contemporary critics. See Hedda Hopper, "Hedda Hopper's Hollywood," *Los Angeles Times*, April 22, 1941.

53. Don Raye, Red Mack, and Gene de Paul, "Gimme Some Skin, My Friend" [publisher leadsheet] (New York: Leeds Music, 1941). Vic Schoen's 1941 arrangement of "Gimme Some Skin, My Friend" for the Andrews Sisters (released on disc as Decca 3871) reflects a number of melodic, harmonic, and rhythmic variations from the published leadsheet.

54. Red Mack (a.k.a. McClure Morris) was omitted from the April 1941 copyright registrations for "Gimme Some Skin, My Friend," although his name is included on the Leeds published leadsheet.

55. Don Raye, Hughie Prince, and the Ritz Brothers, "Rhumboogie" [leadsheet] (New York: Leeds Music, 1940). "Rhumboogie" was featured by the Andrews Sisters in the film *Argentine Nights* (Universal, 1940).

56. [Goldberg], *By Word of Foot I*. Perhaps the song accompanied the infamous "Porto Rico" clown as he chased unsuccessful amateur-night acts off the Apollo stage; see Fox, *Showtime at the Apollo*, 109–10.

57. The "Ballin' the Jack" dance is described as "bending over and putting the hands upon the knees and then swinging the knees from side to side in a crescent path" in Knowles, *Tap Dance Dictionary*, 15. For a somewhat different account, see Stearns and Stearns, *Jazz Dance*, 98–99.

58. At the time of this writing, the complete "Gimme Some Skin" sequence from *In the Navy* is available online; the moment cited occurs at 2:09 into the posted video clip. See "Andrews Sisters - Gimme Some Skin, My Friend," *YouTube*, accessed October 18, 2015, https://www.youtube.com/watch?v=kIFN13-a1iA.

59. The dance director credited in *In the Navy* was Nick Castle, who had choreographed Hollywood appearances for acts including the Nicholas Brothers. See Stearns and Stearns, *Jazz Dance*, 281.

60. The "Hicky Ricky" score is held in DEC, Series 1A (Oversize), box 427, folder 7 (listed as folder 8).

61. Among other engagements circa 1940–41, Whaley supplied material for stage shows at the Apollo and Broadway's Hurricane nightclub. Dance, *World of Duke Ellington*, 48.

62. Schoen is the only music arranger cited in the credits for *In the Navy*.

63. "Gimme Some Skin, My Friend" is issued on the Andrews Sisters, *50th Anniversary Collection Vol. 1* (MCA CD-4426, 1990).

64. Lawrence F. LaMar, "Chocolateers Are Held-Over in West," CD, May 31, 1941.

65. Sam Abbott, "Night Club Follow-Up Reviews," *Billboard*, January 24, 1942, 19; "'Chocolateers' in Republic Picture"; "Three Chocolateers Get Role in Republic's New Musical," BAA, June 6, 1942. Produced in April 1942, *Moonlight Masquerade* was released the following summer, and distributed again in late 1943. "Three Chocolateers Perform for Movies," NYAN, December 18, 1943.

66. The "new dance sensation" descriptor had also been included in the 1941 copyright deposit.

67. "The Hicky Ricky," copyright deposit, July 20, 1942 (E pub. 106386), U.S. Library of Congress. Charles Previn and Ted Cain are credited as the musical director and music supervisor, respectively, in *In the Navy.* Cy Feuer is credited as musical director for *Moonlight Masquerade.*

68. "Chocolateers Will Show Off New Dance," CD, August 30, 1941.

69. The 1942 version of "Peckin'" was released by Soundies Distribution on November 9, 1942, as provided in Stearns and Stearns, *Jazz Dance*, 416; the film is available on [Three] Chocolateers, "Peckin'," *Music Clips from the Swing Years: Dance Your Old Age Away* (Unforgettable DVD-12122 B, 2004). The Chocolateers returned to "Peckin'" again in 1953; the resulting audio disc has been reissued on *Rockin' at Midnight at the Parrot Club* (Relic CD-7027, 1992).

70. A 1941 study of the American popular music industry claimed an average of thirty-five to forty new songs placed on the publishing market each week, including "novelties" and "rhythm numbers." These publishing "industry estimates" are offered in MacDougald, "Popular Music Industry," 176.

71. Another example of cultural fusion in *In the Navy* is the Andrews Sisters' performance of Gene de Paul and Don Raye's "Hula-ba-luau" (E unp. 254543)—also published by Leeds Music—combining boogie-woogie and Pacific island influences.

72. Mack recorded "Gimme Some Skin—Mah Friend" for the Hollywood-based Gold Seal label, presumably ca. 1946; Campbell and Pruter, "Gold Seal."

73. Monson, "Abbey Lincoln's *Straight Ahead*," 175.

74. Regarding opportunities for African American entertainers and jazz musicians in 1930s Shanghai, see Jones, "Black Internationale," 230–31.

75. "Willett [*sic*] Heads Music Firm," CD, June 29, 1944; "Willett [*sic*] Artists Bureau Newest Newsreel Feature," PC, February 1, 1947; Charley Cherokee, "National Grapevine," CD, November 25, 1944. Regarding Willet and Robbins Music, see Billy Rowe, "Chappie Willet Signed," PC, April 30, 1938.

76. "Film Reviews: Hi-de-Ho," *Variety*, May 14, 1947, 15; *Hi-De-Ho/The Duke Is Tops*, Classic Musicals DVD (Mill Creek Entertainment, 2005). Calloway made multiple films under the *Hi-De-Ho* title.

77. "Willet's New Jive Tune on the Hit List," PC, September 13, 1941.

78. Llewellyn Crawford and Chappie Willet, "Eh! Now," copyright deposit, September 3, 1941 (E unp. 268863), U.S. Library of Congress.

79. Use of the phrase *spank the plank* can be found in Chester L. Washington Jr., "Ups and Downs: Reflections from Life," PC, May 9, 1942; Dan Burley, "Back Door Stuff," NYAN, September 19, 1942; "Camp Lee Has Own Tin Pan Alley Songs Show," BAA, April 17, 1943; Dan Burley, "Back Door Stuff," NYAN, September 25, 1943.

80. A manuscript piano accompaniment part for "Eh! Now," copied in pencil by Willet, is held in DEC; the copyright deposit leadsheet reflects the vocal melody and lyrics only.

81. "New Song Wows Gang in New York's Harlem," CD, September 13, 1941. See also "New Singing Sensations," NYAN, September 20, 1941.

82. "Peters Sisters in a Pix Made in New York," CD, October 4, 1941.

83. "Bye Sisters Say Bye to Early Ambitions as Stage Claims Trio," BAA, September 27, 1941.

84. Major Robinson, "Through Harlem," CD, July 11, 1942. Regarding plans for the Hampton tour, see Alvin Moses, "Alvin Moses Says," CD, March 28, 1942; Billy Jones, "Star Twinkles," CD, June 20, 1942.

85. The aircheck recording of "Eh! Now" is held in the collection of Ben Young.

86. Whaley's manuscript score and orchestra parts for "Eh! Now" are held in DEC. The orchestra parts include additional material not reflected in the score.

87. A study in *Radio Research 1941* describes a popular song to be "classified as a hit" after achieving sheet-music sales of 75,000 copies; for recordings, an "average hit" was marked by the sale of 250,000 discs. MacDougald, "Popular Music Industry," 176.

88. "Music Notes," *Billboard*, April 13, 1935, 15.

89. For example, see "Music Notes: 10 Best Records," *Billboard*, November 2, 1935, 61. Prior to its weekly jukebox rating system, *Billboard* offered listings of the "10 Best Records" and "Sheet-Music Leaders" as "reported by . . . record firms" or "leading jobbers and retail music outlets"—unspecified sources that were almost certainly as open to manipulation as later "payola"-based disc-jockey rating systems.

90. Magee, *Uncrowned King*, 145.

91. Erenberg, *Swingin' the Dream*, 85.

92. The AFM recording ban of 1942 to 1944 has often been cited as a contributing factor behind the rise in popularity of some vocalists during this period. For example, see Erenberg, *Swingin' the Dream*, 216–17. An alternative analysis is offered in Townsend, *Pearl Harbor Jazz*, 179–80.

93. Mundy's manuscript score for "These Foolish Things" is held in BGP.

94. Sinatra's alterations to the original "East of the Sun" lyrics are usually maintained in later interpretations of the song. The vocal melody reflected in Willet's conductor score and piano part for Lunceford does not include the lyrics, leaving the arranger's preference unclear.

95. A period discussion of ostinato scoring is offered in Otto Cesana, "Use of Ostinato Reduces Monotony in Arrangements," *Metronome*, February 1942, 47.

96. Porter Grainger and Chappie Willet, "Nothin' to Do but Love," copyright deposit, April 28, 1938 (E unpub. 165622), U.S. Library of Congress; Rowe, "Chappie Willet Signed."

97. Forte, *American Popular Ballad*, 7–8, 12–14, 16–17, 20–23.

98. See ibid., 32.

99. Townsend, *Pearl Harbor Jazz*, 179.

100. Bauer, "Louis Armstrong's 'Skid Dat De Dat,'" 134.

101. Perea, "Voices from the Jazz Wilderness," 230.

Chapter 9. Jungle Madness

1. Bernhardt, *I Remember*, 126.

2. Artie Shaw, as quoted in the documentary film *Artie Shaw: The Quest for Perfection* (British Broadcasting Corporation/Associated-Rediffusion Television, 2003).

3. Dinerstein, *Swinging the Machine*, 167.

4. *Jimmie Lunceford at His Rare of All Rarest Performances Vol. 1* (Kings of Jazz LP-20016, n.d.). Partial manuscript orchestra parts for "Hallelujah" are held in FDCJLO.

5. Bernhardt, *I Remember*, 120.

6. Manuscript orchestra parts or scores for the cited medleys are held in FDCJLO, ASC, CBC, and LAHM. The Armstrong medley parts cite no arranger, but are copied by Maceo Jefferson, who did other copy work for Willet during 1944 and 1945.

7. Magee, *Uncrowned King*, 39.

8. Magee, *Uncrowned King*, 152–53; Ellington's treatments of "Tiger Rag" are discussed in Schiff, *Ellington Century*, 63–67.

9. A relevant discussion of "I Got Rhythm" contrafacts is provided in Tackley, *Benny Goodman's Famous*, 44.

10. Although "Rhythm Jam" debuted on the *Fleishmann's* program a couple of weeks earlier than "I Got Rhythm," the latter arrangement was almost certainly created first, and may well be the Willet arrangement cited among Armstrong's repertoire as early as January 1936 (alongside "Blue Rhythm Fantasy," "Jungle Madness," and "Tiger Rag"). Allan McMillan, "Hi-Hattin' in Harlem," CD, January 11, 1936.

11. "Jungle Madness" and "Prelude to a Stomp"—the latter title also performed by Armstrong on the 1937 *Fleischmann's* show (issued as "Will You Do a Stomp?")—similarly received their debut recordings by the Mills Blue Rhythm Band in February 1937.

12. The chord progression used in "Washington and Lee Swing" and the final strain of "Tiger Rag" is generally acknowledged to predate either composition, including precedents in nineteenth-century marching band music.

13. Morrison Ryder, "'Chappie' and Band Score Hit at Daniel Boone Hotel," [West Virginia State College] *Yellow Jacket*, November 1, 1932.

14. "Washington and Lee Swing" is issued on Louis Armstrong, *Fleischmann's Yeast Show and Louis' Home-Recorded Tapes* (Jazz Heritage Society CD 5289147, 2008).

15. For example, see Isadora Smith, "Cab Calloway, Nicholas Brothers Reach Peak in the Cotton Club's Latest Broadway Offering," PC, October 22, 1938; "Radio Reviews: Let's Dance," *Billboard*, December 15, 1934, 9.

16. Precedents for exotic strategies found in early twentieth-century European classical and American jazz and popular music are overviewed in Locke, *Musical Exoticism*, 214–75.

17. Ibid., 251.

18. Lange, *Arranging*, 181–82.

19. Elements of Ellington's "jungle" style are described in Tucker, *Ellington*, 133, 216, 224. See also Schuller, *Early Jazz*, 339.

20. "Apollo," advertisement, NYAN, March 9, 1935.

21. Gifford's "Chant of the Jungle" manuscript score is held in GGC.

22. "Jungle Madness" is issued on *Mills Blue Rhythm Band 1936–1937* (Classics CD-731, 1993).

23. Korall, *Drummin' Men*, 55.

24. Goodman's different renditions of "Sing, Sing, Sing" are outlined in Tackley, *Benny Goodman's Famous*, 93–100.

25. McMillan, "Hi-Hattin' in Harlem."

26. The possibility of creative contributions to "Blue Rhythm Fantasy" by Teddy Hill, who is also credited for other compositions, cannot be completely dismissed. Nevertheless, it was common practice for Swing Era bandleaders to add their names to the copyrights of pieces they had commissioned or debuted on record.

27. "Apollo," advertisement, NYAN, October 19, 1935. "Uptown Rhapsody," another Hill band arrangement attributed to Willet, certainly dates from that fall, if not earlier; the composer credits of "Uptown" include saxophonist Chu Berry, who left the Hill band shortly after the Apollo engagement.

28. Hill's performances of "Blue Rhythm Fantasy" are noted in Vail, *Swing Era Scrapbook*, 65, 157. In addition to personnel replacements, the second Hill recording of "Fantasy" added a second trombone player—uncredited in most discographies, but probably Wilbur DeParis—and includes a trombone background riff behind the trumpet solo that is absent in the 1936 recording.

29. Hill's summer 1937 European tour is traced in Howard Rye, "Visiting Firemen 6: Teddy Hill and the Cotton Club Revue," *Storyville* 100 (April 1982): 144–46.

30. Bryant's performances of "Blue Rhythm Fantasy" during summer 1937 are noted in Vail, *Swing Era Scrapbook*, 223, 231, 232, 237, 245, 265, 295. Bryant also performed Willet's "Prelude to a Stomp" during this period; see Vail, *Swing Era Scrapbook*, 147, 239.

31. Edward Murphy, "Nightclub-Vaudeville Reviews: Golden Gate, San Francisco," *Billboard*, January 23, 1943, 16.

32. Chappie Willet and Teddy Hill, "Blue Rhythm Fantasy" [stock arrangement], arranged by Edgar Battle (New York: Exclusive Publications, 1936). The copyright for "Blue Rhythm Fantasy" was filed on October 16, 1936, probably upon (or soon after) the release of the Hill recording. The "Fantasy" stock arrangement parts include advertising for a Mills Music arrangement of "Caravan," first recorded in December 1936; a publicity photo of Willet that includes a copy of the "Fantasy" leadsheet indicates a print date no later than December 1937.

33. Chappie Willet and Teddy Hill, "Blue Rhythm Fantasy" [publisher leadsheet] (New York: Exclusive Music, 1936). The stock arrangement and leadsheet are copied in the same hand and reflect a similar formal routine (as well as what appear to be similar pitch errors).

34. Regarding the exotic jazz-modernist characteristics of "Caravan," see Locke, *Musical Exoticism*, 253.

35. Ferde Grofé, *Metropolis: A Blue Fantasie* [piano score] (New York: Robbins Music, 1928).

36. The *New York Evening Post* review is cited in Rayno, *Paul Whiteman*, 214. A relevant musical analysis of Grofé's *Metropolis* is provided in Howland, *Ellington Uptown*, 154–57.

37. "Blue Rhythm Fantasy" is issued on Teddy Hill, *Uptown Rhapsody* (Hep CD-1033, 1992).

38. Another potential parallel between "Blue Rhythm Fantasy" and *Metropolis* is their shared alternation between the tonalities of E-flat major and C minor—among other key areas—though again, the relationship here is loose.

39. Don Redman, "Chant of the Weed" [stock arrangement], arranged by Don Redman (New York: Gotham Music Service, 1932). Gotham Music's "sole selling agent" is listed as Mills Music.

40. The "Chant of the Weed" timing provided references a comparable passage in Redman's 1931 recording (though for expanded instrumentation), issued on Don Redman, *Shakin' the Africann* (Hep CD-1001, 2002). The stock arrangement's strikingly dissonant E-natural in the brass against the saxophone's E-flat in this passage is consistent with later manuscript versions of the arrangement held in DRP.

41. A transcribed score of Redman's whole-tone "Chant of the Weed" theme, along with its chordal accompaniment voiced in parallel half-step motion, is offered in Sturm, *Changes over Time*, 74. See also Schuller, *Swing Era*, 369.

42. "Bebop" is issued on Dizzy Gillespie, *The Ultimate Collection* (Stardust Records, 2009).

43. Gillespie also recalled Willet anecdotally, reportedly asking: "You remember Chappie Willet? He used to write a lot of way out things for the Millinder band in crazy times-three-eight; five-eight; twelve-eight; sixteen-ninety-five—you name it"; Shipton, *Groovin' High*, 367 n. 9. Gillespie may have also performed Willet's music while playing in the Philadelphia band of Frank Fairfax—the former manager of Willet's own Greystone Ballroom Orchestra—during 1935 and 1936; see Wriggle, "Chappie Willet, Frank Fairfax," 13–16.

44. Neither triplet figure appears in the stock publication, which omits the original shout chorus entirely.

45. Paul Denis, "Nightclub-Vaudeville Reviews: Paramount, New York," *Billboard*, January 10, 1942, 24.

46. Himmelstein, liner notes to *Dizzy Gillespie: 16 Rare Performances*; McCarthy, *Big Band Jazz*, 286. McCarthy also describes "Fantasy" as "rather theatrical."

47. Billy Rowe, "Billy Rowe's Notebook," PC, June 17, 1950. Willet's midtown office address remained listed in the AFM (Local 802) union directory through 1952.

Conclusion

1. Shih, "Spread of Jazz," 181–82.

2. Louis Armstrong, correspondence to Don Redman, May 19, 1939, DRP.

3. Regarding perceptions of black music's "distance from the perceived normalcy of a civilized, unemotional, and hence inauthentic white populace," see Radano, "Hot Fantasies," 465.

4. A discussion of jazz's role(s) as a distinct cultural entity during the Swing Era is offered in Erenberg, *Swingin' the Dream*, 78–83.

5. For example, the exclusion of "rhythm 'n' blues" from jazz histories is discussed in Townsend, *Pearl Harbor Jazz*, 157–70.

6. Period references to the Chocolateers' "Harlem antics" include "Night Club Follow-Up Reviews," *Billboard*, January 24, 1942, 19.

7. For example, see the discussion of Mingus's business concerns included in Goodman, *Mingus Speaks*, 158–86.

8. For example, John Lewis's 1959 third-stream composition "Sketch for Double Quartet" pits a composed string quartet performance against an improvising jazz quartet. Performances by the Art Ensemble of Chicago in the 1970s have likewise been heard to utilize familiar tropes of genre and style, relying on audience perceptions of dramatic "intermusicality"; see Steinbeck, "Intermusicality, Humor, and Cultural Critique," 135–54.

9. Teal, "Beyond the Cotton Club," 145.

10. Decker, *Music Makes Me*, 128–68.

11. Bogle, *Bright Boulevards*, 224–32.

12. See Howland, "Jazz with Strings." Nelson Riddle discusses his own career and arranging philosophy in Riddle, *Arranged by Nelson Riddle*, 164–80, 193–95.

13. Stewart, *Making the Scene*, 132–75.

14. Jones, *Q: The Autobiography of Quincy Jones*, 228–46.

15. Berish, *Lonesome Roads*, 217.

16. Murray, *Stomping the Blues*, 196.

17. Goodman, *Kingdom of Swing*, 152.

Bibliography

Ake, David. "Crossing the Street: Rethinking Jazz Education." In *Jazz/Not Jazz: The Music and Its Boundaries*, edited by David Ake, Charles Hiroshi Garrett, and Daniel Goldmark, 237–63. Berkeley: University of California Press, 2012.

Albert, Kurt, and Klaus Bleis. "The Buster Brown Story: To Buster with Love." *International Tap Association Newsletter* 13, no. 2 (Fall 2002): n.p.

Alexander, Van, with Stephen Fratallone. *From Harlem to Hollywood: My Life in Music.* Albany, GA: BearManor Media, 2009.

Allen, Walter C. *Hendersonia: The Music of Fletcher Henderson and His Musicians.* Highland Park, NJ: Walter C. Allen, 1973.

Antrim, Doron K., ed. *Secrets of Dance Band Success.* New York: Famous Stars, 1936.

Armstrong, Louis. *Swing That Music.* London: Longmans, Green, 1936.

Atkins, Cholly, and Jacqui Malone. *Class Act: The Jazz Life of Choreographer Cholly Atkins.* New York: Columbia University Press, 2001.

Axtell, Dan. "Hello, Ev'rybody, Yes Indeed: A Centennial Salute to Charity Bailey." Accessed October 18, 2015. www.danaxtell.com/CharityBailey.

Badger, Reid. *A Life in Ragtime: A Biography of James Reese Europe.* New York: Oxford University Press, 1995.

Bakan, Jonathon. "Jazz and the 'Popular Front': 'Swing' Musicians and the Left-Wing Movement of the 1930s–1940s." *Jazz Perspectives* 3, no. 1 (April 2009): 35–56.

Bakan, Michael B. "Way Out West on Central: Jazz in the African-American Community of Los Angeles before 1930." In *California Soul: Music of African Americans in the West*, edited by Jacqueline Cogoell Djedje and Eddie S. Meadows, 23–78. Berkeley: University of California Press, 1998.

Bañagale, Ryan Raul. "Rewriting the Narrative One Arrangement at a Time: Duke Ellington and 'Rhapsody in Blue.'" *Jazz Perspectives* 6, nos. 1–2 (2012): 5–27.

Baraka, Amiri [Leroi Jones]. *Blues People: Negro Music in White America.* New York: HarperCollins, 1963.

Barnet, Charlie. *Those Swinging Years.* Baton Rouge: Louisiana State University Press, 1984.

Basie, Count, and Albert Murray. *Good Morning Blues: The Autobiography of Count Basie*. New York: Da Capo Press, 2002.

Bastin, Bruce. *Never Sell a Copyright: Joe Davis and His Role in the New York Music Scene 1916–1978*. Chigwell, UK: Storyville, 1990.

Bauer, William. "Louis Armstrong's 'Skid Dat De Dat': Timbral Organization in an Early Scat Solo." *Jazz Perspectives* 1, no. 2 (November 2007): 133–65.

Baumgartner, Michael. "Duke Ellington's 'East St. Louis Toodle-Oo' Revisited." *Jazz Perspectives* 6, nos. 1–2 (2012): 29–56.

Bennett, Robert Russell. *The Broadway Sound: The Autobiography and Selected Essays of Robert Russell Bennett*. Edited by George J. Ferencz. Rochester, NY: University of Rochester Press, 1999.

Bennett, Tom. "Arranging Music for Radio." In *Music in Radio Broadcasting*. NBC–Columbia University Broadcasting Series, edited by Gilbert Chase, 76–90. New York: McGraw-Hill, 1946.

Benson, Bruce. *The Improvisation of Musical Dialogue: A Phenomenology of Music*. Cambridge: Cambridge University Press, 2003.

Berger, Edward. *Basically Speaking: An Oral History of George Duvivier*. Studies in Jazz, no. 17. Metuchen, NJ: Rutgers Institute of Jazz Studies and Scarecrow Press, 1993.

Berger, Edward, Morroe Berger, and James Patrick. *Benny Carter: A Life in American Music*. Vol. 1. Lanham, MD: Scarecrow Press, 2002.

Bergmeister, Horst J. P., and Rainer E. Lotz. Liner notes to *Live from the Cotton Club*. Bear Family Records 16340, 2003.

Berish, Andrew S. *Lonesome Roads and Streets of Dreams: Place, Mobility, and Race in Jazz of the 1930s and '40s*. Chicago: University of Chicago Press, 2012.

Berliner, Paul. *Thinking in Jazz: The Infinite Art of Improvisation*. Chicago: University of Chicago Press, 1994.

Bernhardt, Clyde, with Sheldon Harris. *I Remember: Eighty Years of Black Entertainment, Big Bands, and the Blues*. Philadelphia: University of Pennsylvania Press, 1986.

Bierman, Benjamin. *Listening to Jazz*. New York: Oxford University Press, 2015.

Bindas, Kenneth J. *Swing, That Modern Sound*. Jackson: University Press of Mississippi, 2001.

Blesh, Rudi. *Shining Trumpets: A History of Jazz*. New York: Alfred A. Knopf, 1946.

Bogle, Donald. *Bright Boulevards, Bold Dreams: The Story of Black Hollywood*. New York: Random House, 2005.

Bomberger, E. Douglas. *An Index to Music Published in 'The Etude' Magazine, 1883–1957*. Lanham, MD: Scarecrow Press, 2004.

Boras, Tom. *Jazz Composition and Arranging*. Belmont, CA: Thomson Schirmer, 2005.

Brodsky, Warren. "Joseph Schillinger (1895–1943): Music Science Promethean." *American Music* 21, no. 1 (Spring 2003): 45–73.

Broyles, Michael. *Beethoven in America*. Bloomington: Indiana University Press, 2011.

Bryant, Clora, Marshal Royal, Lee Young, Fletcher Smith, Coney Woodman, William Woodman, Britt Woodman, et al. *Central Avenue Sounds: Jazz in Los Angeles*. Berkeley: University of California Press, 1998.

Buehrer, Ted, and Robert Hodson. "Metric Dissonance in Jazz: The Stride Piano Performances of Thelonious Monk and James P. Johnson." Paper presented at the Society for Music Theory/American Musicological Society conference, Seattle, November 2004.

Burke, Patrick. *Come In and Hear the Truth: Jazz and Race on 52nd Street*. Chicago: University of Chicago Press, 2008.

Burley, Dan. *Dan Burley's Original Handbook of Harlem Jive*. [New York: Dan Burley], 1944.

Calloway, Cab, and Bryant Rollins. *Of Minnie the Moocher and Me*. New York: Crowell, 1976.

Campbell, Robert L., and Robert Pruter. "Gold Seal." October 17, 2013. Accessed November 10, 2013. http://myweb.clemson.edu/~campber/goldseal.html.

Carlin, Richard, and Kinshasha Holman Conwill, eds. *Ain't Nothing Like the Real Thing: How the Apollo Theater Shaped American Entertainment*. Washington, DC: Smithsonian Books, 2010.

Cesana, Otto. *Course in Modern Dance Arranging*. New York: Modern Music Publications, n.d. [ca. 1938].

———. *Course in Modern Harmony*. New York: Modern Music Publications, n.d. [ca. 1938].

Charters, Samuel, and Leonard Kundstadt. *Jazz: A History of the New York Scene*. Garden City, NY: Doubleday, 1962.

Chilton, John. *McKinney's Music: A Bio-Discography of McKinney's Cotton Pickers*. London: Bloomsbury, 1978.

———. *Who's Who of Jazz: Storyville to Swing Street*. New York: Da Capo Press, 1985.

Chilton, John, and Max Jones. *Louis: The Louis Armstrong Story, 1900–1971*. London: Studio Vista, 1971.

Clarke, John L., Jr. "Archie Bleyer and the Lost Influence of Stock Arrangements in Jazz." *American Music* 27, no. 2 (Summer 2009): 138–79.

Clarkson, Austin. "Stefan Wolpe in Conversation with Eric Salzman." *Musical Quarterly* 83, no. 3 (Autumn 1999): 378–412.

Clayton, Buck, and Nancy Miller Elliott. *Buck Clayton's Jazz World*. New York: Oxford University Press, 1987.

Cogswell, Michael. *Louis Armstrong: The Offstage Story of Satchmo*. Portland, OR: Collector's Press, 2003.

Cohen, Harvey G. *Duke Ellington's America*. Chicago: University of Chicago Press, 2010.

Coker, Jerry. *The Jazz Idiom*. Englewood Cliffs, NJ: Prentice-Hall, 1975.

Collier, James Lincoln. "Jazz (i); §II, 5: The Emergence of Hot Music." In *The New Grove Dictionary of Jazz*, edited by Barry Kernfeld, 582–83. New York: St. Martin's Press, 1994.

Combs, Paul. *Dameronia: The Life and Music of Tadd Dameron*. Ann Arbor: University of Michigan Press, 2012.

Connor, D. Russell. *Benny Goodman: Listen to His Legacy*. Studies in Jazz, no. 6. Metuchen, NJ: Scarecrow Press and the Institute of Jazz Studies, 1988.

Cox, Bette Yarbrough. *Central Avenue—Its Rise and Fall (1890–c. 1955)*. Los Angeles, BEEM, 1996.

Cray, Ed. *Ramblin' Man: The Life and Times of Woody Guthrie*. New York: W. W. Norton, 2004.

Cullen, Frank, Florence Hackman, and Donald McNeilly. *Vaudeville, Old and New: An Encyclopedia of Variety Performers in America*. New York: Routledge, 2007.

Cuny-Hare, Maud. *Negro Musicians and Their Music*. Washington, DC: Associated, 1936.

Dance, Stanley. Liner notes to Jimmie Lunceford, *The Complete Jimmie Lunceford 1939–40*. CBS LP-66421, 1981.

———. *The World of Count Basie*. New York: Charles Scribner's Sons, 1980.

———. *The World of Duke Ellington*. New York: Da Capo Press, 1970.

———. *The World of Earl Hines*. New York: Charles Scribner's Sons, 1977.

———. *The World of Swing*. 2nd ed. New York: Da Capo Press, 2001.

Decker, Todd. *Music Makes Me: Fred Astaire and Jazz*. Berkeley: University of California Press, 2011.

Determeyer, Eddy. *Rhythm Is Our Business: Jimmie Lunceford and the Harlem Express*. Ann Arbor: University of Michigan Press, 2006.

DeVeaux, Scott. *The Birth of Bebop: A Social and Musical History*. Berkeley: University of California Press, 1997.

———. "Constructing the Jazz Tradition: Jazz Historiography." *Black American Literature Forum* 25, no. 3 (Autumn 1991): 525–60.

———. "Review of *Swing Changes: Big-Band Jazz in New Deal America*, by David Stowe." *American Music* 16, no. 1 (Spring 1998): 87–91.

DeVeaux, Scott, and Gary Giddins. *Jazz*. New York: W. W. Norton, 2009.

Dietrich, Kurt. *Duke's 'Bones: Ellington's Great Trombonists*. Rottenburg, Germany: Advance Music, 1995.

Dinerstein, Joel. *Swinging the Machine: Modernity, Technology, and African American Culture between the World Wars*. Amherst: University of Massachusetts Press, 2003.

Dixon, Robert M. W., John Godrich, and Howard Rye. *Blues and Gospel Records 1890–1943*. 4th ed. New York: Oxford University Press, 1997.

Dixon Gottschild, Brenda. *Waltzing in the Dark: African American Vaudeville and Race Politics in the Swing Era*. New York: St. Martin's Press, 2000.

Dixon-Stowell, Brenda. "Between Two Eras: 'Norton and Margot' in the Afro-American Entertainment World." *Dance Research Journal* 15, no. 2 (Spring 1983): 11–20.

Driggs, Frank. "Don Redman, Jazz Composer-Arranger." In *Jazz Panorama: From the Pages of the Jazz Review*, edited by Martin Williams, 91–104. 1962. Reprint, New York: Da Capo Press, 1979.

Driggs, Frank, and Harris Lewine. *Black Beauty, White Heat: A Pictorial History of Classic Jazz 1920–1950*. New York: Da Capo Press, 1996.

Duxbury, Janell R. *Rockin' the Classics and Classicizin' the Rock: A Selectively Annotated Discography*. Westport, CT: Greenwood Press, 1985.

Eastman, Ralph. "'Pitchin' Up a Boogie': African-American Musicians, Nightlife and Music Venues in Los Angeles, 1930–1945." In *California Soul: Music of African Americans in the West*, edited by Jacqueline Cogoell Djedje and Eddie S. Meadows, 79–103. Berkeley: University of California Press, 1998.

Edison, Harry. Interview by Stanley Dance, May 1981. Jazz Oral History Project, Smithsonian Institution Division of Performing Arts, Washington, DC. Transcript on file at the Institute of Jazz Studies, Rutgers (Newark).

Edwards, Vernon, and Michael Mark. "In Retrospect: Clarence Cameron White." *Black Perspective in Music* 9, no. 1 (Spring 1981): 51–72.

Ellis, Norman. *Instrumentation and Arranging for the Radio and Dance Orchestra.* New York: G. Schirmer, 1936.

Erenberg, Lewis. *Swingin' the Dream: Big Band Jazz and the Rebirth of American Culture.* Chicago: University of Chicago Press, 1998.

Everett, Walter, ed. *Expression in Pop-Rock Music: Critical and Analytical Essays.* New York: Routledge, 2008.

Feather, Leonard. *The Encyclopedia of Jazz.* New York: Horizon Press, 1955.

———. Liner notes to *The Jazz Arranger, Vol. 1.* Columbia Jazz Masterpieces. CBS Records LP-45143, 1989.

Fernett, Gene. *Swing Out: Great Negro Dance Bands.* New York: Da Capo Press, 1993.

Firestone, Ross. *Swing, Swing, Swing: The Life and Times of Benny Goodman.* New York: W. W. Norton, 1993.

Floyd, Samuel A., Jr. "African Roots of Jazz." In *The Oxford Companion to Jazz,* edited by Bill Kirchner, 7–16. New York: Oxford University Press, 2000.

———. *The Power of Black Music: Interpreting Its History from Africa to the United States.* New York: Oxford University Press, 1995.

Forte, Allen. *The American Popular Ballad of the Golden Era, 1924–1950.* Princeton, NJ: Princeton University Press, 1995.

Fox, Ted. *Showtime at the Apollo.* New York: Da Capo Press, 1993.

Franceschina, John. *Duke Ellington's Music for the Theatre.* Jefferson, NC: McFarland, 2001.

Francis, David. Interview by Milt Hinton [n.d.; ca. 1972–84]. Jazz Oral History Project, Smithsonian Institution Division of Performing Arts, Washington, DC. Transcript on file at the Institute of Jazz Studies, Rutgers (Newark).

Frank, Rusty E. *Tap! The Greatest Tap Dance Stars and Their Stories, 1900–1955.* New York: William Morrow, 1990.

Fritts, Ron, and Ken Vail. *Ella Fitzgerald: The Chick Webb Years and Beyond.* Ken Vail's Jazz Itineraries, no. 2. Lanham, MD: Scarecrow Press, 2003.

Gabbard, Krin. *Jammin' at the Margins: Jazz and the American Cinema.* Chicago: University of Chicago, 1996.

Gavin, James. *Stormy Weather: The Life of Lena Horne.* New York: Simon and Schuster, 2009.

Gentieu, Norman P. "McKinney's Cotton Pickers: Don Redman's Masterpiece." *IAJRC Journal* 14, no. 1 (January 1981): 8–16.

Gerber, Alain. Liner notes to *Louis Armstrong 7: Satchmo's Discoveries 1936–38.* Jazz Heritage Series, vol. 27. MCA Records LP-1326, 1980.

Giddins, Gary. Liner notes to American Jazz Orchestra—Benny Carter, *Central City Sketches.* Musical Heritage Society LP-922211F, 1988.

———. *Satchmo.* New York: Doubleday, 1988.

Gillespie, Dizzy, with Al Fraser. *To Be or Not . . . to Bop*. 1979. Reprint, New York: Doubleday, 1985.

Gillis, Frank J. "Hot Rhythm in Piano Ragtime." In *Ragtime: Its History, Composers, and Music*, edited by John Edward Hasse, 220–31. New York: Schirmer, 1985.

[Goldberg, Jane]. *By Word of Foot I, Tap Masters Pass On Their Tradition, John Bubbles and Albert Gibson* [videotape]. Jane Goldberg's Wandering Shoes Tap(h)istory featuring Tip Tap Top Tapes, Tapalogues, Tapology and Tapperabilia. New York: Changing Times Tap Dancing Company, 1980. New York Public Library Performing Arts Library, Jerome Robbins Dance Division.

Goldberg, Marv. "The 3 Chocolateers." *Marv Goldberg's R&B Notebooks*. Accessed August 2, 2014. www.uncamarvy.com.

Goode, Catherine L. "Thomas Le Roy Whaley." In *The African American National Biography*, edited by Henry Louis Gates Jr. and Evelyn Brooks Higginbotham. *Oxford African American Studies Center*. Accessed October 11, 2014. www.oxfordaasc.com.

Goodman, Benny, and Irving Kolodin. *The Kingdom of Swing*. Armed Services ed. Harrisburg, PA: Stackpole Sons, 1939.

Goodman, John F. *Mingus Speaks*. Berkeley: University of California Press, 2013.

Green, Abel, and Joe Laurie Jr. *Show Biz from Vaude to Video*. New York: Henry Holt, 1951.

Gridley, Mark C. *Concise Guide to Jazz*. 6th ed. Upper Saddle River, NJ: Pearson Education, 2010.

Gushee, Lawrence. "Analytical Method and Compositional Process in Some Thirteenth- and Fourteenth-Century Music." In *Forum Musicologicum* [Basler Beiträge zur Musikgeschichte III], 165–91. Winterthur, Switzerland: Amadeus Verlag, 1982.

———. "Improvisation and Related Terms in Middle-Period Jazz." In *Musical Improvisation: Art, Education, and Society*, edited by Gabriel Solis and Bruno Nettl, 263–80. Urbana: University of Illinois Press, 2009.

———. *Pioneers of Jazz: The Story of the Creole Band*. New York: Oxford University Press, 2005.

Hagert, Thornton. "Band and Orchestral Ragtime." In *Ragtime: Its History, Composers, and Music*, edited by John Edward Hasse, 268–84. New York: Schirmer, 1985.

Hall, Al. Interview by Phil Schaap, September 17, 1986, WKCR-FM, New York.

Hampton, Lionel, and James Haskins. *Hamp: An Autobiography*. New York: Warner Books, 1989.

Handy, W. C. *Negro Authors and Composers of the United States*. New York: Handy Brothers Music, n.d. Reprint, Ann Arbor, MI: UMI Out-of-Print Books on Demand, 1992.

Harker, Brian. "Louis Armstrong, Eccentric Dance, and the Evolution of Jazz on the Eve of Swing." *Journal of the American Musicological Society* 61, no. 1 (Spring 2008): 67–122.

Harrison, Max. "Swing Era Big Bands and Jazz Composing and Arranging." In *The Oxford Companion to Jazz*, edited by Bill Kirchner, 277–91. New York: Oxford University Press, 2000.

Haskins, James. *The Cotton Club*. New York: Random House, 1977.

Henderson, Horace. Interview by Tom McClusky, April 9–12, 1975. Jazz Oral History Project, Smithsonian Institution Division of Performing Arts, Washington, DC. Transcript on file at the Institute of Jazz Studies, Rutgers (Newark).

Hennessey, Thomas. *From Jazz to Swing.* Detroit: Wayne State University Press, 1994.

Hill, Constance Valis. *Brotherhood in Rhythm: The Jazz Tap Dancing of the Nicholas Brothers.* New York: Rowman and Littlefield, 2000.

———. *Tap Dancing America: A Cultural History.* New York: Oxford University Press, 2010.

Himmelstein, David. Liner notes to *Dizzy Gillespie: 16 Rare Performances.* RCA LPV-530, 1966.

Hinton, Milt, and David G. Berger. *Bass Line: The Stories and Photographs of Milt Hinton.* Philadelphia: Temple University Press, 1988.

Hitchcock, H. Wiley. *Music in the United States: A Historical Introduction.* Englewood Cliffs, NJ: Prentice-Hall, 1969.

Hodeir, André. *Jazz: Its Evolution and Essence.* Translated by David Noakes. New York: Grove Press, 1956.

Hoefer, George. Liner notes to *The Sound of Harlem.* Jazz Odyssey, vol. 3. Columbia C3L-33, 1964.

Howland, John. *Ellington Uptown: Duke Ellington, James P. Johnson, and the Birth of Concert Jazz.* Ann Arbor: University of Michigan Press, 2009.

———. "Jazz with Strings: Between Jazz and the Great American Songbook." In *Jazz/Not Jazz: The Music and Its Boundaries*, edited by David Ake, Charles Hiroshi Garrett, and Daniel Goldmark, 111–47. Berkeley: University of California Press, 2012.

Hughes, Langston. *The Collected Works of Langston Hughes.* Vol. 6. Edited by Leslie Catherine Sanders. Columbia: University of Missouri Press, 2004.

Hurwitt, Elliott S. "W. C. Handy as Music Publisher: Career and Reputation." PhD diss., City University of New York, 2000.

Ioakimidis, Demêtre. "Jazz Quiz." *Jazz Hot*, March 1957, 30.

Jackson, Quentin. Interview by Milt Hinton, June 1976. Jazz Oral History Project, Smithsonian Institution Division of Performing Arts, Washington, DC. Transcript on file at the Institute of Jazz Studies, Rutgers (Newark).

Jones, Andrew F. "Black Internationale: Notes on the Chinese Jazz Age." In *Jazz Planet*, edited by E. Taylor Atkins, 225–43. Jackson: University Press of Mississippi, 2003.

Jones, John Bush. *The Songs That Fought the War: Popular Music and the Home Front, 1939–1945.* Waltham, MA: Brandeis University Press, 2006.

Jones, Max. *Talking Jazz: Profiles, Interviews, and Other Riffs on Jazz Musicians.* New York: Da Capo Press, 2000.

Jones, Quincy. *Q: The Autobiography of Quincy Jones.* New York: Doubleday, 2001.

Kart, Lawrence. "The Avant-Garde, 1949–1967." In *The Oxford Companion to Jazz*, edited by Bill Kirchner, 446–58. New York: Oxford University Press, 2000.

Kernfeld, Barry. "Nightclubs and Other Venues." In *The New Grove Dictionary of Jazz*, edited by Barry Kernfeld, 844–915. New York: St. Martin's Press, 1994.

Kernodle, Tammy. *Soul on Soul: The Life and Music of Mary Lou Williams.* Boston: Northeastern University Press, 2004.

Klauber, Bruce. *World of Gene Krupa: That Legendary Drummin' Man*. Ventura, CA: Pathfinder, 1990.

Knight, Arthur. *Disintegrating the Musical: Black Performance and American Musical Film*. Durham, NC: Duke University Press, 2002.

Knowles, Mark. *The Tap Dance Dictionary*. Jefferson, NC: McFarland, 1998.

Korall, Burt. *Drummin' Men: The Heartbeat of Jazz—The Swing Years*. New York: Oxford University Press, 2002.

———. "Jazz Drumming." In *The Oxford Companion to Jazz*, edited by Bill Kirchner, 681–95. New York: Oxford University Press, 2000.

Krummel, Donald. "Printing and Publishing of Music §II, 4." In *Grove Music Online*, ed. L. Macy. Accessed January 2, 2010. www.grovemusic.com.

Krupa, Gene. *Gene Krupa Drum Method*. Edited by Rollo Laylan. New York: Robbins Music, 1938.

Lajoie, Steve. *Miles Davis and Gil Evans: Historic Collaborations (1957–1962)*. Rottenburg, Germany: Advance Music, 2003.

Lange, Arthur. *Arranging for the Modern Dance Orchestra*. 1926. Reprint, New York: Robbins Music, 1927.

Lapham, Claude. *Scoring for the Modern Dance Band*. New York: Pitman and Sons, 1937.

Lasker, Steven. "Duke's Brass, 1937–38." *International Duke Ellington Music Society Bulletin* 4, no. 2 (August–November 2004).

Lees, Gene. *Arranging the Score: Portraits of the Great Arrangers*. New York: Cassell, 2000.

Levin, Floyd. "Reminiscing with Van Alexander." *International Association of Jazz Record Collectors* 34, no. 3 (Fall 2001): 25–31.

Levinson, Peter J. *September in the Rain: The Life of Nelson Riddle*. New York: Taylor Trade, 2005.

———. *Trumpet Blues: The Life of Harry James*. New York: Oxford University Press, 1999.

Locke, Ralph P. *Musical Exoticism: Images and Reflections*. New York: Cambridge University Press, 2009.

Lord, Tom. *The Jazz Discography*. Vancouver, BC: Lord Music Reference, 1996.

Lott, R. Allen. *From Paris to Peoria*. New York: Oxford University Press, 2003.

Lotz, Rainer E., and Ulrich Neuert. *The AFRS "Jubilee" Programs: An Exploratory Discography*. Vol. 1. Frankfurt: Norbert Ruecker, 1985.

Love [Jackson], Candice. "Black and Tan Clubs." In *Encyclopedia of the Harlem Renaissance*, vol. 1, edited by Carl Wintz and Paul Finkelman, 121–22. New York: Routledge, 2004.

Luty, Bryce. "Jazz Education's Struggle for Acceptance—Part 1." *Music Educator's Journal* 69, no. 3 (November 1982): 38–39, 53.

MacDougald, Duncan, Jr. "The Popular Music Industry." 1941. Reprinted in *Mass Communication and American Social Thought: Key Texts 1919–1968*, edited by John Durham Peters and Peter Simonson, 174–80. Lanham, MD: Rowman and Littlefield, 2004.

Magee, Jeffrey. *The Uncrowned King of Swing: Fletcher Henderson and Big Band Jazz*. New York: Oxford University Press, 2005.

Maher, James T. Liner notes to *Hal Kemp and His Orchestra*. The Great Dance Bands of the '30s and '40s. RCA Victor LPM-2041, 1959.

Major, Clarence, ed. *Juba to Jive: A Dictionary of African-American Slang.* New York: Penguin Books, 1994.

Malone, Jacqui. *Steppin' on the Blues: The Visible Rhythms of African American Dance.* Urbana: University of Illinois Press, 1996.

Mancini, Henry. *Sounds and Scores.* 2nd ed. Northridge, CA: Northridge Music, 1967.

Mancini, Henry, with Gene Lees. *Did They Mention the Music?* New York: Contemporary, 1989.

Martin, Denis-Constant. "Review of *Lying Up a Nation: Race and Black Music*, by Ronald Radano." *Journal of the American Musicological Society* 59, no. 3 (Fall 2006): 755–64.

Martin, Henry, and Keith Waters. *Jazz: The First 100 Years.* 3rd ed. Boston: Schirmer, 2011.

Martyn, Barrie. *Rachmaninoff: Composer, Pianist, Conductor.* Aldershot, UK: Scolar Press, 1990.

Mather, Dan. *Charlie Barnet: An Illustrated Biography and Discography of the Swing Era Big Band Leader.* Jefferson, NC: McFarland, 2002.

McCarthy, Albert. *Big Band Jazz.* New York: Exeter, 1974.

———. Liner notes to Jimmie Lunceford, *Harlem Express: Jimmie Lunceford and His Orchestra 1934–1936.* MCA Coral Records CP-21, [1970?].

McClellan, Lawrence, Jr. *The Later Swing Era, 1942 to 1955.* Westport, CT: Greenwood Press, 2004.

McRae, Barry. *Dizzy Gillespie, His Life and Times.* New York: Universe Books, 1988.

Mellor, Richard N. *Spotlights of Fame: The World's First Theme Song Book.* N.p.: Richard N. Mellor, 1953.

Metzer, David. *Quotation and Meaning in Twentieth-Century Music.* Cambridge: Cambridge University Press, 2003.

Mezzrow, Mezz, and Bernard Wolfe. *Really the Blues.* New York: Random House, 1946.

Middleton, Richard. *Studying Popular Music.* Bristol, PA: Open University Press, 1990.

Miller, Dan. "Freddie Webster: 'The Best Sound on Trumpet since Trumpet Was Invented.'" *Dan Miller.* Accessed July 15, 2009. www.danmillerjazz.com.

Miller, Glenn. *Glenn Miller's Method for Orchestral Arranging.* New York: Mutual Music Society, 1943.

Mills Music. *A Portfolio of Great Jazz for Music Decision Makers.* New York: Belwin-Mills Music, 1976.

Monson, Ingrid. "Abbey Lincoln's *Straight Ahead*: Jazz in the Era of the Civil Rights Movement." In *Between Resistance and Revolution: Culture and Social Protest*, edited by Richard Fox and Orin Starn, 171–94. New Brunswick, NJ: Rutgers University Press, 1997.

Moore, Allan F., and Anwar Ibrahim. "'Sounds Like Teen Spirit': Identifying Radiohead's Idiolect." In *The Music and Art of Radiohead*, edited by Joseph Tate, 139–58. Burlington, VT: Ashgate, 2005.

Morgenstern, Dan. "Hot Chocolates." In *Living with Jazz*, edited by Sheldon Meyer, 605–16. New York: Pantheon, 2004.

———. Liner notes to Louis Armstrong, *Rare Items 1935–1944.* Decca LP-9225, 1967.

———. "Louis Armstrong and the Development and Diffusion of Jazz." In *Louis Armstrong: A Cultural Legacy*, edited by Marc. H. Miller, 95–145. New York: Queens Museum of Art and University of Washington Press, 1994.

Murphy, Lyle. *Spud Murphy's Swing Arranging Method*. New York: Robbins Music, 1937.

Murray, Albert. *Stomping the Blues*. New York: Random House, 1976.

Nanry, Charles A. "Swing and Segregation." In *America's Musical Pulse: Popular Music in Twentieth-Century Society*, edited by Kenneth J. Bindas, 185–94. Westport, CT: Praeger, 1992.

Nauert, Paul. "Theory and Practice in 'Porgy and Bess': The Gershwin-Schillinger Connection." *Musical Quarterly* 78, no. 1 (Spring 1994): 9–33.

Nelson, Margaret, ed. *Lyrics for Song Hits*. New York: Avon House, 1942.

Nelson, Stanley. *All about Jazz*. London: Heath Cranton, 1934.

Nicholson, Stuart. *Reminiscing in Tempo: A Portrait of Duke Ellington*. Boston: Northeastern University Press, 1999.

Oliphant, Dave. *The Early Swing Era, 1930 to 1941*. Westport, CT: Greenwood Press, 2002.

Oja, Carol. *Making Music Modern: New York in the 1920s*. New York: Oxford University Press, 2000.

Panassié, Hugues. *Cinq Mois à New York*. Paris: Éditions Corrêa, 1947.

———. *Hot Jazz: The Guide to Swing Music*. Translated by Lyle Dowling and Eleanor Dowling. New York: Witmark and Sons, 1936.

Panassié, Hugues, and Madeleine Gautier. *Guide to Jazz*. Translated by Desmond Flower. Boston: Houghton Mifflin, 1956.

Perea, Jessica Bissett. "Voices from the Jazz Wilderness: Locating Pacific Northwest Vocal Ensembles within Jazz Education." In *Jazz/Not Jazz: The Music and Its Boundaries*, edited by David Ake, Charles Hiroshi Garrett, and Daniel Goldmark, 219–36. Berkeley: University of California Press, 2012.

Peterson, Bernard L., Jr. *Early Black American Playwrights and Dramatic Writers*. New York: Greenwood Press, 1990.

———. *Profiles of African American Stage Performers and Theatre People*. New York: Greenwood Press, 2001.

Porter, Eric. "Incorporation and Distinction in Jazz History and Jazz Historiography." In *Jazz/Not Jazz: The Music and Its Boundaries*, edited by David Ake, Charles Hiroshi Garrett, and Daniel Goldmark, 13–30. Berkeley: University of California Press, 2012.

Porter, Lewis, ed. *Jazz: A Century of Change—Readings and New Essays*. Belmont, CA: Wadsworth, 2004.

Procope, Russell. Interview by Chris Albertson, March 1979. Jazz Oral History Project, Smithsonian Institution Division of Performing Arts, Washington, DC. Transcript on file at the Institute of Jazz Studies, Rutgers (Newark).

Prouty, Kenneth. "The History of Jazz Education: A Critical Reassessment." *Journal of Historical Research in Music Education* 26, no. 2 (April 2005): 79–100.

Radano, Ronald M. "Hot Fantasies: American Modernism and the Idea of Black Rhythm." In *Music and the Racial Imagination*, edited by Ronald M. Radano and Philip V. Bohlman, 459–80. Chicago: University of Chicago Press, 2000.

———. *Lying Up a Nation: Race and Black Music*. Chicago: University of Chicago Press, 2003.

Ramsey, Guthrie P. *Race Music: Black Cultures from Bebop to Hip-Hop*. Berkeley: University of California Press, 2003.

Rapport, Evan. "Bill Finegan's Gershwin Arrangements and the American Concept of Hybridity." *Journal of the Society for American Music* 2, no. 4 (November 2008): 507–30.

Rattenbury, Ken. *Duke Ellington, Jazz Composer*. New Haven, CT: Yale University Press, 1990.

Rayno, Don. *Paul Whiteman: Pioneer in American Music*. Vol. 1. Studies in Jazz, no. 43. Lanham, MD: Scarecrow Press, 2003.

Reed, Leonard. Interview by Fred Strickler (ca. 1997). Oral History Project, Dance Collection, New York Public Library.

Riccardi, Ricky. *What a Wonderful World: The Magic of Louis Armstrong's Later Years*. New York: Pantheon, 2011.

Riddle, Nelson. *Arranged by Nelson Riddle*. Van Nuys, CA: Alfred Music, 1985.

Ruppli, Michel. *The Decca Labels: A Discography*. Vols. 1–3. Westport, CT: Greenwood Press, 1996.

Russell, Ross. "Bebop." In *The Art of Jazz: Essays on the Nature and Development of Jazz*, edited by Martin Williams, 187–214. New York: Oxford University Press, 1959.

Russo, William. *Jazz Composition and Orchestration*. Chicago: University of Chicago Press, 1968.

Rust, Brian. *Jazz Records 1897–1942*. 5th ed. Chigwell, UK: Storyville, 1982.

Rye, Howard. "Curtis Mosby." *The Oxford Encyclopedia of Music*. Accessed August 4, 2009. www.oxfordmusiconline.com.

———. "Maceo Jefferson." *The Oxford Encyclopedia of Music*. Accessed July 9, 2009. www.oxfordmusiconline.com.

Rye, Howard, and Robert Ford. "Tosh Hammed." *Names and Numbers* 64 (January 2013): 28–33.

Salemann, Dieter. "Eugipelliv: Footprints of an Arranger." *International Association of Jazz Record Collectors* 34, no. 3 (Fall 2001): 32–34.

Sampson, Henry T. *Blacks in Blackface: A Sourcebook on Early Black Musical Shows*. 2nd ed. Lanham, MD: Scarecrow Press, 2014.

Sauter, Eddie. Interview by Bill Kirchner, August 1980. Jazz Oral History Project, Smithsonian Institution Division of Performing Arts, Washington, DC. Transcript on file at the Institute of Jazz Studies, Rutgers (Newark).

Savran, David. *Highbrow/Lowdown: Theater, Jazz, and the Making of the New Middle Class*. Ann Arbor: University of Michigan Press, 2009.

Schaap, Phil. *Roy Eldridge Festival Handbook and Discography*. 3rd printing. New York: Jazz Session—Phil Schaap, 1987.

Schiff, David. *The Ellington Century*. Berkeley: University of California Press, 2012.

Schiffman, Jack. *Uptown: The Story of Harlem's Apollo Theatre*. New York: Cowles, 1971.

Schillinger, Joseph. *The Schillinger System of Musical Composition*. Vols. 1–2. New York: Carl Fischer, 1946.

Schuller, Gunther. "Arrangement." In *The New Grove Dictionary of Jazz*, edited by Barry Kernfeld, 32–39. New York: St. Martin's Press, 1994.

———. *Early Jazz: Its Roots and Musical Development.* 1968. Reprint, New York: Oxford University Press, 1986.

———. *The Swing Era: The Development of Jazz, 1930–1945.* New York: Oxford University Press, 1989.

———. "Third Stream." In *Musings: The Musical Worlds of Gunther Schuller,* 114–18. New York: Oxford University Press, 1986.

Sebesky, Don. *The Contemporary Arranger.* 1974. Reprint, Van Nuys, CA: Alfred, 1994.

Serralheiro, Paul. "Charting Musical Flights: The Arranger, Part 2." *La Scena Musicale* 8, no. 7 (April 2003). Accessed July 12, 2008. www.scena.org/lsm/sm8-7/The_Arranger.htm.

Shaw, Arnold. *The Jazz Age: Popular Music in the 1920s.* New York: Oxford University Press, 1987.

———. *Let's Dance: Popular Music in the 1930s.* Edited by Bill Willard. New York: Oxford University Press, 1998.

Shih, Hsio Wen. "The Spread of Jazz and the Big Bands." In *Jazz: New Perspectives on the History of Jazz by Twelve of the World's Foremost Jazz Critics and Scholars,* edited by Nat Hentoff and Albert McCarthy, 171–88. 1959. Reprint, New York: Da Capo Press, 1975.

Shipton, Alyn. *Groovin' High: The Life of Dizzy Gillespie.* New York: Oxford University Press, 1999.

———. *Hi-De-Ho: The Life of Cab Calloway.* New York: Oxford University Press, 2010.

Simon, George T. *Glenn Miller and His Orchestra.* New York: T. Y. Crowell, 1974.

———. *The Big Bands.* 4th ed. New York: Schirmer, 1981.

———. Liner notes to *Gene Krupa: Drummin' Man.* Columbia C2L-29, 1963.

———. *Simon Says: The Sights and Sounds of the Big Band Era, 1935–1955.* New Rochelle, NY: Arlington House, 1971.

Singer, Barry. *Black and Blue: The Life and Lyrics of Andy Razaf.* New York: Maxwell Macmillan, 1992.

Skinner, Frank. *New Method for Orchestra Scoring.* New York: Robbins Music, 1935.

Smith, W. O. *Sideman: The Long Gig of W. O. Smith.* Nashville: Rutledge Hill Press, 1991.

Southern, Eileen. *The Music of Black Americans: A History.* 3rd ed. New York: W. W. Norton, 1997.

Spellman, A. B. "Herbie Nichols." *Jazz,* October 1964, 12.

Spencer, Jon Michael. *The New Negroes and Their Music: The Success of the Harlem Renaissance.* Knoxville: University of Tennessee Press, 1997.

Spring, Howard. "Changes in Jazz Performance and Arranging in New York, 1929–1932." PhD diss., University of Illinois at Urbana-Champaign, 1993.

———. "Swing and the Lindy Hop: Dance, Venue, Media, and Tradition." *American Music* 15, no. 2 (Summer 1997): 183–207.

Stearns, Marshall, and Jean Stearns. *Jazz Dance: The Story of American Vernacular Dance.* 1968. Reprint, New York: Da Capo Press, 1994.

Steinbeck, Paul. "Intermusicality, Humor, and Cultural Critique in the Art Ensemble of Chicago's 'A Jackson in Your House.'" *Jazz Perspectives* 5, no. 2 (August 2011): 135–54.

Steinman, Patrice Madura. "Musical Training and Compensation in the Big Band Era: A Case Study of Madura's Danceland from 1930–1950." *Journal of Historical Research in Music Education* 24, no. 2 (April 2003): 164–77.

Stewart, Alex. *Making the Scene: Contemporary New York City Big Band Jazz*. Berkeley: University of California Press, 2007.

Stewart, Earl. *African American Music: An Introduction*. New York: Schirmer, 1998.

Stowe, David. "Jazz in the West: Cultural Frontier and Region during the Swing Era." *Western Historical Quarterly* 32, no. 1 (February 1992): 53–73.

———. *Swing Changes: Big-Band Jazz in New Deal America*. Cambridge, MA: Harvard University Press, 1994.

Stratemann, Klaus. *Duke Ellington: Day by Day and Film by Film*. Copenhagen: JazzMedia, 2002.

———. *Louis Armstrong on the Screen*. Copenhagen: JazzMedia, 1996.

Sturm, Fred. *Changes over Time: The Evolution of Jazz Arranging*. Rottenburg, Germany: Advance Music, 1995.

Sudhalter, Richard. *Lost Chords: White Musicians and Their Contribution to Jazz, 1915–1945*. New York: Oxford University Press, 1999.

Suskin, Steven. *The Sound of Broadway Music: A Book of Orchestrators and Orchestrations*. New York: Oxford University Press, 2009.

Tackley, Catherine. *Benny Goodman's Famous 1938 Carnegie Hall Jazz Concert*. New York: Oxford University Press, 2012.

Tanner, Rosamond. "Classic Swing." *Music Educators Journal* 27, no. 4 (February 1941): 64–66.

Tansman, Alexandre. Notes to *Sonatine Transatlantique* [solo piano score]. Paris: Éditions Musicales, 1930.

Taylor, Deems. *The Well Tempered Listener*. New York: Simon and Schuster, 1940.

Teachout, Terry. "Jazz and Classical Music: To the Third Stream and Beyond." In *The Oxford Companion to Jazz*, edited by Bill Kirchner, 343–56. New York: Oxford University Press, 2000.

———. *Pops: A Life of Louis Armstrong*. New York: Houghton Mifflin Harcourt, 2009.

Teal, Kimberly Hannon. "Beyond the Cotton Club: The Persistence of Duke Ellington's Jungle Style." *Jazz Perspectives* 6, nos. 1–2 (2012): 123–49.

Timner, W. E. *The Recorded Music of Duke Ellington and His Sidemen*. 5th ed. Studies in Jazz, no. 54. Lanham, MD: Institute of Jazz Studies and Scarecrow Press, 2007.

Townsend, Irving. Liner notes to *Artie Shaw and His Orchestra 1939 Vol. 4*. Hindsight Records LP-149, 1980.

Townsend, Peter. *Pearl Harbor Jazz: Change in Popular Music in the Early 1940s*. Jackson: University Press of Mississippi, 2007.

Tucker, Mark. "Count Basie and the Piano That Swings the Band." *Popular Music* 5 (1985): 45–79.

———. *Ellington: The Early Years*. Urbana: University of Illinois Press, 1995.

———. "In Search of Will Vodery." *Black Music Research Journal* 16, no. 1 (Spring 1996): 123–82.

———, ed. *The Duke Ellington Reader*. New York: Oxford University Press, 1993.

Tucker, Sherrie. *Swing Shift: "All-Girl" Bands of the 1940s*. Durham, NC: Duke University Press, 2000.

Vail, Ken. *Dizzy Gillespie: The Bebop Years 1937–1952*. Ken Vail's Jazz Itineraries, no. 1. Lanham, MD: Scarecrow Press, 2003.

———. *Swing Era Scrapbook: The Teenage Diaries and Radio Logs of Bob Inman, 1936–1938*. Studies in Jazz, no. 49. Lanham, MD: Scarecrow Press, 2005.

van de Leur, Walter. *Something to Live For: The Music of Billy Strayhorn*. New York: Oxford University Press, 2002.

van der Merwe, Peter. *Origins of the Popular Style: The Antecedents of Twentieth-Century Popular Music*. 1989. Reprint, Oxford: Clarendon, 1992.

Waggoner, Susan. *Nightclub Nights: Art, Legend, and Style 1920–1960*. New York: Rizzoli International, 2001.

Wald, Elijah. "Louis Armstrong Loves Guy Lombardo." In *Jazz/Not Jazz: The Music and Its Boundaries*, edited by David Ake, Charles Hiroshi Garrett, and Daniel Goldmark, 31–48. Berkeley: University of California Press, 2012.

Warner, Alan. *EMI Professional Song Catalog*. Vol. 4. New York: EMI Music, 1992.

Washburne, Christopher. "The Clave of Jazz: A Caribbean Contribution to the Rhythmic Foundation of an African-American Music." *Black Music Research Journal* 17, no. 1 (Spring 1997): 59–80.

———. "Does Kenny G Play Bad Jazz? A Case Study." In *Bad Music: The Music We Love to Hate*, edited by Christopher Washburne and Maiken Derno, 123–47. New York: Routledge, 2004.

Watkins, Mel. "That Vaudeville Style: A Conversation with Honi Coles." *Alicia Patterson Foundation Reporter* 2, no. 6 ([1979]). Accessed August 6, 2014. http://aliciapatterson.org/stories/vaudeville-style-conversation-honi-coles.

Weeks, Todd Bryant. *Luck's in My Corner: The Life and Music of Hot Lips Page*. New York: Routledge, 2008.

Welburn, Ron. "Jazz Magazines of the 1930s: An Overview of Their Provocative Journalism." *American Music* 5, no. 3 (Autumn 1987): 225–70.

Wells, Dicky, as told to Stanley Dance. *The Night People: The Jazz Life of Dicky Wells*. Rev. ed. Washington, DC: Smithsonian Institution Press, 1991.

Westerberg, Hans. *Boy from New Orleans: Louis "Satchmo" Armstrong on Records, Films, Radio and Television*. Copenhagen: Jazzmedia, 1981.

Weirick, Paul. *Dance Arranging: A Guide to Scoring Music for the American Dance Orchestra*. New York: M. Witmark and Sons, 1934.

Whaley, Tom. Interview by Milt Hinton, 1979–80. Jazz Oral History Project, Smithsonian Institution Division of Performing Arts, Washington, DC. Transcript on file at the Institute of Jazz Studies, Rutgers (Newark).

Wilkinson, Christopher. *Big Band Jazz in Black West Virginia, 1930–1942*. Jackson: University Press of Mississippi, 2012.

———. *Jazz on the Road: Don Albert's Musical Life*. Berkeley: University of California Press, 2001.

Willard, Patricia. Liner notes to *Artie Shaw and His Orchestra 1938 Vol. 2*. Hindsight Records LP-140, 1979.

Willems, Jos. *All of Me: The Complete Discography of Louis Armstrong*. Studies in Jazz, no. 51. Lanham, MD: Scarecrow Press, 2006.

Williams, Ennis. "Wilfred C. Bain: A Reminiscence in Memoriam." *College Music Symposium* 38 (1998): 1–5.

Woideck, Carl. *Charlie Parker: His Music and His Life*. Ann Arbor: University of Michigan Press, 1996.

———. ed. *The Charlie Parker Companion*. New York: Schirmer, 1998.

Wollen, Peter. "The Auteur Theory, Michael Curtiz, and Casablanca." In *Authorship and Film*, edited by David Gerstner and Janet Staiger, 61–76. New York: Routledge, 2003.

Wooding, Sam. Interview by Chris Albertson, April 22–May 8, 1975. Jazz Oral History Project, Smithsonian Institution Division of Performing Arts, Washington, DC. Transcript on file at the Institute of Jazz Studies, Rutgers (Newark).

Wriggle, John. "Arranger." In *New Grove Dictionary of American Music*, 2nd ed., vol. 1, edited by Charles Hiroshi Garrett, 191–92. New York: Oxford University Press, 2013.

———. "Chappie Willet: A Jazz Arranger in Swing Era New York." *Annual Review of Jazz Studies* 14 (2009): 101–88.

———. "Chappie Willet, Frank Fairfax, and Phil Edwards' Collegians: From West Virginia to Philadelphia." *Black Music Research Journal* 27, no. 1 (Spring 2007): 1–22.

———. "Chappie Willet and Popular Music Arranging in Swing Era New York." PhD diss., City University of New York, 2011.

———. "Jazzing the Classics: Race, Modernism, and the Career of Arranger Chappie Willet." *Journal of the Society for American Music* 6, no. 2 (May 2012): 175–209.

———. "Jimmy Mundy." In *The African American National Biography*, vol. 6, edited by Henry Louis Gates Jr. and Evelyn Brooks Higginbotham, 84–85. New York: Oxford University Press, 2008.

Youngren, William H. "European Roots of Jazz." In *The Oxford Companion to Jazz*, edited by Bill Kirchner, 17–28. New York: Oxford University Press, 2000.

Zamecnik, J. S. *Sam Fox Moving Picture Music*. Cleveland: Sam Fox, 1913.

Author Interviews and Correspondence

Alexander, Van. Telephone interview by author, April 6, 2004.

Bufalino, Brenda. E-mail correspondence, May 22 and 23, 2004.

Cromer, Harold. Interview by author, May 7, 2004, New York City.

Hayes, Cleo. Telephone interview by author, November 14, 2006.

Hicks, Cleophas "Chico." Telephone interviews by author, May 1, 8, and 29, 2004, and January 7, 2005.

Kerr, Brooks. Telephone interview by author, November 8, 2004.

Leavitt, Hart. Telephone interviews by author, December 30, 2003; January 7 and 20, 2004; and February 25, 2004.

Murphy, Lyle "Spud." Telephone interview by author, February 12, 2004.

Reed, Leonard. Telephone interview by author, December 2, 2002.

Wilson, Gerald. Telephone interviews by author, April 1 and 15, 2004.

Periodicals and Newspapers

Allegro

Atlanta Daily World

Baltimore Afro-American

Billboard
Charleston Daily Mail
Chicago Daily Tribune
Chicago Defender
Cornell Daily Sun
Directory and Instrumentation [American Federation of Musicians Local No. 802]
Down Beat
Ebony
Etude
Fort Lauderdale Sun-Sentinel
Gramophone
International Musician
Los Angeles Times
Manhattan Telephone Directory [New York Telephone Company]
Metronome
New Journal and Guide [Norfolk]
New York Age
New York Amsterdam News
New York Post
New York Sun
New York Times
New York World Telegram and Sun
New Yorker
Philadelphia Tribune
Pittsburgh Courier
Seattle Times
Tempo [Los Angeles]
Time
U.S. Copyright Renewals
U.S. Copyright Report
U.S. Bureau of the Census [www.ancestry.com]
Variety
Wall Street Journal
Washington Post
Westchester County Directory [New York Telephone Company]
Yellow Jacket [West Virginia State College]

Index

Note: Page numbers in italics refer to illustrations. For individual song titles also see Appendix.

JOHN WRIGGLE is a musicologist, composer, arranger, and trombonist. He has taught for the City University of New York, Rutgers University, and Boston University.

MUSIC IN AMERICAN LIFE

Only a Miner: Studies in Recorded Coal-Mining Songs *Archie Green*
Great Day Coming: Folk Music and the American Left *R. Serge Denisoff*
John Philip Sousa: A Descriptive Catalog of His Works *Paul E. Bierley*
The Hell-Bound Train: A Cowboy Songbook *Glenn Ohrlin*
Oh, Didn't He Ramble: The Life Story of Lee Collins, as Told to Mary Collins *Edited by Frank J. Gillis and John W. Miner*
American Labor Songs of the Nineteenth Century *Philip S. Foner*
Stars of Country Music: Uncle Dave Macon to Johnny Rodriguez *Edited by Bill C. Malone and Judith McCulloh*
Git Along, Little Dogies: Songs and Songmakers of the American West *John I. White*
A Texas-Mexican *Cancionero*: Folksongs of the Lower Border *Américo Paredes*
San Antonio Rose: The Life and Music of Bob Wills *Charles R. Townsend*
Early Downhome Blues: A Musical and Cultural Analysis *Jeff Todd Titon*
An Ives Celebration: Papers and Panels of the Charles Ives Centennial Festival-Conference *Edited by H. Wiley Hitchcock and Vivian Perlis*
Sinful Tunes and Spirituals: Black Folk Music to the Civil War *Dena J. Epstein*
Joe Scott, the Woodsman-Songmaker *Edward D. Ives*
Jimmie Rodgers: The Life and Times of America's Blue Yodeler *Nolan Porterfield*
Early American Music Engraving and Printing: A History of Music Publishing in America from 1787 to 1825, with Commentary on Earlier and Later Practices *Richard J. Wolfe*
Sing a Sad Song: The Life of Hank Williams *Roger M. Williams*
Long Steel Rail: The Railroad in American Folksong *Norm Cohen*
Resources of American Music History: A Directory of Source Materials from Colonial Times to World War II *D. W. Krummel, Jean Geil, Doris J. Dyen, and Deane L. Root*
Tenement Songs: The Popular Music of the Jewish Immigrants *Mark Slobin*
Ozark Folksongs *Vance Randolph; edited and abridged by Norm Cohen*
Oscar Sonneck and American Music *Edited by William Lichtenwanger*
Bluegrass Breakdown: The Making of the Old Southern Sound *Robert Cantwell*
Bluegrass: A History *Neil V. Rosenberg*
Music at the White House: A History of the American Spirit *Elise K. Kirk*
Red River Blues: The Blues Tradition in the Southeast *Bruce Bastin*
Good Friends and Bad Enemies: Robert Winslow Gordon and the Study of American Folksong *Debora Kodish*
Fiddlin' Georgia Crazy: Fiddlin' John Carson, His Real World, and the World of His Songs *Gene Wiggins*
America's Music: From the Pilgrims to the Present (rev. 3d ed.) *Gilbert Chase*
Secular Music in Colonial Annapolis: The Tuesday Club, 1745–56 *John Barry Talley*
Bibliographical Handbook of American Music *D. W. Krummel*
Goin' to Kansas City *Nathan W. Pearson Jr.*
"Susanna," "Jeanie," and "The Old Folks at Home": The Songs of Stephen C. Foster from His Time to Ours (2d ed.) *William W. Austin*
Songprints: The Musical Experience of Five Shoshone Women *Judith Vander*
"Happy in the Service of the Lord": Afro-American Gospel Quartets in Memphis *Kip Lornell*

Paul Hindemith in the United States *Luther Noss*
"My Song Is My Weapon": People's Songs, American Communism, and the Politics of Culture, 1930–50 *Robbie Lieberman*
Chosen Voices: The Story of the American Cantorate *Mark Slobin*
Theodore Thomas: America's Conductor and Builder of Orchestras, 1835–1905 *Ezra Schabas*
"The Whorehouse Bells Were Ringing" and Other Songs Cowboys Sing *Collected and Edited by Guy Logsdon*
Crazeology: The Autobiography of a Chicago Jazzman *Bud Freeman, as Told to Robert Wolf*
Discoursing Sweet Music: Brass Bands and Community Life in Turn-of-the-Century Pennsylvania *Kenneth Kreitner*
Mormonism and Music: A History *Michael Hicks*
Voices of the Jazz Age: Profiles of Eight Vintage Jazzmen *Chip Deffaa*
Pickin' on Peachtree: A History of Country Music in Atlanta, Georgia *Wayne W. Daniel*
Bitter Music: Collected Journals, Essays, Introductions, and Librettos *Harry Partch; edited by Thomas McGeary*
Ethnic Music on Records: A Discography of Ethnic Recordings Produced in the United States, 1893 to 1942 *Richard K. Spottswood*
Downhome Blues Lyrics: An Anthology from the Post–World War II Era *Jeff Todd Titon*
Ellington: The Early Years *Mark Tucker*
Chicago Soul *Robert Pruter*
That Half-Barbaric Twang: The Banjo in American Popular Culture *Karen Linn*
Hot Man: The Life of Art Hodes *Art Hodes and Chadwick Hansen*
The Erotic Muse: American Bawdy Songs (2d ed.) *Ed Cray*
Barrio Rhythm: Mexican American Music in Los Angeles *Steven Loza*
The Creation of Jazz: Music, Race, and Culture in Urban America *Burton W. Peretti*
Charles Martin Loeffler: A Life Apart in Music *Ellen Knight*
Club Date Musicians: Playing the New York Party Circuit *Bruce A. MacLeod*
Opera on the Road: Traveling Opera Troupes in the United States, 1825–60 *Katherine K. Preston*
The Stonemans: An Appalachian Family and the Music That Shaped Their Lives *Ivan M. Tribe*
Transforming Tradition: Folk Music Revivals Examined *Edited by Neil V. Rosenberg*
The Crooked Stovepipe: Athapaskan Fiddle Music and Square Dancing in Northeast Alaska and Northwest Canada *Craig Mishler*
Traveling the High Way Home: Ralph Stanley and the World of Traditional Bluegrass Music *John Wright*
Carl Ruggles: Composer, Painter, and Storyteller *Marilyn Ziffrin*
Never without a Song: The Years and Songs of Jennie Devlin, 1865–1952 *Katharine D. Newman*
The Hank Snow Story *Hank Snow, with Jack Ownbey and Bob Burris*
Milton Brown and the Founding of Western Swing *Cary Ginell, with special assistance from Roy Lee Brown*
Santiago de Murcia's "Códice Saldívar No. 4": A Treasury of Secular Guitar Music from Baroque Mexico *Craig H. Russell*

The Sound of the Dove: Singing in Appalachian Primitive Baptist Churches *Beverly Bush Patterson*
Heartland Excursions: Ethnomusicological Reflections on Schools of Music *Bruno Nettl*
Doowop: The Chicago Scene *Robert Pruter*
Blue Rhythms: Six Lives in Rhythm and Blues *Chip Deffaa*
Shoshone Ghost Dance Religion: Poetry Songs and Great Basin Context *Judith Vander*
Go Cat Go! Rockabilly Music and Its Makers *Craig Morrison*
'Twas Only an Irishman's Dream: The Image of Ireland and the Irish in American Popular Song Lyrics, 1800–1920 *William H. A. Williams*
Democracy at the Opera: Music, Theater, and Culture in New York City, 1815–60 *Karen Ahlquist*
Fred Waring and the Pennsylvanians *Virginia Waring*
Woody, Cisco, and Me: Seamen Three in the Merchant Marine *Jim Longhi*
Behind the Burnt Cork Mask: Early Blackface Minstrelsy and Antebellum American Popular Culture *William J. Mahar*
Going to Cincinnati: A History of the Blues in the Queen City *Steven C. Tracy*
Pistol Packin' Mama: Aunt Molly Jackson and the Politics of Folksong *Shelly Romalis*
Sixties Rock: Garage, Psychedelic, and Other Satisfactions *Michael Hicks*
The Late Great Johnny Ace and the Transition from R&B to Rock 'n' Roll *James M. Salem*
Tito Puente and the Making of Latin Music *Steven Loza*
Juilliard: A History *Andrea Olmstead*
Understanding Charles Seeger, Pioneer in American Musicology *Edited by Bell Yung and Helen Rees*
Mountains of Music: West Virginia Traditional Music from *Goldenseal* *Edited by John Lilly*
Alice Tully: An Intimate Portrait *Albert Fuller*
A Blues Life *Henry Townsend, as told to Bill Greensmith*
Long Steel Rail: The Railroad in American Folksong (2d ed.) *Norm Cohen*
The Golden Age of Gospel *Text by Horace Clarence Boyer; photography by Lloyd Yearwood*
Aaron Copland: The Life and Work of an Uncommon Man *Howard Pollack*
Louis Moreau Gottschalk *S. Frederick Starr*
Race, Rock, and Elvis *Michael T. Bertrand*
Theremin: Ether Music and Espionage *Albert Glinsky*
Poetry and Violence: The Ballad Tradition of Mexico's Costa Chica *John H. McDowell*
The Bill Monroe Reader *Edited by Tom Ewing*
Music in Lubavitcher Life *Ellen Koskoff*
Zarzuela: Spanish Operetta, American Stage *Janet L. Sturman*
Bluegrass Odyssey: A Documentary in Pictures and Words, 1966–86 *Carl Fleischhauer and Neil V. Rosenberg*
That Old-Time Rock & Roll: A Chronicle of an Era, 1954–63 *Richard Aquila*
Labor's Troubadour *Joe Glazer*
American Opera *Elise K. Kirk*
Don't Get above Your Raisin': Country Music and the Southern Working Class *Bill C. Malone*

John Alden Carpenter: A Chicago Composer *Howard Pollack*
Heartbeat of the People: Music and Dance of the Northern Pow-wow *Tara Browner*
My Lord, What a Morning: An Autobiography *Marian Anderson*
Marian Anderson: A Singer's Journey *Allan Keiler*
Charles Ives Remembered: An Oral History *Vivian Perlis*
Henry Cowell, Bohemian *Michael Hicks*
Rap Music and Street Consciousness *Cheryl L. Keyes*
Louis Prima *Garry Boulard*
Marian McPartland's Jazz World: All in Good Time *Marian McPartland*
Robert Johnson: Lost and Found *Barry Lee Pearson and Bill McCulloch*
Bound for America: Three British Composers *Nicholas Temperley*
Lost Sounds: Blacks and the Birth of the Recording Industry, 1890–1919 *Tim Brooks*
Burn, Baby! BURN! The Autobiography of Magnificent Montague *Magnificent Montague with Bob Baker*
Way Up North in Dixie: A Black Family's Claim to the Confederate Anthem *Howard L. Sacks and Judith Rose Sacks*
The Bluegrass Reader *Edited by Thomas Goldsmith*
Colin McPhee: Composer in Two Worlds *Carol J. Oja*
Robert Johnson, Mythmaking, and Contemporary American Culture *Patricia R. Schroeder*
Composing a World: Lou Harrison, Musical Wayfarer *Leta E. Miller and Fredric Lieberman*
Fritz Reiner, Maestro and Martinet *Kenneth Morgan*
That Toddlin' Town: Chicago's White Dance Bands and Orchestras, 1900–1950 *Charles A. Sengstock Jr.*
Dewey and Elvis: The Life and Times of a Rock 'n' Roll Deejay *Louis Cantor*
Come Hither to Go Yonder: Playing Bluegrass with Bill Monroe *Bob Black*
Chicago Blues: Portraits and Stories *David Whiteis*
The Incredible Band of John Philip Sousa *Paul E. Bierley*
"Maximum Clarity" and Other Writings on Music *Ben Johnston, edited by Bob Gilmore*
Staging Tradition: John Lair and Sarah Gertrude Knott *Michael Ann Williams*
Homegrown Music: Discovering Bluegrass *Stephanie P. Ledgin*
Tales of a Theatrical Guru *Danny Newman*
The Music of Bill Monroe *Neil V. Rosenberg and Charles K. Wolfe*
Pressing On: The Roni Stoneman Story *Roni Stoneman, as told to Ellen Wright*
Together Let Us Sweetly Live *Jonathan C. David, with photographs by Richard Holloway*
Live Fast, Love Hard: The Faron Young Story *Diane Diekman*
Air Castle of the South: WSM Radio and the Making of Music City *Craig P. Havighurst*
Traveling Home: Sacred Harp Singing and American Pluralism *Kiri Miller*
Where Did Our Love Go? The Rise and Fall of the Motown Sound *Nelson George*
Lonesome Cowgirls and Honky-Tonk Angels: The Women of Barn Dance Radio *Kristine M. McCusker*
California Polyphony: Ethnic Voices, Musical Crossroads *Mina Yang*
The Never-Ending Revival: Rounder Records and the Folk Alliance *Michael F. Scully*
Sing It Pretty: A Memoir *Bess Lomax Hawes*

Working Girl Blues: The Life and Music of Hazel Dickens *Hazel Dickens and Bill C. Malone*
Charles Ives Reconsidered *Gayle Sherwood Magee*
The Hayloft Gang: The Story of the National Barn Dance *Edited by Chad Berry*
Country Music Humorists and Comedians *Loyal Jones*
Record Makers and Breakers: Voices of the Independent Rock 'n' Roll Pioneers *John Broven*
Music of the First Nations: Tradition and Innovation in Native North America *Edited by Tara Browner*
Cafe Society: The Wrong Place for the Right People *Barney Josephson, with Terry Trilling-Josephson*
George Gershwin: An Intimate Portrait *Walter Rimler*
Life Flows On in Endless Song: Folk Songs and American History *Robert V. Wells*
I Feel a Song Coming On: The Life of Jimmy McHugh *Alyn Shipton*
King of the Queen City: The Story of King Records *Jon Hartley Fox*
Long Lost Blues: Popular Blues in America, 1850–1920 *Peter C. Muir*
Hard Luck Blues: Roots Music Photographs from the Great Depression *Rich Remsberg*
Restless Giant: The Life and Times of Jean Aberbach and Hill and Range Songs *Bar Biszick-Lockwood*
Champagne Charlie and Pretty Jemima: Variety Theater in the Nineteenth Century *Gillian M. Rodger*
Sacred Steel: Inside an African American Steel Guitar Tradition *Robert L. Stone*
Gone to the Country: The New Lost City Ramblers and the Folk Music Revival *Ray Allen*
The Makers of the Sacred Harp *David Warren Steel with Richard H. Hulan*
Woody Guthrie, American Radical *Will Kaufman*
George Szell: A Life of Music *Michael Charry*
Bean Blossom: The Brown County Jamboree and Bill Monroe's Bluegrass Festivals *Thomas A. Adler*
Crowe on the Banjo: The Music Life of J. D. Crowe *Marty Godbey*
Twentieth Century Drifter: The Life of Marty Robbins *Diane Diekman*
Henry Mancini: Reinventing Film Music *John Caps*
The Beautiful Music All Around Us: Field Recordings and the American Experience *Stephen Wade*
Then Sings My Soul: The Culture of Southern Gospel Music *Douglas Harrison*
The Accordion in the Americas: Klezmer, Polka, Tango, Zydeco, and More! *Edited by Helena Simonett*
Bluegrass Bluesman: A Memoir *Josh Graves, edited by Fred Bartenstein*
One Woman in a Hundred: Edna Phillips and the Philadelphia Orchestra *Mary Sue Welsh*
The Great Orchestrator: Arthur Judson and American Arts Management *James M. Doering*
Charles Ives in the Mirror: American Histories of an Iconic Composer *David C. Paul*
Southern Soul-Blues *David Whiteis*
Sweet Air: Modernism, Regionalism, and American Popular Song *Edward P. Comentale*
Pretty Good for a Girl: Women in Bluegrass *Murphy Hicks Henry*

Sweet Dreams: The World of Patsy Cline *Warren R. Hofstra*
William Sidney Mount and the Creolization of American Culture *Christopher J. Smith*
Bird: The Life and Music of Charlie Parker *Chuck Haddix*
Making the March King: John Philip Sousa's Washington Years, 1854–1893 *Patrick Warfield*
In It for the Long Run *Jim Rooney*
Pioneers of the Blues Revival *Steve Cushing*
Roots of the Revival: American and British Folk Music in the 1950s *Ronald D. Cohen and Rachel Clare Donaldson*
Blues All Day Long: The Jimmy Rogers Story *Wayne Everett Goins*
Yankee Twang: Country and Western Music in New England *Clifford R. Murphy*
The Music of the Stanley Brothers *Gary B. Reid*
Hawaiian Music in Motion: Mariners, Missionaries, and Minstrels *James Revell Carr*
Sounds of the New Deal: The Federal Music Project in the West *Peter Gough*
The Mormon Tabernacle Choir: A Biography *Michael Hicks*
The Man That Got Away: The Life and Songs of Harold Arlen *Walter Rimler*
A City Called Heaven: Chicago and the Birth of Gospel Music *Robert M. Marovich*
Blues Unlimited: Essential Interviews from the Original Blues Magazine *Edited by Bill Greensmith, Mike Rowe, and Mark Camarigg*
Hoedowns, Reels, and Frolics: Roots and Branches of Southern Appalachian Dance *Phil Jamison*
Fannie Bloomfield-Zeisler: The Life and Times of a Piano Virtuoso *Beth Abelson Macleod*
Cybersonic Arts: Adventures in American New Music *Gordon Mumma, edited with commentary by Michelle Fillion*
The Magic of Beverly Sills *Nancy Guy*
Waiting for Buddy Guy *Alan Harper*
Harry T. Burleigh: From the Spiritual to the Harlem Renaissance *Jean E. Snyder*
Music in the Age of Anxiety: American Music in the Fifties *James Wierzbicki*
Jazzing: New York City's Unseen Scene *Thomas H. Greenland*
A Cole Porter Companion *Edited by Don M. Randel, Matthew Shaftel, and Susan Forscher Weiss*
Foggy Mountain Troubadour: The Life and Music of Curly Seckler *Penny Parsons*
Blue Rhythm Fantasy: Big Band Jazz Arranging in the Swing Era *John Wriggle*

The University of Illinois Press
is a founding member of the
Association of American University Presses.

University of Illinois Press
1325 South Oak Street
Champaign, IL 61820-6903
www.press.uillinois.edu